not slaves
not citizens

PETER BISKUP

not slaves
not citizens

The Aboriginal Problem
in Western Australia
1898-1954

University of Queensland Press
ST. LUCIA

Crane, Russak & Company, Inc.,
NEW YORK

Text set in Times New Roman 10/12, and printed on 100 gsm Unglazed Woodfree. Printed and bound by Dai Nippon Printing Co. (International) Ltd., Hong Kong.

Designed by Cyrelle

National Library of Australia card number and ISBN 0 7022 0729 2

Distributed by Angus & Robertson (U. K.) Pty. Ltd.
Great Britain–Europe–Africa

Published in the United States by:
Crane, Russak & Company, Inc., 52 Vanderbilt Avenue, New York, N.Y. 10017

Library of Congress Catalog No. 72–900–72
ISBN 0 8448 0122 4

Preface

This book is not primarily about the aborigines of Western Australia. It is about the "aboriginal problem" — the unending debate among the white Western Australians, going back to the early days of settlement, about how the original inhabitants of the country should be subjugated, tamed, exploited, controlled, protected, preserved, bred out, uplifted, or developed. In other words, the book will tell the reader, if he is an Australian of European origin, as much about himself and his society as it will tell him about the aborigines. In a modest way, the book is also a study in colonialism, using the term in the widest sense: Australia, like the Union of South Africa or the Union of Soviet Socialist Republics, "contains its colonial problems within itself".[1]

A study of this kind is faced with the unavoidable problem of striking a balance between the chronological, geographical, and thematic approaches. Because of the fairly long time-span covered, the material has been arranged primarily upon a chronological basis, around certain easily discernible landmarks: the transfer in 1898 of aboriginal affairs from the imperial to the state government, the 1905 Roth Royal Commission, the 1935 Moseley Royal Commission, the outbreak of the war in the Pacific, and the 1948 Bateman Inquiry. Within these periods the treatment is either by subject or by area, or both. Chapter one, by way of introduction, follows the spread of settlement from the southwest to the northwest (in this study, unless otherwise stated, the name always includes the Ashburton and the Gascoyne) and to the Kimberleys. Chapter two examines the aboriginal problem in 1898. Chapter three looks at some of the changes in aboriginal policy and administration after 1898, culminating in the passing of the 1905 Aborigines Act. Chapter four gives a bird's eye view of the next thirty years; chapters five to seven examine three separate aspects of the period. Chapter eight begins with the 1935 Royal Commission and ends just before the outbreak of the war in the Pacific. Chapters nine and ten survey the war-time scene and the developments of the first decade after the war (the title of the book is borrowed from two articles which appeared in the *West Australian* in October 1952). The study concludes with the passing of the 1954 Native Welfare Act which repealed most of the restrictive provisions of existing legislation and gave the aborigines of Western Australia "reasonable equality" before the law. The choice of 1954 as a cut-off point was a deliberate decision: so much has happened since 1954 that another study would be required to do the intervening years full justice.

Although the book is the product of original research, it owes a great deal to published and especially unpublished works by others. Chapter one draws heavily on Paul Hasluck's study of the nineteenth century, *Black Australians,* and to a lesser degree on L. R. Marchant's thesis, "Native Administration and Welfare in Western Australia 1886–1905." Among other unpublished works which were of considerable assistance must be mentioned theses on various aspects of the aboriginal past by R. A. Fink, E. A. Gibson, F. Goddard, S. R. Marks, A. H. and H. L. West, and J. and K. Wilson; the dozen or so student investigations by trainee teachers from the Claremont and Graylands Teachers' Colleges, preserved in the Battye Library of West Australian History; and G. C. Bolton's and R. D. Sturkey's studies of the pastoral industry. Others, not mentioned here, will recognize the nature and extent of their influence on the shaping of the book.

Personal thanks are due to many people for their advice or encouragement, or both, and especially to these: Professors R. M. Berndt and G. C. Bolton of the University of Western Australia, Professor F. K. Crowley of the University of New South Wales, Professor Emeritus A. P. Elkin of the University of Sydney; Mr. R. G. Hausfeld of the School of Tropical Medicine and Hygiene, University of Sydney; Professors K. S. Inglis and C. D. Rowley of the University of Papua and New Guinea; Mr. R. B. Joyce of the University of Queensland; Miss M. Lukis, Librarian of the Battye Library of West Australian History; Mr. S. G. Middleton, formerly Commissioner of Native Welfare in Western Australia; and Professor W. E. H. Stanner of the Australian National University. There are many others, including a handful of aborigines, to whom I am also grateful.

PETER BISKUP
Port Moresby, 1969

Contents

Contents

List of Illustrations

List of Abbreviations

A.	Aborigines Department
A.F.	Department of Aborigines and Fisheries
A.R.	*Annual Report* of the Aborigines Department and its successors
C.S.D.	Colonial (Chief) Secretary's Department
C.S.O	Colonial Secretary's Office
D.N.	*Daily News*
G.G.	*Government Gazette*
M.H.	*Morning Herald*
N.A.	Department of Native Affairs
N.W.	Department of Native Welfare
N.WT.	Department of the North-West
P.D.	*Parliamentary Debates*
S.T.	*Sunday Times*
V. & P.	*Votes and Proceedings* (listed in Selected Bibliography as *Parliamentary Papers*)
W.A.	*West Australian*

Author's Note

For the convenience of readers, monetary sums wherever mentioned have been converted to decimal currency.

1. The Colonial Period
1829-1897

The aborigines and their culture

At the time of the foundation of the Swan River Colony, in June 1829, the aboriginal population of what is now Western Australia consisted of some one hundred tribes comprising perhaps 55,000 individuals. There is some disagreement among the authorities regarding this figure. A. R. Radcliffe-Brown, writing in 1930, estimated that Western Australia contained originally "not less than 52,000 aborigines, and more probably 55,000";[1] eight years later D. S. Davidson put the original numbers at between 55,000 and 63,000.[2] This difference is of little importance. What matters is the smallness of the estimated total, a fact determined by the available food supply, since the aborigines were hunters and food-gatherers. This also meant that the density of aboriginal population varied considerably. What is today the southwest land division supported between 12,500 and 15,000 individuals; the Murchison and the eastern goldfields had a combined population of approximately 5,000; the northwest supported between 24,000 and 29,000 individuals; the Kimberleys had a population of about 9,700. The rest of Western Australia was peopled very sparsely even by aboriginal standards, supporting an estimated total of 3,000 – 4,000.[3] With one exception, these figures are far from reliable, since they are based mainly on ecological grounds; only the estimate for the Kimberleys, based on ethnological research, can be regarded as fairly accurate.

The aborigines' way of life represented an ingenious adjustment to the Australian environment, maintained by an intricate system of social, legal, and technical customs. The largest unit in the aborigines' social structure was the tribe. The tribe was a group of people who spoke the same language or dialects of that language, had the same or similar customs and inhabited a definite territory; it was *not* a political unit, had no chiefs, and its members did not assemble together at any one time. Tribes were divided into local groups, sometimes called hordes. These were small in number and each "owned" the hunting and food-gathering rights over its territory (in the sense of "looking after them" for all its members — past, present, and future).[4] Membership of the local group was determined in two ways: men were born into it and remained members all their lives, while women became members by marriage, leaving their own groups and taking up residence with their husbands. Local groups were divided into families. These were the basic social and economic units and consisted of a man, his wives, and their children. The aborigines' everyday life was regulated by kinship, that is by the fact that an aborigine was related to every other aborigine with whom he came into contact; by a ritual attitude towards nature known as totemism; and by the authority of old men who were the repositories of sacred lore and tribal sanctions. It was a way of life which changed little from generation to generation, but it was not incapable of change: kinship structures, for instance, show evidence that in the past certain changes must have taken place, as do alterations in the style of aboriginal mural art, for such changes could not have occurred without many psychic and social concomitants.[5]

From the point of view of the contact situation three traits of aboriginal culture were of utmost importance. The first was the absence of a discernible political structure. The aborigines were not, as some would have it, "people without politics",[6] but authority in pre-contact times was always "limited, and qualified by claims of kinship . . ."[7] Insofar as it is possible to speak about political organization among the aborigines, the political unit was the local group. Each had a headman whose position depended not only on his knowledge and wisdom but also on the support of other men. He had no special privileges and lived in the same way as the rest of the group. Occasionally, headmen of adjoining groups would confer together on matters of common interest, but political co-operation did not extend beyond that. This fact had several consequences. Firstly, the aborigines found it difficult to present a united front to the invaders; as Governor Stirling put it in 1837, they had "never felt the effect of combination".[8] Secondly, their societies were not considered to be "sovereign tribes". All land was declared Crown land and the aborigines' right of possession was disregarded. "Although it might be granted that on the first taking possession of the Colony", said a New South Wales judge in 1836, "the aborigines were entitled to be recognized as free and independent, yet they are not in such a position with regard to strength as to be considered free and independent tribes. They have no sovereignty . . ."[9] Finally, after pacification, lack of discernible political structure made it exceedingly difficult to "find the chiefs" through whom it might be possible to rule the subjected population; in Western Australia, attempts to appoint aboriginal "governors" elected by the aborigines ended in abysmal failure.

The second trait of aboriginal culture important in the context of early contact was what J. A. Barnes has called an "unusually strong attachment to specific sites".[10] The aborigines did not practise agriculture and had no domestic animals except the dog; they were hunters, fishermen, and food-gatherers. But they were not true nomads, since their wanderings were confined to well-defined areas. Because of this the "policy of flight"[11] (normal reaction of a food-gathering people to white encroachment) was not readily open to them; they could not bring themselves to abandon their tribal grounds. In the long run, there was no real basis for a compromise between the aborigines' claim for continued access to their tribal grounds and the settlers' conflicting claim for undisturbed occupation of the land. But in the early stages of European conquest there was little or no closer settlement, and since the settlers needed labour, some aborigines found employment on farms or pastoral stations. "The stage was thus set for the partial elimination of the aboriginal population, and its partial conversion to a peon class attached to White pastoral properties."[12]

The third trait of aboriginal culture relevant here centred on the fact that the aborigine "was endowed with a tenacious, if not unique inability to detect meaning in any way of life other than his own", an "inability to live outside the framework of his own culture".[13] According to C. M. H. Clark, this was in a sense a blessing. It prevented the Europeans from using the aborigines for their own ends and relieved them from the evil consequences of reducing them to slavery or semi-slavery. "It protected the aborigine from such slavery or some form of forced labour, but at the price of the total destruction of the Tasmanian aborigine, and the gradual destruction of the aboriginal culture on the mainland."[14]

Analytical framework for a historical study of culture contact in Western Australia

It is a truism to say that the aborigines' reaction to the white invasion was culturally determined, but it is a truism worth restating: aboriginal attitudes towards the Europeans were conditioned by their "social, economic and political organization, by the degree of their cultural self-sufficiency and integration, and to some extent by their numbers".[15] Similarly, the Europeans were conditioned by their cultural background, including their experience with aboriginal peoples in other continents. In Australia the Europeans found people without central political organization, without sited villages or gardens, and soon formed the impression that the aborigines were savages on the lowest scale of humanity. It is against this background that we should view the Europeans' utter disregard of aboriginal customs and values, and their failure to realize that the land was not only occupied but also used. Later, some aborigines recognized that there was some good in the culture of the invaders, and attempted to combine what they learnt with what was left of their own way of life, while some Europeans came to see the intrinsic value of the aborigines' culture. But this did not really alter the facts of the situation; after all, is the concept of assimilation not based on the assumption that the European and aboriginal cultures are "two vessels unequally filled" and that they "have only to be connected up for their contents to find a common level"?[16]

This deep cultural gulf between the aborigines and the Europeans, and the fundamental conflict of interest between them, gave the process of culture contact a kind of relentless logic of its own. A. P. Elkin has outlined this process in the article "Reaction and Interaction: A Food Gathering People and European Settlement in Australia", where he has postulated several stages or phases of aboriginal reaction to European presence. Firstly, the aborigines make "a nervous and tentative approach", and, if not rebuffed, show a readiness to help the trespassers in small ways. Next comes a period of covert or overt warfare called "clash". Once the aborigines accept as inevitable the Europeans' presence, the stage of "external adaptation" follows. This is the core phase — an equilibrium, a *modus vivendi* is reached, manifesting itself, particularly in the marginal regions, in "intelligent parasitism", in an "adaptation to the settler and other persons and institutions". The equilibrium is eventually upset, usually within a generation, and there follows either a social and cultural breakdown ("pauperism") and depopulation, or an "intelligent appreciation" of the European way of life and of the part they might play in it. The success of this phase depends largely on European attitudes; it can "only be attained by the Aborigines if the white man intends that they should, and helps them to do so".[17] Failure of this phase results in "listlessness and disillusionment", resentment (particularly among part-aborigines), defiance, and "return to the mat", in an attempt to recapture the past. The final stage is assimilation, either "guarded" or "intelligent", again depending on European attitudes.

Discussion of European attitudes and reactions to the aborigines' earlier reactions forms an integral part of A. P. Elkin's model; "the process was one of interaction".[18] Early European attitudes, in spite of the usurpation of aboriginal lands, were based on the notion of aborigines as British subjects, to be civilized and converted to Christianity. The failure of this policy of "amity and trust"[19] ushered the phase of pacification by force which operated partly officially and partly unofficially. The third phase, from about 1870 onward, was protection. In the marginal regions, the policy involved the application of the principles of good animal husbandry; in the settled parts it consisted of "smoothing the dying pillow" of a race destined to die out before long. Finally, during the 1930s, the negative policy of protection was replaced by a more positive policy directed towards assimilation and full citizenship. The second half of the thirties was a period of gestation; after 1945 the policy has been implemented over ever-widening fields, both geographical and socio-economic.

How useful is this conceptualization of the Australian culture contact situation from the historian's point of view? Elkin's model seems to beg two questions. First, it postulates the existence of "The Wistful Aboriginal"[20] whose main ambition in life is to become a brown Australian; and second, it does not distinguish clearly between assimilation as a fact and as a desideratum. Most aborigines, and even most part-aborigines, are not assimilated; rather, to use R. M. and C. H. Berndt's phrase, they are "involved in processes which *could* lead to assimilation".[21] Having said this much let us see how the model can help in the writing of history. To start with, it serves as a reminder that, historically, European-aboriginal contact was far from uniform in Western Australia: there were, and still are, both "civilized" and "uncivilized" aborigines, with many gradations between them, individuals being assimilated on one side and "bush" aborigines just coming into contact with Europeans on the other. It is therefore impossible to speak of *the* official policy at any given time — different policies were applied in different areas, or to different groups in the same area. In the 1850s, following the settlement of the Champion Bay district, the policy of pacification by force was applied in the region, while in the southwest depopulation had already set in. By the time the Champion Bay district had been pacified, pastoral settlement in the northwest added another dimension to the aboriginal problem. The expansion into the Kimberleys, in the 1880s, added yet another: while the Kimberley tribes were pacified, protective measures were being tentatively applied in the northwest, while south of the Murchison rapid depopulation obviated the need for any policy at all. The goldrushes of the 1890s brought more clashes and more pacification by force. During the first decade of this century the growth of part-aboriginal population in the south created a new problem and brought in its wake the policy of partial segregation or social isolation of the part-aborigines. In the 1920s depopulation among the Kimberley full-bloods led to the extension of protective policies to that area. Only the Second World War, with its pervading though still far from uniform effects on all except the "bush" aborigines, brought some sort of unity and focus into the total picture.

The model can be put to another use. The sequence of the phases need not be constant; it is "reversible, and variable, according to local circumstances at a particular time".[22] The most important variable in this context was the difference in the strength of the aboriginal societies and of the invaders. In the southwest land division, and later on the eastern goldfields, the Europeans established themselves quickly, firmly, and in comparatively large numbers; the result was dispossession, social and cultural breakdown of aboriginal societies, swift depopulation, and the reduction of the remnants to penury. Elsewhere, European penetration was slow, tentative, and the numbers involved small. The aborigines had time to adjust to new conditions, and the settlers to learn to "accept the natives as a part of the situation — often a very necessary part to them".[23] This mutual intelligent adaptation was not publicized either by the aborigines or the settlers. As a result, a myth grew up that the process of contact throughout Australia was one of complete disinheritance. Nothing could be farther removed from the truth. In the marginal regions, there developed an almost classical colonial situation: political and economic power was in the hands of the Europeans, while the aboriginal societies retained much of their traditional characteristics. In the closely settled regions the process of contact was one of "conquest and disinheritance", followed by the disappearance of the aborigines. This dichotomy provides a useful framework for a historical study of the culture contact situation in Australia; it also points to the conclusion that the "solution" of the aboriginal problem in the marginal regions, or some marginal regions, could well lie in the direction of decolonization rather than assimilation. The part-aborigines do not quite fit into this framework: they are a minority largely of our own creation. For this reason the part-aboriginal problem will be dealt with separately.

Early contact in the southwest

Strangely enough, there was little in the nature of first contact to forebode the developments just discussed. The first settlers were regarded by the aborigines as the returning spirits of the dead, frightening perhaps, and unpredictable, but at least beings who could be explained in terms of their own experience, if not related to them through kinship.[24] Assuming the spirits to be temporary visitors, the aborigines eventually showed some willingness to help the settlers in a number of small ways.[25] But the colonists soon dispelled the aborigines' belief that their stay was only temporary. Before long, the main settlement on the Swan River attained an air of permanency, and smaller settlements sprang up at Albany, at Augusta, at the Vasse, at Mandurah and along the lower Murray. Some colonists crossed the Darling Range and established small farming communities around York, Northam, and Toodyay. From this beginning the frontiers of settlement spread northwards to Bolgart and the Victoria Plains district, and eastwards from York. The absence of villages and cultivated fields gave the colonists an impression that their actions could interfere but little with the aborigines' way of life. "They seemed to be as nomadic as the kangaroos and emus which they hunted, and the settlers felt that they had every right to military protection when selecting such of the aborigines' tribal lands as they chose to occupy and put to better use."[26] Unwilling to flee, and yet unable to put up effective resistance, the aborigines retaliated by spearing the settlers' stock, raiding their homesteads, and attacking lone farmers and shepherds. But bitter experience had taught them that retaliation was not the best policy, and that in order to survive they would have to adjust to the white man's presence and his use of their land. On the Swan and Canning rivers all opposition by the aborigines had ceased by 1832, while the Murray River tribe gave no further trouble after it had been decimated two years later by a posse of settlers and soldiers, in what has become known as the "Battle of Pinjarra".[27] By the middle forties all resistance had ceased and the "most perfect tranquility"[28] prevailed in the colony.

The violence which accompanied the early contact was largely unavoidable. Because of the cultural gulf between the settlers and the aborigines, the "clash" was a conflict in which there was little room for sympathy on either side, and hardly any opportunity for human impulses to assert themselves; nor was there any real basis for a compromise between the aborigines' and settlers' conflicting claims to the land. As time went on, however, some settlers found themselves increasingly dependent on aboriginal labour, while the aborigines, as a result of ecological changes caused by the introduction of new crops and animals, experienced considerable difficulty in obtaining sufficient quantities of their traditional food. And it was not long before they acquired a taste, if not a decided preference, for the colonists' fare. Where a group of aborigines customarily camped on a farm or a sheep run, an understanding usually grew up between them and the settler. If they wanted it, there was always some "tucker" to be had at the homestead; when the settler needed help, he could always find the aborigines down at the camp. It was, on the whole, a satisfactory arrangement: the aborigines were not paid, but they were not exploited. Although their labour was disinterested and inefficient, the settlers had for the most part no alternative. Indeed, they had to feed not only the workers and their families but also the rest of the group, including the old men, who remained the real masters of their helpers.[29]

During the first two decades of settlement the government of the young colony was faced with two distinct problems. The first was pacification, a task known in those days as "maintenance of law and order". This was not hypocrisy. Neither the officials nor the majority of the settlers saw themselves initially as competing with, or conquering the aborigines, and envisaged some sort of accommodation which would be beneficial to both races. In 1829, on the proclamation of the founding of the colony, Governor Stirling warned that anyone "behaving in a fraudulent, cruel or felonious manner towards the aborigines of the country"[30] would be prosecuted as though the offence had been committed against Europeans. Even later, after attacks by aborigines resulted in wholesale reprisals by the settlers, official policy remained one of restraint; while condoning direct action by the colonists in cases of "legitimate self-defence", the government tried to mitigate the violence of the conflict and to protect the aborigines from unnecessary cruelty. In the late 1830s the British government, under pressure from the humanitarians at home, appointed a number of protectors (also known as guardians of aborigines) to the Australian colonies. Two were sent to Western Australia; one was stationed at Perth, the other at York. Their task was to help to apply the law to the aborigines for criminal offences against Europeans, to institute proceedings against the latter for criminal offences against the aborigines, to check acts of hostility on the part of the settlers generally, and to minimize the annoyance caused by the aborigines' appearing uncloaked in public, brawling within town boundaries, begging, and pilfering. The protectors took part in criminal proceedings against aborigines, either for the prosecution or on behalf of the defence (a practice continued later by the police, in their capacity as "protectors of aborigines") to ensure that the accused, as British subjects, were given a fair trial. But the fiction of legal equality was too difficult to maintain for any length of time. As pagans, the aborigines could not be expected to take a Christian oath in court, and in 1841 the rules of court procedure were amended to allow them to give information and evidence without the sanctions of an oath. Eight years later the Legislative Council passed an ordinance providing for summary trial and punishment of aboriginal offenders in certain cases. It empowered two or more justices of the peace not interested in the matter before the court (one had to be a guardian of aborigines or a resident magistrate of the district) to try aborigines summarily for all criminal offences except murder, arson, and rape. Maximum sentence was six months' imprisonment, with an optional two dozen lashes in the case of male offenders.

The aborigines were expected to play an important part in these early attempts to maintain law and order. Sometime in the early 1840s the government appointed a number of Native Constables, as a rule "the best behaved, the most intelligent and influential individuals"[31] who were made "responsible" for the maintenance of peace in their districts, in return for a pound of flour a day. If peace was broken, the ration was stopped, but the deficiency was made up when they produced an individual or individuals willing to admit responsibility for the disturbance (Native Constables should

not be confused with aboriginal police troopers, members of the
Native Police established in Victoria in the late 1830s and later also
in Queensland, or with the latter-day aboriginal trackers who were
personal servants of white policemen and not members of the police
force). If the term rule can be applied to this early experiment in local
government, then it was direct rule, if only because the authorities
knew next to nothing about the power structure of aboriginal societies.
Later, in 1852, the government tried another experiment when it
appointed the first group of "elected" aboriginal "governors" or
"kings", as an "influence for the maintenance of order".[32] Among the
best known were King Tom at Albany, King Jerome at Wagin, King
Winjan at Pinjarra, and King Billy, the "upright native gentleman"
friend of John Forrest. King Billy's "investiture" by Governor Weld
at the Geraldine mine near Northampton was witnessed by the
pioneer S. Mitchell who later described it in his memoirs:

After admonishing the blacks to give up fighting and stealing, and ordering
a supply of flour, tea, sugar and tobacco (the custom on such occasions),
Governor Weld proceeded to select the most suitable man amongst them
to be the King of the Tribes in the district. This exalted position fell to
a native locally known as left-handed Billy . . . The newly-made monarch
was duly invested with a flag-like emblem of his authority — which he
planted at the entrance to his Breakwind Palace.[33]

This was in the early 1870s. Mitchell's subsequent description of
the "revolt" of King Billy's "subjects" underlines one reason for
the failure of the experiment; the tone of his remarks suggests another.
It could be argued, of course, that the acephalous structure of
aboriginal societies foredoomed to failure any attempt to associate
the aborigines with the process of enforcing the new laws which the
government found necessary to impose. Still, the negative attitude
of most settlers (and some officials also) must have contributed to
the failure of the experiment. King Billy, it is true, finished up roaming the streets of Geraldton, with a brass plate inscribed "King Billy
of Geraldton" dangling from his neck.[34] Others, however, such as
King Winjan or King Jerome, remained with their people; the latter
is said to have performed marriage ceremonies which the Wagin
aborigines regarded as binding.

The second problem facing the government at this stage concerned
the place and status of aborigines in the colonial society. Were they
to be a group apart, with their own customs and institutions, or were
they to be encouraged to embrace the European way of life? The

Europeans of the late eighteenth century, influenced by the notion of the "noble savage", were on the whole tolerant in their attitudes towards the indigenous peoples with whom they had been brought into contact. About the turn of the century, however, there occurred an important change in public morality, particularly in Great Britain. In the colonial field, this change manifested itself in demands for the abolition of slavery, and later in general concern with the wider problems of indigenous peoples under British rule. The period which followed the 1832 Reform Act was an era of aborigines' protection societies and of humanitarian interest in the spiritual welfare of the indigenous peoples.[35] It was also an era of laissez-faire. The two strains produced in the colonial field the twin design of promoting the commercial interests of Great Britain and of "imparting the blessings of civilization",[36] largely through the propagation of Christianity, to the indigenous peoples under British rule. The application of this policy to Western Australia was entrusted to Governor Hutt who succeeded Stirling in 1839. Unlike his predecessor, Hutt took a personal interest in the aborigines and their welfare; his instructions, furthermore, enjoined him to "prevent and restrain all violence and injustice" against the aborigines, and to take all measures "necessary for their conversion to the Christian faith, and for their advancement in civilization".[37] Hutt saw his civilizing mission as having two aspects. He inaugurated the practice of financial assistance to churches and missionary societies which has been a feature of Western Australia's aboriginal policy ever since. Between 1840 and 1845 three aboriginal schools were opened by the Church of England and one by the Wesleyans, with financial assistance from the government. In 1846 a Roman Catholic mission was established at New Norcia by Father Salvado, a Spanish Benedictine monk; it was given government subsidy in 1859. Hutt also introduced a system of bounties for the training of adults. A colonist who could prove that he had retained the services of an aborigine for at least two years and had succeeded in teaching him certain farming skills (in the case of a female servant, cooking and dressmaking skills), could claim a remission of $36 in the purchase of land; a settler who managed to teach an aborigine a trade or a handicraft could claim a reduction double that sum.[38] But the scheme was not a success, and only ten bounties were granted before the offer was rescinded in 1848. Most settlers apparently preferred to hold their aboriginal labour by means of written agreements, also called indentures, which were enforceable in courts. Others showed a predilection for assigned aboriginal convicts, particularly during the late forties and early fifties when aboriginal prisoners, instead of being sent to the penal establishment on Rottnest Island (established in 1841 to train aborigines "in the habits of civilized life"), were employed on the roads, used for carrying mails, or let out to work for the settlers.

An important corollary of the policy of imparting the blessings of civilization was the insistence that British law should apply to Her Majesty's aboriginal subjects in its entirety, not only in their relations with the settlers but also with one another. In a theoretical sense this has always been so, for Australian courts have consistently held that the whole of the law at any given time applied to the aborigines and whites alike "except to the extent that the legislature had seen fit to make differences or to allow exceptions".[39] How was this rule to be applied in practice? The mid-twentieth century mind boggles at the enormity of the problems raised, but the colonial officials of the period were confident of ultimate success. Thus Lieutenant (later Sir George) Grey, the future Governor of New Zealand and Cape Colony, thought that the best method of civilizing the aborigines was to punish them, slightly at first but always consistently, for all violations of British laws; allowing them to keep their own "savage and traditional customs" would ensure their continued barbarism. His ideas, contained in a report presented in 1840 while he was resident magistrate at King George Sound, were endorsed by the Colonial Office as fit for adoption all over the continent.[40] Hutt, more realistically, was convinced that aborigines "cannot be taught civilization", but believed that by constant contact they would become "infected" with it and gradually abandon their customs and superstitions.[41] In Western Australia Hutt's view prevailed, and during his term of office (1839–1846) the government ignored all acts of violence committed by aborigines against one another in accordance with tribal custom. The aborigines were British subjects only in their relations with the Europeans; in their own haunts they were to be left alone. We can only speculate as to future developments had this system of legal dualism been allowed to continue. Hutt's successor, Governor Fitzgerald, soon after taking office laid down a strict policy of taking cognizance of tribal murders and aggravated assaults committed by aborigines among themselves; this has been official policy ever since, at least on paper.

The fifties and the early sixties

The occupation of the Champion Bay district, from 1850 onwards, and the introduction of convicts which coincided with it, led to two important changes in aboriginal policy: the replacement of the ideal of protecting Her Majesty's aboriginal subjects by the precept of "paramountcy and protection",[42] and the gradual abandonment of the policy of imparting the blessings of civilization. These changes were due to several factors. One was the increase of European population and the expansion of settlement. Between 1850 and 1860 the area under cultivation more than trebled, the European population increased from less than 6,000 to over 15,000; the boundaries of settlement were extended to the Victoria Plains district and to Champion Bay in the north, and as far as Kellerberrin, Williams, and Kojonup in the east and southeast, while some of the older districts were settled more closely. Another factor was the introduction of convicts, a factor which lessened the settlers' dependence on aboriginal labour. The third was the waning of concern in Great Britain over the aborigines: by the 1850s humanitarian influence on British colonial policy had been overshadowed by the "Manchester men" who demanded economy in governmental expenditure at home and in the colonies. The interaction of these factors can be seen in the changed attitudes towards the pacification of the new areas. Although aboriginal affairs remained a reserved imperial subject until 1897, seven years after the granting of self-government, the decisions which really counted were being made increasingly in the colony, often independently of the government. The ideal of protecting the aborigines from violence and cruelty was replaced by the policy of paramountcy and protection, implemented frequently by the settlers themselves. Governor Fitzgerald gave the settlers in the new districts a *carte blanche* for dealing with the aborigines, intervening only if they overstepped the mark. In the settled parts of the colony, protectors of aborigines became increasingly concerned with the protection of the colonists rather than of their aboriginal charges, and in 1848 their official title was changed to guardians of aborigines *and* protectors of settlers. In 1854 the Colonial Office stopped paying their salaries, and the office was abolished. From 1855 until 1886 (when the system of protectorship was revived in a different form), the colony was without an aboriginal administration in the proper sense of the term. "Protection" was entrusted to the police or to resident magistrates, and in 1865 the latter were formally authorized to distribute rations to destitute aborigines "incapable of seeking their own livelihood".[43]

The second, and by far the more important change in European attitudes lay in the abandonment of the policy of planned advancement towards civilization. All evidence seemed to show that aborigines were totally unfit for civilized life; even when treated with kindness, those who had been subjected to prolonged contact appeared overcome with lassitude and seized with despair for which there was no cure, as if some mysterious law of nature had doomed them to disappear from the face of the earth. For there was little doubt that this was in fact happening in the settled parts of the colony. By the time of the first census, held in 1848, the aboriginal population of Perthshire had decreased to 553 (from an estimated 1,500 in 1829); in the Sussex district it had shrunk to 150, and in the Murray district to a mere 73. The disappearance of the aborigines can be explained by two related factors: the nature of the early contact in the southwest and the structure of aboriginal life and their beliefs. To start with, there was an overwhelming disparity of power between the two groups; the aborigines were simply overawed by the superior technology of the invaders. Many aborigines were wiped out by influenza, measles, smallpox, and other simple ailments unknown in pre-contact times. The Europeans also introduced tuberculosis, gonorrhoea, and syphilis. Changes in diet brought deficiency diseases such as scurvy. The wearing of clothing caused respiratory diseases since it was kept on even when wet. Camps became unhygienic. Traditionally, the aborigines would move camp when surroundings became too squalid, but this was not always possible in the changed circumstances. The result was gastro-intestinal infections, particularly among the children.[44]

The second reason for the disappearance of the aborigines was the "mere presence of the European";[45] "the smell of the white man is killing us" (*jangga meenya bomunggur*) was the plaint heard by Daisy Bates everywhere.[46] "The impact of the outside world came as a rude shock. Things were happening outside the framework of what the Aborigines conceived to be the established order of life, both physical and social . . ."[47] The aborigines believed that their way of life, and the life and stability of nature, depended on their adherence to the ways and beliefs which had been worked out in the past. These had an almost superhuman sanction for the aborigines, for they thought that unless they kept the laws and customs of their ancestors disaster would overtake both themselves and nature. In the words of A. P. Elkin, their philosophy of life was

centred in the concept of the "eternal dreaming", the creative time of the great heroes and ancestors whose spirits are still present — a state which is not limited by space and time, but which is past, present and future. Into conscious appreciation of this state, every male passes gradually after initiation, when he becomes a custodian of its earthly symbols, rites and myths and of the rules of everyday life. Conversely, to lose one's "dreaming", that is, one's conscious connection with this sacred world is to lose direction of life, and to flounder about in an apathetic way — in short, to become psychologically sick, and morally and socially unstable.[48]

The doubts as to the aborigines' capacity to become civilized were further strengthened by the doctrine of social Darwinism which saw all history as a progressive movement from savagery to civilization. It was not an altogether new theory, for it had been formulated before Darwin by Condorcet, Klemm, and Gobineau, to name a few.[49] But the majority of social thinkers of the first half of the nineteenth century, as D. J. Mulvaney has demonstrated,

were conditioned by the Mosaic time-scale and the static concept of culture which it implied . . . As only six thousand years had passed since Adam and as there was evidence of higher civilization going back almost to his time, any concept of cultural change or progression was impossible. Instead, a retrogression from civilization was accepted as a norm in primitive societies.[50]

Before the publication of the *Origin of Species* the aborigines, although savages, were at least human. The theory of evolution and the concept of the survival of the fittest gradually changed this belief, and in the ensuing "great dispute between apes and angels, the aborigines were ranged firmly on the side of the apes".[51]

The conviction (or was it a convenient myth?) that the aborigines were doomed to eventual extinction affected all European attitudes towards the aborigines, and in particular towards their education. By the middle fifties all four aboriginal schools, started with such high hopes in the previous decade, were abandoned; "however bright the blessings of civilization might be pictured, it became difficult to hold these inexplicable people from leading their own lives".[52] In the early 1850s, it is true, two new institutions were established, one at Albany by a Mrs. Camfield, and another by the Sisters of Mercy in Perth, but their concept of education was a far cry from the ideas of the 1840s. Education now meant training or, better still, conditioning, "taming".[53] An aborigine was "civilized" if he wore clothing, could speak enough broken English to be able to understand orders, was not cheeky, and appreciated the kindness bestowed upon him by the Europeans.[54] Anything more would have been too much trouble, and for no good reason; the race was going to disappear anyway.

The belief that the aborigines were doomed to extinction also affected European attitudes towards pacification. If it was pointless to educate the aborigines beyond a certain point, it was equally pointless to protect them unduly from violence: if a man is going to die, does it matter if he dies sooner or later? Put like this, the assertion sounds rather cynical, and the settlers would have been the first to deny it. But the ways of human subconsciousness are devious, and the contempt which many settlers felt for the aborigines must have affected their actions. Indeed, it could be said that the eventual extinction of the aboriginal race was the premise on which the aboriginal policy of the nineteenth and early twentieth century had been erected — even such humanitarian expedient as the establishment of reserves was meant to complete the process of dying out, "peaceably and at a distance".[55]

The occupation of the northwest

The pastoral expansion north of the Tropic of Capricorn and eastward towards the South Australian border, embarked on in the early sixties, added yet another dimension to the aboriginal problem. The De Grey and Harding River districts were settled in 1863, and shortly after the first sheep station was established on the Gascoyne. About the same time pearling operations started at Shark Bay and at Cossack, attracting Europeans as well as a number of Asians. A few settlers established themselves in the coastal lands stretching towards the South Australian border, first in the Esperance district and later at Fraser's Range, Balladonia, and Eucla. In the seventies the scrub and spinifex country south of the existing settlement at Roebourne was occupied, and by about 1885 all the habitable areas of the northwest were settled. Meanwhile, the white population of the colony had increased by approximately 10,000 between 1860 and 1870 alone, reaching 32,000 at the time of the 1881 census.

The relations between the settlers and the aborigines in the newly settled districts followed, at least initially, the broad pattern set in the earlier period. Although very few reliable accounts have survived, there can be little doubt of the fierceness of the conflict or of the harshness of the settlers' reprisals: "in these lonely outposts, the squatters developed the habit of making their own law."[56] Early in 1868 some 150 aborigines were said to have been shot near Cossack "while resisting arrest" by a posse sent to revenge the killing of a party of settlers.[57] The pastoralists on the De Grey, suspecting an aboriginal plot to kill them while they were watching a corroboree, taught the aborigines "a lesson they have never forgotten".[58] At times the pastoralists tended to exaggerate the danger, but this was only natural; outnumbered and separated from one another by long distances, they were inclined to see every aborigine as a potential thief or killer. The government, on its part, while continuing to pay lip service to the idea of protecting the aborigines from physical violence, left the settlers free to "pacify" them in their own way. Governor Hampton (1862–1868) tended to ignore all situations in the outlying districts which were beyond his capacity to handle, and as long as the pastoralists did not use more violence "than may be necessary except in actual self-defence",[59] there were no repercussions. In 1869, for instance, when the Dempster brothers reported that an aborigine had been shot near Esperance and others had been marooned on an island until they could be handed over to the police, the Colonial Secretary replied that there was "no intention on the part of the Government to interfere with the action taken by the settlers at Esperance Bay so long as no complaint is preferred".[60] This policy was reversed by Governor Weld (1869–1875). In 1872 Weld ordered the arrest of a pastoralist, a member of the Perth establishment, for the shooting of an aborigine who had allegedly tried to escape from his "custody" after being caught stealing a saddle, and subsequently suspended the magistrate for reducing the charge from that of manslaughter to one of shooting with intent to do bodily harm. In 1873 Weld issued a general warning that he intended to use all legal means at his disposal to "detect and punish"[61] acts of violence against the aborigines. Finally, the Governor introduced certain changes in the summary trial of aborigines, in an attempt to make the criminal law more effective in the marginal regions. In 1859 the maximum sentence to which an aborigine could be sentenced summarily was increased from six months to three years. In 1874, on Weld's initiative, the maximum sentence was reduced to six months, and the requirement that one of the justices had to be a protector of aborigines or a resident magistrate was dropped. If a full bench as required by the 1849 and 1859 ordinances was available, the old maximum penalty of three years' imprisonment still applied.

There were, however, important differences between the clash in the new pastoral regions and the earlier clashes in the southwest and around Champion Bay. The aborigines were not "dispossessed of their lands",[62] at least not in the same way in which this happened in the southwest. The 1864 Land Regulations explicitly recognized the aborigines' right to enter, at all times, the unenclosed or enclosed but otherwise unimproved parts of any pastoral lease, for the purpose of seeking sustenance in their accustomed manner. This right applied to all Crown land north of the Murchison River and east from halfway between Hopetoun and Esperance, with the exception of a coastal strip two miles wide.[63] After the occupation of the Kimberleys the regulation was extended to that area and was later incorporated into the 1898 Land Act. Another difference arose from the ban on the employment of convicts and ticket-of-leave men north of the Murchison River. Consequently, the pastoralists came to depend almost entirely on aboriginal labour. "A sympathetic attitude on the part of the settlers had led to a definite friendliness between the two groups. The settlers offered the aborigines food, protection from warrior tribesmen on the Tableland, and treatment during sickness."[64] The aborigines offered the settlers their labour. The resulting "adaptation" was as swift as the initial clash was violent. As early as 1868, for instance, a mob of 2,000 sheep on the De Grey station was shepherded entirely by aborigines, some of whom were said to be equal to the best white station hands. By 1881 a total of 2,346 aborigines was employed by the settlers, mainly in the pastoral industry, compared with 245 in 1859. Gradually whole groups of aborigines became voluntarily and permanently associated with the various stations, gave up their roaming habits (except for their "walkabouts" which now coincided with the slack season), started to wear white man's clothing, and some even learned his language. The emphasis is on the word voluntarily. C. H. Berndt, writing in 1950, described the beginnings of a pastoral station in the Northern Territory, and her comments may be usefully repeated here. Initially, each station possessed a small group of labour fed and clothed by the pastoralist, while the "outside" aborigines remained hostile. As the station groups dwindled and station boundaries were expanded, these outside groups were drawn into employment. Eventually, even those aborigines who were not themselves working tended to congregate about the station camp and to regard the property as "their" station.[65] Mission stations originated in much the same way.

Curiosity brought the first natives to the newly established Mission [said Rev. J. R. B. Love of the Port George IV mission, opened in 1911]. Some kept paying repeated short visits, others stayed longer. Those who helped in the outdoor labour that was going on . . . were given food, tobacco, tea and sugar . . . Some of the more readily adaptable soon became almost permanent residents of the Mission, though we have always periodically sent all hands "bush", to keep contact with their tribal institutions. . . .[66]

The pearlers and the bêche-de-mer gatherers, on the other hand, found it more difficult to attract aboriginal labour, which thus had to be "recruited". Because of the high incidence of kidnapping and the use of fraud to induce aborigines to join the pearling crews, a series of acts was passed between 1870 and 1875 which prohibited the employment of aborigines in the pearling industry unless engaged under contract witnessed by a justice of the peace or a police constable. The acts also prescribed penal sanctions for breaches of contract by the master pearlers, prohibited the employment of aboriginal women as divers, and provided for minimum rations for aboriginal employees and for their repatriation after the completion of the term of contract.[67] The ban on the employment of aboriginal women as divers (they were apparently better workers than the men) led to the engagement of Malay (mainy Koepanger) divers and crews. During the second half of the seventies the Dutch prohibited the employment abroad of their East Indies subjects, but the ban was lifted soon after, and the Malays returned in large numbers. After about 1880, pearling ceased to be a "suitable" occupation for the aborigines; in 1913, for instance, only sixty-five of the 2,642 men employed in the industry were aborigines or part-aborigines.

Such were the beginnings of the policy of protection; in 1886, after the establishment of the Aborigines Protection Board, it was applied throughout the colony, with the exception of the newly opened Kimberleys (another aspect of protection, the establishment of aboriginal reserves, goes back to 1872). The policy was a response to purely local needs, but it also reflected the wider changes in attitudes in the eastern colonies. In Victoria, the process of detribalization was virtually completed by about 1850, and in 1860 a

Board for the Protection of Aborigines was appointed; South Australia and Queensland passed similar protective legislation in 1880 and 1897 respectively, and New South Wales created a board in 1883 but it was not given legislative sanction for its operations until 1909. The new policy, said A. P. Elkin, was "in part continuous with the early attempts to bring Christianity to the natives but now the outlook had become pessimistic and negative", and had been adopted largely under pressure from the humanitarians in the capital cities, men and women who had "little, if any, experience of natives, and no recollection of the clash with them in the early days . . ."[68] For this reason, the policy was never fully applied in the outback: the main beneficiaries were the dying remnants of the settled regions.

The expansion into the Kimberleys

The first half of the 1880s saw two important developments: the opening of the Kimberleys and the appointment of a commission to inquire into the treatment of aboriginal prisoners and "certain matters relating to aboriginal natives" — the first general inquiry into the aboriginal problem. The occupation of the Kimberleys (by sheepmen from the south in the west, by cattlemen from Queensland in the east) followed the by then only too familiar pattern. The first recorded attack by the aborigines occurred in 1882 at Yeeda station, the oldest pastoral property in West Kimberley. On the upper Fitzroy, settled later, animosities did not start until the middle eighties, when several white men were killed by marauding aborigines. In 1888 the King Sound Pastoral Company claimed to have lost 7,000 sheep to aboriginal depredations in one year. In East Kimberley, settled later still, aboriginal reprisals were not reported until 1890. No one knew even the approximate number of the aborigines but it was believed to be large, perhaps 30,000 or more. The settlers felt particularly unsafe, especially in East Kimberley where they were vastly outnumbered by the aborigines. In these circumstances it was hardly surprising that the administration should have abandoned all pretences of impartiality. The number of aborigines shot by the settlers, miners (there was a shortlived gold-rush in 1886, centred on Hall's Creek), and the police can be only guessed. "Hundreds of men, women and even children were shot down in this period",[69] wrote a pioneer; another old-timer, portrayed by Mary Durack in the novel *Keep Him My Country,* boasted of the notches on a gun which "tally up the blacks it shot after Mick Condon was speared".[70]

The antagonism between the settlers and the aborigines was brought to a head by the exploits of a group of aborigines led by the notorious "outlaw" Pigeon. His real name was Sandamarra, and he came from West Kimberley. In 1890, he was sentenced in Derby to twelve months' hard labour for cattle-killing, became a police tracker after his release, acquired the "whitefeller" name of Pigeon, and discharged his duties in an exemplary fashion for over three years. In November 1894, with the help of another tracker by the name of Captain, Pigeon killed his constable while they were returning from one of the periodical expeditions to bring in aboriginal cattle-killers, stole all guns and ammunition, freed the prisoners, and escaped into the hills. The fact that Pigeon was a "good" aborigine before turning to crime calls for comment. Ion Idriess, who wrote a book about him, claims that Pigeon had been influenced by another outlaw of forceful personality, Lillimarra, a prisoner of the returning party;[71] it has also been said that the constable had been making advances to Pigeon's woman.[72] This is largely speculation. What is relevant is the fact that both Pigeon and Captain were former police trackers, part-acculturated aborigines who had acquired a tincture of European civilization and who prided themselves on their knowledge of white man's ways. They were outlaws in a double sense, no longer fitting into the tribal society, their assimilation into the European society incomplete. Violence was a form of catharsis for them. Other notorious outlaws, for instance Major, Nippy, and Dibby, who terrorized parts of East Kimberley in 1908, were also former police trackers, and so were many other "trouble-makers". Rev. E. R. B. Gribble, the somewhat forbidding superintendent of the Forrest River mission, once reprimanded one of his flock for some misdemeanour. "Me police boy one time," replied the aborigine, "and me no afraid; I savee."[73]

After the murder Pigeon and Captain, together with all the freed prisoners, took refuge in the Oscar Range. Soon after two drovers were ambushed near the place of the first killing, and their guns and ammunition made a welcome addition to the armoury of the insurgents. Widespread rumours of a general uprising began to circulate, and an urgent appeal was sent to Perth for more men, arms, and ammunition. Late in December a senior police official arrived from Roebourne to "assume command of the whole force and the direction of operations against natives".[74] Meanwhile, unrest had spread to Oobagooma station north of Derby where the aborigines, led by two former stockboys, tried to kill the manager and the white stockmen. The police, however, soon had the situation under control. According to official reports, twenty-seven Oobagooma aborigines were killed by a police party late in January 1895; another seventy were "dispersed" near Fitzroy Crossing by means of "extreme measures".[75] Pigeon, accompanied by a small group, managed to escape, and for the next two and a half years the outlaws roamed the limestone country between the Leopold and the Barrier ranges, evading all pursuers, until they were cornered near Fairfield station in the Oscar Range. In the resulting state of tension, said G. C. Bolton, whenever the settlers "sighted natives of whose intentions they were doubtful, they were inclined to shoot first and ask questions afterwards".[76]

Meanwhile, the situation in the northwest was gradually assuming some of the complexity which was to mark race relations in this area at a later stage. By the middle eighties aboriginal labour had become "a most useful factor in the prosperity of the settlers",[77] particularly to the east of the North West Cape where the aborigines did nearly all the shepherding, shearing, and stock-riding. But there were signs that the demand for aboriginal labour had already passed its peak. The system of paddocking, introduced in 1878 on the De Grey station and gradually adopted by other stations, diminished the need for aboriginal shepherds. Indentured Chinese servants were slowly taking the place of aboriginal domestic help. Following the discovery of gold (on the Pilbara and the Nullagine in 1888, a year later on the Ashburton), white labour was available for the first time in many areas, and aborigines and Europeans began to compete for the same jobs. In the region south of the North West Cape, however, conditions remained unsettled, and the pastoralists were becoming increasingly exasperated with continued depredations. "I think if the Government would shut their eyes for six months," said a young squatter by the name of C. F. Gale before a magistrate inquiring into sheep-killing in the Murchison and Gascoyne districts, "and let the settlers deal with the natives in their own way it would stop their depredations effectually"[78] (this was in 1882; twenty-five years later Gale was appointed Chief Protector of Aborigines). In 1883 the Legislative Council increased the range of offences for which an aborigine could be tried summarily, and an itinerant magistrate was appointed to deal with the offenders on the spot. As a result, the population of the Rottnest Island Penal Establishment doubled in less than a year.

In the pacified parts of the northwest, the precarious adjustment which had been worked out in the seventies was slowly breaking down. There were signs of depopulation on the De Grey and Harding rivers and on the Murchison.[79] A new generation of men and women were growing up who knew nothing of the life before the white man's arrival. Sensing that many customs and beliefs of their people were baseless, the young tended to ignore the old men's knowledge and authority, only to discover that the Europeans were not willing to share their way of life with them. This led to disillusionment and conflict. Many young people became resentful, unreliable as workers, and "cheeky" towards their employers and Europeans in general. In the closely settled parts of the colony the aborigines were dying out; by the eighties only small detribalized remnants were left, eking out a miserable existence on charity and government rations. Some tribes along the coast had disappeared almost completely, while others had shrunk to insignificant groups. In 1891, only eleven full-bloods were counted in the Perth magisterial district, twenty-eight on the Murray, and twenty-four and twenty-nine in the Wellington and Sussex districts respectively. The aboriginal problem in the southwest was close to its final solution.

The Aborigines Protection Board

It is against this background that the findings of the 1883 Native Commission should be viewed. Its report, based on the premise of a gradual extinction of the aborigines, stressed the government's duty to "see that the natives be kindly treated; that they be helped with food and clothing; that missions be encouraged; and that the old, the infirm, and the sick be provided for". Since the aborigine would never "be more than a servant of the white man", his education should be limited to "useful instruction" and entrusted to Christian missions, "liberally supported by the State". But, warned the commission, it was futile trying to change the aborigines' natural way of living: "If good could easily have been done, it would have been done long ago."[80] On the administrative side, the commission recommended the setting up of a board to organize the distribution of relief to aboriginal paupers and to supervise aboriginal reserves, and the appointment of protectors of aborigines to act as agents for the board. The recommendations were implemented by the 1886 Aborigines Protection Act which set up an Aborigines Protection Board whose members were appointed by, and responsible to the Governor alone. The powers and duties of the board were defined in s.6 of the act. It was responsible for the apportioning of moneys granted by the legislature for the benefit of aborigines; it distributed rations, clothing, blankets, and medicine to "sick, aged and infirm" aborigines; it "managed and regulated" the use of aboriginal reserves; and exercised "general supervision and care" over all matters affecting aborigines. The act also set up a rudimentary field organization, by authorizing the appointment of protectors of aborigines with powers similar to those held by the guardians of aborigines appointed in the forties. The position was an honorary one (in the sense that it involved no additional remuneration) and devolved as a rule upon resident magistrates, police officers, and constables, as part of their official duties, or upon justices of the peace. In 1892 a paid travelling inspector was appointed to supplement the work of the part-time protectors, particularly in the northwest. In 1896 two more appointments were made, one for the goldfields and one for the Kimberleys.

These were promising signs. Equally heartening was the revival of missionary activity and its encouragement by the government, in the form of land grants and subsidies. In 1884, after several false starts, a Roman Catholic mission was established by Father McNab, formerly in charge of an aboriginal settlement at Durundur in Queensland, at Disaster Bay on the western shore of King Sound. It was abandoned soon after, but in 1890 Bishop Gibney founded a mission at Beagle Bay in West Kimberley, with the help of the French order of La Trappe. In 1885 the Anglicans sent Rev. J. B. Gribble, a pioneer clergyman in the Riverina whose travels had brought him into contact with the remnants of the Murrumbidgee River aborigines, to start a mission on the Gascoyne, not far from Carnarvon. The venture ended in an angry quarrel between the Reverend and the squatters — the celebrated, rather squalid, "Gribble affair", during which the welfare of aborigines was "obscured in an all-round blackening of reputations".[81] Gribble was a tactless, headstrong, and self-righteous man, as well as something of an idealist. In 1886 he published a book entitled *Dark Deeds in a Sunny Land,* in which he accused the Gascoyne settlers, as a body, of maltreating the aborigines. As many a humanitarian after him,

Gribble had overstated his case; the fact that he was a "t'othersider" only made things worse. He was ostracized by the settlers, refused supplies, threatened with violence, and in the end literally driven out. In 1890 the Church of England established another, smaller mission on the outskirts of Carnarvon, but it was closed in 1896.

Western Australia acquires full control of aboriginal affairs

Unlike the eastern colonies, Western Australia did not acquire full control of aboriginal administration when it achieved responsible government. On the insistence of the Colonial Office, s.70 of the 1889 Constitution Act provided that, even after the granting of responsible government, aboriginal affairs should remain the responsibility of the Aborigines Protection Board rather than of a Minister of the Crown, and that in directing the board the Governor should continue to act independently of his constitutional advisers. As a further precaution, the act prescribed that a minimum of $10,000 or 1 per cent of gross colonial revenue, whichever was greater, should be appropriated annually to the welfare of the aborigines (in New Zealand Britain retained responsibility for the Maoris — and the cost of fighting them — for seven years after the grant of responsible government in 1856). It was an anomalous provision, included in the act as a condition of the granting of responsible government, under pressure from British philanthropists. Constitutionally, it was incompatible with the spirit of self-government, and it was largely unworkable politically. With a sympathetic government the board was unnecessary; with a government hostile to the aborigines, it was next to useless.[82] And the colonial government was anything but friendly. It was particularly unhappy about the financial provisions of s.70. As a result of the gold discoveries of the first half of the nineties, colonial revenue reached a level unimaginable in 1886: in 1897 1 per cent of gross revenue devoted to the welfare of aborigines amounted to $33,912. The first attempt to have the board abolished was made in 1892, and in 1894 parliament passed legislation repealing s.70 of the 1899 Constitution Act, but the bill lapsed while the Colonial Office was trying to make up its mind whether to veto it or not. The board was eventually abolished early in 1898, after the Premier, John Forrest, while in England, persuaded the Secretary of State for the Colonies, Joseph Chamberlain, to relinquish control of aboriginal affairs. On 1 April 1898 the functions of the board were formally taken over by the Aborigines Department, and the people of Western Australia

received into their care the sacred charge of several thousand human beings. The Imperial Government ended its rule of uncertainty, inconsistency and neglect and handed on a charge that was ill-kempt, contaminated, hopeless and despised.[83]

2. The Aboriginal Problem in 1898

Distribution of aboriginal population

In April 1898, when Western Australia acquired full control of aboriginal affairs, the white population of the colony had surpassed 166,000 and the aboriginal population had decreased to somewhere between 20,000 and 23,000. This estimate is little more than a guess, nor can it be anything else, given the conditions prevailing in Western Australia during the nineteenth century. To study the demographic characteristics of any population two types of data are required: adequate census returns and vital registrations. Neither of these are available for the colonial period. The first census, conducted in 1848, enumerated only the aborigines "in the located parts of the colony"; the censuses of 1854, 1859, 1870, and 1881 listed only aborigines in private employment; those of 1891 and 1901 enumerated the "civilized" aborigines, that is those who could be reached by normal census-taking procedures. As for vital registrations, no attempt was made during the nineteenth century to enforce the registration of births, deaths, and marriages, not only with respect to full-bloods but also as regards part-aborigines. Other potential sources of information, such as settlers' reminiscences or reports of early explorers, are equally inadequate; in 1901, for instance, F. S. Brockmann put the number of aborigines in North Kimberley alone at 10,000. How then, it may be asked, was the above estimate arrived at? Every count of aboriginal population, until quite recently, had always comprised two sub-totals: "civilized" aborigines and aborigines "beyond the confines of civilization". In 1899, according to "an approximate census", based on police returns, there were 12,183 aborigines and part-aborigines in the settled regions of the colony, excluding the Kimberleys east of Leopold Range.[1] If we add the figure of about 3,000 for East and North Kimberley, we get a total of approximately 15,000 aborigines in various stages of contact. As for aborigines "beyond the confines of civilization", contemporary guesses put their numbers at between 20,000 and 30,000.[2] This was clearly an overestimate: a total of 6,000–8,000 would have been more realistic.

The grouping of the surviving aboriginal population differed greatly from the original distribution.[3] In 1829 there were approximately 18,000 aborigines south of the Gascoyne River; by the end of the century the full-blood population of the same area (excluding the still uncharted country between the eastern goldfields and the South Australian border) had decreased to about 3,000. In the southwest land division, which may have originally supported a population of 12,500–15,000, there were only some 850 full-bloods left, including a number of northwest aborigines brought down by the settlers as farm labourers or personal servants. Some southwest tribes had disappeared without a trace; others were represented by one or two survivors (these were collected in 1901 on the Maamba reserve near Welshpool). Portents of similar developments could be seen on the eastern goldfields and along the south coast which accounted for about 1,150 individuals, evenly distributed between the two regions. On the goldfields the miners and prospectors had appropriated all natural water resources, forcing the aborigines to congregate around townships or mining camps where they could get water from condensers or wells. In 1903 the travelling inspector of aborigines reported that he could see no children among the goldfields tribes,[4] and in 1908 the district police officer at Coolgardie prophesied that in a few years time the goldfields aborigines would be "as extinct as the dodo".[5] Along the south coast the full-bloods had almost disappeared; the remnants became attached to pastoral properties. Daisy Bates, who visited the area in 1908–1909 and again in 1912, found only two survivors of the original Esperance group, and "not half a dozen natives" along the coast between Esperance and Eucla; at Eucla she counted thirty aborigines camped in the vicinity, but only one of the original Eucla group.[6] On the Murchison, all of the thousand or so surviving full-bloods had settled on pastoral properties or around townships; in the East Murchison, where there was no substantial pastoral settlement, the country was almost devoid of aboriginal population.

The remaining settled parts of the colony had an aboriginal population of perhaps 12,000, in various stages of sophistication. On one end there were the "civilized" aborigines living in or around townships or on pastoral and mission stations; at the other end were the "bush" aborigines living their traditional lives but becoming increasingly aware of, and accustomed to, the white man's presence. In the northwest, where perhaps 3,500 aborigines had become more or less permanently attached to white settlements,[7] nomadic aborigines formed a small portion of the total aboriginal population. The coastal tribes were in the process of dying out, although this was not apparent at the time. "The inlanders were even in those years coming . . . to replace the coast groups that had died out", Daisy Bates noticed in 1901, while droving cattle from Broome to her property in the Ophthalmia Range, "until they, in their turn, succumbed to the new conditions"[8] (in 1886 Curr reported an increase in numbers of the Ngurla which may have been due to a coastward drift of inland groups).[9] In the more recently settled Kimberleys, nomadic aborigines outnumbered those who had attached themselves to pastoral properties, while some tribes in North and Northwest Kimberley were yet to make their first contact with civilization; around Broome, by then the centre of the colony's pearling industry, "the tribes of the place were but a remnant".[10]

The part-aboriginal population of the colony in all probability exceeded 1,000. The census of 1891, the first to make a separate count of part-aborigines, recorded 571 "half-castes" (this term was used until 1936 to denote all part-aborigines irrespective of caste). Ten years later the official figure was 957 but the actual number was almost certainly higher because of the nomadic habits of some part-aborigines, especially on the Murchison and in the northwest. At the time of the 1901 census part-aborigines formed over 45 per cent of the total aboriginal population of the southwest land division, and were fast becoming a major social problem. Their rapid increase was due largely to intermarriage and interbreeding. "These were robust, meat-eating people — the women big like the men and as vigorous. The family heads were mostly first-cross people. They travelled the country with their camel carts, horses, buggies, and what not, in family groups, and they were good, hard workers. They were a people apart, and intermarriage was inevitable".[11]

About the turn of the century, then, the aborigines of Western Australia could be divided into three groups. In the southwest, along the south coast and on the eastern goldfields the full-bloods were dying out and the numbers of part-aborigines were increasing. In the pastoral north the aborigines had on the whole adjusted to European presence and preserved much of their traditional way of life. In North Kimberley, the Great Sandy Desert, the Gibson Desert, and the Western Australian portion of the Great Victoria Desert and the Nullarbor Plain roamed the "bush" aborigines for whom the white man was but a rumour. The distinction between the pastoral north and the closely settled south is of fundamental importance. The pastoral regions were part of "colonial Australia";[12] in 1901 the northwest and the Kimberleys had a European population of 5,467, "ruling" over approximately 12,000 aborigines and 4,000 Asians whose labour was essential for the pearling and the pastoral industries. In the south, the part-aborigines and the remaining full-bloods had no economic role to play: they were an unwanted and increasingly despised minority group.

The Kimberleys

In the pastoral north, the Aborigines Department was called upon to deal with two distinct problems. In the northwest, by then almost completely pacified, aboriginal administration was concerned primarily with the twin issues of providing the pastoralists with aboriginal labour, and, increasingly, protecting aboriginal workers from maltreatment. In the Kimberleys, on the other hand, except for the coastal fringe, the main task of aboriginal administration was continued protection of settlers from aboriginal attacks and depredations. But there was a difference between the earlier mode of maintaining "law and order", when a settler could shoot a few "niggers" in reprisal, without any fear of consequences, and the later method of pacification. By about 1900 the great wave of expansion was nearly over, and, with the pioneering days drawing to a close, the government sought to assert its monopoly of justice, and later, as the settlers took the local aborigines into their employ,[13] to lay down the conditions of employment as well. The implementation of this policy was hampered by three factors: the huge areas involved, the distance from the centre of government in Perth, and the persistence of "settler attitude" among the Europeans, often including government officials. This emerges clearly from the following account. In February 1901 the East Kimberley pastoralist J.J. Durack was shot by two aboriginal servants on the verandah of his Dunham River homestead. As was customary on such occasions, a party of police and special constables (settlers sworn in for the occasion) were sent out from nearby Wyndham and apprehended the presumed murderers; they were eventually tried in Perth, one being sentenced to ten years' imprisonment, the other acquitted. Contrary to the explicit instruction of the Commissioner of Police, the resident magistrate at Wyndham appointed as the leader of the posse the Wyndham clerk of courts, Sir Alexander Cockburn-Campbell, the eldest son of the one-time editor of the *West Australian*, Sir Thomas Cockburn-Campbell, and a "man with an unenviable reputation and not fitted to such a position".[14] When this became known in Perth, the local humanitarians protested to the Premier, George Throssell, who subsequently ordered an investigation into the circumstances of Cockburn-Campbell's appointment. The East Kimberley settlers, for their part, tried to represent the isolated shooting as part of a general uprising. In a telegram to the Premier, Durack's partner warned that the aborigines north of Hall's Creek were out of hand and that the settlers would have to abandon their holdings unless stern action was taken. In the event, the posse returned to Wyndham without any incidents, since the police had been instructed not to use firearms unless absolutely necessary.

In addition to its stated opposition to reprisals, the government tried to impress upon the settlers that it was determined to prosecute and punish them for all acts of violence committed against the aborigines. The application of this principle left much to be desired. Many assaults on aborigines remained undetected, for there was usually no one to report them. The pastoralist who had beaten up or perhaps seriously wounded an aborigine could not be expected to do so, and the recipients of such treatment hardly ever did. Convictions were difficult to obtain, since the case against the settler usually rested on the evidence of aboriginal witnesses who did not understand the importance of exact testimony. Witnesses were frequently intimidated and would sometimes disappear before the trial, or they would retract in court statements made during the preliminary investigation.[15] Friends would occasionally warn a settler of his impending arrest and help him to get away; in 1901, for instance, East Kimberley settlers collected $600 to enable a Turkey Creek pastoralist, about to be arrested for the alleged murder of two aborigines, to escape to South Australia. If the case was a minor one, it was sometimes decided by the local justice of the peace (rather than a magistrate) — perhaps a friend of the person before him, usually a fellow settler, and always a member of his colour group. In 1904 a white man assaulted an aborigine in the main street of Wyndham, the incident having been witnessed by several Europeans prepared to testify against him. The local justice of the peace dismissed the case, saying that he was not going to punish a white for assaulting a black man, adding that the incident would not have happened "if the blacks kept to themselves".[16] If the offence was punishable by death, the case was tried by a judge and an all-white jury, with predictable results. No matter what the evidence, juries consistently refused to convict a European: white prestige was felt to be at stake.

The settlers, on their part, expected from the government full protection for themselves and their stock, especially in East Kimberley where conditions were to remain unsettled until about the beginning of the First World War (in West Kimberley sheep-killing had almost died out by about 1900). Some pastoralists persuaded the more troublesome groups to camp near their homesteads and "no more killem bullock", by giving them regular rations of meat and flour, or they tried to placate them by gifts of tomahawks, pipes, and tobacco. Most pastoralists, however, insisted on police protection. The police, understaffed and overworked, did their best, but this was not good enough for some settlers who expected the police to act as boundary riders and to arrest suspected cattle-killers en masse, only to fail to prosecute after arrest. In 1895 Patrick B. Durack, an East Kimberley pioneer, recorded in his diary "a heated discussion with Inspector Orme, who openly asserted that the squatters were afraid to venture far enough afield to properly round up their cattle. I defiantly threw back the taunt".[17] The police tended to delegate much of their work to aboriginal trackers — mostly discharged cattle-killers or even serving prisoners. A tracker was a personal servant of his constable and not a member of the police force; his master received a special allowance of up to 30 cents a day to keep him in food and uniform. Since aboriginal trackers were invariably "engaged" without a contract or any other authority of office, they had no legal power to make arrests or to be left in charge of prisoners.[18] This did not prevent them from discharging their duties with utmost efficiency. If an aborigine speared a beast, the members of his group usually shared his kill, and, since the possession of even a small portion of the carcass was deemed to be sufficient evidence, whole groups were arrested when surprised in their feast. Since a constable could claim a daily living allowance of 24 cents "per knob" for all aborigines arrested, women and children were usually brought in as "witnesses" in order to swell the number of prisoners. Between January 1902 and October 1904, government expenditure under this heading amounted to $6,916, and one enterprising constable managed to collect $924 in nine months.[19] Arrests were usually made without a warrant or written information, and witnesses were always detained without any legal authority. Although the chaining of prisoners was prohibited (unless they were of "desperate character" or had been arrested at a considerable distance from the police station),[20] the men were usually chained together to prevent them from escaping. They were connected together with a long metal chain, weighing seven ounces per foot, looped around each man's neck. The loop was fairly loose, but not loose enough for the prisoner to be able to escape, and it was padlocked. There was a length of chain of about five feet between the prisoners, allowing them plenty of room when marching.

The trial of aboriginal cattle-killers was governed by the 1883 Aboriginal Offenders Act, as amended in 1892 and 1893. The cattle-killers were dealt with summarily, either by a magistrate or by two justices of the peace. If another could not be found within twenty miles, one justice could hold court — sometimes the very man whose cattle the aborigines had killed (in 1893 an amendment lifted the disqualification which had hitherto precluded a justice of the peace from adjudicating in a matter which concerned him personally). Maximum penalty was three years' imprisonment for the first offence, and five years for all subsequent offences, with or without flogging. In the customary absence of defence, the proceedings were something of a formality. The aborigines were herded into the dock, often in large groups. The prosecution was usually conducted by the arresting constable. Cross-examination was either in Pidgin or through an interpreter, as a rule the aboriginal tracker who had assisted with the arrest. The accused almost always pleaded guilty, by answering all questions with the standard "might be", or, having earlier admitted their offence to the constable, by saying nothing at all. On one occasion, according to camp-fire yarns, a constable returning from patrol fed his prisoners on pollard and water, a diet which soon swelled their stomachs. After every meal he would smack his stomach and say "good fella tucker", until they started to imitate him. In Wyndham the magistrate repeated the procedure, the natives chorused "good fella tucker", and, having pleaded guilty, were duly convicted.[21]

Sentences varied from six months' to five years' imprisonment, two to three years being the rule. Short-term prisoners served their sentences in one of the aboriginal prisons located at Broome, Wyndham, Roebourne, and Carnarvon; long-term prisoners, before 1903, were sent to the Rottnest Island Penal Establishment (the gaol was closed in that year). The prisoners in the northern gaols spent their terms in neck-chains, except those "farmed out" as trackers to the police, or as rouseabouts to telegraph linesmen and other government officials. Chained to one another or to their wheelbarrows, they were put to work on road repairs or other public works, while at night they were fastened to rings attached to prison walls. For all its obvious cruelty, life in gaol had some compensation for most aborigines: their diet was exactly the same as that given to white convicts, consisting of generous helpings of rice, vegetables, bread, and tea, and twelve ounces of meat a day. Little wonder that discharged cattle-killers, "healthy, fat and sleeky",[22] thought nothing of another spell in prison. The whole elaborate system of pacification was in fact losing its effectiveness, but it took ten years and a near-crisis in East Kimberley before it was changed.

The northwest

In the northwest, aboriginal administration was concerned largely with the twin issue of providing the pastoralists with aboriginal labour and protecting aboriginal workers from maltreatment. The problem of labour supply arose out of several factors. One was the gradual breakdown of the phase of "intelligent parasitism", due partly to depopulation, and partly to the new tensions resulting from the conflict between the old and the more acculturated young generation. Perceiving that some of the customs and beliefs of their fathers appeared to be baseless, the young people tended to ignore the old men, only to find that the Europeans were not prepared to share their "tribal secrets" with them.[23] An old man told John Wilson (of the Department of Anthropology, University of Western Australia) how, in his youth, his group had persistently tried to camp near a station in order to learn more of the white man's ways, only to be chased away with equal persistency. Like Pigeon and his band of Kimberley outlaws, the younger people found themselves suspended between two cultures; "as they became more acculturated in the new system so they became more dissatisfied".[24] This dissatisfaction expressed itself in unwillingness to engage as workers, "laziness", "insolence", "independent demeanour", and desire for a "change", that is wandering from station to station. Naturally, there were exceptions, and pastoralists who had the "knack of getting on with natives" had usually little trouble on their stations. The treatment to which station aborigines appear to have responded best was" firmness with gentleness"[25] and, above all, consistency, which made them feel they knew where they stood with the pastoralist. Most of the early pioneers seem to have had this aptitude. Isolated from the outside world, they lived in close social proximity to their workers, often camping with them in the same camp. "They were sometimes tough", observed an old station hand, "but they were good old daddies."[26] Their sons, or the managers representing the growing number of absentee owners, had usually different ideas. Some expected the government to ration their workers when they became destitute, and favoured the "well-behaved" aborigines and their dependents when distributing food, clothing, and tobacco. This created dissatisfaction and psychological disturbance. To be "knocked back" meant more than having to go without food or a smoke; it was the "repudiation of a social tie".[27]

A second factor affecting the supply of aboriginal labour, at least in some parts of the northwest, was due to a geographical accident. The Pilbara and the Nullagine had deposits of alluvial tin. The metal was discovered in 1892 on the Shaw River, southwest of Marble Bar, and later at Cooglegon and at Moolyella, twelve miles north and east of Marble Bar respectively. Because of a slump in the price of tin, the fields were abandoned soon after the discovery, but the miners returned when prices rose again in 1899 — and with them came the aborigines. Daisy Bates, who passed through the district in 1900, saw many aborigines specking out for gold or working the alluvial tin deposits, using a typically aboriginal method known as yandying — "a peculiar way . . . of shaking with their hands, extracting the tin as clean as possible".[28] In 1904 the police counted about 70 aborigines on the Shaw field alone; two years later about 150 were reported yandying on the Shaw and the same number at Moolyella. A good worker could earn a tidy sum; in 1904, when the price of tin was $90 a ton, some aborigines earned up to $12 a month or 5 cents per pound if they were paid by results.

In contrast with most other colonial areas, the problem of labour supply was not a serious one in pastoral Western Australia. There were no professional recruiters in the colony, for none were needed. The pastoralist was his own recruiter. His main problem was how to teach his workers "steady" habits, and to keep them from running away or disappearing from time to time. This is where contracts of service, called agreements, fitted in: they were, as a rule, used to keep one's labour, not to acquire it in the first place. Under the master and servant legislation, going back to 1841, a servant who had entered into a contract of service could be sentenced summarily to up to three months' imprisonment for absenting himself without an adequate reason or for neglecting his work, being also entitled to speedy redress for non-payment of wages or mistreatment. Written agreements were used occasionally in the southwest during the forties and the fifties; during the seventies and eighties they were fairly common on the Murchison and, to a lesser extent, also in the northwest. As can be imagined, the system was readily open to abuse. When short of labour, a pastoralist would produce a piece of paper purporting to be a contract of service, lay a complaint against the aborigine named in the document, and ask the police to catch the fellow for him. As far as the aboriginal servant was concerned, the protective clauses of the master and servant legislation were of little use to him, for his normal way of registering dissatisfaction with his employer was not to complain to a magistrate but to run away. Some of the abuses inherent in the use of agreements were remedied by the 1886 Aborigines Protection Act. The legislation provided that a contract of service was not enforceable in court unless it had been made in the prescribed manner, and reduced the maximum penalty for absconding from service to one month's imprisonment. The act did not specifically state that the master and servant legislation no longer applied to aborigines, but by prescribing certain protective conditions in contracts of service with aborigines it appears to have deprived them in practice of the benefits previously conferred upon them by that legislation. It was not until 1892, however, that aboriginal servants were explicitly excluded from the application of the master and servant legislation. By another act, passed during the same session of parliament, the maximum penalty for a breach of contract was increased to three months and the employer's liability for a similar breach was reduced to a nominal fine. The act also reintroduced flogging, abolished in 1883, and subsequent regulations prescribed in considerable detail the size and shape of the cat-o'-nine tails to be used for such punishment. It was not to weigh more than five ounces and the lashes were to be "small cord, about a quarter of an inch in diameter, with the

ends tapering off, but seized with small twine to prevent un-
ravelling, and no knobs are permitted anywhere on the lashes".[29]
Finally, in 1893, another act removed the disqualification preclud-
ing a justice of the peace from adjudicating in a case which concerned
him personally: the already considerable power in the hands of the
settlers became authority. In 1899 a Murchison pastoralist sentenced
one of his aborigines to two months' hard labour with flogging. The
cat-o'-nine tails used on that occasion, reported the *Sunday Times,*
weighed twenty-two ounces and had a "handle made of the butt of
a billiard cue and nine thongs of leather each half an inch thick".[30]

This formidable array of penal sanctions, it should be remembered,
applied only to aborigines employed under contracts of service. Since
these were not registered, there is no way of establishing the proportion of aborigines employed in this manner at any given time (in
1904, according to the *Report of the Royal Commission on the
Conditions of Natives,* the exact figure was 369, or just under one-
tenth of all aborigines in employment).[31] The incidence of agreements varied from area to area, without any clear pattern of distribution. About the turn of the century they were common in certain
parts of the Murchison and the Gascoyne, mainly on properties
near the main roads where aboriginal station hands were
frequently enticed by travellers or neighbouring pastoralists (it was
here that some of the well-publicized floggings had occurred). In
the Kimberleys, where the pastoralists had not yet come to rely on
aboriginal stockmen, contracts of service were unnecessary. The
link between the station aborigines and their tribal country was still
unbroken, and since there was a sort of code of honour among the
pastoralists not to interfere with each other's aborigines, a runaway
stockman had usually no choice but to return to his station. This
was no longer the case in the northwest where many aborigines were
said to be "cheeky", "independent", "unreliable", and liked to
wander from station to station. For this reason the pastoralists
preferred indentured workers, but the aborigines refused to sign on.
Since most stations depended heavily on aboriginal labour, even for
shearing, this left the pastoralist at the mercy of his aboriginal
workforce, especially on the Pilbara and the Nullagine where the
aborigines would abandon their jobs whenever they felt like a spell
on the tinfields. When the price of tin was high a mass exodus of
station aborigines would take place, leaving the surrounding properties with hardly any labour. "Money in hand" was a new ex-

perience for the aborigines. Some spent it on drink, willingly supplied by the white miners or storekeepers. Others bought shotguns, and not only to shoot kangaroos. In 1904 a contractor, Tresillian Hallet, overheard two Pyramid station aborigines discussing preparations for a rebellion. At a given signal, all pastoralists in the Roebourne and Port Hedland districts were to be killed; in the case of government intervention, the insurgents were going to "shoot the bloody government" as well.[32] The police were put on full alert and all Europeans were issued with rifles, but the precautions turned out to be unnecessary. The Aborigines Act, passed in the following year, made it an offence for an aboriginal native to use or carry a gun without "having in force a licence, in writing, in the prescribed form granted to him by a protector"; if an aborigine could not produce a licence on demand, any policeman could "lawfully" confiscate his gun.

The pastoralists paid their station labour in kind, with few exceptions — in the Shark Bay area they paid cash wages in order to stop their workers from drifting into other jobs, such as pearling and fishing (by 1910 small cash payments had become common in the Roebourne district also); and part-aborigines, at this stage, were as a rule paid a white man's wage. The system of payment in kind was due not only to the profit motive — the supply of money was scarce everywhere until the late 1880s, and besides, outside the coastal areas nothing could be bought with it, or only from the pastoralists. Under the prevailing system, a station worker was paid in food, clothing, and a few luxuries such as tobacco. If an aborigine was employed under contract, the quantity was prescribed in the agreement (no minimum was prescribed by legislation); otherwise it was left to the employer's discretion. The food was mainly flour, meat, sugar, and tea, in varying quantities. At Minderoo station in the Ashburton, partly owned by the Forrest family, aboriginal workers were given as much meat and other staples as they could eat. On Boolardy station in the Murchison, the weekly ration for a married couple consisted of fourteen pounds of flour, two pounds of sugar, a quarter of an ounce of tea, and two sticks of tobacco, and the aborigines were expected to supplement this with native game. Elsewhere they were given no tea or sugar, as on Mount Clere station in the Murchison, where rations consisted of meat, flour, and tobacco. In West Kimberley rice was often substituted for flour; at Roebuck Plains station a couple received a weekly ration of twelve pounds of rice, twelve pounds of meat, two pounds of sugar, and the customary two sticks of tobacco. The food was usually prepared and consumed in the camp. Clothing was as a rule issued once a year. Men received a blanket, a shirt, a pair of trousers, and a hat. Women were given a blanket and one or two cheap cotton dresses. On one station, in the early 1890s, male workers were given a shirt, and the choice between a pair of trousers and a blanket.[33]

Is it fair to describe these conditions as "bond service bordering on slavery", "little better than slavery", "a species of slavery", or "exploitation"? Such charges, about the turn of the century, came mainly from outsiders or the local "relics of the Exeter Hall",[34] and were given wide circulation in the English and eastern Australian press. The philanthropists making these sweeping accusations based their case almost entirely on the existence of penal sanctions in labour contracts, whereas the proportion of aborigines employed under indenture was in fact negligible. Furthermore, there is no evidence to suggest that free labour was better-off than contract labour. An aborigine employed under contract, while liable to corporal punishment or imprisonment, was entitled to free medical treatment and prescribed rations, and was also protected from dismissal during slack periods. Nor does the incidence of convictions for absconding from service (fifteen in 1900–1901, nine in 1901–1902, four in 1902–1903, and seven in 1903–1904) indicate a widespread dissatisfaction among contract labour. The most objectionable feature of the contract system was the indenturing of children for domestic work, from the age of eight onward, but the number of such "indentures of apprenticeship" was small, amounting to a mere fifty in 1902. As for payment in kind, did this amount to "exploitation"? Two questions are relevant here: was aboriginal labour cheap, and was it efficient? In the absence of an accurate survey of these issues, the answers must be necessarily inconclusive. The pastoralists maintained, not without some justification, that aboriginal labour was not really cheap. They had to keep their workers and their dependents not only in food but also in clothes and tobacco; they also had to supply their contract workers with "medicines and medical services where practicable and necessary" (after 1905 this obligation was extended to all workers). Were the aborigines, materially speaking, worse off than before the arrival of the white man? The savings effected by the pastoralists employing aboriginal instead of white labour (when they could get it) must have been minimal. The old stockman was not an expensive employee. His weekly wage was rarely higher than $5, his keep consisted mainly of salt beef and damper, and his quarters were not much better than those of the station aborigines. The pastoralists also claimed, again not without some justification, that aboriginal labour was inefficient, though the customary assertion that "it took three natives to do one white man's job properly" was no doubt an exaggeration.[35] Most aborigines on pastoral properties, said A. P. Elkin, did no more work "than will ensure rations and some extras. It is bare, subsistence labour . . . for the most part uninterested and inefficient".[36] Finally, it should be added that Christian missions also paid their native workers in kind, yet they were not, at this stage, accused of exploiting them.

It seems, therefore, that if the charges of "slavery" and "exploitation" are to be taken seriously, they must be based on other grounds than the existence of penal sanctions and the absence of cash wages. The Dutch scholar, H. J. Niebour, writing in 1900, stated that the presence or absence of slavery in a society depends on the economic state of that society. Slavery (or some form of forced labour) as a rule will not occur in a situation where people are prepared to work for wages "voluntarily"; it will occur in a situation where it is possible to make a living without the help of capital or where unoccupied land is freely available.[37] How does this explanation fit the conditions in "colonial" Australia? It is true that, as their traditional sources of food dwindled, most aborigines had no alternative but to join the ranks of subsistence station labour. At the same time, there is little evidence to suggest that the aborigines were dismayed at the prospect; on the contrary, pastoral employment had considerable appeal for the aborigines who were quick to succumb to the attractions of white man's food and stimulants. W. E. H. Stanner, who was one of the first to make a study of this phenomenon, relates that his Northern Territory informants told him how their appetites for tobacco and tea became so intense that no one could do without them.

Jealousy, ill-will and violence arose over the division of the small amounts which came by gift and exchange . . . Individuals, families and parties of friends simply went away to places where the avidly desired things could be obtained. The movement had phases and fluctuations, but it was always a one way movement.[38]

This should serve as a reminder that the question of relationship between the pastoralists and aborigines is a complex one. For all its hardship, station life was not without a bright side for most aborigines. One only has to dip into the writings of Mary Durack to realize that the life of an aboriginal stockman was not one of unmitigated misery, particularly if the owner lived on the property.[39] Ideally, the relationship between a pastoralist and "his" aborigines was not unlike the contractual relationship between a European feudal lord and his serfs, involving reciprocal obligations based on the recognition of certain common interests. The pastoralist was bound by law to allow the aborigines to roam the unimproved parts of his lease, and in any case he dared not antagonize them beyond a certain point, for if he did they were wont to exercise their "right of revolt" — by walking off his station or killing his stock.

No sign of the slave about him up in the Far North [said Henrietta Drake-Brockman] whatever may be said in the press from time to time. He'll work for you . . . but somehow you understand quite well that if he didn't wish to, he'd walk off "bush" in a second. Servility is unknown. He looks you in the eye, human to human; if he doesn't call you Missi or Boss, the chances are he'll call you by your Christian name.[40]

The south

In comparison with the pastoral north, the aboriginal problem in the remainder of Western Australia was thought to be comparatively simple — the full-bloods were dying out, while the part-aborigines were still few in number. The main task of aboriginal administration was the distribution of rations, blankets, and medicines — a job discharged since 1865 by resident magistrates as part of their official duties. Initially only those "utterly destitute and incapable of seeking their own livelihood"[41] were rationed, but the rule was gradually relaxed, and by the end of the century most of the surviving full-bloods in the southwest were on relief. Adult ration was 16 pounds of flour, $5\frac{1}{4}$ pounds of meat, $1\frac{1}{2}$ pounds of sugar, and $1\frac{1}{2}$ ounces of tea a week, plus an occasional stick of tobacco. The blankets and clothing issued to aboriginal paupers remained the property of Her Majesty, and it was an offence to dispose of them without the sanction of a protector or a justice of the peace. As an added precaution, the blankets were dyed in imperial colours.

Very few full-bloods had permanent jobs. Some worked for the police as trackers or as stable-boys, others found employment as farm hands, while the girls and women were always in demand as domestic servants. Rates of pay were approximately the same as for white unskilled labour — $6 to $10 a month and keep for men, up to $4 a month and keep for women. Most full-bloods preferred to live on government rations, even when jobs were offering, wandering around in small groups and taking on casual clearing, fencing, or shearing jobs. Pauperism was most pronounced on the eastern goldfields where full-bloods had been precluded by the Mining Act from obtaining employment on any mining tenement without the permission in writing of the warden (because of an oversight, they could however acquire a miner's right, and in the early 1930s several Mount Margaret mission inmates availed themselves of this opportunity). Forced to congregate around the wells and condensers, the surviving full-bloods wandered from one mining camp to another "like tribes of Arabs," begging, pilfering, and bartering their women for liquor.[42] "They are certainly a most degraded lot", reported the travelling inspector of aborigines in 1903, "they appear to be utterly spoilt by the whites, and are now absolutely useless."[43]

The part-aborigines became a recognized problem sometime during the 1890s. In 1891 there were 571 "half-castes" in the colony; ten years later the number had gone up to 951 (691 in the southwest land division and the metropolitan area alone). The first generation of half-castes was the product of circumstances occurring all over Australia. For many years, most of the frontier settlements consisted almost entirely of men who, not unnaturally, found certain emotional comfort in the company of aboriginal women. As a rule, these casual associations were not marked (at least outwardly) by jealousy of aboriginal men towards the European partners. On the contrary, they sometimes encouraged them as means of procuring food and particularly stimulants. The women, for their part, felt attracted to the white men who alone could provide these novel and desirable goods. As in other parts of Australia, aboriginal women were occasionally kidnapped or demanded under threat of violence, but this was exceptional; it was the aboriginal women who came to the conquerors; it was they who were the first agents of contact. Some of these early unions were often marriages in all but name; indeed, in Western Australia, during the first three decades of settlement, intermarriage was officially encouraged by means of financial grants for the purchase of Crown land which was then settled on the aboriginal wife and her children. As the number of white women in the colony increased and something like a normal ratio between the sexes was established, the policy was abandoned but casual mating between white men and aboriginal women continued, particularly in the newly opened areas; as a northwest proverb has it, "necessity is not only the mother of invention but also the father of the half-caste". In the settled parts of the colony, as the pioneering days were drawing to a close, upright citizens began to voice stern disapproval of these "depravities", but it was not until 1905 that an attempt was made to control them. At the same time, there was an increasing tendency to blame the lower classes, particularly the kangaroo hunters and the convicts, for the continued "corruption" of native women. "Sexual intercourse" said an official in 1857, "to a great extent exists and must exist between the native women and this class of men and drink is the natural and palatable equivalent paid to the native husbands for their complaisance."[44] Needless to say, many a respectable colonist had also sown his wild oats in those days. After about 1880 miscegenation was limited largely to the "sin-sodden" north, but the part-aboriginal population of the colony continued to grow as a result of interbreeding.

By about 1870, as the offspring of the early white-aboriginal unions were reaching maturity, the question of their status was brought to the forefront. There may have been 200 of them in the colony at that time, perhaps more. Their position in society was fairly clear: they were "half-British". Some had been begotten by men of substance who as a rule did all they could to have them educated and to give them some sort of start in life. The well-known school for aboriginal children, opened by Mrs. Camfield in Albany in 1852 (with government assistance), had by 1858 several half-caste children among its pupils; by 1871, when it was transferred by Bishop Hale to Perth, all but "two or three" were of mixed parentage, "some light enough in complexion to pass quite easily for Europeans".[45] In 1878 the Church of England opened a second institution for aboriginal children, Ellensbrook, at Busselton. Some of the half-caste boys educated in these institutions found employment as messengers with the Perth Telegraph Office; others became farm-hands, and a few acquired properties of their own. The girls were usually sent to service in the country where they eventually married white men.

The position of adult half-castes was slightly more equivocal. Legally, there was a slow but steady erosion of their status from 1874 onward, but the facts of life were often different. Most part-aborigines of the nineteenth century were true half-castes, the

off-spring of white men. As "sons of white men, they demanded the
rights of the white men",[46] and were as a rule accepted as such.
There is no evidence of colour prejudice among the white Australians
at this time; if a coloured man could "stand up", he was generally
accepted as an equal. Tom Collins, in *Such is Life,* a documentary
novel set in western New South Wales, depicted the half-caste of the
eighties as "a sturdy fellow and every bit as insolent to his employer
as his white peers".[47] As late as 1906, a year after the introduction in
Western Australia of "exemption certificates", a part-aboriginal
farmer from the Bridgetown district, Edwin Turner, was refused
drink in a Bridgetown hotel because he did not have a certificate.
His complaint to the Chief Protector, in impeccable English, regarding "this unwarranted insult on the part of the authorities to a law
abiding citizen" earned him not only a certificate (without an
application) but also a prompt official apology.[48]

In the legal sphere, the first reduction in the status of part-
aborigines occurred in 1874. In 1849 the Legislative Council passed
an ordinance providing for summary trial of aborigines for all
offences except murder, arson, and rape, with sentences not to exceed
six months' imprisonment. The ordinance was extended to "persons
of the half-blood" in 1874. Summary trial of all aborigines was
abolished by the 1902 Criminal Code, but this was largely nullified
by a subsequent amendment, passed in the same year, providing that
in proceedings before justices, where an aboriginal native charged
with an offence not punishable by death pleaded guilty, the case
could be dealt with summarily. The 1880 Wines, Beer and Spirit
Sale Act, on the other hand, which prohibited the supply to aborigines of intoxicating beverages, by licensed or unlicensed persons,
did not apply to part-aborigines. The 1886 Aborigines Protection
Act, the first comprehensive attempt to regulate the aboriginal
problem, applied only to half-castes or to children of half-castes who
were "habitually associating and living with" other aborigines; in
the absence of conclusive evidence, the fact of "association" was to
be decided by a justice. In the 1891 census, however, part-aborigines
were counted with the white population of the colony, and in 1893
those who possessed the required qualifications were also given the
right to vote. The real deterioration in their legal status occurred in
the decade before the First World War and will be discussed in
chapter seven.

3. New Policies Take Shape 1898-1905

The Aborigines Department

The Aborigines Department came into existence on 1 April 1898, replacing the Aborigines Protection Board as the agency responsible for the administration of aboriginal affairs. It was a small, unimportant department near the bottom of the colonial administrative structure. It was established as a sub-department of the Treasury and its entire staff consisted of two clerks (the number was reduced to one in 1899) and a permanent head, the Chief Protector of Aborigines. The duties of the department were defined by legislation and were discharged through part-time protectors of aborigines. The first Minister in charge of the Aborigines Department was the Colonial Premier and Treasurer, John Forrest. The first Chief Protector of Aborigines was H.C. Prinsep, Under-Secretary of Mines since 1894.

Forrest's decision to take on an additional portfolio, when he was fully occupied as Premier and Treasurer (and as Colonial Secretary until the temporary abolition of that department late in April 1898), was due to two reasons. The portfolio, while insignificant in the context of local politics, was an important one from the point of view of imperial relations, and was to retain some of this importance even after the establishment of the Commonwealth of Australia. Also, Forrest was something of an expert on aboriginal affairs. Unlike many Western Australian politicians of this period, he was born in Western Australia. He grew up in Bunbury before the local aborigines had died out and later, as explorer, he made a study of aboriginal customs.[1] He was accessible to any aborigine with a real grievance, and the stables behind "The Bungalow" were always open to his aboriginal acquaintances. As Minister, he made his own policy, and his reasons for the choice of Prinsep as Chief Protector are obvious. Prinsep lacked forcefulness and knew little about aborigines. He was born in Calcutta where his father had been Advocate-General in the Bengal government, and received most of his education in England. As a young man of twenty-two he visited Western Australia where his family owned a large property in the southwest, and decided to stay after the estate had been attached for debt and sold. In 1872 he joined the public service as a draughtsman, and was Under-Secretary of Mines at the time of his appointment as Chief Protector of Aborigines. Although he had spent most of his adult life in the public service, Prinsep was not a public servant at heart; he painted, dabbled in poetry, and achieved a measure of notoriety in the Perth amateur theatre.

Repeal of s.70 of the 1889 Constitution Act

Some of the early decisions made by Forrest and Prinsep had lasting effects. The act which abolished the Aborigines Protection Board also repealed s.70 of the 1889 Constitution Act guaranteeing the board an annual grant of $10,000 or 1 per cent of gross colonial revenue, whichever was greater. The Aborigines Department was given a minimum annual grant of $10,000 instead. Although supplementary grants kept departmental expenditure during Prinsep's tenure of office at a level at least double that figure,[2] this was still considerably less than the $33,912 spent by the Aborigines Protection Board during its last year of existence. The repeal of s.70 augured ill for the colony's aboriginal population. The fields to be affected most by the resulting reduction in expenditure were the system of travelling inspectors, distribution of relief, and mission subsidies. The travelling inspectors of aborigines (one appointed in 1892, the other two in 1896) were dismissed. Some of their functions were taken over by resident magistrates, resident medical officers, and district police officers who were appointed ex-officio protectors and charged, as part of their public duties, with assisting the Chief Protector "in promoting the welfare of the aborigines and in providing relief to the aged, infirm and the sick".[3] It was a retrograde step. Protectorship became a part-time, in a sense unpaid job, regarded by some officials as an irksome addition to their already manifold duties. Administratively, the system did not work very well; as the *Report of the Royal Commission on the Conditions of Natives* was to point out in 1904, the Chief Protector lacked the authority to give orders to these officials and depended on their voluntary co-operation in the execution of departmental policy. The savings effected by the dismissal of the travelling inspectors proved to be illusory. As a part of the drive to reduce departmental expenditure, stricter control was introduced over the distribution of rations to aboriginal paupers. All except "sick and infirm" aborigines had to produce a medical certificate before being placed on the permanent ration list, and claims by private individuals for reimbursement of expenses incurred in connection with the rationing of aboriginal indigents had to be certified, wherever possible, by a protector of aborigines. The new system broke down within a year. Some settlers claimed that they could not afford to keep a lot of idle aborigines (one said that he employed more labour than he actually needed, "for humanity's sake"),[4] and a few went as far as to state publicly that they felt entitled to a share of the taxpayers' money spent on aboriginal relief ($14,394 in 1898–1899 on food alone, out of a total direct expenditure on aboriginal administration of $21,648). As a result, the department had to appoint in 1899 a travelling inspector of aborigines whose main duty was to corroborate settlers' claims for reimbursement; since the appointee, G. S. Olivey, was a medical practitioner *manqué*, he also acted as an unofficial travelling medical inspector. His two *Reports on Stations Visited by the Travelling Inspector of Aborigines* cover most of the state except East and North Kimberley and contain a wealth of information about the pastoral industry. They reveal, for instance, that some settlers had worked out an elaborate system of defrauding the government. They purchased rations wholesale and charged the department retail prices, distributed smaller quantities of food than those charged for, and occasionally even employed aborigines who were on government rations. These practices were almost universal along the south coast, though they were by no means limited to that area. The appointment of a travelling inspector had a salutary effect and reduced the number of permanently rationed aborigines by about one-third, from 750 in 1898–1899 to 516 in 1901–1902; when the office was abolished in 1903 (the reasons for this are not clear), the figure went up to 833 in one year.

The abolition of the Aborigines Protection Board and the repeal of s.70 of the 1889 Constitution Act also affected government-missions relations. The control of aboriginal affairs was now in the hands of men whose attitude towards Christian missions differed from that of the Colonial Office; while not opposed to missions in principle, they did not harbour many illusions about the practical value of their work among the aborigines. The record of the existing missions (with the exception of the Church of England children's institutions at Busselton and Perth – transferred to the Swan in the late 1880s — which were technically industrial schools) gives some support to this belief. At New Norcia the Benedictines had been unable to prevent the extinction of the local aborigines (the last Victoria Plains full-blood died in 1913); the mission, as its critics were increasingly wont to stress, was nothing but a huge latifundium run with the help of aboriginal labour. It held some 18,000 acres of good wheat and pastoral land, grazed about 20,000 sheep, and had flourishing outstations at Wyeming, Marah, and Berkshire Valley. New Norcia itself, reminiscent of the Spanish missions on the west coast of the United States, consisted of a monastery, a "huge quadrangular two-storied pile of buildings"[5] housing about sixty fathers and brothers, surrounded by gardens, orchards, and vineyards, a three-storied mill, a macaroni factory (the only one in the colony), and many smaller buildings, including a row of cottages for the aborigines. The wealth of the mission provided an excellent argument for a cessation or a decrease of government subsidy. In the case of Beagle Bay it was failure rather than success which provided the government with a similar argument. A contemplative order, the Trappists made little effort to cultivate the land or to look after the cattle, for meat was excluded from their diet for religious reasons. They "led a life of rigorous poverty, intensified in this barren remote land to the point of starvation".[6] Daisy Bates, who visited the mission in 1900, found it "but a collection of tumble-down, paper-bark monastery cells, a little bark chapel and a community room of corrugated iron, which had been repeatedly destroyed in bush fires and hurricanes".[7] Yet the Trappists had shown great wisdom; they taught the children in Nyul-Nyul, made a study of the local customs, and were careful not to interfere with those which they thought compatible with Christianity. But they did not publicize this aspect of their work, and in any case it is doubtful if this would have influenced the bureaucrats in Perth.

The only other mission which would have been affected by the impending reduction in subsidies, the Church of England mission at Forrest River, was speared out of existence just after the abolition of the board. The mission lasted little over one year. It was established in June 1897 by Harold Hale, the son of the Bishop of Perth, on the site of an abandoned sheep station on the western shore of the Cambridge Gulf. Whether there was any connection between this fact and subsequent events we do not know. For nine months the missionaries were unable to establish contact with the aborigines who appeared to take no notice of their presence. Then, in March 1898, Hale was speared while trying to interview a tribesman; in May the aborigines stole the mission cutter and removed portions of the ironwork for speartips; in July the cutter disappeared once more and one of the missionaries was wounded when trying to recover it. Soon after the aborigines stole the dinghy, and speared the sole occupant of the homestead while other missionaries were searching for it. The mission was abandoned in August 1898 when another missionary was almost clubbed to death.

After the abolition of the Aborigines Protection Board the missions were left without any indication as to the assistance they could expect. The future looked bleak, and the recent separation of Church and State (1895) made a complete cessation of mission grants a real possibility. When the new subsidies were finally announced, some missions at least must have felt relieved, in spite of the severe reduction.[8] Indeed, it was not the severity of the cut but the way in which the new subsidies were arrived at which caused more resentment. During the nineteenth century the government used two methods of subsidizing missions. The early church schools and the New Norcia and Beagle Bay missions were given an annual lump sum, while the later Church of England children's homes were subsidized on a per capita basis, the scale being only slightly below that applying to similar institutions for white children established under the 1874 Industrial Schools Act. After the setting up of the Aborigines Protection Board, subsidies became the subject of a bitter sectarian controversy. The Roman Catholic Church maintained that the system penalized its institutions, but this was not quite true. Beagle Bay and New Norcia derived considerable income from their vast land holdings, leased to them by the government at a peppercorn rental, whereas the Church of England children's homes had no such source of revenue. In 1893 Governor Robinson suggested that subsidies ought to be calculated according to the proportion of the various religious denominations in the population of the colony, but the proposal had little appeal for the Roman Catholic missions as it would have halved their share of subsidies;[9] instead, they asked for "equality" with the Church of England institutions.

The new subsidy scale, based on "need" rather than "fairness", was even more discriminatory from the point of view of the Roman

Catholic missions. The Church of England children's homes continued to receive assistance at the daily rate of 10 cents per child;
the subsidy to New Norcia was reduced by about one half; the Beagle
Bay grant ceased altogether. In the case of New Norcia the subsidy
was for work with children (though still below the scale which
applied to the Church of England homes); adult aborigines, reasoned
Forrest, should be looked after by the mission, since their labour
contributed to its prosperity. In the case of Beagle Bay, Forrest
withdrew the subsidy because he was convinced that it was largely
wasted. Prinsep, in a rare display of resoluteness, tried to convince
Forrest that the Roman Catholics ought to receive approximately
the same share of the taxpayers' money as the Anglicans, but he
was overruled by the Premier. "It was bad under the Aborigines
Board, very bad", wrote Bishop Gibney to Prinsep, "but under you
it is worse . . ."[10]

John Forrest and the aboriginal problem

L. R. Marchant, in the thesis, "Native Administration in Western
Australia 1886–1905", took Forrest to task for some of his early
policy decisions. Thus, on the issue of the distribution of relief, he
said that Forrest, "in contrast with the more liberal attitude of the
Aborigines Board, ceased to distribute assistance except to the
chronically incapacitated, holding that the term 'welfare' meant that
the natives should be forced to work, or sent back to the bush out
of harm's (and cost's) way". He also criticized Forrest for openly
favouring the Anglican missionaries.[11] Both assertions simplify the
issues involved. The second fails to take into account several facts.
The standard of institutional care in the Swan Native and Half-Caste
Home (Ellensbrook had only handful of inmates) was higher than
in the Roman Catholic missions. The curriculum followed closely
that of the state schools, and the institution was regularly inspected
by the Education Department. Most of the children were part-
aboriginal, and it was not uncommon for them to reach standard
four or even five. At New Norcia and Beagle Bay, on Marchant's
own admission, education was "utilitarian in character" and "based
on a policy of indoctrination",[12] and only two to three hours daily
were devoted to classroom work. The fact has already been mentioned that New Norcia was prosperous and that it owed its prosperity partly to aboriginal labour; Beagle Bay, under a different
management, could have also prospered. For Beagle Bay, in fact,

the withdrawal of the subsidy turned out to be a blessing in disguise. It forced Bishop Gibney to replace the French Trappists by the more practical Pallotines, a German order with flourishing missions in the Cameroons. The transfer took place in January 1901, for a sum of $5,280 of which $2,000 was borne by the Bishop himself. The subsidy was reinstated in the same year.

Marchant's criticism of Forrest's views of aboriginal "welfare" fails to take into account the fact that the new regulations were directed as much against the settlers as against the aborigines. The Aborigines Protection Board was indeed liberal with the taxpayers' money, but some of it found its way into the pockets of the settlers. And if Forrest's concept of "welfare" excluded hand-outs, he should not be criticized for it. His attitudes towards the original owners of the country were a survival from an age which believed, or wanted to believe, that the aborigines had a place, however humble, in white society. Late in 1900 Prinsep submitted for Forrest's approval a draft amendment of the 1886 Aborigines Protection Act. The proposal envisaged the introduction of employment permits, the creation of aboriginal reserves to which any aborigine "not lawfully employed" (that is employed without a permit) could be removed, and the establishment of "white reserves" from which aborigines not employed by "trustworthy" persons could be excluded. It also proposed to give the Chief Protector the right to remove an aboriginal child up to the age of sixteen "from any place and cause him to reside in any other place". Forrest's comments were devastating. On the margin of the preamble which spoke of the need for closer protection of aborigines in the interest of their "health and morals", Forrest scribbled: "They have them [morals], try well-being." He dismissed outright the proposed establishment of reserves to which aborigines could be forcibly removed: "This would make prisoners of these poor people in their own country — *for their own good* — *it would be said*" [Forrest's italics], adding: "By what means? By being placed in irons?" On the proposed establishment of white reserves from which aborigines could be excluded, Forrest commented: *"This too is a monstrous infringement of the liberty of a native. It is manufacturing offence with a vengeance."*[13] Some eight years later, at Williams, a group of aborigines protested to the future Premier, James Mitchell, then a junior Minister in the Moore government, against being turned out from town at six o'clock in the evening. "They said that as Lord Forrest had left the country", recalled

Sir James in 1929, "and as I was the same 'Budgera' and brother that he was, they claimed my help."[14]

Prinsep at the helm

Section 51 of the constitution of the Commonwealth of Australia, which came into force in January 1901, precluded the federal parliament from legislating on behalf of the aboriginal race. The constitution also provided, in s.127, that aborigines should not be counted in reckoning the numbers of the people of the Commonwealth or a state. The reasons for making aboriginal affairs a "residual" state power can only be surmised, for the matter was not even raised at the 1897–1898 conventions. The constitutions of the United States of America and of the Dominion of Canada, to which the founding fathers of the Commonwealth looked for guidance, made the care of the indigenous population a federal matter, and one would have expected the framers of the Australian constitution to follow this example. It may be that the representatives of the older colonies accepted the then current view that the aborigines would soon disappear, while the representatives of the younger colonies, including Western Australia, had their own reasons for not raising the issue at all. As for s.127, it was not intended to deprive aborigines of citizenship (as suggested by Brian Fitzpatrick)[15] but was directed solely at the reckoning of people. The framers of the constitution, in the light of the prevailing conditions, thought that an accurate count would be difficult to achieve and might give an unfair advantage to particular states in such matters as the representation of the states in the federal political system and financial relations between the states and the Commonwealth.[16]

Although the establishment of the Commonwealth of Australia left the administration of aboriginal affairs with the state government, it deprived it of the services of its ablest politician, John Forrest, who had resigned from the Premiership in February 1901 to take up a seat in federal parliament. His departure was followed by a period of political instability. There were four different ministries in 1901 alone, and it was not until June 1902, when Walter James formed a government which was to remain in office until August 1904, that the situation became stabilized. Prinsep's department suffered as a result; from February till May 1901 it was under the Premier, George Throssell; for the next six months it was in the charge of Frederick Illingsworth, the Colonial Secretary in the Leake ministry; from November till December 1901 it was under M. L. Moss, Colonial Secretary in the Morgans ministry, and from December 1901 until July 1902 once more under Frederick Illingsworth, the Colonial Secretary in the second Leake ministry. None of these men equalled Forrest in expertise or determination, and on the whole left the Chief Protector alone. Prinsep made little use of this opportunity. The years between Forrest's departure and the passing of the 1905 Aborigines Act were, in fact, singularly devoid of concrete achievements. "The principal efforts of the Department", said Prinsep in his report for 1901–1902, "have, as usual, been devoted to the proper and efficient relief of all natives reported to be aged, crippled or destitute through other causes . . ."[17] There were, of course, proposals aplenty. Prinsep's mind, for instance, was occasionally "exercised" by the growing number of part-aborigines,[18] but he did nothing, claiming that he lacked legal authority to deal with the problem. On several occasions he asked for an amendment of the 1886 Aborigines Protection Act (along the lines of the draft bill he had submitted to Forrest in 1900), but his Ministers did not think the matter important. The aboriginal question in East Kimberley, said Prinsep in 1903, "demanded attention",[19] but again there was no action — in fact, the Chief Protector had never visited the northwest or the Kimberleys while in office. The only important scheme which he managed to put into effect ended in failure. In 1901 he collected the remnants of the southwest tribes on a "refuge" near today's Welshpool — a reserve of 200 acres at the foot of the Darling Range. It was the first aboriginal settlement in Western Australia, but it bore little resemblance to the later settlements at Carrolup and Moore River, for the aborigines were free to come and go as they pleased. Prinsep hoped to make the settlement self-supporting. Each family was given a few acres of land on which they were to grow vegetables, fruit, and flowers for the Perth market. Additional income was to be derived from the sale of bricks, boots, and nets produced by the inmates. But the dying remnants of the southwest tribes showed little interest in these money-making schemes. Some left when they realized that they were expected to work; those who remained were rationed on behalf of the department by a part-time "working" superintendent. Daisy Bates, who spent some time on the reserve late in 1904, described her impressions in the book, *The Passing of the Aborigines*. Every fortnight the department sent the inmates "liberal rations of flour, tea, sugar and tobacco, with meat and jam

added". Each hut had a fireplace, a bed, a spring mattress, blankets,
and even crockery, but the aborigines, while intensely proud of their
"villas", built themselves bush shelters outside them, where they
slept with their dogs. Occasionally "those who were able, wandered
restlessly away to their own *kalleep*" (home country), only to return
dispirited with "finding no friendly fires, and the houses and fences
of the white man everywhere . . ."[20]

Prinsep lacked not only drive but also imagination. In 1899 a
former trader by the name of Sydney Hadley established a mission
on Sunday Island, a small granite islet near the entrance to King
Sound. Hadley was a most unusual missionary. He was not a
minister of religion, nor even an adherent of any particular faith.
A man of superior birth, educated at Cambridge, he came from an
old English seafaring family with profitable connections in the City,
and was said to have sufficient naval honours to gain him access to
the Queen. Before becoming a missionary Hadley was a beach-
comber, feared and respected by the aborigines as the possessor of
special magical powers. In 1884 he took up a pastoral lease at Lombadina on the Dampier Peninsula, in partnership with a shipwright
named Harry Hunter (after the two separated, Hunter was convicted
for having "as many concubines as Solomon").[21] Hunter built the
boats and Hadley worked them, trading in pearl-shell, bêche-de-
mer, and trepang. In 1897, while in England, he was said to have
"got religion" and returned to Western Australia intent on making
amends for his misdeeds. He joined the Anglican mission at Forrest
River and was wounded in one of the attacks which led to the closing
of the mission. In July 1899, accompanied by another Forrest River
missionary, Ormerod, he started a non-denominational mission
among the Sunday Island Bardi whom he had "exploited" as a
trader. Since Hadley did not ask for a subsidy (he proposed to support the mission by fishing and trade), Prinsep grudgingly allowed
him to remain on Sunday Island, but he took the precaution of
granting him the tenure of the island "at will" of the department.
In any case, he did not expect the mission to last. But the Bardi
obviously liked their unorthodox missionary. Hadley could speak
their language, did not insist that they wear clothing, permitted
traditional marriages, burials, and even such practices as tooth
evulsion, maintained the segregation of sexes and moieties in church
and school, and was said to have been initiated into the tribe and
given three wives. All this did not endear him to his two European

assistants, who left the island in mid-1901 after a heated argument over mission policy. Writing from Derby where he had taken refuge, Ormerod told Prinsep that Hadley preached "Christianity which is entirely his own", and enclosed for good measure a letter from the mission cook, a Japanese, testifying that Hadley had taken two young girls "as wives".[22] Prinsep immediately cancelled Hadley's tenure of the island and sent Ormerod to take charge of the mission, but Hadley insisted on a public inquiry of the charges and threatened to take "his" aborigines with him if he were forced to leave. Hadley was eventually reinstated, but the relations between the mission and the department remained strained for some time; the Derby police, for instance, were asked to keep an eye on Hadley, only to find him "most abstemious" whenever he came to collect supplies for his mission.[23] He remained on the island until December 1923 — a term exceeded only by another equally controversial missionary, R. S. Schenk of Margaret River.

The pastoralists and their treatment of aborigines

If the years between Forrest's departure for federal politics and the passing of the 1905 Aborigines Act saw little by way of concrete achievements, they were certainly not devoid of animated public discussion of certain aspects of the aboriginal problem, and in particular the treatment of aborigines by the pastoralists. We have seen that there was much to condemn in the pastoral north, but with each successive accusation and counter-accusation the issue became little more than a pretext for a trial of strength between the humanitarians and the pastoralists in which the aborigines and their welfare were all but forgotten. In order to understand the passion generated by the conflict, one must go back to the days of the anti-slavery campaign in England during which the leaders of the movement developed certain techniques enabling them to excite, direct, and maintain emotions among large groups of people over considerable periods. These techniques were later taken over by the successors of the anti-slavery movement, such as the Aborigines' Protection Society, and were put to good use by the Western Australian "relics of Exeter Hall", the local "honorary prickers of conscience".[24] The pastoralists, in a sense, had only themselves to blame for the violence of the humanitarians' attacks. The average settler saw himself "intellectually and morally superior to the savage tribes",[25] often believing this state of affairs had been ordained by God himself. "The niggers are protected beyond the squatters' endurance", complained the author of *Darkest West Australia,* proposing that aboriginal cattle-killers, instead of being sent to prison, should be emasculated and indentured to pastoralists. This expedient would solve two problems: it would save the government the cost of upkeep of aboriginal prisoners, and it would make the castrated aborigines "more contented" and consequently more useful as workers. Whites should not shoot in the presence of aborigines unless they were first-class shots, and should not be familiar with the "niggers" — the more you gave them, the more they wanted, and the more you fraternized with them, the bolder and more insolent they became.[26] *The Golden West,* a periodical devoted mainly to publicizing Western Australia overseas, described the aborigine as

brutish, faithless, vicious, the animal being given fullest loose, a natural liar and a thief, and only approached by his next-of-kin, the monkey, for mischief . . . A goldfields clergyman of the early days was wont to refer to the native as "God's image cut in ebony", and it is doubtful if anything more offensive to White Christians could have proceeded from the lips of a blasphemous bullock driver. The Australian black may have a soul, but if he has, then the horse and the dog — infinitely superior in every way of the black human — cannot be denied the possession of that vital spark of heavenly flame.[27]

The pastoralists, for their part, felt irritated by the constant stream of abuse from people thousands of miles away who "met in public halls shrieking and yelling shame on a considerable body of respectable settlers".[28] And not without reason. Most humanitarians knew little about life in the pastoral north and, furthermore, they tended to condemn the pastoralists as a class. "For every sheep killed by the blacks . . .", said Bishop Gibney in 1892, "God has punished the settlers by taking away 100 or more sheep in the drought."[29] A year later the *W.A. Record,* commenting on the gradual disappearance of the aborigines, claimed that this was not due to their inability to adapt to civilization but because the settler, "beyond the cognizance of law, shoots straight, and shoots often".[30] In addition to the philanthropists and the churches, the anti-pastoralist coalition drew considerable support from a section of the press (the *Sunday Times,* the liberal *Morning Herald* — between 1896 and 1909 Perthites had the choice of two morning dailies, the *West Australian* and the *Morning Herald* — the *Northam Advertiser,* the *Kalgoorlie*

Miner, and the *Sun,* a goldfields weekly) ready to embrace any cause which would embarrass the government. It could also count on the support of the Labour Party and the trade unions who were quick to raise the cry of slavery and exploitation in times of adverse economic conditions. The party, of course, had no aboriginal policy as such, but it subscribed to the maxim that aboriginal labour should not be used if white labour was available. The first Labour government, formed in 1904 under Henry Daglish, stopped the practice of employing aboriginal prisoners on public works and was considering the introduction of cash wages in the pastoral industry in order to reduce competition from aboriginal workers.[31]

The first major trial of strength between the humanitarians and the pastoralists occurred in the mid-eighties, during the already mentioned Gribble affair. The outcome was inconclusive, but the resulting publicity gave the colony a bad reputation in the eyes of British philanthropists, and was partly responsible for the withholding of aboriginal affairs from local control when the colony achieved self-government in 1890. Between 1890 and 1897 colonial parliament, dominated by pastoral and rural interests, passed several acts which gave the pastoralists a decisive say in most matters affecting the employment of aborigines. After the abolition of the Aborigines Protection Board, which they regarded as yet another victory for the pastoralists, the humanitarians took the offensive. The campaign was well organized, and the press in eastern Australia and Great Britain was never short of a good copy about "slavery under British flag in Western Australia".[32] The campaign was given further impetus by the establishment of the Commonwealth of Australia, for after 1901 adverse publicity overseas was a matter which concerned all Australians. In July 1901 the member for Coolgardie, Hugh Mahon, moved in federal parliament for the appointment of a Royal Commission to investigate the conditions of Western Australian aborigines north of the 30th parallel and to look into the advisability of transferring the administration of aboriginal affairs throughout Australia to the federal government.[33] In Western Australia, the demand for an inquiry into aboriginal affairs was taken up by the *Northam Advertiser,*[34] and in August 1901 the member for Roebourne, Dr. J. T. Hicks, moved formally in the Legislative Assembly for the appointment of a commission of inquiry.[35] In December 1901 the London *Daily News* published a scathing attack by Walter Malcolmson, an Englishman who claimed

to have spent several years in the northwest, mainly in Marble Bar.
Using somewhat emotional language, Malcolmson spoke of "brutal
slavery still in full swing" in Western Australia's pastoral north and
quoted specific instances of ill-treatment of aborigines by the pastoralists and the police.[36] The article achieved the desired effect: the
Secretary of State for the Colonies sent it to the Governor of Western
Australia with a discreet request for comment. The police were asked
to investigate, but found no evidence to substantiate Malcolmson's
charges (in 1900 Daisy Bates "investigated" similar charges by the
Times and found them equally unfounded. The only charge she
could prove was that of "giving offal to natives instead of good
meat" and of "sending them away from stations without food when
work was slack". Later she discovered that offal was an aboriginal
delicacy and that aborigines preferred traditional food on their
walkabouts).[37] As a result of the interest shown by the Colonial
Office, however, the 1902 Criminal Code repealed all discriminatory
legislation relating to the trial of aboriginal offenders, except for the
retention of whipping and public hanging (this was largely nullified
by a subsequent amendment which provided that in proceedings
before justices, where an aborigine charged with an offence not
punishable by death pleaded guilty, the case could be dealt with
summarily). In addition, the practice of providing free legal representation for aborigines charged with serious crimes, discontinued
for financial reasons in 1898, was revived, and the courts were instructed to forward for departmental perusal records of proceedings
in which an aborigine was interested as a plaintiff, defendant, or
accessory.

These minor reforms, however, failed to silence the anti-pastoralist
coalition. In September 1902 the member for Gascoyne, N. E.
Butcher, moved in the Legislative Assembly for the appointment of
a Royal Commission to inquire into all aspects of aboriginal administration, but the motion was lost.[38] In October the *Morning
Herald* — by then the most outspoken critic of the government —
went even further: the inquiry should be entrusted to an "independent expert", preferably the Assistant Protector of Aborigines
for Queensland, Dr. W. E. Roth, an Oxford-educated surgeon and
ethnologist of repute.[39] But it was left to Walter Malcolmson to
deliver the most violent attack. "The inhuman legislators of Western
Australia", said the self-appointed guardian of Western Australian
aborigines in the London *Times,*

pretend to wax very indignant at any reputable commission being appointed
to inquire into the subject; for they have good reason to know that such
an inquiry would end their cheap labour, and they are all aware that they
would be proved utterly unfit to deal justly with the natives, but they very
generously offer to hold an inquiry themselves. Such a commission would
be a farce, and on par with a jury of burglars, presided by a garotter,
trying a prisoner for robbery.[40]

This was a challenge which the government, itself claiming to
subscribe to liberal ideals, could hardly ignore. In April 1904 the
Premier, Walter James, approached Dr. Roth, who agreed to undertake a survey of aboriginal administration; he was formally appointed
Royal Commissioner on 31 August. In the meantime, the government was defeated in the June general election but remained in office
until 10 August. This gave it time to bring down an amendment of
the 1886 Aborigines Protection Act which was taken over with a
few minor changes by the Labour government formed by Henry
Daglish in August. The bill was debated at some length in September
1904 and referred to a select committee which reported shortly before
the Christmas recess.[41] There was little point in proceeding with
the bill while Dr. Roth was still conducting his inquiry.

The Roth Royal Commission

Dr. Roth's report, presented in the last days of January 1905, became
the subject of an immediate controversy. Even before its contents
were fully known to the public (it was published seriatim in the press)
Captain Hare, the Commissioner of Police, accused Dr. Roth of
"inaccuracy and prejudice" and of having based his conclusions on
the evidence of the "scum and riffraff of the North"[42] (among the 110
witnesses examined by Dr. Roth were forty police officers, fourteen
pastoralists and, as Dr. Roth was quick to retort, the Commissioner
of Police himself). Similar views were expressed by Octavius Burt,
the Comptroller-General of Prisons, and Captain Smith, the Fremantle Shipping Master. John Forrest, then in Perth, thought Dr.
Roth's appointment a "foolish action", saying: "Why he was asked
to report I do not know. Surely West Australians know as much
about the aborigines of their own state as anyone else . . ."[43] The
report was also criticized by the *West Australian* for its failure to
suggest an effective policy for future guidance.[44] Other newspapers,
notably the *Daily News* and the *Morning Herald,* gave it unqualified
support; the former thought the moment propitious for reprinting

J. B. Gribble's *Dark Deeds in a Sunny Land* (first published in 1886),
with a new sub-title *Blood-Curdling Cruelty: a Chapter of Horrors*.
The Council of Churches, comprising the Baptist, Methodist, Church
of Christ, and Presbyterian denominations, was also behind Dr.
Roth, as was the Roman Catholic Church. Only the Anglicans
maintained an attitude of cautious neutrality; according to Bishop
Riley, the "whole of Dr. Roth's time has been more or less wasted".[45]

The controversy over the report[46] is all the more surprising in
view of the fact that Dr. Roth refuted almost all charges of cruelty
and maltreatment of aborigines by the pastoralists; indeed, the inquiry was largely a vindication of the settlers — and a grave indictment of the administration, particularly the Aborigines and the
Police departments. Dr. Roth found that the Chief Protector had
no power to enforce the provisions of the Aborigines Protection Act,
for he could not, as a matter of right, command obedience from any
government official outside his own department in the execution of
his instructions. There was no regular system of inspection, and
distribution of relief was not properly supervised. But the brunt
of Dr. Roth's criticism was reserved for the "most brutal and outrageous condition of affairs" in connection with the arrest of aboriginal cattle-killers, the long sentences imposed by the courts,
and the harsh treatment of aboriginal prisoners. As a remedy, he
recommended that the government should establish a rudimentary
field organization, by appointing in each magisterial district one
official (preferably a resident magistrate or a senior police officer)
who would be directly responsible to the Chief Protector and receive
a small honorarium in addition to his regular salary. Distribution
of relief was to be entrusted to district police officers, and aboriginal
indigents were to be collected on small reserves where their rationing
could be properly supervised. The police should be ordered not to
arrest suspected cattle-killers without warrants, neck-chains were
to be replaced by wrist-cuffs, and courts should impose shorter
sentences on aboriginal cattle-killers, since long imprisonment "does
not do them the least bit of good".

Although the report had refuted the charges of deliberate cruelty
by the pastoralists, they did not emerge from the inquiry without
a censure. The customary absence of employment contracts, for
instance, worked almost entirely in the pastoralists' favour. It did
not prevent them from invoking the assistance of the police when
a worker had run away, and it relieved them of the obligation to

supply their labour with minimum rations and medical care (in the case of indentured workers Dr. Roth found that only the penal clauses regarding the aborigines were enforced). Most pastoralists also expected the government to ration indigent aborigines on their properties. His recommendations in the field of employment were twofold: the introduction of employment permits, renewable every year, and the payment of a minimum monthly wage of 50 cents ($1 for workers on pearling boats), to be decreased or wholly remitted in proportion to the number of indigents rationed by the pastoralists. Another recommendation affecting the pastoral industry was the proposal to create large hunting reserves in marginal regions, partly on humanitarian grounds and partly to diminish friction between the pastoralists and the "bush" aborigines. The right of the aborigines to hunt on the unimproved parts of pastoral leases, granted to them in 1864, was worth little under the fast changing conditions: native game was disappearing and aboriginal waterholes were being appropriated by the settlers' stock. The choice was between losing a few pounds from rents or sacrificing many human lives.

Another issue discussed at some length in the report was miscegenation. "Along the whole coastline extending from a few miles south of La Grange to the Eastern shores of King Sound", observed Dr. Roth, "drunkenness and prostitution, the former being the prelude to the latter, with consequent loathsome disease, is rife amongst the aborigines." To minimize this evil, Dr. Roth recommended that the police should be given the right to order the pearling crews back to their boats and that small reserves be set aside where alone the pearling crews could land to collect wood and replenish their water supply. Dr. Roth also spoke with some concern about the prevalence of "komboism" throughout the pastoral north and the absence of administrative powers to prevent Europeans and Asians from cohabiting with aboriginal women. In another section, dealing with the half-caste problem in general, the report criticized the fact that it was not compulsory for a reputed European father of a half-caste child to support his offspring, and expressed approval for the suggestion, made previously by Prinsep, that the Chief Protector should become legal guardian of all aboriginal children and minors up to the age of eighteen. As for Christian missions, the report dismissed the subject in a few sentences. They should be regularly inspected and subsidized for their work with children: ". . . it would be wiser to make the pecuniary sacrifice rather in the interest of the infant than in those of the adult full-blood."

Taken as a whole, the report was not the prejudiced document its critics made it out to be; nor did it lack, as the *West Australian* suggested, effective proposals for future guidance. But Dr. Roth was an outsider, a "t'othersider", and this alone made him suspect in the eyes of most locally born Western Australians. Most of his recommendations were taken from the Aborigines Protection and Restriction of the Sale of Opium Act, passed by the Queensland parliament in 1897 — hardly a progressive piece of legislation. But this did not save him from being labelled a dangerous radical. His most important recommendations — the establishment of large hunting reserves and the payment of minimum cash wages by the pastoralists — were not implemented, while some of the reforms introduced by the government after the inquiry turned out to be shortlived. But all this was still in the future. Immediately after the publication of the report, the Executive Council ordered the immediate release from gaol of all juvenile prisoners, and the police were instructed to arrest aboriginal "witnesses" only when absolutely necessary and to purchase provisions for aboriginal prisoners en route when returning from patrol. On 20 February the Commissioner of Police, Captain Hare, was suspended for having disregarded the provisions of the Public Service Act which prohibited public servants from making public statements on matters affecting their departments (he was reinstated in April). The Chief Protector, the Comptroller-General of Prisons, Octavius Burt, and the Fremantle Shipping Master, Captain Smith, all of whom had publicly commented on Dr. Roth's report, were reprimanded.[47] In mid-May the government prohibited the use of neck-chains in aboriginal prisons and reduced the daily hours of prison labour to six. The police were instructed not to assist with the roundup of runaway workers not employed under contract and to arrest suspected cattle-killers only when direct evidence was available. In the last week of May cabinet decided that the office of the Chief Protector should be moved to Broome or Derby and instructed Prinsep to make appropriate arrangements immediately. Some of these reforms turned out to be paper innovations only. Prinsep remained in Perth. Most settlers refused to sell provisions to returning police patrols, and the police reverted to the old method of rationing prisoners from their own pocket and claiming expenses incurred. In July a deputation of Kimberley pastoralists told the Commissioner of Police that the new regulations regarding arrest of suspected cattle-killers had done "incalculable damage" and that they would be forced either to take the law into their own hands or to abandon their holdings if the regulations were strictly enforced.[48] No evidence of a formal reversal of policy by the government has been preserved, but the fact that early in 1909 similar regulations were gazetted (not to mention a steady increase in the number of arrests) suggests that the police had reverted to their old ways.

By the time the government introduced amending legislation in parliament, in August 1905, the public interest aroused by the inquiry had waned, and some of Dr. Roth's recommendations had been shelved. But there were still the humanitarians in eastern Australia and in Great Britain to reckon with. Late in March 1905 the Conservative member for Saint Helen's, Sir Henry Seton-Karr, said in the House of Commons that Dr. Roth's report reminded him of "cruelties committed in the Dark Ages", and the Secretary of State for the Colonies described as "deplorable" the state of affairs revealed in the report.[49] The latter also disclosed that he had cabled the Governor of Western Australia about the government's intentions regarding the implementation of Dr. Roth's recommendations. Soon after parliament convened for the winter session, in July 1905, the Daglish government brought down an amendment of the 1886 Aborigines Protection Act implementing a number of Dr. Roth's proposals, but the ministry was defeated soon after when it was announced that it intended to buy out a private railway company for what was thought to be too large a sum. The new government, led by H. C. Rason, adopted the bill without any alterations, though it probably had reservations about some of its provisions. The bill was passed before the Christmas recess, after a perfunctory debate. There was general agreement that it had to be passed, if only as a piece of window-dressing. The only clause which had been discussed at some length was eventually left intact. It limited the size of aboriginal reserves to 2,000 acres in any magisterial district, and had been inserted by the 1904 select committee. The 1904 bill subscribed to the idea of large "hunting" reserves, but the select committee reduced their size to 2,000 acres, ostensibly on the ground that "any scheme proposing to bring together in large reserves natives of different tribes is foredoomed to failure . . ."[50] (one legislator, with more courage, thought them unnecessary because the aborigines already

had "full liberty all over the country").[51] In 1905 the feeling of the
lower house was against what one member described as "kaffir
locations", and the limitation was consequently struck out. It was
reinstated in the Legislative Council.

The 1905 Aborigines Act

The 1905 Aborigines Act (entitled "An Act to make provision for the
better protection and care of the Aboriginal inhabitants of Western
Australia") was as important for what it did not contain as for what
it did. It failed to establish the independent departmental field organization recommended by Dr. Roth; it did not provide for the
payment of cash wages by the pastoralists; and it limited the size
of aboriginal reserves to 2,000 acres. The main provisions of the act
can be summed up under several headings. Administratively, it
raised the status of the Aborigines Department from a sub-department
to a department and increased its minimum annual grant from
$10,000 to $20,000. In the field of employment, the act prohibited
the engagement of children under the age of sixteen, abolished
indentures of apprenticeship, retained contracts of service, and
introduced compulsory employment permits. These were either
single (allowing an employer to employ a single aborigine named in
the permit) or general, had to be renewed annually, and could be
revoked at any time. Employers were under the obligation to provide
their workers with "good and sufficient" rations, clothing and
blankets, and medicine and medical attention "when practicable and
necessary". The Governor, in addition to the right to reserve for the
use of aborigines areas of Crown land not exceeding 2,000 acres in
any magisterial district, was also given the power to order the removal
of any aborigine not "lawfully employed" to such reserves (the
provision introducing a system of passes allowing an aborigine to
absent himself from a reserve was never applied). He could also
declare, "whenever in the interest of the aborigines he thinks fit",
any town, municipal district, or any other place a "prohibited
area" for any aborigine not in lawful employment. Other provisions
increased the powers of the Chief Protector: s.8 made him legal
guardian of every aboriginal and half-caste child up to the age of
sixteen; s.33 gave him the right to undertake the general care,
protection, and management of the property of any person under
the act, including the right to "take possession of, retain, sell or
dispose of any such property, whether personal or real"; s.34 entitled

him to proceed, with the approval of the Minister, against the father of an illegitimate child with view to maintenance, if the child was cared for in an aboriginal institution at the government's expense; s.42 prohibited marriages of "female aboriginals" to non-aborigines without his written permission. Cohabitation between white men and aboriginal women became a punishable offence, and the supply of liquor to any aborigine, by licensed or unlicensed persons, was prohibited. Finally, the police could arrest, without warrant, any aborigine offending against the provisions of the act.

Tucked away among the sixty-six clauses of the 1905 Aborigines Act was a short definition of persons "deemed to be aborigines" for the purposes of the act. The definition embraced four categories: aboriginal inhabitants of Australia, half-castes (defined as persons of an aboriginal parent on either side, or the children of such persons) who lived with an aborigine as wife or husband, half-castes who otherwise "habitually lived or associated with" aborigines, and half-caste children, irrespective of their mode of life, whose age did not apparently exceed sixteen years. The 1886 Aborigines Protection Act classified as aborigines only those half-castes who habitually associated with full-bloods. The new definition was considerably wider and embraced all "half-castes" up to the age of sixteen, whether "assimilated" or not, and certain adult quadroons as well. Viewed in this context, and against the background of the rapidly increasing part-aboriginal population, the act was not a measure "for the better protection and care" of Western Australia's aborigines but an instrument of control, and ruthless control at that. In the pastoral north, for all its manifest shortcomings, the act was a step in the right direction; in the south, it relegated the part-aborigines to the status of second-class citizens. It is true that any aborigine "under the act" could apply to be exempted from application of the act, but such exemptions were to be exceedingly difficult to obtain and could be revoked at any time for any reason, whereupon the act applied to the formerly exempted person "as if no such certificate had been issued". Seen in this light, the legislation was the formal acknowledgment of the demise of the policy of "imparting the blessings of civilization", abandoned in practice more than a generation earlier.

4. The Perspective
1906-1935

The legislative framework

The 1905 Aborigines Act remained the cornerstone of aboriginal administration until 1936. In retrospect, the most serious shortcoming of the legislation was its negative spirit, due partly to the generally accepted assumption that the full-bloods were doomed to die out, and partly to the belief in their cultural and mental inferiority. The act provided for the "protection and care" of tribal and semi-tribal groups in the northwest and the Kimberleys, at least on paper, and for a fairly effective regime of "dole and control"[1] for the rest of the aborigines and for the part-aborigines. Although the act sanctioned the establishment of aboriginal reserves, by limiting their size to 2,000 acres it reduced them to mere receptacles for the collection of aboriginal vagrants. The act also recognized the existence of the part-aboriginal problem but failed to face it squarely — the impression one gathers from contemporary records is one of optimism, of hope that the half-caste, like the man who wasn't there, would somehow go away. And yet, in the hands of determined men, the act could have been a fairly effective instrument, especially after its amendment in 1911 when parliament partially removed the restriction on the size of reserves — the old limitation of 2,000 acres now applied only to land held under lease or licence from the Crown — and accorded the aborigines greater measure of legal protection in criminal proceedings, by stipulating that a plea of guilty by the accused should be disregarded by the court unless it had been made with the explicit approval of a protector. There was nothing in the act, for instance, to prevent the Chief Protector or the Minister from subsidizing missions more generously (they had the power to "apportion" the departmental grant as they "saw fit"). It was their explicit duty to "provide for the custody, maintenance and education" of aboriginal children, to supply medicine and medical attendance to the needy, "as far as practicable", and to protect all aborigines against "injustice, imposition and fraud". They could ask the Governor to issue regulations on any matter relating to the administration of the act including, specifically, the payment of wages to aboriginal workers and the inspection of aborigines employed under the provisions of the act. These facts should be mentioned because of the recurring official pronouncements, particularly during the twenties and the early thirties, about the lack of appropriate powers to deal with this or that problem. Some of these complaints were justified, but others were merely an excuse for procrastination: with one or two exceptions, the men who made and implemented the decisions affecting the lives of Western Australian aborigines and part-aborigines were mediocrities, men without courage, devoid of new ideas and often downright hostile to new suggestions. They meant well, but they were not up to the job, for theirs was a truly difficult task: they had to fight a running battle with an indifferent cabinet and parliament, their actions were circumscribed by niggardly finance, and they were opposed by powerful special interests. Above all, they got very little support from public opinion.

The administrators and the policy-makers

Who were the men who had helped to shape aboriginal policy and administration between 1906 and 1935? We have already met H. C. Prinsep, Chief Protector of Aborigines from 1898 until 1907. He was an amiable but somewhat ineffectual man. The 1905 Aborigines Act cannot be really attributed to him, for it was his inaction, as much as anything else, which helped to precipitate the Roth Royal Commission and the subsequent amendment of the 1886 Aborigines Protection Act. During his nine years in office he had never been farther north than Geraldton. "He should never have been appointed", said the *Morning Herald* in 1905, "to a post which demands the best energies of a younger and more active man than Mr. Prinsep when the position was conferred upon him."[2] Unknowingly, Prinsep the amateur play producer had assessed Prinsep the Chief Protector when he wrote, in the *Prologue to the Presentation of Colleen Bawn:*

> If here and there we show a want of skill,
> To represent the part we have to fill,
> If points be missed, or gestures overdone,
> Remember that perfection waits on none.[3]

C. F. Gale, who replaced Prinsep in December 1907 and lost his

position in somewhat unusual circumstances in March 1915, was
a man of almost diametrically opposed qualities. He was exceedingly
active, physically, an "expert" with first-hand knowledge of aborigines, and as a young man he had spent a number of years pioneering
in the Carnarvon district. He joined the Public Service in 1893 as
assistant inspector of sheep in the Lands Department, was retrenched three years later, rejoined the service in 1897 as inspector
of fisheries for the Shark Bay district, and became Chief Inspector
of Fisheries in 1899. His joint appointment as Chief Protector of
Aborigines and Chief Inspector of Fisheries, in December 1907,
was a shrewd political move; by appointing an official with a fairly
high classification (and saving money by amalgamating the two positions), said the Public Service Commissioner, we shall "convey to
the public at large, including those of Exeter Hall, that authority
appreciates the importance of the native question by placing it in
charge of a higher paid official".[4] Gale's qualifications for the job
were his "experience as pioneer and squatter".[5] He was a somewhat
vain man, impulsive, with a "solution" to almost every problem up
his sleeve, but found it often difficult to bring his ideas to fruition.
He did not get on with his Ministers, and in particular with J. D.
Connolly who was in charge of the department from the beginning
of 1907 until October 1911 (it was Connolly who made the decision
to separate the offices of Chief Protector and Chief Inspector of
Fisheries, in August 1910, while Gale was on a tour of inspection).
Gale's record is difficult to evaluate. The lock hospitals for the treatment of venereal disease, opened while he was in office, were decided
on in principle before his appointment; Moola Bulla, the first aboriginal cattle station, owed its existence as much to Connolly as to
Gale; and the 1911 amendment of the Aborigines Act embodied
mainly Connolly's ideas. In spite of his squatting background (or
perhaps because of it), Gale managed to keep the pastoralists in
their place; in 1909, for instance, he persuaded most station owners
to ration, free of charge, aboriginal indigents on their properties.
The reasons for his dismissal, on 30 March 1915, are not entirely
clear. Early in July 1914 Gale left for Japan on long service leave,
but was forced to return by the outbreak of the war. In October he
applied to the Public Service Commissioner for permission to resume
duty on 1 December, before the expiry of his leave, and was told that
there would be no objection. On 23 November, however, the Premier,
John Scaddan, reorganized his cabinet, and in the resulting reshuffle

of portfolios the Department of Aborigines and Fisheries was assigned to the Minister without Portfolio, R. H. Underwood. The new Minister immediately notified the Chief Protector, through the Public Service Commissioner, that he should complete his long service leave. Gale eventually resumed duty in February 1915, only to be retrenched on 30 March "owing to the reorganisation of certain departments".[6] Gale's dismissal had almost certainly nothing to do with matters of policy, and appears to have been due to a clash of personalities; in 1909, for instance, in one of his rare forays into aboriginal affairs, Underwood told the Legislative Assembly that Gale lacked "ability and energy to carry out the work properly", and called the attention of the house to the "fishy business"[7] in the Department of Aborigines and Fisheries. Gale's dismissal caused something of a stir in the public service and was the subject of an inquiry by a select committee of the Legislative Council, appointed on the motion of a personal friend of the former Chief Protector, Walter Kingsmill. All witnesses called by the committee agree that Gale's work had been always satisfactory. The Crown Solicitor volunteered the opinion that Gale had been dismissed without cause: he had not reached the retiring age, had not committed any offence, and his office had not been abolished. The Public Service Commissioner testified that Gale had been dismissed without his recommendation. In October 1915 the committee finally reported that Gale's dismissal was "illegal" and recommended his immediate reinstatement,[8] but Underwood had different ideas — he even ordered that all back pay due to the former Chief Protector should be withheld until Gale formally renounced his stated intention to take legal action for wrongful dismissal.

A. O. Neville, who had replaced Gale in April 1915, held the position of Chief Protector of Aborigines (after 1936, Commissioner of Native Affairs) until March 1940. At the time of his appointment he had no relevant experience for the job except his eighteen years in the public service. The son of a Church of England clergyman, he had migrated to Western Australia from England, early in 1897, and joined the public service soon after, following a brief engagement as a shipping clerk. By 1902 he had achieved the position of clerk-in-charge of correspondence in the Colonial Secretary's Department. In 1911 he became Secretary in the Department of Immigration, Tourism and Information and supervised in that capacity the immigration of some 40,000 British settlers. He was a thorough administrator. Soon after his appointment as Chief Protector he reorganized the departmental records and introduced registers of permits, agreements, and reported deaths (none were kept before 1915), as well as an annual "census" of aboriginal population based on figures supplied by the police. His *bête noire* was the missionary. "I sometimes wondered", said he after his retirement, "whether missions were needed for the blacks — to convert them to Christianity, or the blacks for the missions — to create a job for someone. I fear the latter has sometimes been the motive behind their establishment".[9] Not surprisingly, government-missions relations (and mission subsidies) reached their nadir while he was in office. His relations with the pastoralists were only a little better, mainly because of his conviction that aborigines in pastoral employment should be paid cash wages. He was one of the foremost advocates of social isolation of the part-aborigines: it was during his tenure of office that the Carrolup and Moore River aboriginal settlements were established. He was the author of *Australia's Coloured Minority,* written after the abortive 1944 referendum on increased federal powers. It is a remarkable book, at once a panegyric on the advantages of federal control of aborigines, an apology of Neville's own record in Western Australia, an attack on Christian missions, and a guide for future action. It sums up the spirit of an era: "The native must be helped in spite of himself! Even if a measure of discipline is necessary it must be applied, but it can be applied in such a way as to appear to be gentle persuasion . . . *the end in view will justify the means employed*"[10] [italics supplied].

Of the dozen or so Ministers who had guided the fortunes of the department between 1905 and 1935 only four had held the position long enough to warrant discussion: J. D. Connolly, J. M. Drew, H. R. Underwood, and H. P. Colebatch. Connolly was a Queenslander who came to Western Australia in 1893 and made a modest fortune as a mining speculator and building contractor. He started his political career in 1901 when he was elected to represent the north-west province in the Legislative Council. In May 1906 he became Colonial Secretary in the Moore ministry and was in charge of the department from January 1907 until October 1911. His greatest achievement was the creation in 1911 of a four-million-acre aboriginal reserve in East Kimberley. In 1905 a similar proposal by Dr. Roth was killed by the pastoral lobby; six years later Connolly, through the sheer force of his personality, succeeded in converting his lukewarm cabinet colleagues to his own views, in the face of contrary advice from such Kimberley "experts" as the explorer F. S. Brockman, who thought that tribal aborigines, rather than being confined to reserves, should be "absorbed and utilized" by the pastoralists.[11] Connolly's relations with the Chief Protector were initially friendly, at least outwardly, but after 1909 a marked deterioration took place. Connolly and Gale were men of different temperaments: the latter was impulsive and a poor administrator, while the former was more of a realist with a practical twist of mind. During 1910 the two men had clashed over staffing matters, mission subsidies, wages in the pastoral industry, and the draft of a bill to amend the 1905 Aborigines Act which became law early in 1911. The separation of the offices of the Chief Protector and the Chief Inspector of Fisheries (Gale retained the former position) added new tensions, and the relations between the two men must have been near breaking point when Connolly was ousted from office.

Connolly's successor, J. M. Drew, was in charge of the department for nine years, from October 1911 until November 1914, and from April 1924 to April 1930. Born in Western Australia, he was the first owner of the *Geraldton Express* and entered politics as member for the central province in the Legislative Council. Considering the length of his stay in office, his record as Minister is not very impressive. During the first period he displayed a penchant for negative decisions: in 1912 he would not sanction the opening of more aboriginal cattle stations in the Kimberleys; in the following year he refused to authorize the establishment of an aboriginal settlement in the south; and in 1914 he failed to co-operate with the Education Department in providing education for the children of southern part-aborigines. During his second term of office, from 1924 to 1930, he had allowed himself to be dominated by Neville, only to leave him to the wolves when the pressure was on; in 1927, for instance, he reversed his decision to compel all employers of aboriginal labour to pay cash wages, after the first signs of opposition from the pastoral lobby.

R. H. Underwood was responsible for the department between November 1914 and July 1916, as Minister without Portfolio in the Scaddan government, and (after his defection from the Labour Party) from November 1917 to March 1919, as Minister without Portfolio in the Lefroy ministry. Born in Victoria, he was a bootmaker by trade, and came to Western Australia during the goldrushes.

Possibly because he had no other departments to distract him, the "Ballarat bootmaker" was one of the most determined Ministers the department had ever had, even though his energy was sometimes misdirected — his dismissal of Gale, and certainly its manner, was one such occasion. His 1915 decision to withdraw the subsidy to New Norcia, and his 1916 proposal to close the Beagle Bay mission — averted only by the fall of the Scaddan government — look like symptoms of anti-Roman Catholic or xenophobic sentiments, or both (Underwood was an Anglican, the New Norcia Benedictines were Spanish, and most of the Beagle Bay Pallotines were German). But he was equally tough with the pastoralists; only a week before the Scaddan government was toppled, for instance, he was ready to go ahead with the introduction of minimum cash wages in the pastoral industry. Underwood and Neville got on exceedingly well, had almost identical ideas on most issues, and knew what they wanted. It was a formidable team, in fact, and its premature break-up was in many ways something of a loss.

H. C. Colebatch was in charge of aboriginal affairs from July 1916 to November 1917 and again from early 1920 until June 1923. An Englishman by birth, he had settled in Western Australia in 1895, worked as a journalist on the liberal *Morning Herald,* and in 1905 became the editor and owner of the influential country newspaper, the *Northam Advertiser.* His main contribution to aboriginal administration was a new formula for the allocation of mission subsidies which he devised as Colonial Secretary in the second Wilson government. Instead of the "unequal method of making [lump sum] grants on no definite basis",[12] missions were now paid a fixed amount for each child or indigent who would otherwise be the care of the state, the actual sum depending on the location of the mission and whether or not it owned freehold land or held free government land grants. Later, as Minister for the North-West in the Mitchell government, he continued to display pro-mission sentiments, and was partly responsible for the 1923 Native Mission Stations Act which gave the Drysdale River and Forrest River missions greater security of tenure over the land on which they were built.

The department

The department administered by these men was one of the least important agencies, politically, and one of the smallest as well. The

1905 Aborigines Act, it is true, had raised its status from a sub-department to a full department, but this amounted to a change in nomenclature only. The department had little "pull" in the corridors of political power, for the simple reason that the vast majority of Western Australians were in no way affected by what it did or did not do. Aboriginal affairs were not a political issue in this period — it was not until the 1953 general election that all major parties had a "native plank" in their electoral platforms — and the few groups which showed a sporadic interest in aboriginal welfare did not count electorally. So the aborigines, except during brief flare-ups of public interest occasioned by violence on either side or a sensational news-paper article, came always last in the calculations of the politicians. "Possibly a State Government which dared to do the right thing to its fullest extent would no longer command the confidence of the public. It would be said 'our own people first'; indeed, that has been said."[13]

This lack of political "pull" was reflected, firstly, in the position of the Aborigines Department in the administrative structure, and secondly, in the size of the departmental grant. There was no separate portfolio of aboriginal or native affairs during this period and the department was usually assigned to the Colonial (after 1923, Chief) Secretary, as one of his manifold responsibilities. For a brief period, from August 1905 until May 1906, it was under the Minister for Labour and Commerce; from May until December 1906 it was under the Colonial Treasurer (who was in addition Minister for Education, Works, and Mines and Railways); from November 1914 until July 1916 and again from November 1917 until March 1919 it was in the charge of the Minister without Portfolio. Between 1909 and 1915 the department was amalgamated with the Department of Fisheries, and from 1915 until 1920 it was part of the combined Department of Aborigines, Fisheries and Immigration. Between 1907 and 1911 the Chief Protector was also the Chief Inspector of Fisheries, and after 1915 he also held the position of Secretary in the Department of Immigration, at least on paper (there was practic-ally no immigration after the outbreak of the war). Between 1920 and 1926 aboriginal administration was divided between the Depart-ment of the North-West which was responsible for aboriginal affairs north of the 25th parallel, and the Department of Fisheries which looked after aboriginal affairs south of the 25th parallel; the Chief Protector of Aborigines was during this period also the Secre-

tary for the North-West, while the Chief Inspector of Fisheries also
acted as Deputy Chief Protector. Of all conceivable administrative
arrangements, this one was probably the most unfortunate. There
was little or no liaison between the Chief Protector and his deputy;
in 1922, for instance, the Colonial Secretary decided to close the
Carrolup aboriginal settlement without even consulting the Chief
Protector. It was only after the abolition of the Department of the
North-West, in 1926, that aboriginal affairs became again the responsibility of a single agency, the Aborigines Department.

Although the grant at the disposal of the department was always
higher than the minimum of $20,000 per annum stipulated by the
1905 Aborigines Act, it was never sufficiently high to allow the
department to discharge properly the functions laid down by legislation. In 1905–1906, when gross state revenue was approximately $8
million, the department was given $30,250; in 1909–1910 the depart-
mental grant amounted to $49,718; in 1910–1911 it was $91,876[14]
(the highest until 1937–1938); and in 1914–1915, $66,172. During
the First World War departmental expenditure averaged about
$52,000, went up to $69,388 in 1920–1921, down to $49,288 four
years later, and up again, to $60,724, in 1928–1929 (gross state
revenue had by then surpassed $20 million). During the depression
the grant was stationary around the $56,000 mark, started to climb
in 1934, and reached $64,400 in 1935–1936.

How was this money spent? The largest single item of expenditure
was always the cost of relief: in 1905–1906 $17,066 or about 56.5
per cent of the departmental grant, was spent on the rationing of
aboriginal indigents. The expenditure on rationing remained fairly
constant during the next fifteen years, fell to $12,334 in 1918–1919,
showed an upward trend during the depression, and reached $27,200
in 1935–1936. The second largest item of expenditure devoted directly
to native welfare was the cost of clothing, blankets and medicines
($3,356 in 1909–1910, $2,314 in 1917–1918, and $5,484 in 1935–1936).
Mission subsidies accounted for $5,950 in 1905–1906 (the highest
figure until 1947–1948), dropped to $5,454 in 1913–1914, showed a
further downward trend during the next fifteen years, and were consistently below $2,000 during the early thirties, with the exception of
1933–1934 when exactly $2,000 was distributed to subsidize Christian
missions. Before and during the First World War, when venereal
disease was a major problem, the lock hospitals on Dorre and Bernier
islands took a large slice of the departmental budget ($14,924 in

1909–1910, including the cost of shipping to and from the islands, and a record $19,672 in 1911–1912).

Salaries and wages of head office personnel and the staffs of the aboriginal cattle stations and settlements accounted for most of what remained of the departmental grant ($2,888 in 1907–1908, $5,838 in 1917–1918, and $11,950 in 1934–1935). The head office establishment was small. In 1906 the Chief Protector had one clerk to assist him; thirty years later the head office consisted of the Chief Protector, a clerk-in-charge, and five clerks. The two travelling inspectors of aborigines (one for the Kimberleys and the northwest excluding the Ashburton, the other for the remainder of the state), appointed early in 1907, were technically also head office staff; the services of the latter were dispensed with in 1910, and the former was retrenched in 1913. In 1925 a travelling inspector for the whole of the state was appointed, only to be dismissed in 1930 on grounds of economy. This is indicative of departmental priorities during the period: field staff were something of a luxury which could be done away with whenever funds were short. The result was a complete dependence on "outsiders" for the execution of departmental policy. In May 1906, in pursuance with s.7 of the 1905 Aborigines Act, all government residents, resident magistrates, and inspectors and sub-inspectors of police were appointed protectors of aborigines, and in the following month sixteen police constables and fifteen private individuals (pastoralists, ministers of religion, and missionaries) were similarly appointed. Women protectors were first appointed in 1913, following agitation by women's organizations. As time went on protectors were drawn increasingly from the ranks of the police. The limitations on the freedom of action on the part of the department, inherent in such an arrangement, are too obvious to be dwelt upon. At its best, the dual role of a policeman, combining "welfare" and penal sanctions, meant that his work as protector was of secondary importance. Even a sympathetic policeman, bound as he was by loyalty to his oath and his superior officers, could do little for his aboriginal charges; "we only came to kill their dogs", recalled E. Morrow in his memoirs.[15] At its worst, a policeman protecting an aboriginal was like "a hawk protecting a pigeon":[16] the police "held the lives of the natives in their hands to make or mar".[17] The aborigines, for their part, divided Europeans into two groups, "whitefella" and "pleeceman",[18] while those not proficient in Pidgin used the following words to denote a policeman: fierce, severe-looking, sour, salty, the chaining horseman.[19]

Organized interest groups

During the thirty years under review five groups influenced, or
attempted to influence, aboriginal policy and administration in
Western Australia: the pastoral lobby, organized labour, local
government authorities, parents' and citizens' associations, and the
humanitarians. The first four were "organized" groups, and their
interests were clearly defined: the pastoralists wanted to preserve
the status quo in the north; organized labour sought to secure
preference for white labour in the pastoral industry; local government authorities and parents' and citizens' associations demanded
partial segregation or social isolation of the aborigines and part-
aborigines in the closely settled parts of the state. The last group, the
humanitarians, lacked organizational continuity; its aims were vague,
changing, and occasionally diverging. During the twenties, to mention one example, the churches and missionary societies campaigned
for inviolable reserves under mission management, while the "scientists" advocated the setting aside of reserves from which all non-
aborigines, including missionaries, would be debarred.

The pastoral lobby was the most effective, and at the same time
the least conspicuous interest group: the northern pastoralists had
always possessed an influence out of all proportion to their members.
Like other groups concerned with the preservation of the status
quo, the pastoral lobby did not require a tight organization to
express its influence: it operated subtly through powerful allies in
parliament, the civil service, and the press. L. R. Marchant, writing
in 1954, assessed the influence of the pastoralists between 1886 and
1905 in the following words:

From the time of the first Aborigine Act of 1886 the application of the
law has been affected by a legislative body that found itself idolizing the
pioneer spirit of the settlers. Whenever this spirit was at odds with a
desire to protect the natives, the Aborigines Acts were modified accordingly.
They . . . were changed by administrations which interpreted the badly
worded actions to suit their ends.[20]

This was also the position after 1905, with one important qualification: the introduction in that year of employment permits, renewable
annually, made it possible for the department to apply more pressure
on the pastoralists, especially in matters affecting departmental
expenditure, such as the rationing of indigents on pastoral properties.
As regards the more important issue of remuneration of aboriginal

workers, on the other hand, the pastoralists managed to preserve the old-established custom of payment in kind. While Gale was in office they were in no danger; in 1910, when a Franco-German syndicate planning to start large-scale cultivation of cotton in West Kimberley proposed to pay aboriginal workers 5 cents a day, the Chief Protector told them that it was "not desirable that the natives should be in possession of any spending money".[21] Neville's ideas were diametrically opposed to Gale's, but they remained ideas during his entire twenty-five years in office.[22] His first attempt to force all employers of aboriginal labour to pay their workers in cash, made in 1916, came to naught when the government fell, just a week after his submission had been approved by Underwood. He tried again in 1922, only to see his proposal turned down by a cabinet committed to northern development (and cheap aboriginal labour). Three years later he made another attempt but his submission was pigeon-holed, allegedly because of drought. He tried once more in 1927, again without success; before his proposal could reach cabinet a group of parliamentarians, led by the member for Kimberley, A. A. M. Coverley, had a friendly chat with his Minister, with predictable results. In 1928 the proposal found its way into a draft bill to amend the 1905 Aborigines Act but was subsequently deleted in cabinet. The bill itself, a non-party measure, was soundly defeated in December 1929 by the joint efforts of the opposition and a group of Labour members led by Coverley; the people of the north, the member for Kimberley told the lower house, objected to the bill because it gave the department too much power to interfere with their affairs.

All this time the Pastoralists' Association of Western Australia (formed in 1907)[23] remained safely in the background and refrained from making any public statements or direct approaches to the government. Only once, during the height of the depression, did the association depart from this principle. The issue in question was the hospitalization of aboriginal employees. In a letter to the Chief Protector, early in 1932, the association claimed that its members were not legally responsible for hospital expenses incurred by their aboriginal workers receiving a weekly wage of $2 or less (very few received more), on the ground that white workers in the same position were entitled to free hospital treatment, even though they did not pay any hospital tax. Neville referred the complaint to the Crown Solicitor who ruled that the Aborigines Act was quite explicit on the matter: an aboriginal worker was not liable to pay hospital tax, but neither was he entitled to free hospital treatment. It was one thing to lay down the law, however, and another to enforce it: whenever an aboriginal worker became sick or injured, an unscrupulous pastoralist would discharge him first and then send him to the hospital, disclaiming all responsibility upon receipt of the hospital bill.

The trade unions had one simple objective: to ensure preference for white labour in the pastoral industry. This demand can be traced to the closing years of the nineteenth century. Before the gold discoveries of the nineties a wide range of jobs, skilled and unskilled, was opened to the aborigines. After the goldrushes, there was, for the first time since 1829, a surplus of labour in most parts of the colony, and white workers "did not like to compete on equal terms with the aborigines . . . they did not like to see the aborigines employed in positions they had their eyes on . . ."[24] It was during this period that most of the European stereotyped attitudes towards the natives developed. "It was said that native shearers 'cut sheep', that 'natives rode horses to death', that they were, in fact, quite incapable of acting in a European-like manner, and so were not fit to be employed in similar jobs."[25] Opposition to aboriginal labour was most pronounced during periods of adverse economic conditions. The slump of 1906–1907, for instance, brought a spate of angry complaints from the unemployed whites. One trade unionist accused the squatters of the Eucla district of encouraging sexual intercourse between their white stockmen and the local women, thereby assuring themselves of a supply of cheap half-caste labour. Another condemned the "white trash" on the Murchison and the eastern goldfields for employing aborigines in preference to men of their own colour, just to save a paltry pound or two. In 1908 a deputation of Kimberley shearers told the travelling inspector of aborigines that the pastoralists should not be allowed to employ aborigines if white men could be found to do the job. Later, during the great depression, similar complaints were voiced with monotonous regularity. In 1932, for instance, the State Executive of the Labour Party, acting on the initiative of the Derby branch of the Australian Workers' Union, asked the Chief Protector to order the pastoralists to employ more white labour;[26] when the government failed to act, the union took their case to the federal arbitration court, only to have their application for the extension of the shearers' award to aborigines rejected in most emphatic terms by Judge Detheridge.

Nor were such demands confined to bad times. In 1912 the State Executive of the Labour Party wanted the government to segregate the tribal and semi-tribal aborigines on state-owned cattle stations and to ban the employment of aboriginal labour on private properties.[27] In 1922 the leader of the Labour Party, Phillip Collier, attacked the government for employing aboriginal prisoners on Wyndham roads, and J. C. Willcock, then still plain member for Geraldton, took it to task for using aboriginal prison labour to lay a water pipeline in Broome.[28] The objective was sometimes couched in moral terms. In 1911, after a Sydney conference of the Australian Workers' Union condemned the "vile and abject system of slavery" in the Kimberleys, the *Truth* exhorted all trade unionists to take

an active and intelligent interest in native labour and its *abolition* [italics supplied] and the alleviating of the horrible and revolting conditions under which the defenceless original owners of the soil are exploited. This demand is made more imperative by the fact that, although the white toilers may be superior in intelligence and morals to the aborigines, the white workers have to compete in the same industrial market, and therefore their economic interests are the same.[29]

This was a few months before Labour came to power. In 1912 the government brought down the Shearers' and Agricultural Labourers' Accommodation Bill which was meant to achieve the next best thing to the "abolition" of aboriginal labour demanded by the *Truth*: by extending the definition of a shearer and agricultural labourer to aboriginal natives, the government hoped to bring about the virtual closing of these two avenues of employment to the aborigines. The fact that it was the "reactionary" Legislative Council which foiled the scheme speaks for itself — organized labour, for all its cries of "slavery", was just as indifferent as the pastoralists to the real interests of the aborigines, if not more so.

Local government authorities and parents' and citizens' associations, too, had a well-defined aim: social isolation of the growing part-aboriginal population and the surviving full-bloods in the closely settled parts of the state. Their influence on aboriginal policy in the south was all-pervasive: the virtual exclusion, by 1915, of aboriginal children from state schools; the establishment of the Carrolup and Moore River aboriginal settlements, in 1915 and 1918 respectively; the inadequate health services for aborigines in country areas; the existence of many "prohibited areas" or "anti-native reserves", as they were originally called — all this was the direct or indirect outcome of their lobbying. Since their activities affected mainly the part-aborigines, they will be discussed in detail in chapter seven.

The humanitarian lobby before the Onmalmeri massacre

The influence of the humanitarian lobby on aboriginal policy and administration is somewhat difficult to evaluate. Speaking broadly, it was negligible before about 1927, and more marked after that date, though even then the humanitarians did not determine the direction of official policy; rather, they set limits beyond which the government or other interest groups dared not go. The comparative ineffectiveness of the humanitarians was due to several factors. Unlike other groups, they sought to influence governmental action indirectly, through public opinion; they lacked organizational continuity, and, more often than not, continuity of interest; their aims were vague and changing; and they occasionally spoiled a good case by overstating it. Above all, they were not united: individuals like Daisy Bates or M. M. Bennett fought their own battles on behalf of the dispossessed aborigines; the missions (or some missions) would have liked to make the aborigines their sole responsibility; the anthropologists had their own notions of how to save a dying race; assorted "do-gooders" wanted to do good without quite knowing what. But the main reason for the humanitarians' ineffectiveness was public indifference: the man in the street took little interest in the aborigines, and even less in their proposed solutions to the aboriginal problem.

Until about the mid-twenties humanitarian interest in Western Australia's aboriginal population came largely from outside the state, first from Great Britain and later from eastern Australia. The main issue at stake was physical maltreatment of the aborigines. The problem, as we have seen, had been aired by Dr. Roth; his report, unfortunately, did nothing to whitewash the state's reputation in this respect. In June 1907, two and a half years after the inquiry, the Secretary of State for the Colonies asked the Governor of Western Australia whether his government had done anything about replacing neck-chains by wrist-cuffs; the reply, drafted by Prinsep, defended the existing practice as the most "practicable and humane"[30] method of securing the safety of the prisoners in conditions prevailing in the Kimberleys. This was not just a rationalization — medical opinion, for instance, was in favour of chaining as the "best" or "most

humane" method,[31] and even the Bishop of Bunbury admitted:
"Although all one's British sentiment is against the chain, I do not
see what alternative is possible"[32] (the unfortunate cattle-killers also
"preferred" neck-chains to hand-cuffs since they left the hands free
to play cards and to deal with the flies and the mosquitoes).[33] Such
arguments were unlikely to convince the English humanitarians,
however. Following questions in the House of Commons, in July
1907, the Secretary of State undertook to impress upon the Western
Australian government the "objection which the continuance of this
practice cannot fail to excite in this country".[34] In Western Australia,
the issue was taken up by the Aborigines' Amelioration Movement,
founded in 1906 by one F. Lyon Weiss, fond of referring to himself
as an "Australian Briton". In 1907, soon after the appointment of a
Royal Commission to investigate charges of "nigger-hunting" by
the Canning exploring party (about which more will be said later),
the society petitioned parliament to "prevent the evil deeds of a
sordid, heartless influential few from continuing to bring discredit on
the many", and to appoint yet another Royal Commission to inquire into all aspects of aboriginal affairs in order to "show the
civilized world that ninety-nine hundredths of the citizens of Western
Australia were disposed to have the aborigines treated with humanity
and justice".[35] The subsequent exoneration of Canning, followed by
such tangible reforms as the opening of lock hospitals for the treatment of venereal disease and the establishment of aboriginal cattle
stations, did much to placate the local humanitarians and the Exeter
Hall circles in Great Britain. By about 1910 Western Australia's
aborigines had ceased to "excite" the attention of the British public.
In a sense, this was largely a reflection of the changing political
realities and of the growing importance of the Commonwealth
government in the political life of Australia (after 1906 the states
were dependent on federal parliament for much of their income; in
1909 the Commonwealth took over state debts; in 1910 per capita
payments were substituted for the earlier book-keeping system
whereby three-quarters of the customs and excise revenue had been
given to the states; in 1911 the Commonwealth took over from
South Australia the administration of the Northern Territory). One
of the earliest indications of this change was the "Canning affair".
In 1905 the government sent a party, led by the surveyor A. W.
Canning, to explore the country between Willuna and Hall's Creek
and to report on the feasibility of establishing a stock route between

the Kimberleys and the eastern goldfields. Canning returned early
in 1906, and parliament gave him a warm reception. In October
1907 the party cook, one Blake, made a number of startling allegations against Canning and his men, charging them with chaining
aborigines who had refused to lead the party to water, immorality
with native women, and wanton damage to aboriginal water-holes.
Although the charges were first made public in the *Morning Herald*,[36]
it was their publication in the Melbourne *Age*[37] and the action of the
member for Coolgardie, Hugh Mahon, who brought the article to
the official notice of the Prime Minister, which prompted the government to appoint a Royal Commission to inquire into the matter.
The man appointed as Royal Commissioner was C. F. Gale, the
Chief Protector of Aborigines. His report, presented in February
1908, exonerated Canning and his men, except for the charge of
immorality with aboriginal women, for which there was a "slight
foundation".[38] Commenting on the outcome of the inquiry, the
West Australian announced: "An expedition in the desert may surely
claim some of the rights which are supposed to justify a military
leader in commandeering guides from the noncombatants of the
country he traverses", adding ". . . the way in which the Commissioner insisted on hearing all available evidence bearing on the case
is a notable contrast to the unfortunate error of Dr. Roth, some
years ago".[39]

The body which gradually replaced Exeter Hall as the keeper of
the government's conscience, the Association for the Protection of
Native Races in Australia and Polynesia, was founded in Sydney in
1910. Despite its imposing membership (among the foundation
members were Andrew Fisher, Joseph Cook, Alfred Deakin, the
Lord Mayors of Sydney and Melbourne, and several bishops), the
association's influence was negligible, at least in Western Australia;
it was largely a matter of taking notice of its existence and placating
its officials. Late in 1911, after the first party attempting to overland
cattle along the Canning stock route had been ambushed, a punitive
expedition "dispersed" the first group of aborigines encountered
near the scene of the ambush. There was nothing extraordinary about
the incident, which went largely unnoticed in Western Australia. In
December 1911, however, the Sydney press ran an article about the
ambush and the subsequent reprisal,[40] and soon after the Premier,
John Scaddan, received a somewhat belligerent letter from the association's secretary, Archdeacon Lefroy. The main point of the com-

munication was a demand for the elucidation of the term "dispersal". The Premier, perhaps too busy with more important matters, did not even bother to reply. He also ignored the Archdeacon's follow-up letter which was even more unfriendly than the first one. The infuriated Archdeacon then released the story to the press and hinted that there was more to follow. When it looked as if the government was going to be saddled with another scandal, Sir Winthrop Hackett, the editor of the *West Australian* and a counsellor of many a Premier, advised Scaddan to be more circumspect: "I am afraid the Archdeacon is on the warpath, and as he has nothing to occupy him at present he is certain to exercise himself to our discomfort."[41] The Premier took the hint, the Archdeacon was mollified, and the "dispersal" was forgotten.

Another eastern Australian philanthropic body which showed an occasional interest in Western Australian aborigines was the Aborigines' Friends' Association. Founded in Adelaide in 1858, the association became increasingly active on the national scene after the establishment of the Commonwealth of Australia; its main preoccupation, at this time, was inviolable reserves. The only development in Western Australia which can be directly traced to its activities was the gazetting of the Western Australian portion of the central Australian reserve. The reserve was first suggested early in 1914 by two leading members of the association, Dr. Herbert Basedow and Rev. Howard, and was eventually created after the war (Western Australia gazetted its portion in 1920, and the Commonwealth and South Australian governments in 1921). It was one of the earliest examples of successful humanitarian action on a national scale.

On the local scene, before the mid-twenties, one looks in vain for signs of more than sporadic concern for the aborigines and their welfare. The virtual exclusion of aboriginal children from state schools, accomplished by 1915, evoked no protests from the local (or outside) humanitarians; the closing of the Carrolup aboriginal settlement, in 1922, went unnoticed except for a solitary protest from the Australian Aborigines' Mission. After the disintegration of the Aborigines' Amelioration Movement, in 1908, only women's organizations such as the Women's Service Guild and the National Council of Women displayed an occasional interest in the aboriginal question; in 1913, for instance, women protectors were appointed after a deputation from women's organizations had told Drew that such a step was "absolutely essential from a moral point of view".[42] In addition, a few dedicated individuals tried to help the aborigines in their own way. Between 1899 and 1912 Daisy Bates, the legendary *kabbarli* (grandmother from dreamtime), "driven by compassion to direct action",[43] worked tirelessly to alleviate the suffering of what she thought was a dying race (she was also collecting material for a "history" of the Bibbulmun "nation", commissioned by the government in 1904). By the time of her death, in 1951, she was something of a national figure, but in 1912, when she left Western Australia, hurt by the refusal of the government to publish her "history", she was unknown, and her efforts unappreciated. In Kalgoorlie a Church of England clergyman, Canon Collick, had for many years served a "Blackfella Kismas" dinner to the local aborigines. The feasts ceased in 1922 (they were prohibited by the police), but the aborigines did not forget their "Goodfella Collicke". As with Caesar, the name of the person became synonymous with the designation of the office, and even after the Canon's departure, in 1924, the local aborigines insisted on calling all clergymen "Collicks".[44]

The Onmalmeri massacre

It took "murder most foul" to shake the Western Australian humanitarians from their peaceful slumber. In May 1926 an East Kimberley settler was found dead on his station, bordering the Marndoc reserve, with a spear in his body. A posse of police and settlers, sworn in at nearby Wyndham, rode out into the reserve and killed all aborigines they could lay their hands on, taking extraordinary precautions to hide their work by burning the bodies of their victims. It took the government almost seven months to appoint a Royal Commission to inquire into the murders. Prompted by rumours, the Wyndham sergeant of police, who did not accompany the posse, tried to delve into the matter, but no one would talk. Next, the superintendent of the Forrest River mission, Rev. E. R. B. Gribble, "a hardworking, obstinate, tactless man",[45] made his own inquiries and reported the conclusions to the local protector of aborigines. For the remainder of the year Wyndham was subjected to repeated visits by the Broome and Perth police, and in January 1927, following the discovery of charred human remains along the route taken by the posse, magistrate T. G. Wood was appointed Royal Commissioner to inquire into the alleged murders. He found it difficult to sift the truth. In Wyndham public sympathy was entirely with the posse, and a fund was started to pay for their legal representation. Several aboriginal witnesses had disappeared during the investigation, after someone had threatened them that they would be hanged. Although the Commissioner was unable to present enough evidence to justify prosecution on charges of murder, he put on record his unequivocal belief that the aborigines had met their deaths while in the custody of the posse.[46] Subsequently two policemen were arrested for murder, tried, acquitted, and promoted out of the district. Actually, two hordes of the Andedja tribe had been virtually annihilated by the settlers and the police, and even "nowadays, now, at Onmalmeri, you can hear ghosts crying in the night, chains, babies crying, troopers' horse, chains jiggling".[47]

Things were never to be quite the same, after Onmalmeri. In Perth, there was a public outcry over the massacre, followed by a flare-up of interest in the wider aspects of the aboriginal problem. In January 1927 the *Daily News* called for complete segregation of the surviving full-bloods; this would protect them from further contamination with civilization, and would also speed up the development of the north, since the aborigines would have to be replaced by white workers.[48] A public meeting was held in Perth, and a spate of letters to the editor appeared in the metropolitan press, calling for a variety of measures ranging from demands for stern action against the pastoralists to appeals for regular medical inspection of all aborigines. Even earlier, in November 1926, the "better-class" part-aborigines had formed a union "in order to obtain the protection of the same laws that govern white man", because they were "tired of being robbed, and shot down, or run into miserable compounds".[49] In March 1928 an aboriginal deputation, led by the part-aborigine William Harris, asked the Premier to grant all aborigines south of Carnarvon full rights as British subjects; "we want to live up to the white man's standard," said Harris, "but in order to be able to do this we should be exempted from the Aborigines Act."[50] A few days later the *West Australian,* in an editorial of unprecedented earnestness, reminded its readers:

It is no longer taken for granted that the Australian aborigine has been given by Nature a very limited mentality which he cannot transcend. It is true that these people were in a condition similar to that prevailing in Europe in the Neolithic age and were discovered to be one of the most primitive peoples on earth .... Now it has been proved that, notwithstanding the restless habits of possibly thousands of years of hunting and mental torpor, the aboriginal is capable of intellectual and moral education. The blacks make good station hands, competent craftsmen, and admirable domestic servants. Given favourable opportunities, their numbers cease to decline. It is already apparent that there is no need for them to die out, and many people are beginning to look to the aborigines as the solution of the labour problem in the North, where already their work is proved indispensable for the development of the country.[51]

The government, for its part, after years of procrastination, finally consented to a comprehensive amendment of the 1905 Aborigines Act — something Neville had been asking for since 1919. The innovations which eventually found their way into the amending bill fall under two broad headings: greater control over part-aborigines, and more protection for full-bloods, particularly those in pastoral employment. Brought down as a non-party measure late in 1929, the bill passed the Legislative Council with a comfortable majority, only to be thrown out by the lower house. The defeat of the bill was something of a personal triumph for A. A. M. Coverley, who was to administer the department for almost a decade as Minister for the North-West in the Willcock and Wise governments. Coverley made his political debut in 1924, as an "affable young man"[52] of twenty-nine, when he was elected to the Kimberley seat as the first Labour member ever to represent the district. Those who knew him liked him for his "rough and ready methods" and friendly disposition; he also had a reputation of being "a great believer in the underdog".[53] In 1925, after his attack in parliament on the Department of the North-West, the *Westralian Worker* praised him for "setting an example to the older members in advocating the cause of a section of humanity which does not possess a vote, and which has not the slightest political influence whatsoever".[54] The newspaper obviously mistook an attack on aboriginal administration for a plea on behalf of the aborigines, for two years later, after the Onmalmeri massacre, Coverley criticized in parliament "the stupid system of protecting the aborigines to the detriment of the settlers as a whole".[55] In 1929 he led the opposition to the amendment of the Aborigines Act, arguing that the increased powers of the department would result in a "disadvantage of the white people in the north".[56] Most members must have agreed with him, for only twelve voted for the bill.

The humanitarian lobby after the Onmalmeri massacre

And there things might have remained, for years perhaps, had it not been for certain developments in eastern Australia which were eventually to make themselves felt in the west. Throughout Australia, the early twenties were an era of "unsettlement of spirit", accompanied by a temporary destruction of that "progressive, common-sense liberalism"[57] which marked the Australian ethos before the war. As regards aboriginal affairs, the tide began to turn around the mid-twenties. The two influences which were to make themselves increasingly felt after that date were the humanitarian, vocal through churches and philanthropic organizations, and the academic, represented by the rising generation of Australian-trained anthropologists. The renewal of interest in aboriginal welfare was largely due to changes in international morality, and in particular to the League of Nations' concept of the mandate which, owing to the responsibility of the Commonwealth government for New Guinea and Nauru, brought world opinion to Australia's door. Many influential individuals realized that this could have a definite bearing on aboriginal affairs, in Australia itself, and that our fitness to administer the mandate in New Guinea might well be questioned if we could not advance the welfare of aborigines in our midst. As a sovereign state, Australia was, of course, in no way directly responsible to the League of Nations for the treatment of its aboriginal population, although it was under a moral obligation, laid down in article twenty-three of the covenant, to "secure and maintain fair and humane conditions of labour" for all its inhabitants. As with most causal connections of this kind, it is impossible to demonstrate the precise extent of the influence of world opinion on the aboriginal policies pursued by the four states with substantial aboriginal population and by the Commonwealth government in the Northern Territory. Still, consideration of world opinion did play a part. The Kimberley police atrocities and the subsequent Royal Commission, for instance, were almost certainly among the factors which led to renewed demands for federal control of aboriginal affairs: in the eyes of the world, the responsibility of all incidents involving aborigines lay with the federal government. The earliest proposal of this kind, as we have seen, came from the Western Australian Irishman, Hugh Mahon, in 1901. Nine years later, on the eve of the transfer of the Northern Territory from South Australia to the Commonwealth, the Association for the Protection of Native Races asked the federal government to assume sole responsibility for aboriginal affairs throughout Australia; "the wider the area from which the governing power is derived", argued the association, "and the larger the task set, the wider and more statesmanlike the policy is likely to be."[58] In February 1911 a deputation, chosen a month earlier at the Sydney meeting of the Australasian Association for the Advancement of Science, appealed to the Prime Minister to appoint a commission to inquire into "all the native obligations of the Commonwealth".[59] Both proposals came to naught, as did the suggestion, advanced in 1913 by the latter body, that aboriginal affairs should be relegated to a Permanent Native Commission composed of representatives of the federal and state governments. This would enable Australia, for the first time in her history, to treat the aboriginal problem as a whole, and would create a "national sentiment of sympathy and pity" towards the aborigines.[60] The reopening of the question, in 1927, came less than a month after the Royal Commission into the Onmalmeri massacre concluded its investigation. The initiative, on this occasion, came from the Commonwealth government. In June 1927 the Prime Minister proposed the appointment of an extra-parliamentary Royal Commission to inquire into all aspects of aboriginal affairs in Australia, but the states refused to co-operate.[61] In October, the member for Bass moved in the House of Representatives for the appointment of a joint select committee to inquire into the aboriginal problem, including the feasibility of co-operation with the states in matters affecting aboriginal welfare. The motion was lost, after a debate in which the Onmalmeri massacre (referred to as the Gribble case), and certain comments made by Dr. Roth twenty-two years earlier were given a prominent place.[62] The federal government did the next best thing: it appointed the Queensland Chief Protector of Aborigines, J. W. Bleakley, to report on aboriginal administration in the Northern Territory. Bleakley's report,[63] submitted early in 1929, put forward certain far-reaching proposals which were subsequently discussed at a conference of government officials and representatives of pastoral interests and missionary societies, convened in Melbourne by the Minister for Home Affairs. It was the first meeting of its kind ever held in Australia. Federal control of aboriginal affairs was also considered by the 1927 Royal Commission on the Constitution which concluded its deliberations early in 1929. The commission recommended that aboriginal affairs should remain with the states, since they were in a better position to deal with them by virtue of their control over the police, Crown lands, and the conditions of industry. Three members of the commission disagreed and submitted a contrary recommendation: since the aborigines were the responsibility of the nation as a whole, the federal government should see that all Australians carried their fair share of the financial burden in respect to the aboriginal race, and should accept the responsibility for their well-being.[64]

Federal control of aboriginal affairs was one demand voiced by the humanitarians; the creation of large "inviolable" reserves was another. In this field, as we shall see later, Western Australia was something of a pioneer: before the war, it had reserved for the use of the aborigines four million acres of marginal land in East Kimberley and had established the Moola Bulla aboriginal cattle station, covering over one million acres. It had also co-operated (though with a certain lack of enthusiasm) in the establishment after the war of the central Australian reserve, embracing fourteen million acres in Western Australia alone and extending well into South Australia and the Northern Territory. But none of these reserves were inviolable. South Australia, for instance, revoked in 1922 a portion of its part of the central Australian reserve, after a mining syndicate had applied for a prospecting lease in the area; in Western Australia, also in 1922, a part of the Marndoc reserve was thrown open for selection by returned servicemen. What the humanitarians wanted were reserves set aside for the aborigines' permanent use, preferably under the control of those "most intimately associated with native problems",[65] that is the missionaries — a sort of apartheid with religious undertones. A missionary conference, held in Melbourne in April 1926, which resulted in the formation of the National Missionary Council of Australia, declared: "The only effective way of saving and developing the aboriginal natives of Australia is by a policy of strict segregation under religious influence."[66] Speaking at the 1926 meeting of the Australasian Association for the Advancement of Science, held in Perth, F. Wood Jones, the Elder Professor of Anatomy at the University of Adelaide, called for "properly organized and properly administered reserves" as the only way to preserve the aborigines and, thereby, "justify ourselves in the eyes of the world . . ."[67] In 1927 the Aborigines' Protection League, founded in Adelaide the year before, petitioned federal parliament to establish in the Northern Territory a "Model Aboriginal State", with representation in the federal parliament along the lines of the New Zealand Maoris, to be ultimately "managed" by aboriginal "tribunal" as far as possible according to aboriginal laws and customs. Aborigines were not to be detained in the state against their will; all Europeans, except those "of the highest ability and the very fullest sympathy" would be debarred from entering it.[68] In 1928 the Aborigines' Friends' Association proposed that a part of central Australia (to be known as Aboriginal Territory, Central Australia) be set aside for the permanent use of aborigines, under federal control. None of these proposals would have vested the title to the land in the aborigines, and most of them envisaged the reserves as preserves for the missionaries rather than real reserves for aborigines; only a small band of "scientists" would have debarred all Europeans, including the missionaries and even the police, from entering them.

The second influence to make itself felt after the mid-twenties was the academic. During the nineteenth century the study of Australian aborigines was largely the concern of amateurs — explorers, missionaries, police troopers, government officials, and so on.[69] Although the quality of their contributions leaves much to be desired, we owe them a great deal; for instance, were it not for George Grey, Scott Nind, G. F. Moore, and Bishop Salvado, we should today possess very little information about the aborigines of the southwest. Towards the end of the century these casual studies were replaced by others closer to the spirit of scientific research. The first solid work was *Kamilaroi and Kurnai*, by A. W. Howitt and L. Fison, published in 1880, which "laid down the foundations of scientific study of Australian aborigines".[70] Their successors R. H. Mathews, Baldwin Spencer, and F.J. Gillen brought the aborigines to the prominence they have had in the world of anthropology ever since. Their work, and that of others who followed in their footsteps, was based on the Darwinian analysis of the natural world: they saw the aborigines as a remnant of primitive humanity, and valued the study of their culture only insofar as it helped to trace out the "sequence of ideas by which mankind has advanced from the condition of the lower animals to that in which we find him at the present time, and by this means to provide really reliable materials for a philosophy of progress".[71] Not all students of Australian aborigines, however, subscribed to these ideas. "It is impossible to understand the Australians", said F. Raetzel as early as 1885, "apart from their extensive nomadism, to which all the natural qualities of the land contribute. At the bottom of it lies the deficiency of water, and the unequal distribution of food, plants, and animals, which partly results from this."[72] W. H. R. Rivers, in 1911, expressed a similar view when he called for a more realistic study of Australian aborigines in which ethnological analysis must precede any theoretical use of facts in support of evolutionary speculations.[73] But the man who really buried the "dogma of Australian ultra-primitivism",[74] to use H. R. Lowie's felicitous phrase, was A. R. Radcliffe-Brown. Not a prolific writer himself (he was "a starter and a stirrer"),[75] his influence on the study of Australian aborigines was nevertheless profound, especially during the five years he held the chair of anthropology at the University of Sydney. The chair (the first in Australia, and the third only in the British Empire) was established late in 1925 with financial help from the Commonwealth and state governments, and a generous research grant from the Rockefeller Foundation, as a result of a resolution passed two years earlier by the Second Pan-Pacific Science Congress, held in Melbourne and Sydney. "It was indeed remarkable", said A. P. Elkin, "that just when the Department was founded such a person as Radcliffe-Brown was available and ready to set it going."[76] His work was almost undone by the depression. In December 1930 three states ceased their grants (including Western Australia whose annual contribution was $192), and the Commonwealth government reduced its grant and put it on a yearly basis. This led to Radcliffe-Brown's resignation. The second occupant of the chair, Raymond Firth, left soon after his appointment in June 1931 and was replaced in December 1932 by A. P. Elkin as lecturer-in-charge. In March 1933 the Commonwealth government agreed to extend its financial support for another five years, and at the end of 1933 Elkin was appointed to the chair. Gradually, too, the University of Sydney allowed the department to become its own responsibility; this brought stability and permanence, and made continuity in research projects possible. In marked contrast to their nineteenth century predecessors, Australian anthropologists of the 1920s and 1930s paid considerable attention to the problems of culture change. "Anthropology is no longer to be treated as an academic subject having a purely theoretical interest", announced the inaugural issue of *Oceania,* an anthropological quarterly published with the assistance of the Australian National Research Council, "but can and should be made a science of immediate practical value, more particularly in relation to the government and education of native peoples."[77] A few administrators shared this conviction. "A scientific training in anthropology", said Neville in 1927, "combined with actual training in the field, will go a long way towards the better administration of native affairs in the future, and establish a sympathetic understanding between the people and the officials concerned."[78] Most aboriginal administrators, however, continued to stress the "practical" nature of their work, deprecating unsolicited advice from the scientists; as late as 1945, for instance, when urged to appoint an anthropologist to his staff, Neville's successor, F. I. Bray, replied: ". . . the welfare of the native is not bound up with the advice and guidance of trained anthropologists, and it is not apparent just what advantage would result to the natives."[79] The main contribution of anthropology, however, was to point out a way beyond "segregation" and "protection", by supplying the idea that a major development of aboriginal life from its broken down state was a thinkable possibility.[80] In the late twenties G. M. Morant and H. Woolard demonstrated that the cranial capacity of the aboriginal brain was well within the European range,[81] thereby disproving the lingering belief in the affinity between the aboriginal skull and that of the Neanderthal man. In 1929 S. D. Porteus, Professor of Racial Psychology at the University of Hawaii and one of the pioneers of "culture free" intelligence tests, conducted a series of tests in West Kimberley, central Australia and at the Moore River aboriginal settlement. The results led him to conclude that the aborigines, while not unintelligent in relation to their own environment, lacked the "ethnic capacity" to become civilized[82] (he was later criticized by A. P. Elkin for failing to take into account the higher scores obtained by aborigines with prolonged contact, which at least suggested that they "may have learned to adapt themselves to our hurried way of doing things").[83] Other students of the problem were more cautious: R. Piddington, for instance, thought that the existing intelligence tests had little value and were, in any case, inapplicable to aborigines with little or no formal schooling.[84] This view was confirmed by a later generation of social scientists. Today we believe that the question of whether one ethnic group is as intelligent as another has no acceptable answer, and that we can measure only the "culturally acquired" intelligence which depends almost entirely on the environment and not the "natural" or "innate" intelligence, that is the basic capacity of the nervous system as represented by the genes. The social scientists of the inter-war years were more optimistic, hoping to measure the intelligence of non-literate peoples by means of carefully constructed "culture free" intelligence tests. Inconclusive as their findings may have been, they were none the less seen as a proof that the aborigines were capable of at least partial adaptation to our way of life, and that they could therefore survive as a race. But mere survival was not enough: positive measures in the field of education and welfare were necessary to help them to take an "intelligent place" in our complex social, economic, and religious life. Such was the programme adopted in the early thirties under the influence of A. P. Elkin by the Association for the Protection of Native Races, the National Missionary Council, and other philanthropic organizations. Elkin's 1931 address to the former body — the first formulation of what was to be known as a "positive policy" for the aborigines — was printed in 1933 as a pamphlet, under the title *A Policy for the Aborigines*. The idea, said W. E. H. Stanner recently, had not come out of the blue. "What was radical and startling was the putting into words of the first notion of a 'positive policy', obvious and unadventurous as it may seem now."[85] In that sense, the publication of the pamphlet was a turning point of aboriginal affairs in Australia.

The developments described above had initially only a marginal effect in Western Australia. The physical isolation of the state from the rest of Australia, the feeling of many Western Australians of being cut off from the larger centres of population in the east, and the lack of identity of public interest between east and west, all contributed to this lag. The first to take up the cudgels on behalf of the aborigines (after the brief revival of public interest in the wake of the Kimberley police atrocities) were two women, K. S. Prichard and M. M. Bennett. K. S. Prichard was an authoress of some standing when she wrote *Coonardoo,* a *Bulletin* competition prize-winning novel, published in book form in 1929. It is the story of Coonardoo, the passionate aboriginal girl, and Hugh Watt, the young station owner. There is no happy ending; Coonardoo dies as the "black pearl" of a pearler's crew, her body "rotting away from her".[86] If the novel is marred by a "slightly sentimental humanitarianism",[87] it is also the "first novel to treat the aboriginal as a fully emotional and human being",[88] and the fact that it was written at all is significant in itself. M. M. Bennett's *The Australian Aboriginal as a Human Being,* which appeared in 1930, is an altogether different book; if K. S. Prichard's humanitarianism was slightly sentimental, that of Mrs. Bennett was of the militant kind. The elder daughter of a Queensland pioneer, Mrs. Bennett had worked for some years as matron at the Forrest River mission and at Kunmunya. Her first excursion into creative writing was *Christison of Lammermoor*

(1927), a sympathetic biography of her father describing the trials that beset the life of a Queensland pioneer in the 1860s, and the way her father had won the confidence and goodwill of an aboriginal tribe. *The Australian Aboriginal as a Human Being* was a plea for federal control of aborigines, as well as a scathing attack on Western Australia's aboriginal administration; the fact that a part of the book was devoted to a description of the evils as recorded by Dr. Roth a quarter of a century earlier speaks for itself.[89] The attack by the anthropologist R. Piddington, purporting to describe more recent evils, was a different story. Early in 1932, following a period of field-work in West Kimberley, Piddington publicly accused the government of condoning "virtual slavery" in the pastoral north, and of "utter indifference" to the welfare of the aboriginal population[90] (since Piddington had been sponsored by the Australian National Research Council, Neville brought the case to the official notice of Professor Firth, the chairman of the anthropological committee of the council, advising him that his department would not welcome further field trips by Piddington; Professor Firth, for his part, agreed that in future research workers sponsored by the council would be asked to refrain from making public statements critical of the administration). In the meantime, Mrs. Bennett, in an article in the *West Australian* entitled "Allegations of Slavery", had criticized the government for giving the pastoralists a virtually free hand with the aborigines, and for closing its eyes to the suffering inflicted on aboriginal women by the "cruel institution of polygamy"[91] (three years later the Royal Commissioner asked to investigate these allegations had to admit that the article "really provided nothing specific into which I could inquire").[92] This was in May 1932. In June the Women's Service Guild appealed to the government to take all necessary steps towards the implementation of an "honourable" aboriginal policy.[93] In October the Australian Aborigines' Amelioration Association was founded in Perth, with a platform which included the planks of greater protection for aboriginal women, segregation of full-bloods from the growing part-aboriginal population, and greater Commonwealth participation in aboriginal affairs. In June 1933 the *Daily News,* under a heading in very large type, "Natives are Virtually Slaves", published extracts from a "survey" of Western Australia's aboriginal administration, prepared by Mrs. Bennett for the 1933 Conference of the British Empire League, held in London. The paper was a mixture of valuable observations and unfounded attacks. It criticized the government, and rightly so, for neglecting aboriginal education and for its reluctance to lay down a clear policy in the pastoral regions. It also accused it of deliberately encouraging polygamy (in the interests of the pastoralists) and the practice of placing half-caste women "at the disposal of the police".[94] If the article was intended to force the hands of the government, then it achieved its purpose. In August 1933 the Legislative Assembly, by a unanimous vote, agreed to the appointment of a Royal Commission to inquire into all aspects of aboriginal administration. In February 1934 a Perth police court magistrate, H. D. Moseley, was appointed to investigate all recent allegations of maltreatment of aborigines and to report on the administration of the Aborigines Department in general. Moseley presented two confidential interim reports, one in April, dealing with the "woeful spectacle" of the Moore River native settlement,[95] and another in July, recommending an immediate medical survey of the north, as a preliminary step towards checking the alarming spread of leprosy. His final report, presented in January 1935, disproved all recent allegations of brutality and maltreatment of aborigines, though otherwise it revealed a state of affairs which was far from satisfactory. Its contents will be discussed in more detail in chapter eight.

5. The Pastoral North
1906-1935

Demographic changes and their effect on aboriginal policy

In common with the rest of the Australian outback, the northwest and the Kimberleys were affected by the march of progress during the thirty years separating the Roth and Moseley Royal Commissions. Communications were improved; some long-needed amenities were provided; the advent of the aeroplane and the pedal wireless transmitter did much to overcome the feeling of fear and isolation. Most aborigines shared the benefits of these developments. Those near the coast were provided with a health service which went beyond the application of "painkiller" as a cure-all; in parts of the northwest, during the First World War, they tasted the bittersweet experience of "cash money in hand", after the customary payment in kind had been replaced by cash wages; in the Kimberleys, new missions were established to convert them to Christianity. For all this, the colonial character of the pastoral north remained unchanged. In 1935 the Europeans were still a highly privileged group, retaining all political and economic power: "The dominance of European interests was total, unquestioned, and inexpressibly self-centred."[1] The settlers' dependence on aboriginal labour had not diminished: attempts to develop the north and to populate it with Europeans had failed, the boundaries of settlement had advanced but little after 1906, and no new industries of major importance had been established. The European population had in fact decreased in those years: in 1901 there were 5,467 Europeans in the north (just under 2.8 per cent of Western Australia's European population), ten years later, 6,498, in 1921, 5,663 (2,177 in the Kimberleys and 3,476 in the northwest), and only 5,328, or little over 1.2 per cent of the state's European population, in 1933. About the turn of the century, there were in the north some 12,000 aborigines "in touch with civilization"; in 1935 there were approximately 10,500 — about 6,000 in the Kimberleys, the remainder in the northwest.[2] "Beyond the confines of civiliza-

tion", it was thought, there roamed large numbers of "bush" aborigines, estimated officially at 20,000 until 1916 and at 10,000
between 1917 and 1947 (the figure was reduced to 6,000 in the
following year). These estimates were almost certainly considerably
in error. To start with, they were based on the assumption that the
pre-contact aboriginal population of Western Australia was about
100,000;[3] they also disregarded population movements subsequent
to white contact. All over the north, as the tribes with long contact
decreased in numbers, migrants from inland areas settled on pastoral
properties, to be eventually integrated, with various degrees of
success, into the local communities. In those areas where there were
no or only few local aborigines left, no special gifts of insight were
required to observe this population drift; elsewhere, it was far from
obvious, and difficult to detect without anthropological training.

For this reason alone, official population counts for these years
are at best only rough estimates. None the less, they contain some
useful clues. During the twenties and early thirties, for instance,
children under fourteen accounted for about one-third of the total
population of the northwest, and only for about one-tenth in the
Kimberleys (in the Wyndham district the count for 1935 listed only
ninety children in a total aboriginal population of 1,280). This
observation is in line with other evidence. In 1928 the manager of the
recently established Munja aboriginal cattle station, in northwest
Kimberley, reported that he could count only a dozen children among
the 700-odd aborigines frequenting the institution.[4] From the Presbyterian mission at Port George IV (renamed Kunmunya in the late
twenties), also in northwest Kimberley, we have similar evidence
from the mission superintendent, Rev. J. R. B. Love. The anthropologist Phyllis Kaberry reported that in 1935, except on the Moola
Bulla aboriginal cattle station, she found few children in East
Kimberley aboriginal camps,[5] in spite of the "baby bonuses" —
bribes to produce another generation of stockmen — offered by
most pastoralists (one station owner, F. C. Booty, had apparently no
problem here; a "cultured Englishman", "looking like Bond St."
when presiding over the meetings of Hall's Creek road board, he
was once asked how he got his labour, and replied: "breed it
myself").[6] Depopulation, clearly, was more pronounced in the
Kimberleys than in the northwest. This explains the increasing preoccupation of the administration with the Kimberleys and the relative
neglect of the northwest, especially after the First World War. A

related explanation can be found in the growing economic importance of the Kimberley native. In 1906 the Kimberleys accounted for
only a small proportion of the 4,000 or so aborigines in European
employment; by 1918, there were more aborigines in European
employment in the Kimberleys than in the northwest (2,473 as
against 2,029). So the policy of protection, first applied in the north-
west during the 1880s and later embodied in the 1905 Aborigines
Act, was extended to the Kimberleys. This development was foreshadowed in 1910 when the government, realizing the futility of
arresting aboriginal cattle-killers en masse, decided to feed them
at the taxpayers' expense instead. One year later the government took
a further step by gazetting four million acres of East Kimberley
scrub country as an aboriginal reserve — the first reserve of its kind
in Australia. After the war had taken all eligible men from pastoral
employment, the Kimberley aborigine became almost overnight
an important economic asset. "The future of the aborigines in the
Kimberleys", warned Neville in 1920, "is a matter of immediate
attention. It is, moreover, economically sound to preserve the race
as far as possible in order that it may continue to assist in the development of the Territory, in which it has materially helped in the
past."[7] This remained the guiding principle of the administration
between the wars. The northwest aborigines, pacified a long time
ago, outwardly "happy and contented", required little attention, all
the more so since they showed no signs of dying out. The pastoralists
felt secure, the whole system ran fairly smoothly, and occasional
complaints were put down to personal idiosyncracies of the "trouble
makers".[8] It required an upheaval like the Second World War to
show how unrealistic this assessment had been.

Cattle-killing in the Kimberleys and the establishment of aboriginal cattle stations

In 1906 all this was in the future. The Kimberley aborigine was
still a threat, a pest to be controlled rather than a source
of labour; the main task of aboriginal administration in the
region, as in the past, was still the maintenance of "law and order".
After 1906, however, with the pastoral expansion virtually completed, the primary concern of the government was no longer the
protection of the settler himself but of his stock — to be more precise,
his cattle (in West Kimberley sheep-killing had died out by about
1900). The main culprits were the "semi-civilized" aborigines of East

Kimberley, that is those who had not yet "sat down" and become attached to a pastoral property. The usual method of dealing with the problem, as we have seen, was to arrest whole groups, secure the men by neck-chains, and march them to the nearest magistrate or justice of the peace, who completed the formalities by sentencing all and sundry to two–three years' imprisonment. Dr. Roth's condemnation of this "brutal and outrageous" state of affairs brought certain improvements, but within a year the police reverted to their old, "tried out" methods. Mass imprisonment was fast losing its deterrent value, however; during 1906–1907, 137 aborigines were convicted for cattle-killing, 156 in the following year, and 219 during 1908–1909. The pastoralists were getting restless; one went so far as to suggest the emasculation of convicted cattle-killers, "partially for the first offence, the operation to be completed after the second".[9] The cost of keeping aboriginal prisoners was rising: in 1906–1907 $13,682 was spent on the gaoling of natives, and $18,256 in 1908–1909. Since the expenditure was almost entirely wasted, the idea of feeding the aborigines instead of gaoling them began to gain support. As early as 1906, following the conviction of no less than thirty-nine cattle-killers in one month alone, several East Kimberley pastoralists offered to donate up to one hundred head of cattle for that purpose. In January 1908 a deputation from the Kimberleys asked the Colonial Secretary to establish two feeding depots, one in East and one in West Kimberley. The Chief Protector himself, in his 1908 annual report, argued that the mounting cost of arresting the depredators and then feeding them for two or three years at the government's expense was the best argument in favour of creating a chain of feeding depots across the Kimberleys. Soon after the *West Australian* gave the scheme its blessing, by drawing attention to the "healthy, fat and sleek" condition of aboriginal prisoners; it also claimed that after their release, having become accustomed to prison food, they committed further depredations just to be able to go back for another "spell" in prison.[10] The policy of mass arrests was abandoned in two stages. In February 1909 the police were instructed to arrest only the ringleaders of the cattle-killing gangs, and only on the condition that the owner claiming his cattle had been slain produced the same evidence as would be required if the offence had been committed by a European. At the same time, the practice of paying the police a daily allowance for each aboriginal prisoner or witness brought in was discontinued; instead, stores were supplied to the police in advance, with the government paying only for the actual cost of provisions.[11] The second stage was put into effect soon afterwards. In September 1909 the Colonial Secretary approved the establishment in East Kimberley of a "self-supporting institution for the relief of indigent natives", and in February 1910 the government resumed twenty-eight well-stocked pastoral leases near the Wyndham-Hall's Creek road, at the cost of $42,894. The station, comprising over one million acres, was gazetted as an aboriginal reserve under the Land Act and named Moola Bulla ("plenty tucker"), on the suggestion of Daisy Bates. The institution was "opened" by the Chief Protector who, through an interpreter, explained to the assembled aborigines the purpose of the new "blackfellow" station; they, in turn, signified their willingness to "sit down" and cease depredations on surrounding properties. Despite initial fears as to the aborigines' reaction, the experiment was a success. Cattle-killing on nearby properties ceased, and there was no need for the firearms with which the European staff had been initially provided. Describing his visit to Moola Bulla, the superintendent of the Beagle Bay mission, Father Bischofs, remarked in 1913:

I spent a few days here, and saw some 200 natives, and assisted at the killing of from three to four bullocks every second day . . . I doubt if there is another place in the world where natives find such a compensation for the loss of their country to the whiteman.[12]

Moola Bulla had a twofold aim. Its primary purpose was to act as a buffer between the semi-nomadic aborigines and the marginal pastoral regions, to "deter natives from killing cattle by feeding them at government expense".[13] Its subsidiary purpose was to "civilize" the local aborigines: the government hoped that the property would develop into a self-supporting institution where adults would be trained in tropical agriculture and pastoral pursuits, and children groomed for employment as house servants on adjoining properties (it was this aspect of Moola Bulla which must have prompted A. P. Elkin to comment on the "positive" note of Western Australia's aboriginal policy at this time).[14] But the aborigines refused to regard the station as a "home". In December 1910, for instance, some sixty Ruby Plains station aborigines, taken to Moola Bulla by the police, cleared out within forty-eight hours, and even the local aborigines would not "sit down" permanently; as soon as one group moved in, another would move out. So the institutional aspects of Moola Bulla were neglected, at least until 1929, when the wife of one of the European employees started to teach the station children in her spare time. Up to that time Moola Bulla served primarily as a buffer, run not "in the interests of the natives in the East Kimberley district"[15] but in the interest of East Kimberley pastoralists.

The new method of dealing with aboriginal cattle-killers, followed by the founding of Moola Bulla, brought a sharp drop in the number of convictions on cattle-killing charges: only twenty-two aborigines were gaoled in 1909–1910, and none in 1910–1911. This did not mean that cattle-killing had ceased, of course, but the new system was a step in the right direction and a success financially. The capital cost of establishing Moola Bulla was only a little more than double the annual cost of the gaoling of aboriginal prisoners, and the station (run as a trading concern) was soon to bring steady profits.[16] Consequently, the department would have liked to extend the system throughout the Kimberleys, and made a start in that direction in June 1911 by opening a second feeding depot at Violet Valley near Turkey Creek. The idea received support from somewhat unexpected quarters. The trade unions had always been uneasy about competition from "cheap" aboriginal labour, and in September 1912 the State Executive of the Australian Labour Party asked the government to segregate the northern aborigines on state-owned cattle stations and to prohibit their employment by private persons. But the government failed to act; with the problem of cattle-killing "solved", it saw no need for expenditure which was no longer absolutely imperative.

Early "hunting" reserves

The four-million-acre Marndoc reserve, on the western shore of Cambridge Gulf, gazetted a year after Moola Bulla, had a somewhat different purpose. Moola Bulla aimed to "pacify by feeding"; Marndoc, in the words of J. D. Connolly, was to allow the tribal aborigines, still unspoilt by civilization, to "live their lives in their own native way".[17] There was nothing extraordinary about the mere gazetting of the reserve. Under the powers conferred upon him by the 1872 Land Regulations, the Governor could set aside reserves for the "use and benefit" of the aborigines, and in the intervening years a number of aboriginal reserves (including one on the Fraser River in West Kimberley which covered 600,000 acres) were created. They were meant to "benefit" the aborigines only indirectly, being either "sanctuaries for the detribalized", or held by missions in trust for the aborigines. The idea behind Marndoc was to "preserve the aborigines as a race", by protecting them from all contacts, be it with settlers, miners or prospectors, or missionaries — in other words, segregation. It was a concept which ran counter to the pastoralists' claim that the remaining aborigines should be "absorbed and utilized"[18] by them, and was soon to clash with the missionaries' claim for "free and unfettered preaching of the Gospel . . . bestowed upon [them] by God".[19] Connolly was a member of a government which certainly did not place the interests of the aborigines above those of the pastoralists or the missionaries, and yet he managed to convert most of his cabinet colleagues to his point of view; perhaps he was helped by the fact that most of Marndoc was unsuited for pastoral settlement and carried only a small aboriginal population. Marndoc was actually gazetted by the Scaddan government which replaced the Wilson ministry after the landslide victory of Labour at the 1911 general election; for some reason a second reserve, between the King Edward River and the northwest Kimberley coast, mooted by Connolly at the same time as Marndoc, was not proclaimed by the new government. Nevertheless, by the time Scaddan went out of office, in July 1916, 414,000 acres of marginal land between King Sound and Collier Bay (known as the Yampi Sound reserve), had been declared a "temporary" reserve, that is subject to cancellation should the land be required for other purposes. In 1920 Western Australia gazetted its portion of the central Australian reserve, covering fourteen million acres in Western Australia alone.[20] On this occasion, the government had acted with a marked lack of enthusiasm. The reserve was mooted early in 1914 by a group of Adelaide philanthropists who persuaded the South Australian government to seek the co-operation of the Western Australian and federal governments in the matter. Scaddan's reaction was discouraging: the Western Australian portion of the proposed reserve was too large to be permanently excluded from future pastoral and mining development. The idea was revived during the last year of the war by the South Australian government, after fresh representations from Adelaide philanthropic organizations. Western Australia agreed to set aside its portion in August 1918, as a temporary reserve, and in January 1920 the federal government issued a similar statement regarding the Northern Territory. In June 1920 the Royal Anthropological Institute of Great Britain and Ireland added its support to the proposal.[21] The reserve, covering about forty-two million acres, came into existence in 1921: Western Australia gazetted its portion in December 1920, and the other two governments followed suit soon after.

Aboriginal cattle stations and reserves between the wars

By 1921 Western Australia could boast that it had reserved over twenty million acres for the "use and benefit" of its aboriginal population. On paper, this was an impressive achievement. In reality, the reserves were something of a sham. Most of them were temporary reserves, and even those classified as permanent failed to vest in the aborigines the title to the land or the right to the minerals it contained; nor were they inviolable, since they too could be cancelled, albeit not with the same ease as temporary reserves. In those circumstances, the post-war emphasis on "northern development" augured ill for the northern tribal aborigines. Before the war, the government was at least prepared to admit that it "had a duty in regard to the welfare of the natives",[22] even though the welfare of the north came first; in 1919 a committee appointed to advise on the best means of promoting the development of the Kimberleys saw the aboriginal question as the "greatest barrier to settlement", concluding that it could see no way of reconciling the "material progress" of the region with the "spiritual welfare" of its aboriginal inhabitants.[23] In 1920 a Department of the North-West was created to co-ordinate the work of all departments in the north (including the administration of aboriginal affairs) and to encourage closer settlement, tropical agriculture, and the pastoral industry. With practically all suitable land already taken up, aboriginal reserves were a natural target for prospective settlers. In 1918 the Lands Department, without consulting the Chief Protector, excised 200,000 acres from the Wyndham end of the Marndoc reserve, and leased the land to one of the town's residents (since the reserve had been gazetted only under the Land Act, and not under the Aborigines Act as well, there was little the Chief Protector could do about it; in fact, he learned of the transaction from the *Government Gazette*). In 1919 the Commonwealth Department of Repatriation inaugurated a settlement scheme for returned servicemen; the men were to be trained at Moola Bulla, and, on completion of training, were to be allocated whatever land was available. Forewarned by the earlier cancellation of a part of the Marndoc reserve, Neville succeeded in having Moola Bulla gazetted under the provisions of the Aborigines Act.[24] But his effort to have the Marndoc reserve similarly gazetted failed, and in 1922 880,000 acres of marginal land along the southern boundary of the reserve were thrown open for selection and allocated to returned servicemen.

While northern development was the order of the day, creation of additional reserves was highly unlikely. Still, Neville did his utmost in that direction. Basing his arguments on the gradual reappearance of cattle-killing (in West Kimberley after 1917, in East Kimberley somewhat later), he repeatedly urged the government to set aside more land for the aborigines, especially in northwest Kimberley, and to establish at least two feeding depots in the same area. So great was the aborigines' lust for beef, he told the Minister for the North-West in January 1921, that "nothing will prevent them from killing to obtain it except properly regulated provisions of ample supplies of meat".[25] He might have added: and they will travel a hundred miles, if necessary, to get it. Neville was among the first to observe that the mere gazetting of more reserves would not stop the aborigines from gravitating towards civilization — white man's food and stimulants. For this reason alone, a chain of feeding depots across the Kimberley was essential; if cattle-killing diminished as a result, all the better. But the government was not convinced by this argument, nor would it approve Neville's alternative proposal to put the convicted cattle-killers to work opening new tracks, improving river crossings, and clearing land for tropical agriculture. The pastoralists in the recently opened Durack River country threatened to take the law into their hands unless the government took measures to stop the depredations. In 1926, exasperated by continued stock losses, some East Kimberley settlers did just that. Taking the spearing of a pastoralist for an excuse, a posse of civilians and police killed two hordes of the Andedja tribe and burned the victims' bodies.[26] This more or less solved the cattle-killing problem in East Kimberley. In West Kimberley, similar results were achieved by the expenditure of $15,600 on the resumption in 1926 of the Avon Valley station, on the eastern shore of Collier Bay, and its conversion into an aboriginal cattle station. There was no connection between the two events: negotiations for the resumption of Avon Valley were in their final stage at the time of the East Kimberley killings. The establishment of Munja, as the station became known, was a symptom of a new approach to the problem of the north in general, and to the aboriginal problem in particular, on the part of the Collier government which replaced the Mitchell ministry in 1924. The Department of the North-West, having failed to develop the north, was abolished in 1926. In 1927 Munja was gazetted as an aboriginal reserve, and in the following year 600,000 acres of land between Prince Frederick Harbour and the Admiralty Gulf were similarly gazetted. Finally, in 1929, on the recommendation of A. P. Elkin, just back from field-work in the Kimberleys, one million acres near Mount Hann in central Kimberley were reserved for the aborigines, bringing the total area under reservation to over twenty-three million acres.

Unlike some of the more ardent advocates of segregation who thought of reserves in terms of future, perhaps self-governing, "aboriginal states", Neville saw them largely as a form of insurance against pastoral expansion.[27] For this reason he tried to make the reserves inviolable, that is subject to cancellation only by an act of parliament, and out of bounds to all Europeans, including missionaries. The main danger to aboriginal reserves, at this stage, came from miners and prospectors who could obtain the necessary licences by applying to the Department of Mines. In 1929 Neville sought to have all Kimberley reserves declared "A Class" reserves under the provisions of the 1899 Permanent Reserves Act, but the cabinet deferred its decision until the expiration of all existing mining concessions on aboriginal reserves. After a second, equally unsuccessful, attempt two years later, the department started to bond prospecting parties about to enter a reserve, in an attempt to prevent the "molesting" of aborigines and the acquisition, legally or otherwise, of their weapons and implements. It was largely a face-saving device, for the system was impossible to police, and depended almost entirely on the goodwill of the prospecting parties. In 1932 Neville made another, truly revolutionary, proposal: he asked for the aborigines to be given a share, in the form of royalties, of mineral wealth found on aboriginal reserves. Although such royalties were to be held "in trust" for the entire aboriginal population, and the fund was to be administered by the department, it was a bold innovation none the less. It never received a moment's serious consideration.[28]

By this time the whole concept of segregation was coming under increasing criticism as "negative", undesirable in principle, and largely ineffective, since the aborigines themselves preferred "civilization" to life on reserves. So their inviolability gradually ceased to be an issue. After 1937, when some six million acres were added to the Western Australian part of the central Australian reserve, no new large reserves were gazetted, and nothing was done to develop those already proclaimed (the cancellation of most of them, in the late fifties, went practically unnoticed). Aboriginal cattle stations, on the other hand, retained some of their usefulness, even though the government was not prepared to spend any money on them. Educationally, using the term in its broadest sense, they were a failure; at Munja, said I. L. Idriess in *Over the Range*, "the natives took no particular interest in the beasts, except to eat them".[29] But the anthropologist Phyllis Kaberry was greatly impressed by what she termed the "policy of non-interference" practised by the government at the cattle stations. In 1935 she had witnessed a happy gathering of some four hundred aborigines at Violet Valley; they told her that they met at the station every year, knowing there would be plenty of food and tobacco, that the police and station owners would not molest their dogs, and that no one would interfere with their tribal activities.[30] The closing of the station, early in 1940, was not due to a change of policy but to chance. The manager had apparently gone "too much mad feller, all day chasing blackfellow belong to gun",[31] so the government sold the station after most aborigines had left. Late in 1940 Munja, also suffering from staff problems, was offered to the Presbyterian Church, to be run as a mission, and the negotiations were almost completed when the war in the Pacific broke out. The station was eventually closed in 1948 and handed over to the Presbyterians. The remaining aboriginal cattle station, Moola Bulla, was sold to a Queensland pastoralist in 1955.

Government control of pastoral employment

Government regulation of pastoral industry was based on the permit system, designed to prevent "untrustworthy" persons from employing aboriginal labour. Before 1905 only those aborigines employed under a contract were protected; after 1905 protection was extended to all aboriginal workers (an employer was still free to "sign on" aborigines, but he required a permit to do so). The act itself did not lay down detailed conditions of employment beyond the prohibition of child labour and the stipulation that an aborigine employed under an agreement was entitled to "leave to absent himself" from his work for a specified period, depending on the length of contract. The details were laid down in the permits themselves, at the discretion of the issuing protector, the customary formula being the prescription of "substantial, good and sufficient rations, clothing and blankets, and medicines and medical attendance when practicable and necessary". The permit system was far from perfect, naturally. A protector was free to issue permits as he saw fit; he could grant a permit to himself, his agent or principal, his employer or employee, indeed anyone, and the Chief Protector could not overrule him. An unsuccessful applicant could always reapply in another district where the protector was more lenient. General or blanket permits which simply specified the maximum number of workers an employer was allowed to employ, without naming them, could be used to defeat the whole purpose of the legislation; a pastoralist, for instance, when presented with a hospital bill for one of his employees, could always deny that he had ever laid his eyes on the aborigine. Finally, the effectiveness of the system depended on regular inspection, since the local protectors were usually either unable (as in the case of private individuals) or not unduly eager (as in the case of the police) to do the job properly. But there was no regular inspection between 1913 and 1925, and again from 1930 until 1937, and only for three years, from 1907 till 1910, were there two travelling inspectors on the staff. For all its faults, the permit system had a salutary effect on the pastoral industry. This emerges clearly from the greater willingness of the pastoralists to ration the old and indigent aborigines on their properties. Early in 1909 Gale concluded that the existing system of rationing aboriginal indigents, whereby each "relieving officer" was allowed so much per head (from 5 cents to 10 cents per day) did not work very well, "owing to the few opportunities the Department had of checking the numerous accounts sent in, and ascertaining if they were correct, and if the service had been faithfully performed".[32] The system which replaced it, in February 1909, largely eliminated the possibility of fraud. Rations were now supplied at contract rates, and aboriginal indigents had to report every week to the police who issued ration orders on the contractor, usually the local shopkeeper (in the few districts where the *per capita* system was retained, accounts had to be certified by a resident magistrate and countersigned by the district police officer after he had satisfied himself, to the best of his ability, that the aborigine or aborigines in question had actually received the rations specified in the account). Soon after, Gale sent a circular to those pastoralists who insisted on charging the department for the rationing of aboriginal indigents on their properties. The circular drew attention to the "gratifying" fact that many pastoralists had been discharging this duty for years, without any cost to the government, and appealed to the recipients of the letter not to charge for the feeding of old and sick aborigines, "born in the country from which in many instances large profits are yearly made . . ."; it also hinted that the renewal of permits "may be subject to conditions in the direction of the subject matter of this letter".[33] The response was very satisfactory, resulting in annual savings to the government of $1,700.

The departmental *quid pro quo* for these concessions was not to insist that the pastoralists pay cash wages. This policy was not dictated solely by expediency, however. Prinsep, for instance, was convinced that it would be pointless to pay wages if "nothing could be bought with them, or to a class of people who almost to a man did not know the value of the coin";[34] Gale, soon after taking office, expressed similar sentiments when he said that it was undesirable for aborigines to be "in possession of any spending money".[35] Another and more important reason was the fear that if the pastoralists were forced to pay cash wages they would dismiss most of their aboriginal workers, who would then become a charge upon the state. Since the proposition has never been put to a test (when the Kimberley pastoralists finally agreed to pay cash wages, in 1950, it was public opinion rather than departmental pressure which had forced them to do so), we shall never know whether this was just a convenient rationalization or a genuinely held belief. But early in the century the pastoralists held most of the trumps. To start with, they saved the government a tidy sum by looking after many old men, women, and children. At least periodically, too, white labour was not only available but most willing to supplant their "exploited" fellow-toilers — and nothing would have suited the trade unions better than a policy which would have enabled their members to compete with the aborigines on "equal" terms. In these circumstances, the attitude of the department makes a lot of sense. The present system of employment, said Gale in 1911,

is working smoothly and satisfactorily to all parties. Once disturb this in the direction of compelling the squatters to pay wages to their native servants, or place any other restrictions upon their employment, and the result will be far-reaching and little dreamt of by those who have not studied the economics of the question. There are many who advocate a system of calling upon the employer to pay a weekly sum for every native

employed into a fund to be used for the general benefit of natives throughout the State. Objections might reasonably be taken to such a scheme on
the grounds that the individual native labour would be exploited for the
benefit of others. Apart from this phase, such a scheme would be absolutely
impracticable and would create endless trouble and confusion throughout
the stations in the State . . .[36]

Neville, who replaced Gale in 1915, had different ideas: he was
convinced that the pastoralists should pay cash wages, and did not
take the threat of possible mass dismissals seriously. Wartime
conditions were propitious for the implementation of such a plan.
The pastoral industry, moderately prosperous since about 1905,
was now flourishing; wool and beef prices were high; aboriginal
indigency decreased by two-thirds, from 3,319 registered indigents
in 1914–1915 to 820 four years later; many white men were fighting
overseas; in parts of the northwest, by the end of 1916, wages up to
$4 a week and found had become common, and aboriginal workers,
in the words of a disgruntled squatter, "let one to understand that
they only work to oblige one".[37] In May 1916 the department
issued new regulations reminding the pastoralists that a permit
was still a prerequisite for employing aboriginal labour, and introducing a new procedure as regards applications, which now had
to be addressed, in writing, to the nearest police officer, whose
endorsement was necessary for the grant or renewal of all permits
in his district.[38] In July Underwood put his signature on a long
submission by Neville which laid out in detail the arguments in
support of a scheme equally dear to both men — minimum cash
wages in the pastoral industry, to be paid in part to the worker
himself, and in part into a trust fund to be administered by the
department.[39] As mentioned earlier, the government fell before the
cabinet could consider the proposal, and was replaced by another
more favourably disposed towards the pastoralists. After the war
Neville returned to his pet project on at least four different occasions,
but conditions were never quite as favourable as in 1916. The price
of wool declined after 1924; in the beef industry the good times had
come to an end even earlier; 1925 saw a severe drought; the following
year brought disastrous floods. Neville's Ministers were either
opposed to his plan or, as in the case of the Labourite J. M. Drew,
largely indifferent. Gradually, too, the custom of paying aboriginal
labour in cash was spreading, and by 1927 more than one half of
the 5,000 aborigines in pastoral employment were paid in cash.

Station hands in the northwest were paid weekly wages ranging
from $1 to $4 and found, the only exception being the Tableland and
the Ashburton, where only "trustworthy" station hands were paid
in cash. Men on the Gascoyne and the Murchison commanded similar
wages; female homestead help was also paid, usually 50 cents a week
and found (Carnarvon domestics could command up to 80 cents a
day). Even in the Kimberleys, near the coast, small token payments
to the more sophisticated station hands had become common. In
Broome and Derby aborigines were employed in hotels as handymen,
and female domestic labour was in short supply, in spite of the current wage of $2.50 a week and found; in the former township all
aboriginal workers, even the "semi-bush types", were regularly given
20 cents for the Saturday show at the local cinema.[40] The increasing
sophistication of the native workforce had at least one unexpected
result. In 1925 a station hand, injured while mustering cattle, applied
(apparently on his own initiative) for workers' compensation. Since
there was no precedent to fall back upon, the Crown Solicitor was
asked to rule on his application. His opinion was straightforward:
legally, there was no doubt whatsoever that aboriginal employees
were workers under the Workers' Compensation Act, but compensation might be difficult to compute because of the method by which
most of them were paid. Armed with the ruling, Neville sought the
co-operation of the Department of Labour which was responsible
for the administration of the act.

While it is correct that there is no doubt that the natives come under the
Workers' Compensation Act, [replied the Minister for Labour, Alexander
McCallum] I am equally sure that Parliament never intended that the
schedules set out for compensation in that Act should apply to aborigines.
To seriously contend that the full provisions of the Act should apply
equally with our own people appears to me too stupid to occupy a
moment's consideration.[41]

The onset of the depression forced Neville to abandon all hopes
of reform in the pastoral industry. Late in 1929 the Legislative
Assembly threw out his bill to amend the 1905 Aborigines Act;
in 1930 the Treasury cut his grant and he had to dismiss his only
travelling inspector (appointed in 1925); the trade unions, with one
out of every three white men jobless, were increasingly unhappy
about "discrimination" in the pastoral industry; the pastoralists,
with numerous problems of their own, were in no mood for dictation
from above. The aborigines, for their part, were largely unaffected

by the slump. In the northwest and the Murchison, where cash wages were customary, the depression resulted in a small overall reduction in aboriginal employment, although around Roebourne and Port Hedland there was in fact a slight increase. In the Kimberleys, where cash wages were still something of an exception, there was a substantial increase in the number of aborigines employed, especially in West Kimberley where the sheep industry, largely because of the application of new boring techniques and the resulting utilization of more marginal land, continued to show comparatively high returns. If, before the depression, "there would have been no great pastoral industry" without the aborigines,[42] this was doubly so during the thirties: "native and mixed-race labour was the corner-stone of the sheep and cattle industries in the northern districts. . ."[43] And if it was the "cheapness" of their labour which made this possible, the aborigines did not seem to mind. Since there was no inspection of employment conditions after 1930, we can only speculate as to how many pastoralists reduced wages or economized on rations and clothing; what little evidence there is suggests that the practice, except for the substitution of saccharine for sugar, was not widespread. The depression inflicted little hardship on the northern aborigines — in fact, they suffered less than any other section of the community.

Aboriginal health

The 1905 Aborigines Act contained one short reference to aboriginal health. Section 6, defining the duties of the department, charged it with the supply, "as far as practicable", of medical attendance and medicines to sick, aged, and infirm aborigines. The health of employed aborigines, by virtue of the conditions laid down in the employment permits, was the responsibility of their masters who were under an obligation to provide their workers with "medicines and medical services when practicable and necessary" (in 1910 the Crown Law Department ruled that this responsibility extended to injuries incurred after working hours). The key word, in both cases, was practicable: there were no special hospitals for aborigines at this time, nor any form of special aboriginal health organization. The system went back to the nineteenth century. In the 1860s resident magistrates started administering medicines to sick aboriginal paupers or, in exceptional cases, sending them to the nearest hospital where they were bunked on the verandah or in the yard. By the

1880s this was common practice: "the sick and needy natives are treated by the Government as paupers, and the medical officers in the several districts attend to them gratis, the same way as to any pauper Europeans."[44] The settlers usually looked after the aborigines on their properties, "generally with a good deal of sympathy and care".[45] It was the best the colony could afford: in the pioneering days medical services even for Europeans were inadequate, medical attention was difficult to obtain and, "when available, was expensive and not particularly skilled".[46] The main drawback of the system was its inability to deal with emergencies: when an epidemic of influenza or small-pox broke out little could be done beyond collecting the sick aborigines and hiring someone to look after them until they died.

The first change in this pattern came with the establishment of lock hospitals for the treatment of venereal disease. First noticed in 1842, the affliction was apparently ignored by the authorities;"as far as I knew", said a Geraldton pioneer, [those suffering from it] "never had any medical attention."[47] Earliest signs of real concern appeared about the turn of the century. In 1899, when the department appointed a travelling inspector, one of his duties was to treat the disease with iodoform; four years later Prinsep asked the government to establish at Onslow a hospital for the treatment of venereal disease; in 1905 the Principal Medical Officer made a plea for a strict application of the Contagious Diseases Act to northern areas. Two years later the incidence of the disease reached alarming proportions — up to 15 per cent in certain districts. "The menace to the white population", said Prinsep in his 1907 report, "although probably the seeds of evil have been sown by them in the first instance, is becoming so great . . . that some drastic steps should be taken to check the spread of the disease."[48] In the same year a conference of medical men, attended by the Chief Protector, recommended the establishment of a modern hospital, preferably on an isolated island, for the "treatment in numbers" of sufferers from venereal disease. Acting with commendable promptitude, the government selected two islands west of Carnarvon, Bernier and Dorre; the former was set aside for male, and the latter for female patients. The first group of inmates arrived in October 1908. The usual method of collecting prospective patients was to send a police party into an area, catch as many aborigines as appeared afflicted with the disease, put them into chains and take them to Carnarvon for transhipment, "not only for their own sake, but also for the sake of the community at large"[49] (the Chief Protector, it seems, had doubts about the legality of the procedure, but the police could not suggest an alternative). Daisy Bates witnessed the arrival of one such group at Carnarvon, in 1910:

Shall I ever forget the surge of emotion that overcome me as they saw me, and lifted their manacled hands in a faint shout of welcome, for many of them recognized me? There was a half-caste assistant with [constable] Grey, and the natives were chained to prevent them from escaping on the way, as it was quite probable that they would have been murdered had they attempted to reach their homes through strange country. In one donkey-wagon were forty-five men, women and children, unable to walk.[50]

Once safely on the islands, "barren and forbidding, a horror of flies in summer",[51] the patients were provided with clothing and rations; those strong enough were allowed to hunt or fish for their meat. Progress with the treatment of the disease was "disheartening", for the drugs normally used in the treatment of syphilis — mercury and iodide potassium — turned out to be absolutely useless. The death-rate among the patients was so high that in 1910 the hospital superintendent felt justified in ordering a bone-crusher, in order to "utilize all available organic matter for the object of improving the nutritive value of the soil".[52] Administrative problems added to the difficulties. Staff turnover was high because of inadequate living and working conditions. Until 1912 the responsibility for the running of the hospitals was divided between the Medical Department, in control of professional and technical matters, and the Department of Aborigines and Fisheries, which retained the overall control of the islands. This led to recurring friction, and was partly responsible for the resignation of three medical superintendents in less than three years. Failure to make headway with the treatment of the disease, no doubt, also contributed to low staff morale. In 1910 a bacteriologist from the Central Board of Health spent six months on the islands, but his prescribed treatment proved ineffective. In 1911 the hospitals started to use salvarzan, a potent anti-syphilis drug from Germany, also without any result. The break-through came on the eve of the war when the ailment was finally diagnosed as *granuloma of the pudenda,* a venereal disease peculiar to the aboriginal race. In all, some 800 aborigines were treated in the hospitals before they were transferred to Port Hedland, in 1919. The annual cost of the undertaking ranged from $10,000 to $20,000 — a sum higher than the average total expenditure on aboriginal affairs in South Australia (including, up to 1911, the Northern Territory) and almost equalling that of Queensland during the same period. The money was spent primarily in the interest of the European population, but the expenditure was also, as the Chief Protector proudly announced, an "eloquent testimony to the wisdom of the Government in undertaking a work of such a humanitarian nature".[53] After the move to Port Hedland the hospital eventually became a general aboriginal hospital, with venereal disease accounting for an ever decreasing proportion of its patients. By 1930 it was thought to have been completely eradicated and the special subsidy for the maintenance of lock hospitals, introduced by the federal government eight years earlier, was withdrawn.

Unlike granuloma, leprosy was unknown in traditional aboriginal Australia: it was introduced by indentured Asian labour. The disease was discovered in 1909 at Mardie station, more or less by accident, by the Roebourne district medical officer, Dr. Maloney, formerly in charge of the Moreton Bay leprosarium in Queensland.[54] In 1910 six additional cases were diagnosed, all west of Roebourne, and were immediately isolated on a small reserve near Cossack. Following the discovery of more cases, early in 1911, a temporary leprosarium was opened on Bezout Island near Cossack, to be eventually transferred to either Bernier or Dorre Island. In the meantime Dr. Maloney had been asked to join one of the periodical expeditions collecting aborigines suffering from venereal disease, and used this opportunity to examine the northwest for signs of leprosy. He failed to discover any traces of the disease outside the locality where it was first diagnosed. As a result, the few confirmed cases were left on Bezout Island — hardly an ideal spot, since it was devoid of vegetation except for scattered patches of spinifex, and lacked fresh water. Their care consisted of regular distribution of food, water, and firewood by the Roebourne police, and a periodical examination by the Roebourne district medical officer. His visits ceased after the outbreak of the war.

All this time, the Kimberleys were largely ignored. The first indication of interest came in 1916 when Neville proposed to transfer the lock hospitals to Disaster Bay on the Dampier Peninsula (Port Hedland was chosen instead). In 1921 the Australian Hookworm Campaign, an organization financed jointly by the federal government and the Rockefeller Foundation, sponsored an investigation into the incidence of hookworm in the Kimberleys, where it had been introduced by indentured Asian labour. The disease was found to be endemic in the whole of the Dampier Peninsula, with a staggering incidence of 91.1 per cent at Beagle Bay.[55] In 1922 came the alarming discovery of four cases of leprosy, all around Derby, which prompted the government to ask for Commonwealth assistance, initially in the form of a medical survey of the north. The survey was eventually undertaken in 1924 by Dr. Cecil Cook, an expert in tropical diseases attached to the federal Department of Public Health. Dr. Cook examined 2,340 aborigines and diagnosed eleven cases of leprosy (all in the Kimberleys) and eighty-four cases of granuloma. He made three recommendations: the appointment of a travelling medical inspector, to be stationed at Hall's Creek; the closing of the Cossack leprosarium, since it was too far from the endemic area; and an approach to the federal government with view to the treatment of lepers from the Kimberleys in the Darwin lazaret.[56] The first recommendation was implemented, in part, by the appointment of a travelling inspector of aborigines in the following year. The refusal of the federal government to co-operate took care of the remaining two, at least temporarily (the Cossack leprosarium was eventually closed in 1931 and the patients were transferred to Darwin). Dr. Cook's survey, unfortunately, came too late to check the spread of the disease. In 1928 several cases were discovered at Munja, the Port George IV mission and the Ninety Mile Beach; in 1929 the disease was reported from farther inland, and from the hitherto leprosy-free East Kimberley. By 1931 most of the local authorities had become thoroughly alarmed and appealed for yet another medical survey of the north; the only outcome was an amendment, in 1932, of the Health Act giving government medical officers the right to "medically and physically" examine (if they could find the time) any aborigine within the meaning of the Aborigines Act. The closing of the Cossack leprosarium, in 1931, added more difficulties. The arrangement was to send all lepers to Darwin, with the leprosy compound of the Derby aboriginal hospital (opened in 1926) serving as a staging point. By 1934 the compound held forty-six lepers, some of whom had been waiting for transport for longer than a year. When visited by the Moseley Royal Commission, it was separated from the hospital by a two-strand wire fence, and consisted of a "galvanized iron shed, open on one side and rather less pretentious than the average fowl-house",[57] and a few humpies about three feet high, built of scrap iron and old tins. Little wonder the commission was amazed that "so little action has been taken since Dr. Cook reported on the matter in 1924".[58]

General health services for the aborigines, as distinct from services devoted to the treatment of contagious diseases, were entirely neglected during the first half of the period under review, and still far from adequate in 1935. The first hospital facilities for aborigines were those of the Port Hedland lock hospital which, since its opening in 1919, served increasingly as a general aboriginal hospital for the entire northwest. Derby got an aboriginal hospital in 1926 — the old European hospital made superfluous by the construction of a new one. The only other hospital to admit aboriginal patients was the Australian Inland Mission nursing home in Hall's Creek (this was a condition of an annual subsidy of $100 from the Aborigines Department). Elsewhere, sick aborigines were usually dumped in separate facilities, known in the lore of the north as "dying rooms". Not that the aboriginal hospitals were much better. In 1934, a journalist accompanying Moseley found that at Port Hedland most patients slept in clean sand under a bough shed; the Derby hospital he described as a large wooden hut with a common sleeping room for men at one end, similar accommodation for women at the other end, and a small operating theatre in the middle — "an excellent place for storing boxes".[59] In the absence of adequate facilities some aborigines continued (perhaps preferred) to rely on traditional remedies, while others depended on what medical assistance they could get from the police and the pastoralists, whose medicine chest was as a rule limited to epsom salts, camphor, painkiller, and, after 1924, an influenza remedy labelled "Dr. Atkinson's Nigger Cure-All" (prescribed by the Commissioner of Public Health, Dr. Atkinson, and marketed under that name, somewhat unethically, by Felton, Grimwade and Bickford — a pharmaceutist who had seen a copy of the actual prescription assured the writer that the medicine was "better" than most of the influenza remedies on the market today). Such arrangements, whatever their effectiveness under normal conditions, simply broke down in an emergency. During the Kimberley influenza epidemic of 1920, to take one example, 132 deaths were recorded; in the words of the Chief Protector, the aborigines had "suffered a good deal by reason of their expulsion from the various outlying towns on account of the possibility of their becoming affected and, in turn, communicating the disease to white residents".[60]

6. Christian Missions
1906-1935

The growth of missionary endeavour

In 1906 Christian missionaries had little to show for some sixty years of work among Western Australian aborigines. The Roman Catholics ran two missions, New Norcia and Beagle Bay; the Anglicans had two children's homes, the Swan Native and Half-Caste Home and the much smaller Ellensbrook at Busselton; the fifth mission, Hadley's Sunday Island, was not affiliated with any particular church. These institutions had about 400 inmates — approximately 270 adults, the remainder children in "regular school attendance". In addition, Beagle Bay claimed that about 200 aborigines were under mission influence. Thirty years later there were 358 children in mission schools, and the missions claimed to have about 2,000 aborigines under their influence. This increase was due to the establishment of the following institutions: Drysdale River in 1908, Port George IV in 1911, the Saint John of God Convent in Broome in 1912, Forrest River in 1913, Mount Margaret in 1921, Gnowangerup in 1928, Badjaling in 1930, and Warburton Range in 1933. This brought the number of institutions to twelve (Ellensbrook and the Swan Native and Half-Caste Home were closed in 1917 and 1921 respectively), and the number of missionary societies active in Western Australia to four.

This expansion took place in two waves. The first was ushered by the establishment in 1908 of the Drysdale River mission at Napier Broome Bay, one of the loneliest stretches of the north Kimberley coast. The step was the outcome of the third plenary council of the ecclesiastic hierarchy of he Roman Catholic Church of Australia, held in Sydney in 1905, which authorized the New Norcia Benedictines to proceed with the establishment of a priory in the Kimberleys. The site was selected in 1906 by Bishop Salvado's successor, Abbot Torres, but the mission was not founded until two years later, since the government would not agree to lease the land the mission had applied for under conditions put forward by the mission (the Benedictines finally settled for a forty-nine year lease of 50,000 acres instead of a ninety-nine year lease double that size). The first two years were uneventful, since the missionaries were completely ignored by the local aborigines; the mission, reported Bishop Torres laconically in 1910, "so far, has not done much in the way of civilizing".[1] The first contact was far from friendly; in September 1910 the mission was attacked by some thirty warriors, but the fathers managed to take shelter in a galvanized iron shed, constructed, it seems, with precisely such a contingency in mind. There followed almost three years of fear and apprehension. In 1911, for instance, the fathers mistook an approaching exploring party for "an advance guard" of tribal warriors; "when they saw us coming", said C. Price Conigrave in his reminiscences, "great excitement seemed to be taking place around the mission house. With the glasses we saw a few people running about, and then they went out of sight."[2] By 1913 the fathers were ready to abandon the mission, and on 11 July, the Feast of the Patronage of Saint Benedict, "special prayers were addressed to the Saint, asking him to use his intercessory powers with the Almighty, so that he might soften the hearts of the natives and lead them to truth".[3] Two weeks later, in what must have seemed to him more than a coincidence, a father met in the bush a group of aborigines and induced them to visit the homestead, where they were given presents. After about three months of apparently cordial relations, the aborigines retrieved their clubs and spears and attacked the missionaries, seriously wounding two fathers in the affray. As a result, Gale asked Torres to recall the missionaries, but the Bishop promised to increase the mission staff for greater protection, adding that he had no doubt "that the blood and sufferings of his monks would prove in time very fruitful, [and that] others besides were ready to take the place of the fallen or disabled missionaries".[4]

The Port George IV mission was started by a society new to the Western Australian missionary scene. Later in 1908 the Presbyterian Church of Queensland, a body with a successful missionary record to its credit, sent a lay member to Perth to look into ways and means of spreading Christianity in the north of Western Australia. As a result of the visit, the local church approached the government with a proposal to start a mission in the Kimberleys, asking not only for a substantial grant of suitable land but also for a daily subsidy of 2 cents per inmate or a lump sum of $400 per annum. Gale recommended against a cash subsidy, intimating that the department might reconsider the decision if the mission started an institution for half-caste children, preferably somewhere in the northwest.[5] This the church was not prepared to do: the lure of the far north was stronger than the prospect of financial assistance. In 1910 a party of eight, led by Dr. Yule, left for the Kimberleys in search of a mission site. They selected Walcott Inlet, about 120 miles northeast of Derby, but it was abandoned soon after as completely unsuitable. In 1911 the church applied for a lease of the Forrest River reserve, vacated by the Anglicans in 1898 but still held by them "in trust" for the aborigines, a move which prompted the Perth diocese of the Church of England to vote for the reopening of the mission. In 1912 a second party, led by Rev. R. H. Wilson, selected a new site at Port George IV, not far from Walcott Inlet; significantly, one of the considerations prompting the choice was the short distance between the proposed homestead site and the sea, to enable the missionaries to keep a watch on the mission boat, their only link with the outside world. In the event, the precaution turned out to be unnecessary, for the beginnings of the mission were not marked by the ferocious attacks which had marred the early days of the Forrest River and Drysdale River missions. By 1913 the institution was well established, and the department gave it a small annual subsidy.

Lombadina, opened in 1911, and the Saint John of God Convent in Broome, started in 1912, were branches of the Beagle Bay mission. Situated halfway between Broome and Beagle Bay, Lombadina was from 1909 until 1911 a government feeding depot, run on a part-time basis by Hadley's erstwhile companion Harry Hunter; earlier still, between 1907 and 1909, there was a mission of sorts at nearby Cygnet Bay, under Father Nicholas Emo, one of the Trappists who stayed on after 1900 as a "freelance" missionary.[6] Early in 1911 Hunter was fined for cohabiting with native women, and when the department decided to close the depot, the Pallotines asked Father Emo, then in Drysdale River, to return to Lombadina. Although it was officially classified as a mission, Lombadina remained for years an unsubsidized feeding depot: there were no permanent buildings, the children went without education, and the adults came and went as they pleased. The Broome Convent School for aboriginal and half-caste girls was an altogether different proposition, and the government recognized it as such by giving the Sisters of Saint John of God financial assistance from the outset. The building of the convent was financed in part from the proceeds of a public appeal for funds which resulted in an unfortunate incident and led to the withdrawal of the subsidy soon after. The appeal was conducted on somewhat emotional lines: one potential benefactor in England was informed that the missionaries had earlier appealed for funds in Australia but were told they could have money "for powder and shot to shoot aborigines down, but to save them alive, no!"[7] The subsidy was withdrawn as soon as the department learnt about the letter, despite profuse apologies from the missionaries.

The Forrest River mission was reopened by the Church of England early in 1913. Although the Anglicans had been somewhat unhappy about their poor missionary record for quite some time, it was not until 1911, when the Presbyterian Church applied for a lease of the Forrest River reserve, that a special meeting of the Perth diocese voted to reopen the mission, abandoned in 1898. The enterprise started under a bad omen when a young naturalist who came along with the foundation party, L. N. Burns, drowned while shooting ducks. Within five months the entire mission staff, "new to aborigines and Australia"[8] (they came from central Africa), resigned in frustration, and only the prompt action of the Right Rev. Gerard Trower, the Bishop of the North-West, in sending to Yarrabah for E. R. B. Gribble, the son of the fiery J. B. Gribble, saved the mission from being abandoned a second time. Gribble arrived early in 1914, bringing with him James Noble, a Queensland aborigine who later made history by being ordained as a clergyman in Perth. The mission received its first subsidy in 1921.

All the new missions mentioned so far were in the Kimberleys, among aborigines as yet "uncontaminated by civilization"; the northwest and the south apparently did not present the same challenge to most Christian churches. But there were exceptions. In 1905 the Salvation Army orphanage at Collie admitted the first group of aboriginal boys, and two years later the Kalgoorlie girls' orphanage followed suit. The work was subsidized by the department at a daily rate of 10 cents per child (reduced to 8 cents in 1906), and both institutions claimed that they treated black and white children alike. In May 1908 the Aborigines' Inland Mission, an undenominational society founded three years earlier in Singleton, New South Wales, took over the Welshpool native settlement, and was promised an annual subsidy of $500 by the government. The missionaries set out to work with great zeal and determination. The inmates were told that they would have to work and that only the sick and the disabled would be given free rations. By July the settlement was empty, the mission withdrew from the agreement with the government, and the institution was closed. Some of the former inmates moved to an old aboriginal camping ground in West Guildford, but not for long. As a "nuisance", they were moved by the police to Success Hill, on the bank of the Swan River; in 1910, after more protests by white Guildfordians, they were shifted to a newly created reserve in South Guildford — today's Allowah Grove.

The second missionary society to come from New South Wales, the inter-denominational Australian Aborigines' Mission, was more successful in its work in the west. The society was founded in 1893, under the name of Christian Endeavour Mission, changed its name to New South Wales Aborigines' Mission in 1899, and changed it once again in 1907 when it became known as the Australian Aborigines' Mission, in keeping with an earlier decision to expand its work to other states. In 1908 the society sent Rev. E. J. Telfer and a goldfields aborigine named Wandy, said to have been kidnapped as a boy by prospectors and later taken to New South Wales as a farm worker, to spread the Gospel in the west. The missionaries landed at Albany with 2 cents between them and bicycled to Perth, preaching in aboriginal camps and "relying entirely on the Lord" for their financial needs.[9] In 1909, with the help of Perth non-conformist clergy, they opened an aboriginal orphanage in East Perth. Telfer described its naming in his book *Amongst Australian Aborigines*. Determined to find a suitable aboriginal name for the orphanage, he connected two words from the Dainggati language of northern New South Wales, *dulhi,* meaning child and *gunyah,* meaning shelter. After painting the sign Dulhi Gunyah on a sign-board, he was standing across the road admiring his handiwork, when an old aboriginal woman passed by. He asked her what the words meant in her speech. "In my language", she said, "that means, 'Hold your tongue, you're a big liar' " — an answer which the Reverend found "alarming and altogether disconcerting".[10] In 1910 the society decided to expand its work into the Kimberleys, and sent Telfer and a Mr. Radford to select a site for a mission. They travelled by steamer from Fremantle to Carnarvon and from there by bicycle to Derby, preaching en route to all who would listen. In Carnarvon they visited the aboriginal gaol but "were not favourably impressed" with the treatment of the prisoners; on Bernier Island, on the other

hand, they found that the government was "doing a very praiseworthy job" in the lock hospitals. Near Onslow, Telfer asked an old
aborigine if he knew anything of Christ and he replied: "That's what
my boss say when he swear."[11] At Derby they had an interview
with Sydney Hadley who put before them the proposal that the
mission should take over Sunday Island, or alternatively, start a
branch station on the east side of King Sound, to be run in conjunction with Sunday Island. In the end the A.A.M. council decided not
to proceed with mission work in the north for the time being and to
concentrate its activities in the south — a step with which the department wholeheartedly concurred. In 1912 the mission opened a
"preaching station" on the Katanning reserve, and in 1913 the
government agreed to pay the salary of the teacher in charge of the
education of the Dulhi Gunyah children. In 1917, two years after
the establishment of a government aboriginal settlement at Carrolup,
on the Great Southern, the department withdrew the subsidy and
the orphanage was closed.

The second wave of expansion was ushered in 1921 with the establishment by the A.A.M. of the Mount Margaret mission, near the
mining town of Laverton. The choice of an eastern goldfields site
signalled a departure from the established pattern of missionary
activities: in the past, missions had shown little interest in the "semi-
civilized" northwest and goldfields aborigines, preferring the challenge of the untamed north, or, as a second choice, that of the de-
moralized south. Yet the need for a mission or a government settlement on the eastern goldfields had been apparent for some time. The
vacuum left by the disappearance of the local tribes led to a gradual
westerly and southwesterly drift of aborigines from the semi-arid
regions farther inland, and by 1917 the goldfields had once again a
fair-sized aboriginal population. In 1921 a young New South Wales
businessman turned missionary, R. S. Schenk, applied for permission
to start a mission at Moola Bulla, but Neville suggested the eastern
goldfields: "It is the semi-civilized natives that are in much greater
need of missionary help. The uncivilized natives have a code of
their own which is in a way superior to ours but which seems to
disintegrate as soon as they get in touch with civilization."[12] Schenk
took Neville's advice and went to Mount Margaret. Since the mission
was not subsidized and received only token financial assistance
from the Australian Aborigines' Mission, Schenk sent the inmates
to cut sandalwood which he sold through normal trade channels.

In November 1921 he applied for an exemption from the payment of the royalty on sandalwood, adding: "My sincere love for the natives would lead me to ask big things for them, and I have a tendency to open my mouth too wide on their behalf."[13] This faculty, which Schenk undoubtedly possessed, led him into immediate difficulties. In September 1921 he accused the Laverton police of irregularities in the distribution of relief. Later in the year he sent Neville a somewhat undiplomatic letter in which he criticized the removal to the Moore River aboriginal settlement of a group of Laverton aborigines. In December 1923 he recorded in one of his "prayer-letters": "It is wonderful how Satan can mobilize souls to spend time and energy for him here . . . Some people at Laverton think that the natives ought not to be drawn to Mt. Margaret."[14] By 1924 he was *persona non grata* in the district, particularly with the pastoralists, who were quick to complain that the aborigines were increasingly reluctant to take on pastoral employment unless paid in cash. "Before this so called mission station was established in this district", said the secretary of the Mount Margaret road board, "the natives were a comparatively quiet lot and gave little or no trouble, but now they threaten the sandalwood cutters and the prospectors, marauding up and down the country like a regiment of soldiers."[15] The department, on its part, had certain reservations about Schenk's trading with the aborigines (he bartered goods for dingo scalps) and "exploiting them under the cloak of religion".[16] This aspect of the mission's activities will be discussed later on; all that need be said here is that the biggest losers were almost certainly the Laverton shopkeepers whose monopoly of the dingo-scalp trade had been broken as a result. In 1925 the Mount Margaret road board refused to make further payments, on some obscure technical grounds, for scalps delivered by the mission, and Schenk had to send the skins directly to the Department of Agriculture in Perth.

Other A.A.M. missionaries who came in Schenk's footsteps displayed similar zeal and determination. Late in 1923 Mr. and Mrs. Jago went to Sunday Island, sold to the A.A.M. by Hadley for the sum of $540. In 1928 a missionary couple settled on a private property on the outskirts of Gnowangerup, not far from Albany; others went to the Kimberleys where they established temporary preaching stations, moving from one pastoral property to another and spreading the "Gospel of equality".[17] A split within the mission late in 1928 threatened to undo this work, but the factions were reunited in April 1929, under the name United Aborigines' Mission. In 1930 the society opened a small mission at Badjaling, on the Great Southern, and in 1933 Schenk opened a branch station at Warburton Range near the boundary of the central Australian reserve. By 1935 the U.A.M. had grown into the largest missionary society in Western Australia, with five mission stations under its management, and a staff of thirty.

The work of the Roman Catholic missions

There were important similarities as well as differences between the three Roman Catholic missions active before 1935. The points which they had in common were, first, their foreign character (most of the Benedictines were Spaniards, while the Pallotines were predominantly German), and second, their "air of utter detachment from the world outside".[18] The differences stemmed from divergent goals and methods. New Norcia, as far as its work with aborigines was concerned, had by 1906 become a children's institution rather than the self-contained aboriginal community envisaged by its founder, Bishop Salvado. Of the original Victoria Plains aborigines there remained only a handful (the last was to die in 1913), and the number of adults from other localities was also decreasing. "This New Norcia is no longer a home for the natives at all", complained one inmate in 1910. "They keep a few hands to carry bricks because they are cheap but have no time for a sick native."[19] The children were gathered from a wide area, the parents usually agreeing to their offspring remaining at the mission until they were at least sixteen. After leaving school at fourteen, the boys were trained as farmhands, carpenters, bootmakers, or mechanics, while the girls were employed in the kitchen or doing laundry work, and were encouraged to marry "their own countrymen".[20] The boys eventually drifted into farmwork for the nearby settlers, taking contracts for ring-barking, clearing, and fencing, but they continued to regard the mission as "home". Since it was more than self-supporting, New Norcia was not subsidized during most of the period under review. In 1935 it had sixty-seven children in its care.

Drysdale River, on the other hand, was a "bush" mission par excellence. Its first decade of existence was largely a struggle for survival. By 1919, however, the "confidence and docility of the natives were complete",[21] and in 1922 the department gave the mission its first subsidy. In 1926 it was considered safe enough to be visited by the Governor-General, Lord Stonehaven, and his wife. The aeroplane, almost overnight, brought an end to its crippling isolation. In 1931 a group of Benedictine Oblate Sisters arrived from New Norcia, to work with the women and children; in 1932 an outstation was established at nearby Kalumburu (it became the main mission centre in 1937), and a permanent airstrip was constructed in 1935. Earlier, in 1932, the mission achieved brief worldwide publicity when its inmates saved the lives of the German aviators, Bertram and Klausmann, forced to land on an isolated stretch of the Kimberley coast; among the tangible rewards was a gift of a harmonium from the German government and a radio transmitter from Amalgamated Wireless (Australasia) Ltd. In 1935 the mission could be described as "only a relative success".[22] It had a population of about 100, mainly adults, and some 70 head of cattle and 300 goats; its crops consisted almost entirely of beans and peanuts.

Beagle Bay stood somewhere between these two contrasts. In many ways the most successful of the Roman Catholic missions, it had by 1906 more than made up for the Trappists' neglect of things material. Two years later a visitor described it as a "fair sized village" of over twenty permanent buildings constructed almost entirely from local materials, with a scrupulously clean slaughter-yard, a well-equipped butcher's shop, and a blacksmith's shop with "labour saving machines of all descriptions".[23] The labour was provided by the inmates, under the guidance of the brothers. Finance came from three sources: donations from Germany and Australia, government subsidies, and the sale of cattle and the proceeds of fishing and pearling activities (an attempt to start a sisal hemp plantation, in 1911, ended in failure). Although the mission claimed to be in constant financial difficulties, it expanded its activities whenever an opportunity arose: in 1911 a branch was opened at Lombadina, in 1912 a convent was started at Broome, and in 1934 Rockhole station was acquired in East Kimberley, as another branch. The station was unfortunately too close to Moola Bulla, and rather than incur the displeasure of the department, the mission abandoned the property soon after. In 1935 it claimed to have 340 aborigines under its influence, including 123 children. It also owned 3,500 head of cattle and had ten acres under rice — the earliest instance of successful rice cultivation on a commercial basis in the state.

The mission placed great emphasis on education, especially after the arrival in 1907 of seven sisters of Saint John of God from Subiaco and Kalgoorlie. Parents were asked to "give" their children to the mission until they were sixteen; half-caste children from Broome and other townships were sent to the mission by the department as a matter of course. The stated aim of education was to teach the children all that may be "good and useful" for a life "amidst civilized surroundings"[24] — in practice almost always the mission. Vocational training was stressed, especially blacksmithing, carpentry, tailoring, and stockwork. The fathers tried to balance work, play, and religion; in consequence the youngsters were neither "over-schooled, over-churched or overworked",[25] and impressed the occasional visitor by their "brightness and intelligence".[26]

In the case of the adults the missionaries' policy was to "make haste slowly". Under Father Bischofs, the first Pallotine superintendent and an anthropologist of some repute, the brothers took pains to interfere as little as possible with the traditional life of their charges. In 1908 Dr. Hermann Klaatsch, Professor of Anatomy at the University of Heidelberg, praised the Pallotines for their tolerance: they "knew how to lead the aborigines in an easy way to civilization", thereby demonstrating that "religion need not interfere with the natural pleasure and enjoyment of the aboriginal race".[27] This tradition was carried on after the First World War by E. O. Worms, a trained anthropologist and expert linguist with many years of missionary experience in Equatorial Africa, and by Herman Nekes who joined him in 1935. Known primarily as the authors of the monumental *Australian Languages* (published in 1953 by the Micro-Bibliotheca Anthropos), both men made it their primary task to discover those aspects of aboriginal culture which were compatible with Christianity. The result was "as strange and quixotic a thing as Mother Church has ever attempted in all her history".[28] The anthropologist S. D. Porteus, after witnessing an aboriginal ceremony at Beagle Bay late one night, concluded:

One might almost believe that the fierce note of these songs is struck in challenge to all that the mission stands for. One can hardly believe that these natives, shaking with the vehemence of their singing, can be the same men who knelt so quietly at the vespers. No matter how sincere their religious response may have seemed, one cannot help feeling that the primitive reasserts itself with the first beat of the kylies and that the blackfellow with every note that he sings is voicing a belief in and a passionate attachment to his own folkways. . . The Brothers of the Mission, sitting in their cheerless monastery and hearing this wild chorus night after night, must sometimes wonder how deep their teachings have gone. Perhaps they are wise to give the night to the blacks. To-morrow will be a new day, so why wonder? The black helpers in semi-civilized garb will be back at their tasks. . .[29]

The work of Protestant missions

Port George IV, known since the late twenties as Kunmunya, was one of the most successful missions of the inter-war years, as well as one of the most interesting. Its success was due almost entirely to the wisdom and farsightedness of its superintendent, Rev. J. R. B. Love. Love was born in Ireland and had been educated at the universities of Adelaide and Melbourne. As a school teacher in the north of South Australia he became interested in aborigines, and gave up teaching to become a missionary. In 1913 he was sent by the Presbyterian Board of Missions to Port George IV but enlisted in the A.I.F. in the following year. After the war he spent seven years at the Mapoon mission in Queensland, and in 1927 became superintendent of Port George IV (renamed Kunmunya soon after), remaining there until 1941. Unlike many missionaries, Love was an efficient administrator; A. P. Elkin, who visited Kunmunya soon after Love took over, described it as the "best run mission" he had ever seen.[30] Love was also better educated than most of his fellow-missionaries, and saw his task as something more than the mere preaching of Christianity. He practised "enlightened gradualism", his guiding principle being to "save the black race as a black race, keeping everything in the tribal organization that is good, and using it as a foundation on which to build Christianity".[31] But he was not as lenient as Hadley, for while condoning tribal mutilations, circumcision, and sub-incision, he was strictly opposed to polygamy, child marriages, and the evil influence of the *banmandja* (medicine man). Love believed that the missionary should go slowly, "letting in a better light, that will, of its own power, in time drive out the darkness of an evil tradition".[32] A good example here is his attitude to the customary platform burial of the dead to which he applied his policy of using aboriginal custom as a basis for higher principles. He would hold a Christian funeral ceremony around the platform and, while opposing as spurious the practice of stone marking to determine who had caused each particular death, he participated in shouting farewell to the departing spirit of the dead man.[33] In contrast with most other Protestant missionaries of the period, Love could "hear" the language of his charges and had translated the gospels of Saint Mark and Saint Luke into Worora. Children were allowed to live with the parents while attending school, and were taught in English as well as in their own language. Love's relations with the department were excellent. Mission finance came from the Presbyterian Board of Missions, government subsidies, and the earnings of two boats owned by the mission. In 1935 the institution claimed to have about three hundred aborigines under its influence, with an "average weekly attendance" of about a hundred.

If the good fortunes of Kunmunya were due almost entirely to one man, so were the vicissitudes which beset Forrest River. Admittedly, the mission site was far from suitable, the soil being poor and water in short supply, but its unsatisfactory record must be ultimately laid at the feet of Rev. E. R. B. Gribble, superintendent from 1914 to 1928. Gribble was very much the son of his father: headstrong, self-righteous, and authoritarian, with a permanent chip on his shoulder and a tendency to blame others for his or the mission's misfortunes. "This mission", he wrote in *Forty Years with the Aborigines,* "is the only one in Western Australia which has never received a subsidy from the Government..."[34] (it had been regularly subsidized since 1921). In *A Despised Race,* discussing the failure of his father's Carnarvon mission, he said: "The Church finally abandoned the attempt, and also abandoned my father."[35] Describing a fellow-missionary, Gribble drew a most fitting portrait of himself: he "was very enthusiastic but entirely lacking in that great essential for a Missionary — tact. His zeal was apt to run away with him."[36]

Gribble's zeal certainly ran away with him on more than one occasion. While he sincerely believed that "the welfare of the natives must be paramount",[37] he thought nothing of knocking down an aborigine who did something to displease him, or of "arresting" aborigines caught killing the mission cattle. His role in the events which led to the Royal Commission to inquire into the Onmalmeri massacre did nothing to improve the already strained relations between the mission and the Wyndham European community. In 1927 the Australian Board of Missions asked A. P. Elkin, who was about to leave for the Kimberleys as the Australian National Research Council's first Research Fellow, to report confidentially on Gribble's administration of the mission. Elkin's report amounted to an unqualified condemnation of the superintendent. He found that Gribble's relationship with his staff was a most unhappy one and that there was little trust between the superintendent and other missionaries. Staff living quarters were appalling and the food, consisting mainly of porridge, salted meat, and half-rotten bread, "not quite what one would like even missionaries to have".[38] Gribble's relations with the aborigines were equally strained. Parents who refused to part with their children had their rations stopped. Compound children were kept under constant supervision. On reaching adolescence they were married in complete disregard of tribal custom. Young men who refused to marry were lined up for work with adolescent boys. Family life was discouraged. Couples were allowed to spend the nights together, but in daytime the wives were kept in the "ladies compound" — little wonder the mission was known in nearby Wyndham as Gribble's stud farm.

As a result of A. P. Elkin's confidential report to the Australian Board of Missions in Sydney, Gribble resigned in November 1928[39] and was replaced by his son Jack. Early in 1930 Jack Gribble became implicated in a number of ugly incidents involving flogging of inmates, chaining to posts for sexual offences, and pouring of water over snoring boys.[40] After these had been reported to the department, Neville asked the Archbishop of Perth, Dr. H. L. Le Fanu, to dismiss the superintendent. The Archbishop agreed that Gribble should be relieved, but thought the matter did not warrant immediate action, intimating that he had intended to replace him all along. Only when the possibility of a public inquiry was mentioned did he agree to dispense with Gribble's services and to place the mission in the charge of an officer of the department until a suitable successor could be appointed. A subsequent inspection by the Wyndham district medical officer only underlined the critical situation at the mission. Because of vitamin deficiencies caused by lack of fresh food, all children had various stigmata of rickets, while most adults suffered from boils, infected hands, and other minor disorders. Jack Gribble's successor, appointed in 1931, resigned in the following year, and the mission was once again left in the charge of an official. Suspecting that some of the difficulties may have been due to the mission's location, Neville in 1934 proposed that it be moved farther south to Nulla Nulla station which had been previously acquired by the Wyndham meatworks. The Australian Board of Missions agreed but insisted on retaining the Forrest River reserve as well — a condition which the department found unacceptable. Reporting on his visit a year later, the Chief Protector concluded: "I can see no evidence of progress in many necessary directions."[41]

The work of the non-denominational and inter-denominational missions

The negotiations between Rev. E. J. Telfer of the Australian Aborigines' Mission and Sydney Hadley, mentioned earlier, were not the first occasion on which Hadley sought to enlist the support of an outside body for his mission. As early as September 1900, only a little more than a year after his arrival on Sunday Island, Hadley approached the Aborigines' Friends' Association in Adelaide with a view to financial assistance from the society. Late in 1904, halfway through a routine report to Prinsep, he remarked: "I am sick and tired and I need a break."[42] In 1905 he made overtures to the southwestern diocese of the Church of England, and in the following year he tried to solicit support from the Wesleyans. All these feelers were unsuccessful, for reasons which are not difficult to seek. Except for a small flat near the mission homestead, the island was barren rock, and would apparently never pay its way; also, the thought of the unorthodox Hadley remaining (he did not contemplate leaving at this stage), one suspects, did not make the proposition any more attractive. The department, on its part, would have liked the negotiations to succeed, since it had never become reconciled to the idea of a mission supported entirely by trade. In 1909, on the recommendation of the travelling inspector, J. Isdell, Gale told Hadley to move the mission to the mainland where he could "secure a lease of some pastoral lands, utilise his native labour, raise stock and make the mission self-supporting".[43] Hadley selected some land north of the Oobagooma Cattle Company's holdings, but the transfer did not take place, for Hadley was not eager to move. After 1910, even though the negotiations between the A.A.M. and Hadley had come to naught, the parties kept up the contact, and in December 1922, after several abortive attempts by Hadley to sell his "share" of the mission for $2,000, an agreement was signed by the parties transferring to the A.A.M. all buildings, furniture, and equipment, two cutters, several smaller boats, and twenty-five head of cattle. Hadley received $540.[44]

All this time Hadley somehow managed to keep the mission going — occasionally alone, sometimes with the help of drifters and beachcombers like "Frenchy" d'Antoine, hailing from the Seychelles, most of the time with the assistance of "proper" missionaries sent by one or other missionary society. Except for taking an occasional period of religious instruction, he left the institutional work to his "resident" schoolmaster or schoolmistress (when he had one) — his main job was to provide for "his" aborigines. After 1903 the government gave him a small subsidy, but his most important source of income was shipping cargo to the various coastal stations, "all of which he spends on the Mission; he neither looks for nor reaps any benefits nor remuneration from his labours . . ."[45] His forays into tropical agriculture, on the other hand, ended in failure: in 1904 he started experimenting with coffee, but most of the seeds failed to germinate; in 1905 he could report that he had twenty-one thriving cotton plants, only to see them destroyed by white ants; his small rubber plantation, started with a special subsidy from the Department of Agriculture, met a similar fate; and his banana trees were killed by an unknown disease. His fishing and pearling ventures, on the other hand, prospered. He exported trepang to Singapore and Manila, trochus shell to France and Germany, and just before the war, during one of his periodical trips to England, he signed a contract for the delivery of a large quantity of turtle meat. The war closed some of the markets, and the resulting lean years forced Hadley to send many aborigines back to their own country on the east side of King Sound. Hadley's own life, it would seem, did not change: in 1917, he entertained a group of visitors by playing a new gramophone "which had cost Mr. Hadley 700 dollars in America and it was certainly the finest instrument I have heard in Australia".[46]

The A.A.M. missionaries who took over from Hadley in 1923 adopted a stern attitude towards the "heathen customs" of their charges. They also insisted that the aborigines "work for kind", with the result that whole groups of them left for the mainland. In 1934, on Neville's suggestion, the mission moved to a new site on the mainland, between Yampi Passage and Cone Bay, and was renamed Wotjulum. The move turned out to be a mistake. The new site was close to Cockatoo Island and its huge iron-ore deposits, and was otherwise unsuitable. In February 1937 the department, dissatisfied with lack of progress at Wotjulum, cancelled the mission's lease, and the missionaries returned to Sunday Island.

If the record of the Australian Aborigines' Mission on Sunday Island left something to be desired, its achievement at Mount Margaret more than made up for it. "No station or mission that I have seen in Australia", said J. B. Birdsell, a member of the Harvard-Adelaide Anthropological Expedition, "approaches Mount Margaret as representing the most ideal solution of the native and half-caste problem. The administrative policy of the mission is so well grounded that it is difficult to analyse the elements that have led to its marked success."[47] The American visitor may have misread certain signs, but his general impression was in keeping with the facts. For all his fervent evangelistic zeal, Schenk was an extremely practical man. Deprived of government subsidy (except for bulk supplies of rations for destitute aborigines) and unable to count on regular financial support from the A.A.M., he adopted a "no work, no food" policy from the start, and apparently got away with it. Trade with aborigines was another important facet of Schenk's policy. The mission bought up to five hundred dingo scalps annually, paying as a rule with guns and cartridges — one gun for ten scalps, worth $2 each when delivered in Perth, or one package of cartridges for five scalps. The stress on vocational education, and especially on carpentry, shearing, mechanical engineering, and all aspects of mining, coupled with the employment opportunities for skilled men on the goldfields, gave the aborigines a degree of independence unparalleled elsewhere. Those who could not find outside employment were provided with paid work by the mission, in keeping with the motto "Not Money but Sin Spoils".[48] In 1935 Schenk started a small battery. Taking advantage of a loophole in the Mining Act which prohibited the employment of aborigines on mining tenements, but failed to debar them from acquiring such tenements, Schenk encouraged the aborigines to apply for small mining leases, and crushed their ore for a small fee. As for the weaker sex, young girls were trained not only in domestic work but also as typists and nurses, while older women were given instruction in raffia work and were paid daily for all articles produced.

Schenk's concept of aboriginal welfare was considerably ahead of the times. His was the only mission of the inter-war years with proper hospital facilities and a programme of education which went beyond training in useful skills. During the twenties education at Mount Margaret had a "decided Biblical quality",[49] but this changed in 1933 with the arrival of Mrs. M.M. Bennett from Kunmunya. Mrs. Bennett was not only an outspoken controversialist but also one of the outstanding aboriginal educators in Australia. Her teaching methods, which she later described in the booklet, *Teaching the Aborigines: Data from Mount Margaret,* were simple but effective: she took one class at a time, while other children played, devoted little time to formal education, and used visual aids as much as possible, even for the teaching of arithmetic. Instruction was based on the state school curriculum, with emphasis on personal hygiene, money transactions, and Bible history. Significantly, it was Schenk who had first raised the question, in 1938, of the government supplying mission schools with properly trained teachers — seven years before the Department of Education provided the first teachers for aboriginal settlements, and fourteen years before they were sent to schools run by missions prepared to accept them.

Schenk's attitude towards aboriginal culture was typical of the A.A.M.: he strove for a speedy breakdown of practically all aboriginal customs and traditions. He was opposed not only to those features of aboriginal culture which he considered incompatible wtih Christianity or harmful in themselves, but also such "harmless" customs as avoidance and marriage rules and "totem stick customs".[50] The outward results were most gratifying — the aborigines simply kept much of their traditional life secret. So it must have come as a shock when, in December 1930, "the natives had one of their biggest ceremonies a few miles from here. We are sure Satan is at the back of all these ceremonies . . ."[51] Or so Schenk reported to the mission council. A few years later, while the Moseley Royal Commission was inquiring into the aboriginal problem, Mrs. Bennett publicly accused A. P. Elkin, who had visited Mount Margaret in December 1930, of having deliberately encouraged "sorcery practices" during his stay. The subsequent refusal of the department to sanction the establishment of a branch station in the Warburton Range only strengthened Schenk's suspicions that the "scientists" were attempting to keep aborigines in the "stark and barbarous superstitions of the dark ages". But, as he told Neville, "if they tried to keep these souls just for museum specimens they would find that there are missionaries in Australia prepared to lose their life blood in carrying out the command of our Lord Jesus to preach the Gospel to them".[52] Little wonder that when the anthropologist Phyllis Kaberry visited Mount Margaret, in 1935, she was not well received. "She comes here and pretends to be a Christian and yet, like Dr. Elkin, wants to encourage the natives into all kinds of superstitious rites in opposition to our teaching . . . We want souls to be saved from hell, but scientists and anthropologists turn them back . . . they drag them back to hell."[53]

Government-missions relations

Relations between the missions and the government had their ups and downs during the years between the Roth and Moseley Royal Commissions. Under Prinsep and Gale missionary work, with the exception of children's institutions, was tolerated rather than encouraged; in Gale's view, missions "were not in the best interest of uncivilized natives".[54] Neville regarded them as unnecessary: "Where two or more [natives] have been gathered together the missionary has often barged in quite needlessly, and the native has become the medium for the advancement of the mission, to be followed by pleadings for the material things of life."[55] In practice, Neville's mission policy depended on the exigencies of the political situation and the views of his Ministers. During the war, and especially while Underwood was at the helm, the department pursued an openly anti-mission policy; in the twenties an uneasy truce prevailed, during which the missions were neither supervised nor interfered with; the thirties saw a revival of animosities, culminating in open warfare after the passing of the 1936 Native Administration Act. After Neville's retirement, early in 1940, there occurred a temporary rapprochement between the government and the missions. By 1943, however, the old animosities had reasserted themselves, and relations remained strained until the appointment of S. G. Middleton as Commissioner of Native Affairs, in August 1948.

Gale had inherited from Prinsep a system of subsidies which was hardly designed to eliminate friction between the missions and the government: subsidies were allocated on an *ad hoc* basis, and outside pressures were often brought to bear on the department or the cabinet. In April 1904, for instance, following representations by Bishop Gibney, the James government approved a daily capitation grant of 10 cents for all children at the Beagle Bay mission, thereby bringing it in line with the Church of England children's institutions. This was rescinded, as an "electioneering dodge",[56] by Henry Daglish who replaced Walter James as Premier in August 1904. During the slump of 1906–1907 subsidies were reduced across the board, with Prinsep favouring a withdrawal of all financial assistance to the "large and wealthy firm" of New Norcia.[57] Gale shared Prinsep's sentiments. In 1908 he argued that the time had come to withdraw the New Norcia subsidy, "as it must be the opinion of everyone that a recourse to pecuniary assistance . . . should be only sought when the Mission cannot be carried on without it . . ."[58] Three years later, in a submission to the Colonial Secretary, he again argued that the subsidy to New Norcia should be withdrawn. Connolly told him to wait: without aboriginal institutions of its own the government was not in a position to wield the big stick and would have to compromise until it no longer depended on charitable institutions for the implementation of its aboriginal policy.

Gale encouraged missions to start new industries such as hat-making from cabbage-tree palm leaves, and to experiment with the growing of sisal hemp, rubber, and coffee. This would not only make them self-supporting, but would also enable them to "keep the same controlling influence over adult aborigines as was held over them during school days". Here Gale put his finger on a fundamental problem. "The present system", said the Chief Protector in 1911, "of educating children up to a certain age and then sending them out to service cannot commend itself to anyone giving the matter serious thought. Companionship formed in early youth is often severed . . . and the two sexes instead of being encouraged to marry among themselves drift apart, often with unfortunate results, especially to the weaker sex."[59] Children from "fundamentalist" missions which stressed the total accuracy of the scriptures and preached neophobia, asceticism, and chiliasm, suffered from additional disadvantages: brought up in a closed authoritarian mission society, they found it difficult to adjust when they moved out into the freedom of the wider community.

The Neville-Underwood partnership of the war years posed a serious threat for the missions. In January 1915, two months after taking office, Underwood announced that his department had been asked to reduce expenditure and that he intended to cut mission subsidies to a bare minimum; when the missions protested he promised temporary assistance to all institutions except Beagle Bay, whose management he believed to be "neither economical nor wise".[60] In May 1915 New Norcia and Port George IV were notified that their subsidies would be withdrawn in the coming financial year. A deputation from the Presbyterian Church eventually persuaded Underwood to reverse the decision as far as Port George IV was concerned, but the subsidy to New Norcia was withdrawn, leaving the mission without government assistance for the first time in sixty-six years. Underwood's anti-Roman Catholic bias was not actuated by policy alone. Soon after the outbreak of the war all missionaries of German nationality were detained on Rottnest Island or in the Liverpool internment camp in New South Wales; some, including the Beagle Bay superintendent, Father Bischofs, were later released on parole, while others were allowed to retire to the mother house of German missions in Sydney. Those who returned to Beagle Bay were regarded as security risks and were kept under surveillance by Commonwealth authorities. In June 1916, when it was rumoured that the Commonwealth security police were about to take over the mission, Neville submitted a confidential memorandum for Underwood's approval, proposing the immediate establishment of a large government cattle station on the Dampier Peninsula; this was to be followed by the closing of the Beagle Bay, Lombadina, and Sunday Island missions and the transfer of most inmates to the cattle station (the lock hospitals on Bernier and Dorre islands were to be eventually moved to the station, preferably to Disaster Bay). The proposal was sent for cabinet approval early in July, but the Scaddan government was toppled soon after by the defection of a member to the opposition. The new ministry, led by Frank Wilson, was more sympathetic towards Christian missions. In November 1916 the Saint John of God Convent, whose subsidy was withdrawn by the Labour government in 1913, was given a small annual grant, and in the following year, on the initiative of the Colonial Secretary, H. P. Colebatch, a new system of mission subsidies was put into operation. Missions were divided into two groups, according to whether or not they owned freehold land or held free government land grants. Missions in the first group, located north of the 25th parallel, were to receive an annual subsidy of $10 for every inmate approved by the department; if located south of the 25th parallel they were to be paid $14 a year. Missions in the second group were given $28 annually for every inmate cared for at the request of the department, irrespective of location. It was a fair system, on paper. In practice, the words "at the request of the department" made it still possible for the administration to discriminate between missions or to threaten their very existence. The closing of Dulhi Gunyah and the Swan Native and Half-Caste Home, in 1917 and 1921 respectively, after the department ceased to send "approved" inmates to these two institutions, is a good case in point.

In October 1917, following yet another change of government,

Neville revived his earlier proposal to establish a government cattle station on the Dampier Peninsula, though in a modified form. The original proposal called for the transfer of the lock hospitals to Disaster Bay; the new plan envisaged the establishment of two separate hospitals for the treatment of venereal disease, one for men at Derby, another for women on Finucane Island near Port Hedland. This part was approved by the cabinet in November, but the construction of the hospital at Derby was in the end shelved because of opposition from the local road board, while Finucane Island turned out to be unsuitable in other respects (in 1919, an up-to-date hospital for the treatment of venereal disease was opened on the mainland near Port Hedland and the lock hospitals on Bernier and Dorre islands were closed). The more controversial part of Neville's proposal, involving the closing of the three West Kimberley missions, was approved in December 1917 by Underwood, who had in the meantime joined the government as Honorary Minister for the North-West. The first mission to be closed was Lombadina, but the press got hold of the proposal, and soon after Archbishop Clune called on the Premier, who at once asked Underwood to leave the matter in abeyance. In January 1918 cabinet decided that the proposal should stand over for one year. In 1919 Neville brought up his scheme once again, but without success. In the course of his official life, recalled Neville after his retirement,

a Public Servant is occasionally warned off the grass, so to speak, and given more or less direct hints not to proceed in certain directions, however reasonable it may seem to him to do so in the interests of his duty or charges. In my early years of administration it was "hands off the missions", and so the work was not strictly supervised or interfered with, neither was it greatly encouraged.[61]

After the war the friction between the department and the missions centred largely on the question of security of land tenure. Over the years the missions had come to hold land under a variety of conditions: in fee simple, as regular pastoral leases, as reserves under s.39 of the Land Act, or as Crown grants in accordance with s.42 of the same act under which land could be leased or granted to individuals or to corporate bodies in trust for certain specific purposes. Of the missions then in existence only Beagle Bay held a Crown grant, issued in 1904 in accordance with a promise made by the government in 1888 that a fee simple of 10,000 acres would be granted to the mission after $10,000 had been spent on improvements, to be held

in trust for the aborigines of Beagle Bay. Forrest River and Port
George IV were built on aboriginal reserves, Drysdale River on a
pastoral lease, Lombadina on private land, and Sunday Island was
held by Hadley "at will" of the department. Among the southern
missions only New Norcia held land; its estates consisted of two
pastoral leases, three grazing leases, two conditional purchase
leases, and various leases held in the name of the executors of the
late Rosindo Salvado, in all about 18,500 acres. Following Neville's
attempt to close the three West Kimberley mission stations, the
missions began to press for greater security of tenure. In January
1918 the Drysdale River mission applied for a freehold grant of
5,000 acres. When this was rejected by the department, the mission
asked for a 999 year lease of the same area, and later indicated its
willingness to settle for a freehold grant of a mere 100 acres. In
January 1921 the Church of England applied for a freehold grant of
a small portion of the Forrest River reserve. Neville offered the
mission a twenty-one year lease, adding that he could not sanction
any steps which would in effect deprive the government of the right
to interfere in mission affairs, should this become necessary because
of poor management or as a matter of policy. Early in 1922 the
Drysdale River mission reapplied for a freehold grant, this time asking for 1,000 acres. Neville recommended favourable consideration,
and, having reversed his stand, he then proposed that other missions
should be given similar grants, since it would be unjust, as well as
unwise, to differentiate between the various denominations. This was
approved by the cabinet in February 1922, and in the following year
the Native Mission Stations Act gave the Drysdale River and Forrest
River missions a Crown grant of 1,000 acres each. For some reason
the remaining missions were not included in the act, despite Neville's
belated intervention.

The deterioration in government-mission relations after about
1930 was due largely to the rapid growth of the United Aborigines'
Mission and the subsequent attempts by the department to secure
greater control over missionary activities. During the late twenties
Neville and Schenk, the senior U.A.M. missionary in Western Australia, were on fairly friendly terms. In 1927 Neville made Schenk
responsible for the distribution of relief to indigents in the Laverton
district. In 1928 the department gazetted a small portion of the
mission lease as an aboriginal reserve, thereby giving Schenk some
security of tenure. The pastoralists, on the other hand, kept up their

war of attrition, and in February 1929 asked the department to remove the mission farther inland. Schenk was not averse to the idea, providing the mission was compensated for all capital outlay at Mount Margaret, but Neville told the pastoralists that the mission would not be moved and defended Schenk as a "sensible, level-headed man".[62] As late as November 1930 he said in the *West Australian:* "He was no sluggard, this white man [Schenk]. He put his neck in the yoke and pulled his full weight . . ."[63] After 1930 the relations between the two men began to deteriorate. The U.A.M. differed from other missions in its concept of spreading Christianity: its approach was fundamentalist, and much of the work was done by itinerant missionaries, often without adequate financial support from the mission council. This aspect of the society's activities became pronounced after the temporary split within the mission late in 1928 which brought a "veritable plethora" of itinerant missionaries to the state.[64] Needless to say, their work was not subsidized by the department. Indeed, if Neville had had his way, they would have been prevented from spreading their "radical" views altogether — which was precisely what some pastoralists urged him to do. So when Schenk asked for permission to open a branch on the central Australian reserve, in 1932, Neville told him that he would have to apply for a permit to enter the reserve even temporarily, "like every-one else".[65] In the following year Schenk, in his own words, "decided to obey the command of Christ"[66] and established a small mission in the Warburton Range, just outside the reserve. Neville retaliated by threatening to cancel the Mount Margaret reserve and to revoke Schenk's certificate of protectorship. In 1936 Schenk applied for a goldbuyer's licence, but his application was turned down by the Department of Mines, on Neville's recommendation. Early in 1937 Schenk asked for permission to start a mission at Cosmo Newbery, halfway between Mount Margaret and the Warburton Range, and later applied for a lease of Crown land at Wodjina in the Port Hedland district; in both instances he was refused. By the time the department got around to introducing regulations for the "licensing" of missionaries, in April 1938, relations between the department and U.A.M. had reached the breaking point.

7. The Part-Aborigines
1906-1935

Growth of racial prejudice

In 1898, when Western Australia acquired full control over its aboriginal administration, the aboriginal problem in the south was close to its ultimate solution — all that remained to be done south of the Gascoyne River was to "smooth the dying pillow" of the 3,000 or so remaining aborigines. Suddenly, almost overnight, the government and the country came to realize that they had an additional problem on their hands. Between 1891 and 1901 the part-aboriginal population had almost doubled itself as a result of intermarriage or interbreeding; at the 1911 census, it had increased to 1,471; it had doubled itself again by 1926, to an estimated 2,957, and reached an estimated 4,005 in 1935 (by 1968 the number of part-aborigines had surpassed 13,200). Such rapid growth would lead to difficulties anywhere; but in Western Australia, with its comparatively small white population, an ethnic group which tended to triple itself every generation was naturally bound to create a "social problem of the first order".[1]

During the nineteenth century, as we have seen, the part-aborigines had managed to cling, however precariously, to their "European" status; by the time the first Western Australian fighting men were leaving to help make the world safe for democracy, they had been relegated to the status of second-class citizens, despised and discriminated against wherever they turned. The deterioration in the part-aborigines' position occurred during a period in which Australian society acquired "its own individual character and a set of values peculiar to itself", a period marked by "experiments in the redistribution of national wealth, the greater equalization of opportunity, the passage of humanitarian welfare legislation and the regulation of industrial life by processes of law"[2] — for white Australians. The exclusion of part-aborigines from participation in these experiments was due to their rapid increase and the subsequent emergence of racial prejudice in the southwest (where most part-aborigines could be found) and later in other parts of the state. The two phenomena were obviously related, but the exact nature of this connection is difficult to establish. Racial prejudice used to be thought of as an instinctive reaction to members of another racial group, but this explanation is no longer accepted. Today it is regarded either as displaced aggression caused by frustration or other personality needs stemming from fear, anxiety, insecurity, guilt, and so on, or as resulting from competition between groups for material possessions and desired positions in society. Cultural traditions and social norms also play a role: prejudice can become a part of a given culture and be transmitted like any other attitude. In Western Australia, the emergence of racial prejudice about the turn of the century can be explained partly in terms of the vague dissatisfaction which, on a different level, gave birth to the labour movement, and partly by the potential economic threat caused by the increase in the part-aboriginal population. In the 1870s and 1880s, as L. R. Marchant has demonstrated, a wide variety of occupations was opened to the aborigines. During the 1890s they were forced out of the skilled and even some unskilled positions. As a result of the goldrushes, there was, for the first time since 1829, a surplus of labour in most parts of the colony, and trade unions closed shop as far as aborigines and part-aborigines were concerned.[3] This development coincided with wider changes in the Australian ethos, symbolized by the white Australia policy. Although the policy was not based on racial grounds alone,[4] these were almost certainly uppermost in most Australians' minds:

All that is necessary for us to urge in justification of this measure [said Alfred Deakin during the debate on the Immigration Restriction Bill, expressing the deepest feelings of his generation] is that these people do differ from us in such essentials of race and character as to exclude the possibility of any advantageous admixture or intermarriage . . . They are separated from us by a gulf which we cannot bridge to the advantage of either.[5]

The best expression of the changing mood of the country was the 1905 Aborigines Act. As we have seen, the act was designed primarily for "the better protection and care" of full-bloods, but because it had considerably widened the definition of an "aboriginal native", it applied to most part-aborigines as well (see chapter three, "The 1905 Aborigines Act"). The ideas embodied in the act did not come entirely out of the blue. In 1900, several years before the community began to concern itself seriously with part-aborigines, Prinsep, in a draft bill to amend the 1886 Aborigines Protection Act, proposed that the Chief Protector should become the official guardian of all native children up to the age of sixteen, with the right to remove them "from any place and to cause them to reside at any other place".[6] In 1901 Prinsep asked again for increased powers over part-aboriginal children:

... where there are no evil influences these half-castes can be made into good useful workmen and women ... But, unfortunately, they are more often found in communities whose influence is towards laziness and vice; and I think it is our duty not to allow these children, whose blood is half British, to grow up as vagrants and outcasts, as their mothers now are.[7]

Two years later he asked once more for increased legal powers and money for the establishment of training institutions:

In my opinion it is our duty to make good citizens of them by every means in our power ... During the years that I have had charge of this department numbers of these half-castes have grown from children into adults, and have so slipped out of my hands even were I legally able to influence their lives.[8]

In 1904 he complained:

There is no law at present to enable me to withdraw them from the black race. . .[9]

The Roth Royal Commission had little to say about part-aborigines, and nothing that was favourable. It expressed the opinion that they should be "got at" and spoke of the "evil antecedents to the presence of half-castes in the neighbourhood of townships", reserving the bulk of its comments for certain white men, including some police, "guilty of intercourse with the native women".[10] There were few dissenting voices in parliament, where amending legislation was introduced in August 1904, when George (Mulga) Taylor, the Colonial Secretary in the Daglish government and a stalwart advocate of the rights of working men, defended as absolutely necessary the proposed power of the Chief Protector to place any child born of a half-caste or aboriginal mother in an industrial home:

There is no power to do this now; consequently a half-caste, who possesses few of the virtues and nearly all the vices of whites, grows up to be a mischievous and very immoral subject ... it may appear to be a cruel thing to tear an aborigine child from its mother, but it is necessary in some cases to be cruel to be kind.[11]

The object of the 1905 act was protection. Most part-aborigines, however, felt no need to be protected: they were "educated, and ratepayers, and not savages", so they wanted to be treated "like any other respectable man".[12] The effect of the act on part-aborigines, as one parliamentarian remarked during the debate, "was to make a very invidious and humiliating distinction".[13] Any part-aborigine, classified as an aboriginal native, who was not in "lawful employment", could be removed to a reserve or expelled from any town or municipality which had been declared a "prohibited area". The Chief Protector became the legal guardian of his or her children and had the right to undertake "the general care, protection and management" of his or her property, including the right to "take possession of, retain, sell or dispose of any such property, whether real or personal". A part-aboriginal woman "under the act" could not marry a non-aborigine without official permission, and if she cohabited with any man other than an aborigine, her common law husband was liable to prosecution; in the absence of a proof to the contrary, travelling accompanied by a man who was not an aborigine was deemed to be cohabitation. If she was under sixteen and had left school or "lawful service" without the Chief Protector's permission, the person who had "enticed" her could be prosecuted. Finally, the act contained a clause enabling the Minister in charge of the Aborigines Department to exempt from the provisions of the act any aborigine who, in his opinion, ought not to be subject to the act. Had this provision been applied in a more liberal spirit, much of the harshness of the act could have been mitigated, but such was not to be the case. The Minister's "opinion" was invariably that of the local police, who were always asked to report on the applicant's fitness or otherwise to be exempted from the act. By 1910 it had become virtually impossible for an aborigine to secure a certificate of exemption. If the applicant was known to be addicted to drink, or if the police thought that he might supply other aborigines with liquor, the request was automatically refused. If an aborigine "associated" with other aborigines, including close relatives, he had little chance of being granted an exemption; in 1913 a relatively prosperous Brookton part-aborigine had his application turned down because his two brothers lived on his farm.[14] Moreover, certificates could be revoked at any time, there being no right of appeal, and exempted their holder only from the provisions of the Aborigines Act, leaving unaffected other statutory disabilities except the prohibition on the supply of liquor to part-aborigines introduced by the 1902 amendment of the Wines, Beer and Spirits Sales Act.

The most important among these disabilities was the disqualification from voting. The first step in this direction was taken in 1893 when an amendment of the Constitution Act disenfranchised the colony's full-bloods, "except in respect of a freehold qualification" (a white man could vote also by virtue of a "leasehold" or "household" qualification). In 1899 another amendment gave the right to vote to the colony's women but took it away from all "persons of the half-blood", unless they had a freehold estate of the prescribed value. The 1907 Electoral Act, the cap-stone of political democracy in Western Australia which introduced the principle of one man one vote, disenfranchised all full-bloods and persons of the half-blood (by virtue of the 1902 Commonwealth Franchise Act, this entailed disenfranchisement in the federal sphere as well). Another legal disability which was not affected by the grant of an exemption was based on the discriminatory provisions of the 1898 Land Act: a white selector could be granted a freehold or a lease of an area up to 1,000 acres of Crown land, while in the case of a "person of aboriginal descent" the area could not exceed 200 acres. The Invalid and Old-Age Pensions Act and the Maternity Allowances Act, passed by the Commonwealth Parliament in 1908 and 1912 respectively, on the other hand, applied to persons of the half-blood or less; "civilized" aborigines with more than one-half of aboriginal blood had to wait for these privileges until 1942, and even then they qualified only if they held a certificate of exemption.

Changes in prevalent attitudes towards miscegenation and inter-marriage are another index of the growth of racial prejudice. During most of the nineteenth century, it may be recalled, sexual relations between white men and aboriginal women were tolerated, and during the first three decades of settlement intermarriage was officially encouraged by means of financial assistance for the purchase of Crown land which was settled on the aboriginal wife and her children. By the end of the century miscegenation and intermarriage had become not only undesirable but morally deplorable, and allusions to the "sin-sodden North" and to "disgraceful conduct to which a decent newspaper must refrain from direct reference" were the order of the day.[15] At any rate, such were the feelings of the respectable citizens in the settled south. In the north, where white women were few, most men were quite open about their moral lapses, and "glad enough of the dusky companions whose only terms were the right to live and to serve".[16] The 1905 Aborigines Act tried to tackle the problem of "immorality" by making cohabitation a punishable offence, but in 1906 the Crown Law Department ruled that such cohabitation had to be "continuous", thereby limiting the application of the act to permanent liaisons deserving the least attention. These liaisons were frequently marriages in all but name; the men stayed with their unofficial wives as long as their jobs lasted, and often did all they could for their children (one man left a $1,000 legacy to his son while the latter was still being educated at the Beagle Bay mission). But it is doubtful if greater powers under the act would have made any difference, since the department could not initiate proceedings against an offender and had to rely on the police to prefer charges. Since the offender was often an acquaintance or a friend of the local constable, the police were naturally somewhat lukewarm in the execution of their duties; on one occasion, when Gale asked the constable at Esperance to prefer charges against a local station hand, the department was presented with a bill for incidental expenses incurred. Once proceedings got under way the men might offer to marry their concubines but required official permission to do so. If they came from "good families which should be protected from their follies", permission was as a rule refused; it was usually granted in cases where the union had been blessed with offspring, where the "parties were old and have been living together for years", or where the proposed marriage was "otherwise just and right".[17] Applications by Asians were always refused. A bond of $100 was also required to provide for the woman in case of desertion. Even these strict rules were apparently not stringent enough for some people. Following the prosecution for cohabitation of two Marble Bar men and the subsequent legalization of their de facto unions, the Premier received this telegram, signed by several Marble Bar residents: "Protest Moore Government degrading White Australia by permitting marriage to take place today between black and white Stop Do not want country overrun by half-castes."[18]

If the government was somewhat lax in its attitude towards "komboism", it showed great determination in its opposition to the "abominable and corrupting"[19] influence on aboriginal women of the Asian pearling crews. During the lay-up season hundreds of Japanese, Koepanger, Manilamen, and Malays converged on Broome, where they supplied the aborigines with drink in exchange for the favours of their women. The resulting degradation of the men, "to such extent that they became almost useless", was one cause of official concern; the appearance of a "mongrel race inimical to the quietude of the whole region" was another.[20] Prinsep believed that nothing short of a complete eviction of aborigines from Broome would solve the problem, but he lacked the power to order their removal under the 1886 act. In 1902 the local road board promulgated by by-law under the Health Act prohibiting unemployed aborigines from remaining in town after sundown, and when the regulation was disallowed as being *ultra vires* of the act, the police drove out unemployed aborigines as vagrants. The town was declared a prohibited area in June 1907.

Part-aborigines and land settlement

It was somewhat unfortunate that these changes in white attitudes should have coincided with another development which left a legacy of apathy among the part-aborigines. In 1904, following the end of the goldmining boom, the government embarked on a vigorous policy of land settlement, designed to absorb the unemployed miners and disgruntled prospectors into agriculture and dairy farming. Under the provisions of the 1893 Homestead Act and the 1898 Land Act, prospective farmers could select free homestead farms of up to 160 acres or buy larger blocks under a deferred payment scheme, with initial financial assistance from the Agricultural Bank. This opportunity proved attractive not only to the white men disappointed in their search for gold but also to some enterprising part-aborigines. F. K. Crowley, in the standard history of Western Australia, *Australia's Western Third,* claims that it was impossible for the aborigines "to acquire property, as they were not counted as citizens";[21] however, there is little occasion for dispute about the following facts. The 1872 Land Regulations empowered the Governor to reserve Crown land for the "use and benefit of aborigines", and the 1898 Land Act gave him the additional right to grant or to lease areas of Crown land not exceeding 200 acres to any aborigine or descendant of an aborigine, as a reserve for his or her personal use, that is for the purpose of residence or cultivation. The first recorded grant under the provisions of the 1872 Land Regulations appears to have been made in 1892, and in 1906 six aborigines held land as reserves for their personal use. By then a number of part-aborigines had acquired free homestead farms, while others had bought properties under the deferred payment scheme, particularly around Busselton, Newcastle, and Quairading, where some of the best land in the district was owned by the Kickett family. A dozen aborigines applied for land in 1906 alone; their hopes were summed up by a Norseman full-blood who wanted to become a landowner because he was tired of white men who forgot to pay him wages. But determination to succeed was not enough, for most aborigines lacked the necessary experience and capital. Although they were entitled to financial assistance from the Agricultural Bank, only one, Johnny Dangin, is known to have been granted such a loan. None the less, a few aboriginal farmers did remarkably well. In 1907, for instance, a Newcastle full-blood named Ryder had seventy acres under wheat and a two-acre vineyard, another thirty acres ringbarked, and had recently acquired more land for his son. Johny Dangin, who had been farming since 1904 in the Greenhills district, had by 1908 twenty acres under cultivation, and 120 chains of fencing. Unfortunately, the poor harvest of 1911–1912 which ruined many a white farmer, forced many aboriginal cultivators to abandon their holdings, and after the drought of 1914–1915 only a handful remained on the land. Their ruin was in a sense due to their initial success, for those who had done well were looked upon as men of substance by all their kith and kin and were expected to share with them, on a communal basis, the fruit of their labour.

The failure of aboriginal farming had a number of repercussions outside the economic sphere. "A lot of aborigines have children growing up", observed the Beverley Land Agent in 1913, "and if these children have no land to work they cannot be other than shiftless vagrants and quite apart from their own good, would be as such a veritable nuisance and even a danger in these closely settled parts."[22] Fortunately, not all the children were destined for such a fate. Some found work on farms, others did occasional clearing or fencing, a few became opossum hunters or rabbit trappers, while the girls could always find work as domestics, in Perth as well as in the country. Most work offering for men, however, was seasonal and poorly paid, and it was always a case of "last on, first off" in times of even slight unemployment. In fact, the part-aborigines of the southwest were increasingly discriminated against in almost every walk of life. Although they were entitled to free medical treatment by resident medical officers and to free hospitalization in government and in assisted hospitals, most hospitals outside the metropolitan area were increasingly reluctant to admit aboriginal patients. In 1909 the Principal Medical Officer circularized all assisted hospitals to remind them that in return for the payment of the government subsidy they were expected to provide free medical assistance to all paupers, including aborigines. The directive appears to have had little permanent effect; in 1911 the nursing staff at the Geraldton hospital went on "strike", claiming that they "did not engage to be the servants of the natives".[23] In hospitals where ab- origines were admitted they were almost invariably segregated in separate wards, usually unlined huts of corrugated iron and timber. Private practitioners in country towns were inclined to discourage aborigines from visiting their surgeries, and were not always prompt in answering calls for home visits. The record of one such incident at Beverley has been accidentally preserved for posterity. It concerned Billy Kickett who, as a young man, had accompanied John Forrest on one of his exploring journeys. One evening the Kickett family sent an urgent message to the local doctor: Billy was seriously ill and needed immediate medical attention. But the doctor was apparently too busy to answer the call, and Billy died the same night. A few weeks later an old woman died in similar circumstances. Normally, there would have been no repercussions, but on this occasion the Kickett family wrote to John Forrest in Melbourne, the Principal Medical Officer had to appoint a board of inquiry and the doctor was found guilty of neglect of duty.

The establishment of the Carrolup and Moore River aboriginal settlements

The developments described in the preceding section left their most tragic legacy in the field of education. In 1901 some 31 per cent of part-aborigines over the age of five could read and write, and approxi- mately 30 per cent of part-aboriginal children of school age were "receiving instruction" (twenty-four in state schools, three in private schools, eighty in mission schools, and nine at home);[24] twenty years later these percentages were so low that it was thought prudent not to record them. The relatively unsatisfactory situation in 1901 (by today's standards) was not due to a belief in the part-aboriginal child's mental inferiority but to complications of a different nature. The education of part-aboriginal children was governed by two potentially contradictory enactments. These were the 1871 Elemen- tary Education Act which provided for compulsory school attendance of every child residing within three miles of a state school, and the 1897 amendment of the Aborigines Protection Act which made the Aborigines Department "responsible" for the education of full-blood and part-aboriginal children. The former act implied that a part-aboriginal child had the right to education on equal terms with the white child; the latter made their education the separate concern of a specialist department. During the era of the Aborigines Protection Board this "responsibility" was discharged by the government through financial assistance to missions. After 1898 the Aborigines Department reduced mission subsidies as a matter of policy, hoping to establish its own training institutions; in 1905, as we have seen, the Chief Protector acquired the necessary legal powers. As so often in the history of aboriginal affairs, the decision remained an intention because of the Treasury's insistence on financial stringency. After 1905, too, the part-aboriginal problem was once again, for a brief period, low on the list of departmental priorities; what money was available was spent mainly combating granuloma and on aboriginal cattle stations. So the various religious institutions continued to be the only avenue of education for part-aboriginal children. In 1905 the Salvation Army Industrial School at Collie started to take in selected boys; its Kalgoorlie institution for girls followed suit in 1907. About the same time New Norcia and the Swan Native Half-Caste Home increased their intake of part-aboriginal children, and in 1909 the Australian Aborigines' Mission established the Dulhi Gunyah Orphanage for aboriginal children in Perth.

The third alternative, sending part-aboriginal children to state schools, was at no stage seriously considered by the administration, since they were unacceptable there except in small numbers; in fact, they could be officially prevented from attending. The 1893 Education Act gave the education authorities the right to exclude from state schools any pupil "suffering from any infectious or contagious disease, or whose presence was otherwise injurious to the health or welfare of other children". The first recorded instance of this provision being invoked occurred in 1905. In March of that year an irate group of white parents from Shark Bay asked the Education Department to expel all coloured children from the local school "not because of any unworthy feeling as of white against black but because of the tendency of whites to mimicry; they are given to imitate the black children in tone of voice which is considered a disadvantage and not easily susceptible to subsequent eradication".[25]

If the phraseology of the white parents' petition was somewhat muddled, the reason for their action was simple enough. The coloured people of Shark Bay, where a "lucky genetic crossing of Malay, white and aboriginal"[26] produced a hard-working and self-reliant race of sea-going fishermen, had achieved a standard of living comparable to that of the local whites; the local resident medical officer described their condition as "generally superb".[27] The Education Department expelled the children; for a while there was talk of establishing a separate school for them, but in the end nothing was done. They were the "responsibility" of the Aborigines Department.

The issue came to a head in 1911 in another part of the state. By that time there were some thirty (mainly part-aboriginal) children of school age in the Katanning and Wagin districts, and almost as many in the Quairading, Beverley, York, Mount Barker, Bridgetown, and Busselton districts. In November 1911 the protector of aborigines at Beverley sent an alarming report to the Chief Protector. The local aborigines had told the Beverley teacher that they were going to send their children to school when it reopened in the following year, and they were somewhat belligerent about it. Gale asked the protector to explain to the aboriginal parents that if they wanted their children educated they should send them to a mission, but they would not listen and threatened to "invade" the school if the teacher refused to admit them. In January 1912 the Director of Education made a proposal which, for all its inadequacy, might have solved the problem: he offered to open a separate aboriginal school at Beverley, providing Gale's department agreed to foot the bill for the erection of a tent building and to pay the teacher's salary. The proposal was rejected. When the school reopened, in February 1912, aboriginal children turned up in full strength but were sent away, since, as the teacher said in his report to Perth, they were "anything but clean".[28]

In other country towns, notably at Quairading, Mount Barker, and Katanning, there was no opposition to the sudden influx of aboriginal pupils; in Katanning alone thirteen children were enrolled in February 1912, all over the age of ten. Later in the month Drew asked Gale to prepare an estimate of the cost of establishing separate aboriginal schools in the closely settled parts of the state. The Chief Protector recommended the construction of thirteen schools, involving a capital cost of $5,200 and a recurring annual expenditure of $5,000 on salaries, proposing further that three such schools be opened without delay, one each in the Mount Barker, Wagin, and Katanning districts. Meanwhile, the Beverley aborigines were reported to be "howling" in protest, while at Katanning the white parents were beginning to have second thoughts about aboriginal children attending the local school. Wrote an irate citizen to the editor of the *West Australian:*

Australia boasts of the White Australia policy, and rightly so. I do not blame the children for their skins — God help them that they had no choice in the matter — but it appears to me that if we compel black and white to intermingle in schools we are practically encouraging the future fathers and mothers in this State in the belief that there are no differences in the races . . . The Brotherhood of Man is a very good theory, but the welfare of our little White Australians is of far greater importance than the possible hardship inflicted on, I trust, a very small minority of our citizens.[29]

Early in June the Education Department announced that it would provide "separate instruction" for aboriginal children attending the Katanning state school, but this failed to satisfy the white parents who were now clamouring for the expulsion of all aborigines. The Katanning reserve, just outside the town boundary, was an old aboriginal camping ground, with an aboriginal "hospital" dating back to the days of the Aborigines Protection Board and a number of "shelters" erected by the Aborigines Department in the early 1900s. Throughout 1912 there was a steady influx of women and children to the reserve; the men who in the past led a semi-nomadic existence, moving from farm to farm in search of work, now left their families behind so that the children could go to school. Early in 1913 a group of Katanning citizens came up with an ingenious solution: the establishment of a mission at Carrolup, an aboriginal camping ground some twelve miles away. The Australian Aborigines' Mission, which had opened a preaching station on the Katanning reserve some time earlier, agreed with the idea, but the administration declined to subsidize the proposed mission. In October 1913 a deputation asked the Chief Protector to order the immediate removal of all aborigines from Katanning. "The native child's mind was not as pure as could be wished", they told him, adding that "the natives were a nuisance, and a menace to the morals of the youths of Katanning", and that "the ladies were afraid that they will be interfered with by some black man".[30] Gale must have found these arguments convincing,

for on his return to Perth he recommended the immediate establishment of an aboriginal settlement at Carrolup, though without any
result. By the beginning of 1914 the agitation had spread to other
towns along the Great Southern. In March the headmaster of the
Quairading school complained that white pupils were suffering from
biliousness caused by the "abominable smell from the black children";[31] in the following month the local parents' and citizens' association asked the Education Department to expel the aboriginal
pupils because white children could not "endure their foul smelling
bodies and their dirty habits".[32] At Mount Barker, white parents
had in the meantime taken direct action by withdrawing their children from school, pending the expulsion of aboriginal pupils. In
fairness to the white parents, it should be pointed out that their
complaints were not without foundation; aboriginal families lived
in insanitary humpies, and water was a rare commodity on the
reserves. The only workable solution would have been to establish
separate aboriginal schools, but the divided responsibility for
aboriginal education and the refusal of the Department of Aborigines
and Fisheries to shoulder its financial responsibility as laid down by
the Aborigines Act, made such course of action unlikely. As late as
mid-April 1914 the Education Department did not apparently contemplate a general ban on aboriginal pupils. At an interdepartmental
conference, held in the second week of April, the Director of Education offered to provide separate teaching facilities at Quairading
and Mount Barker (and elsewhere, as the need arose), the expenditure involved to be borne by the Department of Aborigines and
Fisheries. Gale recommended acceptance, but the proposal was set
aside by Drew. On 20 April, the Minister for Education authorized
the expulsion of aboriginal pupils from the Quairading and Mount
Barker schools, and in June, following the resignation of the teacher
in charge of the aboriginal school at Katanning, the Director of
Education notified Gale that he would not be replaced. With
unprecedented promptness, Drew replied that his department would
pay the teacher's salary if another were appointed and that it was,
moreover, prepared to assume financial responsibility for aboriginal
education in general, but the Director of Education had by then
lost all interest in further discussion. It was a point of no return in
the history of Western Australian part-aborigines. The wholesale
expulsion of aboriginal children from state schools set a pattern for
years to come and, coupled with the failure of aboriginal farming,

left a lasting legacy of resentment and bitterness. The determination of the southern aborigines to have their children educated was a symptom of their desire to "pass from an external adaptation, making the best of the inevitable, to an inner understanding of the new way and of the part they might play in it",[33] to become self-reliant members of the wider community. However, as A. P. Elkin has pointed out, such "intelligent appreciation can be attained by the natives only if the white society intends that they should and helps them to do so".[34] Perhaps it would have been too much to expect this from the Western Australians of 1914.

The final scene of this sorry episode took place at Katanning. In January 1915, the police removed the local aborigines to Carrolup and left them to fend for themselves. Faced with a *fait accompli,* the administration had no alternative but to establish a departmental settlement for the unfortunate deportees. The scheme was approved by cabinet in March 1915 and three months later a superintendent was appointed. In May 1916 regulations were gazetted which gave him sweeping disciplinary powers, such as the right to withdraw rations from recalcitrant inmates and the right to inflict summary punishment for a host of offences against camp discipline. Inmates who had been removed to the settlement under "ministerial warrants" could not leave without written permission; recaptured absconders spent the customary two weeks in the settlement "boob". Trusted inmates were appointed as camp police, and in September 1916 fortnightly visits by the Katanning police were arranged. They proved "very beneficial".[35]

The establishment of the Carrolup aboriginal settlement was not a policy decision; the administration simply drifted into it under increasing pressure from the white countryfolk. Once in existence, however, Carrolup was embraced wholeheartedly by the administration, and the policy of partial segregation or social isolation of part-aborigines was on its way. The idea found an outspoken supporter in Neville whose appointment coincided with the opening of Carrolup. Soon after taking office Neville decided that Carrolup should serve as a "home" for all part-aborigines south of the Great Eastern Railway, with its own school and hospital, and a farm where the inmates would grow their own food. It was a perfect solution, on paper, but most part-aborigines showed no desire to move there. Two families from Beverley agreed to go voluntarily, as "scouts"; their report must have been discouraging, for no one followed. Soon after

the expulsion of the Katanning aborigines a group of white citizens
from Quairading asked Neville to "remove the whole of the race
that comes under the Aborigines Act";[36] a rival group, backed by the
Quairading Progress Association and said to represent "moneyed
interests", opposed this. Neville let the aborigines stay. Unlike the
Katanning group, the Quairading aborigines were comparatively
well-off: some were farmers, many earned good wages, and "all
knew their minds on the subject of educating their children".[37]
In February 1915 one Severin E. Jacobs wrote to the Minister of
Education complaining that the teacher would not allow his children
to attend the local school, although they had been examined by a
doctor and declared "fit to attend any school", adding: "I have
been here two years this coming August after setterling down purpose
for sake of my children attending school".[38] Four months later one of
the wealthiest aborigines in the district, John Kickett, sent a similar
complaint to the same Minister. His member of parliament had
told him that his children would be admitted to the local school
"proveiding I lived as a white man and I looked after my children.
Now Sir I am farmeing I have 200 acreas of land and Trying to make
at Liveing out of ot. . . I was teached at a State School and don't
want to see my children degraded."[39] In September 1917 the local
teacher finally agreed to admit Kickett's children to the school, only
to be overruled by the Director of Education. In August 1918
Kickett wrote to his member of parliament: "I want a Little Fair
Play if you will be so kind Enough to see on my Beharfe. . . I have
five of my People in France Fighting Since you were her for your
Election one has been Killed which leaves four. . . as my people
are Fighting for Our King and Country Sir I think they should
have the liberty of going to any State school."[40] The member for
York passed on the letter to the Director of Education, with the
following marginal comment: "The matter of these half-castes is a
problem — the sins of their fathers visited upon their children."[41]

This "cold war in the towns between black and white"[42] was not
limited to the Great Southern. Late in 1914 the Moora and Northampton road boards asked the department to expel all aboriginal
indigents from their districts, and in 1915 the Education Department
excluded all aboriginal pupils from the Mullewa school. In September
1916, following more unrest, approval was given for the establishment
of a second aboriginal settlement at Mogumber on the Moore River;
it opened in March 1918. The aborigines were removed to the settle-

ment under ministerial warrants; in April 1918, for instance, forty-five Guildford aborigines were rounded up by the police and sent to Moore River "in their own interests".[43] Surveying the scene in mid-1919, the Chief Protector made this confident prediction:

As a sociological experiment, our settlements offer an interesting study, particularly having regard to the complex character of the inmates, both male and female. Many of the inmates removed from towns on account of their bad behaviour, women and even murderers are settling down to a new life of peace, contentment and usefulness. There is a complete absence of quarrelling and fighting, the reserves being regarded as common ground when controlled by the Government, the "Big Boss" protector of all tribes. . . Most of the natives have a prejudice against being confined in any particular area, but it is remarkable how soon this prejudice disappears when they realize why they are placed there and what the Department is trying to do for their welfare and happiness. In the light of experience already gained I am satisfied that the reserve and settlement system is the only solution of the native question.[44]

The twenties and the early thirties

During the first half of the 1920s, while the responsibility for the aborigines was divided along geographical lines between the Department of the North-West and the Department of Fisheries, aboriginal administration in the south was limited almost entirely to the distribution of rations and the policing of the Aborigines Act. In 1917 the department introduced a new system of mission subsidies; missions were to be assisted only with respect to "approved" inmates, that is those cared for "at the request" of the government. As a result, all church institutions in the southern part of the state (except New Norcia) had closed by 1921. Their place was to be taken by the Moore River and Carrolup aboriginal settlements (the latter was closed in 1922 as an economy measure and reopened in 1940). However, as time went on, the settlements came to symbolize all that was inhumane and oppressive in aboriginal administration between the wars. The settlements were envisaged as self-supporting institutions, but they turned out to be neither self-supporting nor did they provide any real institutional care. Carrolup had in 1919 only 110 acres under cultivation, and depended heavily on outside supplies to feed its 150 inmates. Absconding was a serious problem, particularly among adolescent girls; if caught, they had their heads shaved or they were "dressed" in old sacks. There were frequent resignations among the staff because of low pay and inadequate accommodation, and occasional dismissals for cruelty and other offences; in 1918 the superintendent, an "ex-Missionary, and a good man, too",[45] had to resign because of his propensity for chaining girls to table legs.

The Moore River settlement had similar problems, and some others. The land was unsuitable for cultivation. In summer there was an acute shortage of water, alleviated only by the fact that the inmates were "content to drink the river water which is slightly brackish".[46] The settlement was constructed to house 200 inmates; after the transfer of the Carrolup aborigines, in June 1922, it had a population of almost 400. In the customary official jargon, the inmates were "perfectly happy and contented", but anyone with eyes to see would have found little to substantiate this claim. Fenced compound, camp police and the settlement "boob" were a part of daily life. Compound inmates were not allowed to leave the compound without written permission from the superintendent or the matron, and outside visitors had to have similar approval. Association of adults and children was prohibited, even in the dining room, where there were separate sittings for women and children. Female inmates were subjected to particularly strict discipline. Girls under the age of fifteen were segregated from older girls who in turn were kept apart from women with young children. Children's dormitories were locked and bolted from the outside at six o'clock in the evening, even in summer. For the "camp" aborigines (those not housed in the compound) institutional care meant little more than a weekly ration of $1\frac{1}{2}$ pounds of sugar, 8 pounds of flour, 4 ounces of tea, 1 stick of tobacco, and $3\frac{1}{2}$ pounds of meat, mainly kangaroo or brush flesh caught by the aborigines themselves. Wages for work performed were nominal. The inmates were also allowed to buy, through the superintendent, such items as books, magazines, sewing material or "anything of improving nature".[47] The education of the one hundred-odd settlement children was entrusted to one teacher. Boys who were not "likely to improve further" were put to work on the farm before they reached school-leaving age, while girls were sent to work in the sewing room or in the kitchen. The spiritual welfare of the inmates was entrusted to a resident Church of England missionary but her work was hampered by recurring clashes with the superintendent who objected to her "familiarity subversive of discipline" and the "lack of dignity which is so essential in one making an attempt to uplift, control and bless this childish race".[48]

It is hardly surprising that the southern part-aborigines should have come to regard Moore River as a prison. Recaptured absconders were invariably sentenced to fourteen days of solitary confinement in the "boob". Habitual absconders were occasionally sentenced to imprisonment in the Fremantle gaol. Girls who became pregnant after being sent to service were sent back under warrant, together with the child — in some cases almost white. Still, it would be wrong to regard the settlement as a concentration camp, or even as a place of permanent segregation. The administration was genuinely convinced that the harsh measures, and in particular the separation of the children from the parents, were absolutely necessary if the young generation was to be uplifted and weaned away from its aboriginal background.[49] With the wisdom which comes from hindsight, it is easy to see why this policy of "tutored assimilation" could not have succeeded. For one thing, it involved the breaking up of aboriginal families and deprived the children of the security which comes from the feeling of belonging. After leaving the settlement to start what they thought was a new and better life, they discovered that they were not accepted by society and became resentful and belligerent, "the men useless and vicious, and the women a tribe of harlots".[50] On the bread and butter level the policy suffered from the almost total lack of employment opportunities outside the settlement. The girls, it is true, could always find work as domestics but the semi-literate and unskilled boys were largely unemployable. The success of the policy was furthermore prejudiced by the insistence of the administration that part-aborigines who wished to be exempted from the Aborigines Act should make a complete break with their aboriginal background. The strictness with which this rule was applied can be gauged from the fact that in 1923 there were in force only forty-one exemptions, covering between 150 and 200 individuals. Applications for exemption were subjected to a thorough scrutiny, and were occasionally turned down for reasons which had little or no bearing on the personal qualities of the applicant. A good example here is the case of four part-aboriginal sisters from Broome whose application, backed by the local police, was turned down by the Chief Protector on the grounds that it would have been "almost impossible for them to get away from their native surroundings".[51] Applicants were sometimes treated in an off-hand manner. A Kimberley part-aboriginal who had waited two years for an acknowledgement of his application wrote to the Chief Protector: "I would like to know the reason for keeping me so long as I can refer you to my Banker and

the local store-keeper in Hall's Creek my carricter is clean I am Head
Stockman on Sturt Creek Station and at any time I would like to
talk to you about this if you have anything against my carricter I
would like you to tell me so that I can defend myself."[52] In 1924
an exempted aborigine was threatened with the revocation of his
certificate unless he stopped associating with his brother. On another
occasion the Crown Law Department ruled that two Moora part-
aborigines were aborigines at law because they played football with
the local aboriginal team.

After the abolition of the Department of the North-West, in 1926,
aboriginal administration became again the responsibility of a single
agency, the Aborigines Department. This administrative innovation
had in itself little effect on official policy, but it coincided with a
pronounced revival of public interest in aboriginal affairs in eastern
Australia, due largely to the untiring efforts of the churches, missionary societies and the rising generation of Australian-trained anthropologists. As we have seen, their influence in Western Australia
was in no way comparable with that exercised in other states, particularly South Australia and New South Wales. Still, Western Australia had its own *cause célèbre* which generated a brief revival of public
interest in aboriginal affairs: the Onmalmeri massacre. The shootings
and the subsequent failure of the Royal Commission to pinpoint
precise responsibility for them had a galvanizing effect on the
"better-class" part-aborigines who, in November 1926, banded
together "in order to obtain the protection of the same laws that
govern the white man".[53] The idea appears to have been the brain-
child of a half-caste farmer from the Morawa district, William
Harris, the son of a Williams shepherd who had been educated at
his father's expense in the Swan Native and Half-Caste Home.
Although it would be far-fetched to describe Harris as the leader
of the discontented part-aborigines, he was the most vocal among
them. In 1906, he had complained to the editor of the *West Australian*
about the treatment of the goldfields aborigines who were being
slowly starved to death by the administration;[54] in March 1913 he
drew attention to the practice by the police of shooting aborigines'
dogs,[55] and in the following month he spoke out against the proposed
segregation of aborigines on state-owned cattle stations: "They
might just as well ask for the imprisonment of all aborigines, for
that is what it would amount to."[56] But Harris was concerned mainly
with the status of part-aborigines. "In the Southern portion of this

State", he said on the same occasion, "hundreds of natives brought up like whites, who pay taxes and whose ideals of life are the same as those of white men, are by law denied the vote and are not permitted into hotels."[57] In November 1926, two months before the appointment of the Wood Royal Commission, Harris wrote to the editor of the *Sunday Times* that the southern aborigines were tired of being "robbed, and shot down, or run into miserable compounds" and that they had decided to form a union in order to fight for their rights as British subjects.[58] An indication how Harris set out to accomplish this formidable task can be found in a letter written by William's nephew Norman Harris to a Perenjori part-aborigine:

Now, Jim we are trying to get some of the natives and half-casts together as a deporation to the Premier as you know what for . . . So that we can get a vote in the country also one law for us all that is the same law that governs the whites also justice for fair play . . . Uncle Bill is going down to Perth at about the end of the month he is going to Yalgoo now. Uncle Bill is going to have a go at the Aboriginal Department. I think he will smash it up also all these compounds of course he wants help from all the natives and halfcasts . . . If the natives and half casts pay a little in for him for a lawyer if we can get every one it will run into a few shillings.[59]

The letter contained the following list of complaints which the deputation intended to take up with the Premier:

Why shouldn't a native have land?
The country belongs to him?
Why segregation in his own land?
Why can't he be alowd in a public Hotel?
Why is he a prisoner in any part of the State?
He can be arrested without a warrant?
Why shouldn't he have a voise in the making of the Laws?
How do they suppose keeping natives in a big reserve?
Why shouldn't a native mother demand Freedom for her child?
Why should the Aboriginal Department put quadroons in Morgumba [i.e. Mogumber]?
How many Schollars have they turned out of Morgumba?
Why is it that the fairest are to the blackest?
Why is it that all letters are opened before going and out to?
Is it so that all girls and boys are found a job by the Dept?
Is it so that all from their have to send their money back?
Is it so that girls are lock up in Dormytorys?
Does children have to work?
What does their food consist of, I bleave Billy Goats?
Do they encourage young people to come their?
Do they stop card playing and gambling their?
Why does anyone who leaves their have to report his movements?

Why is the Act stillover anyone who comes from Morgumba?
Why was those people shifted from Carrollup to Morgumba?
Who has got Carrollup now how much was it sold for?
Who has got the money for it?
I bleave that girls were tied with chains to get punished.
I bleave that girls were made bend forward while the kick from the
  behindn Jist fancy that.
Why was the name change to Aboriginal Department from a Chief
  Protector of Aborigines?
Where does the money go that is set aside for the aborigines?[60]

On the morning of 9 March 1928 a group of immaculately dressed
aborigines entered the Treasury building in Perth, and a few moments
later the first aboriginal deputation to wait on a Western Australian
Minister of the Crown was ushered into the Premier's office. The
deputation consisted of William Harris, his brother Edward and his
nephew Norman Harris, Arthur Kickett from York, Edward Jacobs
from Quairading, Wilfred Morrison, a Toodyay full-blood, and W.
Bodney, said to be partly of West Indian negro stock. William
Harris stated the deputation's case with "no small sign of erudition".
He told the Premier that the aborigines south of Carnarvon did not
want to be owned body and soul by the department, and that they
objected to being herded into the Moore River aboriginal settlement
which was nothing but a prison run by aboriginal police recruited
from the Kimberley cut-throats. Educated aborigines were punished
under British laws, but in all other respects they were treated like
wild blackfellows. "We want to live up to the white man's standard",
concluded Harris, "but in order to be able to do this we should
be exempted from the Aborigines Act, and allowed to live our lives
in our own way."[61]

The deputation achieved little by way of tangible results.[62] The
West Australian conceded the justice of the educated aborigines'
claim to be exempt from the Aborigines Act, concluding with a plea
to "allow aborigines with a desire to make themselves useful members
of the Australian Commonwealth the power to raise themselves.
They should be given free right to education, moral and intellectual,
and employment under decent conditions."[63] The Premier promised
to look into their complaints, and passed on the case to the Aborigines Department for comment. The department, unfortunately,
had been moving for quite some time in the opposite direction,
seeking greater, not smaller, powers over the part-aborigines. In 1922
a part-aborigine was brought before a Carnarvon police court but

the magistrate took the view that since both his parents were second-generation half-castes, he himself was not an aboriginal native within the meaning of the Aborigines Act. Other magistrates followed suit, and an increasing number of part-aborigines took advantage of this loophole to defy the department. Their "recalcitrance" was a matter of mounting concern for Neville; "unless I am given increased powers over all part-aborigines", he told his Minister on one occasion, "the situation will become very serious and a number of coloured children will have to be treated as white."[64] But the cabinet, as we have seen, was consistently opposed to a full-dress debate in parliament which an amendment of the Aborigines Act would have entailed. It was not until 1928, when the publicity accompanying the Kimberley police atrocities made further procastination politically unwise, that Neville was finally given the go-ahead. Most of the changes which found their way into the amending legislation concerned part-aborigines. The definition of an aboriginal was to be broadened to include all male "half-castes" over twenty-one who in the opinion of the Chief Protector were incapable of managing their own affairs, and the term "half-caste" was extended to include all lineal half-blood descendants of aborigines. The Chief Protector was to become the legal guardian of all minors up to the age of twenty-one, and the term cohabitation was to be broadened to include sexual intercourse. Other proposed changes concerned mainly the pastoral industry, making employers of aboriginal labour liable for expenses incurred by the administration on behalf of aboriginal workers in connection with medical and hospital charges arising from injuries suffered in the course of employment. The bill was passed in December 1929 by the Legislative Council where it was defended by a member of the cabinet as being in agreement with "the trend of opinion throughout Australia [which] is in the direction of separating the half-castes from the whites and treating them as akin to aborigines".[65] In the lower house only twelve members voted for the bill. Although the new wider definition of an aboriginal native was strongly opposed by several members, including Sir James Mitchell who said that many part-aborigines were living "clean, decent lives"[66] and should not come under the act, this was not the reason for the defeat of the bill. It was killed by a group of northern members led by the future Minister for the North-West, A. A. M. Coverley, who objected to government interference in the pastoral industry and the increased powers of the department in general.

Meanwhile the events of the southwest were repeating themselves, on a smaller scale, in the north. By the end of the twenties the part-aboriginal population of the state reached about 3,500 (not counting the "half-castes not deemed aborigines" whose numbers, according to departmental estimates, showed wild fluctuations from year to year).[67] In 1930 more than two-thirds of this total lived in the southwest land division. The second largest group was in the Kimberleys which had a part-aboriginal population of some 500, mainly in and around Broome. The northwest accounted for about 400 part-aborigines, and the Murchison for approximately 250. Most of the northern part-aborigines, disclosed the Moseley Royal Commission in 1935, "are not in such great numbers as to cause anxiety, and in habits and temperament they are more black than white".[68] Not so in Broome and Port Hedland where the part-aborigines aspired to white status. But it was an uphill struggle. In Broome the men, although generally educated, found it virtually impossible to get permanent jobs, for they were excluded from membership of the Australian Workers' Union and completely overlooked by the master pearlers. The women had their own problems. As they told the Moseley Royal Commission:

It is very difficult to explain the unhappy position in which we have to live, because most of us do work for white people and by doing so get used to their kind of living . . . Our employers must obtain permits before they can employ us and since most of us do casual work this prevents us from getting work. Sometimes we have a chance to marry a man of our choice, who may be in better circumstances than ourselves. Here again we need the Chief Protector's consent, and are in this respect worse off than the aboriginals who can marry amongst themselves and no questions asked.[69]

The part-aborigines of Port Hedland were in a similar position. Only a handful were paid award rates, and the few who managed to join the Australian Workers' Union were often last in the queue when labour was required at the wharf. Social pressures within the town excluded them from hotels, the cinema, and race meetings. In 1934 these grievances led to the formation of the Euralian Association, a society devoted to the improvement of the status of the Port Hedland part-aborigines (it was disguised as a death benefit society, in much the same way as early trade unions were disguised as friendly societies). The main achievement of the association was the establishment of a part-aboriginal housing settlement on a small lease just outside the town boundary. In 1937 the lease was cancelled, the land was declared an aboriginal reserve open to all aborigines, and the settlement soon deteriorated into another squalid aboriginal camp.

In the south, the depression hit the part-aborigines harder than any other group. At its height only some one hundred southwest aborigines were in employment (including a large contingent of police trackers); the rest subsisted on government rations. Before the depression, an aboriginal indigent was entitled to a weekly issue of $1\frac{1}{2}$ pounds of sugar, 8 pounds of flour, 4 ounces of tea, 1 stick of tobacco, plus a daily issue of $\frac{3}{4}$ pound of meat in "approved" cases. In 1930 the distribution of meat was discontinued. Unemployed aborigines who before the depression earned award rates were also put on the "aboriginal" ration, although they were entitled to the "white" sustenance, worth about 70 cents per week (the "aboriginal" ration was worth about 22 cents weekly). Living conditions on reserves were wretched.

[When a humpy becomes too insanitary,] even beating the sense of decency and comfort of its native occupants, they will move it a yard or two away to a new position, but will not think of cleaning up the old site; so the bones, rags, excreta, and filth remain to carry on the good work of providing more fleas, germs and disease. What cooking is there, is done on small open fires. The utensils are strictly limited and often unwashed. . . Meat is thrown on the ashes and eaten far too raw. Clothing is seldom washed — how can it be when there are no facilities for doing so or even vessels in which to carry sufficient water into the dwelling? The human body goes unwashed because there are no baths and often little water, though a swim now and again, in some not too distant waterhole helps a little.[70]

What of the frame of mind of these people? Early in 1936 Paul Hasluck, a young journalist on the literary staff of the *West Australian,* interviewed scores of southwest aborigines; he found most of the older folk resigned, and the young generation sullen, resentful, and hostile. Only here and there would be met a more intelligent man who would discuss things more fully. One such man told him:

"Of course, a lot of these young fellows won't work more than they need to and a lot of them won't try to build better humpies for themselves. What's the use if they do? You work hard but you can never get anywhere. You try to improve your place but you still can't get any of the privileges that white people get." He was asked about these "privileges". He said that the State schools would not take their children, that even if they had money the local picture show would not let them in, and that they could not go into places (meaning the hotels) where white men could go. In-

cidentally, this ambition to "breast the bar" seems to be a gnawing sore
with some of them. It does not seem that they want to have a drink of
beer so much as to show that they are as good as the white man.[71]

The administration met this challenge in a determined spirit; it
can be summed up in the phrase "they must be helped in spite of
themselves". The part-aborigines, said Neville in 1934, are "fast
becoming an outcast race, increasing in numbers and decreasing in
stamina, unemployed and largely unemployable".[72] Obviously, one
settlement was insufficient to cope with the problem. As early as
1927 Neville proposed the establishment somewhere in the Kimberleys of a Home For Criminally Minded Natives (partly to alleviate
overcrowding at Moore River, and partly to separate the more law-
abiding inmates from those whom Harris and his friends had described as the northern "cut-throats"), but nothing was done. Later
in the year Neville appealed for the reopening of Carrolup but it
was not until 1930 that the cabinet, concerned at the rapidly rising
costs of rationing along the Great Southern, authorized the reposses-
sion of the property which had been leased to private interests in
1922. The decision caused apprehension among the owners of
surrounding properties who feared that the reopening of the settlement would depress land values in the district. In October 1930
a deputation from the Road Boards Association of Western Australia
asked the Chief Secretary to abandon the scheme in favour of "district depots" in selected localities where aboriginal indigents could
be kept under constant supervision by local police. On the advice
of the Narrogin district police officer the cabinet reaffirmed its
decision. Before the property could be repossessed, however, several
Ministers had second thoughts about "the expenditure of public
funds while our people are in need of accommodation",[73] and the
scheme was quietly abandoned. So the department continued to
depend on Moore River, overcrowded, understaffed, and without
proper facilities. In January 1933 eighty-one aborigines — the entire
population of the Northam aboriginal camp — were dumped in the
settlement by the police, with what results can be easily imagined.
The pretext put forward by the Northam municipal council was that
the aborigines were a health risk (they were said to be suffering from
scabies), but only four of the eighty-one deportees were found to be
so infected on arrival in Moore River. The group was detained for
six months, when all except a few were released on condition that
they would never return to Northam.

The ambivalent attitudes displayed by some local authorities while the reopening of Carrolup was under discussion are worth noting. On one hand, they insisted that aborigines should be kept out of towns; on the other hand they opposed their removal from their districts lest they should lose a cheap source of casual labour.

An ideal reserve [said Paul Hasluck] has to be near enough to town to allow natives to call for rations when they are "indigent" and to come under at least occasional surveillance by the police and local protectors, and yet it has to be far enough from white habitations to avoid complaints and to discourage unwelcome visits to the camps by white men.[74]

The distance of the reserve from towns ensured that most parents would not even attempt to send their children to school; those who did were thwarted in other ways. In 1928 an amendment of the Education Act reiterated the right of the Minister of Education to expel from state schools any child "whose presence is injurious to the health, welfare and morality of other children"; subsequent regulations empowered teachers to suspend a pupil temporarily either on their own initiative, or if objections were raised by parents of other children. Suspensions had to be approved by the Education Department, but this was largely a formality. In practice, a single parent could secure the expulsion of aboriginal pupils (as in Narembeen); if several parents objected, expulsion followed more or less automatically. Occasionally, parents would agree to the presence of aboriginal children if the number of white children did not warrant the establishment of a school in the area. When the number reached the required minimum, aboriginal children were often sent home (as in Mawson). The Aborigines Department, while aware of this state of affairs, was in no position to intervene; in 1930, when the Women's Section of the Primary Producers' Association proposed that expulsion should be approved only where it had been requested by the majority of parents in writing, Neville told them that it was better not to press the issue. However, the 1933 general election brought some change. In June 1933 the new Labour Premier, J. C. Willcock, ordered the readmission of several Wagin children who had been suspended by the district inspector of education, and in the following month the Director of Education issued a directive to all headmasters not to suspend aboriginal pupils without prior approval from his department. The instruction appears to have had little permanent effect: early in 1934 the headmaster of the Watheroo school suspended several children because they lived "in

tents without home comforts",[75] and later in the year three boys at
Shark Bay were sent home because of indecent language. Even
quadroons and octaroons were not protected from the white parents'
indignation. In 1933 an English nurse known to most Western
Australians as Sister Kate established a home for quarter-caste
children at Buckland Hill, whence it was later moved to Queen's
Park, another Perth suburb. The Children's Cottage Home was an
outstanding institution by the standards of the day; it was subsidized by the Aborigines Department and the Lotteries Commission,
and was free from "institutional" atmosphere. During the day the
children went to the local state school. Some were lighter in colour
than the children of most Greek and Italian migrants who also
attended the school, but this did not prevent the Queen's Park
Parents' and Citizens' Association from insisting on a separate
classroom for the children from the home. On this occasion, however, the Education Department showed more determination and
the agitation eventually died down.

A Murchison family, 1898 (*Battye Library, Perth*)

On the verandah of one of Broome's pubs, ca.1900 (*National Library of Australia*)

Prisoners from the Broome Gaol, ca.1900 (*National Library of Australia*)

Waiting for Christmas dinner at a northwest station, ca.1900 (*National Library of Australia*)

Women employed at a northwest station, undated (*Battye Library, Perth*)

Prisoners in the Perth Gaol, undated (*National Library of Australia*)

Returning from patrol somewhere in the Kimberleys, ca.1905 (*Battye Library, Perth*)

A group of women at the Carrolup aboriginal settlement, 1916 (*Battye Library, Perth. A. O. Neville photograph*)

Carrolup schoolchildren in front of the settlement school, 1916 (*Battye Library, Perth. A. O. A. O. Neville photograph*)

Carrolup aboriginal settlement: dormitory and "dining room", 1916 (*Battye Library, Perth. A. O. Neville photograph*)

"The Aborigines present a collection of their weapons to General Pau, Head of the French Mission", 1918 (*National Library of Australia*)

The aboriginal camp near Lake Monger at Wembley, a Perth suburb, 1923 (*Battye Library, Perth*)

Integration in a northwest station shearing-shed, ca.1935 (*National Library of Australia. Frank Hurley photograph*)

Little Louise and two goannas, ca.1960 (*Sun-Herald, John Fairfax and Sons Limited*)

8. The Department Gets Tough 1936-1940

The Moseley Royal Commission

The report of the Moseley Royal Commission,[1] presented in January 1935, was a remarkably pragmatic document: it dealt only with matters requiring "immediate attention", leaving the larger issues shelved. Moseley's findings fall under the following broad headings: allegations of maltreatment of aborigines which had appeared in the press since 1930, general administration of the Aborigines Department, social and economic conditions of aborigines and part-aborigines, and laws relating to aborigines and persons of aboriginal origin. Moseley dismissed as unfounded all allegations of maltreatment of aborigines he had investigated, although he was careful to add that he was not "so foolish as to suggest that isolated cases of cruelty to natives do not exist". As regards departmental administration, Moseley found serious deficiencies in the current system of governing aborigines "by one officer having his headquarters in Perth", assisted either by overworked policemen or by honorary protectors who, beyond signing a few employment permits, "have nothing to do with aborigines". His recommended solution was the appointment of what he called divisional protectors (three for a start) — permanent officials who would devote the whole of their time to aborigines in their districts and would be responsible to the Minister alone. This would be followed by the reduction in the number of honorary protectors and the eventual abolition of police protectors: "when called upon to take police action against a native, a constable cannot satisfactorily at the same time act as his Protector." As regards health, Moseley criticized the high aboriginal mortality rate throughout the state, and especially in the Kimberleys, as well as the absence of proper hospital facilities, listing the following as the minimum requirements: aboriginal hospitals at Wyndham, Broome, Roebourne, and Onslow, a clinic at Moola Bulla, a leprosarium at Derby, accommodation for medical and surgical treatment of aborigines at all hospitals in districts where aborigines can be found in numbers, complete examination of all northern aborigines for leprosy and venereal disease, and the establishment of a Natives' Medical Fund to which employers of aboriginal labour should contribute. As regards employment, the report contented itself with such minor suggestions as the formal identification of aborigines in general employment permits and the already mentioned establishment of a medical fund, similar to that in existence in the Northern Territory, with contributions from employers as a condition of employment. Other recommendations with a potential bearing on the pastoral industry concerned the gazetting of additional aboriginal reserves in the Kimberleys, north of the Leopold Range, and the proclamation of all existing reserves as permanent reserves for the exclusive use of aborigines, their purpose not to be altered except by an act of parliament.

As regards part-aborigines, Moseley was fairly optimistic: since they were found mainly in the southwest, the "task of caring for them and training them" was largely a matter of finance and sound administration. At the present time, said the Commissioner, "apart from the work done by a few missionaries, the care of the half-caste child is hopelessly inefficient. It is pathetic to see these children, in many cases so fair in complexion as to be scarcely distinguishable from white children, living in a hut worse by far than the kennel some people would provide for their dogs — whole families of 9 or 10 being huddled together in abject squalor..." Moseley saw the solution in the abolition of aboriginal camps and the establishment of additional settlements: "There is duty on the community to see that half-castes are placed in surroundings and given a training which will fit them later to take their place, if necessary, in a white civilization." The Commissioner, it should be stressed, perceived the cruelty of past attempts to remove part-aboriginal children from the parents' custody: "... there is beyond doubt in the native woman a great love for her child, whether that child's father be black or white." But he also realized that, given the state of public opinion, it would be unrealistic to expect any improvement in the situation, particularly as regards education, if they continued to live in the squalor of aboriginal camps: hence the suggestion that whole families should be sent to settlements. There was to be no more "splitting of generations"; instead, uplift would come through removal, by force if need be, to "surroundings better than those of the native camps".

The last broad group of recommendations pertained to laws relating to aborigines and part-aborigines. Here Moseley made the following proposals: the definition of an aborigine was to be broadened to include "persons of aboriginal origin in a remote degree"; the Minister (not the Chief Protector!) was to become the legal guardian of all part-aboriginal children up to the age of sixteen, with provisions for an extension of the age to twenty-one in certain cases; the minimum penalty for cohabitation was to be increased to six months' imprisonment; and finally, aborigines not exempted from the act were to be prevented not only from obtaining liquor but also from remaining on, or loitering about, licensed premises. All these were minor changes. The only real innovation was the proposal to establish Native Courts to deal with offences arising out of aboriginal custom, including capital offences. Noting, with a certain amount of understatement, that European laws "would seem to operate unfairly" against tribal aborigines, and that the whole procedure, "from the moment of arrest, seems inappropriate", Moseley suggested trial by tribunals which will "enable the native to understand what is going on and the proceedings of which can be listened to and understood by others of the tribe", the penalty to consist of corporal punishment or, for more serious offences, banishment. He did not think that the question of tribal custom as a defence was an important consideration, one way or another.

Some of Moseley's recommendations were implemented almost immediately. In June 1935 cabinet appointed Dr A. P. Davis, a specialist in tropical diseases and for many years district medical officer at Port Hedland, as travelling medical inspector, and approved the establishment of aboriginal hospitals at Broome and Wyndham and the construction of a leprosarium on the outskirts of Derby. Other proposals, notably the appointment of divisional protectors to be responsible directly to the Minister rather than the Chief Protector, and the phasing out of police as protectors, were shelved because of Neville's opposition. Many others were incorporated in an amending bill which the government introduced in September 1936. In spite of its stormy passage (and the 95,000 words or so it took to pass it), the fate of the bill had never been really in doubt, for there was general agreement that reform was long overdue and that the department had to have "requisite legislative authority"[2] if it were to discharge its functions properly.

The 1936 Native Administration Act and subsequent regulations

The 1936 Native Administration Act gave the Department of Native
Affairs unprecedented powers over the daily lives of Western Australian aborigines; in the words of Paul Hasluck, it confined them
within a "legal status that has more in common with that of a born
idiot than any other class of British subject".[3] More constructively,
it could be said that the legislation tried to achieve the right thing in
the wrong way. It attempted to give a greater measure of protection
and care to the full-bloods, and largely succeeded in its aim. At the
same time, by granting the administration greater powers over all
"natives" and by extending the definition of a "native" to practically
all part-aborigines, it made real "uplift" impossible; as a part-aborigine said about similar legislation in Queensland, "the law makes
it easy for the whites to control us, but it makes it harder for us to
live".[4] Among the least objectionable provisions of the act were the
establishment of a Natives' Medical Fund, the extension of employment permits to contract work, and the introduction of the right
of appeal by persons aggrieved by the refusal of a protector to grant
them a permit to employ aborigines or by his cancellation of such
a permit. Trial by jury in proceedings against whites charged with
assaulting an aborigine was abolished, and members of the police
force, in their capacity as protectors of aborigines, were disqualified
from accepting an aborigine's plea of guilty in any trial where they
were connected with the prosecution. Criminal offences by aborigines
against aborigines were relegated to Courts of Native Affairs which
were empowered to take into account, in mitigation of punishment,
any tribal custom proved as the reason for the commission of the
offence. Other provisions of the act were more controversial. The
legal guardianship rights of the Commissioner of Native Affairs
were enlarged to cover all aboriginal minors up to the age of twenty-
one. Cohabitation between white men and women of the half-blood,
as well as between aboriginal men and white women was made a
punishable offence, and the term was broadened to include casual
sexual intercourse. The power of the Commissioner of Native Affairs
to object to the celebration of a marriage between white men and
full-blood women was extended to all marriages involving one or
two aborigines at law, and the grounds on which consent could be
withheld were considerably widened; for instance, he could now
object to a marriage if it contravened tribal custom, if one of the

parties was afflicted with a communicable or hereditary disease, or if there were "any other circumstances" which rendered it advisable that the marriage should not take place. The most controversial provision, however, was the broadening of the definition of a "native" to include all part-aborigines except the following: quadroons under twenty-one who neither associated with nor lived substantially after the manner of the full-bloods, unless ordered by a magistrate to be classed as natives; all quadroons over twenty-one unless classed as natives by a magisterial order; and persons of less than quadroon blood born before 31 January 1936. The new definition embraced practically all persons with an admixture of aboriginal blood, bringing many assimilated and partly assimilated part-aborigines under the Native Administration Act. Finally, the act sanctioned a new denotation of the term "native": the full-bloods and part-aborigines under the act became known as natives, the Aborigines Department became the Department of Native Affairs, and the title of the Chief Protector of Aborigines was changed to that of Commissioner of Native Affairs. "To be called an aboriginal", said Neville at whose insistence the new name had been introduced, "is repugnant to most of the coloured folk who prefer to be known as the people of the soil — the native people. The half-caste is abhorrent to the true aboriginal who calls him a 'yellow-fellow' . . . But the word native has no derogatory implications whatever, it suits all and is literally correct."[5]

Section 68 of the 1936 Native Administration Act empowered the Governor to issue regulations to further implement the provisions of the act. To have the force of law, such regulations had to be gazetted and laid before parliament within fourteen days, if in session, or within fourteen days after the commencement of session. The first regulations under s.68, laying down the procedure for the Courts of Native Affairs, were gazetted in March 1937; they dealt with highly technical matters and escaped the scrutiny of parliament. In July the government gazetted further regulations, pertaining to the Natives' Medical Fund, and requiring employers of aboriginal labour to contribute $2 annually with respect to every aborigine permanently employed ($1 with respect to "trainees" and 50 cents in the case of casual employees). At the same time, the Western Australian branch of the British Medical Association agreed to lower doctors' fees with respect to aborigines covered by the fund (to 50 cents for the initial visit and to 25 cents for all subsequent visits),

and the Medical Department reduced hospital charges for the
members of the fund, to 50 cents a day. Although the scheme had
much to recommend it, late in August the member for north province, J. J. Holmes, warned the administration that if the regulations
were enforced the pastoralists would have to dismiss all aborigines
who were not full-time employees.[6] Early in September the Pastoralists' Association asked the Chief Secretary to withdraw the regulations, and soon afterwards the member for Kimberley, A. A. M.
Coverley, moved in parliament that the regulations be disallowed.[7]
Although the motion was carried, the department, after a conference
with representatives of employers of aboriginal labour, decided to
continue the fund on a voluntary basis, the maximum annual contribution from individual employers being limited to $100 irrespective
of the number of aborigines employed. This concession seems to have
made the fund more acceptable to the pastoralists, most of whom
decided to remain in the scheme.

In April 1938 the government gazetted 156 additional regulations
covering all aspects of aboriginal administration. Some fifty-odd
regulations pertained to aboriginal employment, prohibiting such
practices as the "lending" of workers by one employer to another
who did not possess a permit to employ aborigines, the employment
of aboriginal women on pastoral stations where there were no white
women, and the employment of married aboriginal women anywhere
apart from their husbands. Other regulations defined more closely
the increased powers of the Commissioner of Native Affairs in such
matters as aboriginal marriages, guardianship of aboriginal children
and adolescents, aboriginal trust funds, probate matters, and exemptions. Another group of regulations related to the administration of aboriginal institutions, giving their superintendents considerable disciplinary powers, such as the right of summary punishment
of inmates for a host of minor breaches of discipline, as well as the
right of censoring all in- and outgoing mail. The regulations also
stipulated that in the future prior approval of the Minister in charge
of the Department of Native Affairs would be required before the
establishment of a Christian mission anywhere in the state, and
that all mission workers would have to obtain a licence from the
department before taking up their duties. Finally, the regulations
provided that only those missions which had complied with departmental instructions regarding the education, diet, hygiene, and housing of their inmates would be subsidized by the government.

Not all of these regulations were new; some had been in force since 1916, and several went back to 1909 and even 1906. Of the new regulations, some had been taken from the Child Welfare Department regulations, others from the regulations under the Queensland Aborigines Protection Act, while the regulation relating to the estates of deceased aborigines was drawn up after consultation with A. P. Elkin. Most of the powers conferred by the regulations had been foreshadowed by the 1936 Native Administration Act; in this sense, the regulations simply elaborated the provisions of the act. The licensing of missionaries, which turned out to be the most controversial aspect of the regulations, was not a new idea. It was first mooted in 1924 by the then Minister for the North-West, J. M. Drew, and was brought up again by Neville in 1928, 1932, and 1935. Except for a single sentence hidden among the other provisions of s.68, empowering the Governor to issue regulations "for the establishment of mission stations and the issue of permits to mission workers", the 1936 Native Administration Act made no other mention of missions, and the legislature apparently failed to realize the implications of that sentence when it passed the act. But the introduction, by means of subordinate legislation, of such a controversial measure as the licensing of missionaries, was bound to lead to criticism. On 13 May 1938 two members of the Australian Aborigines' Amelioration Association, Rev. C. S. Hardy and R. Powell, addressed the general assembly of the Presbyterian Church, urging a firm stand against the proposed licensing of missionaries; "the liberties of the Christian Church", said the latter, "must not be subject to a Hitler — a dictator."[8] The meeting passed a resolution calling for the convening of a conference between the representatives of the churches and the administration, but the department did not as much as acknowledge the request. Subsequently, the association embarked on personal attacks on Neville, accusing him of indifference to the welfare of his charges, callousness, and moral laxity. "It would be perfectly unfair to paint the Commissioner as a monster of iniquity, devoid of any compassion and bent only upon the ill-treatment of the whole native race", said the association in its 1938 annual report, adding that "there was something wrong somewhere, and that the Commissioner's good deeds or good intentions constitute no excuse for his less praiseworthy attitude towards the natives or for his hostile manner towards those who have ventured to differ from him".[9] Late in June the Roman Catholic Church joined the ranks of the critics; the proposed licensing of missionaries, said the *Record,* was contrary to the teaching of the Church which "claims a Divine mandate to go spread the gospel to every living creature".[10] Criticism from other quarters was not long in coming. "When man-made laws come into conflict with what we conceive to be our duty to God and our fellow-men", said the *United Aborigines Messenger,* "we can do no other than to declare with the apostles 'we must obey God rather than man.' "[11] Towards the end of August the National Missionary Council, in a published statement, conceded the right of the department to exercise a measure of supervision over the work of the missions, only to claim that the powers conferred by the regulations were excessive and that they should be exercised only after consultation with the denominational authority concerned.[12] But the most severe criticism came from the Association for the Protection of Native Races which, in a submission to the Premier, accused the government of suppressing the freedom of religion guaranteed by the federal constitution; the regulations relating to licensing of missionaries were null and void by virtue of s.109 of the constitution providing that where a state law was inconsistent with that of the Commonwealth, the latter should prevail.[13]

The reaction of the missions and churches must have taken the department by surprise, for it decided not to enforce the regulations for the time being. Later in September, at a conference with the representatives of missions and churches, the department agreed to several minor changes in the regulations, such as the substitution of "permit" for "licence", and the establishment of a Board of Reference, consisting of the Commissioner or his deputy and the nominees of the Church of England, the Roman Catholic Church, the Presbyterian Church, and the non-denominational churches, to hear appeals in the case of a permit being refused. The amended regulations were gazetted on 1 November and tabled on the same day in parliament, where they were almost immediately attacked by both government and opposition members. On 14 November the Labour member for Murchison, W. M. Marshall, was reported by the *West Australian* as having described the regulations as "childish, frivolous and inhuman". Two days later five members — three of them Labour — moved in the Legislative Assembly that some or all the regulations be disallowed, and on 22 November the regulations were attacked in the Legislative Council by H. Seddon, the member for the north-east province. Although Seddon had moved for the disallowance of only certain regulations, his speech was a general indictment of the Department of Native Affairs and its permanent head. "I think, after having perused them", said the member for the northeast province, "that all of them might well be revised . . . Personally I consider that the whole of the regulations might be disallowed."[14] Following Seddon's speech, the member for the south province, J. Cornell, moved for the disallowance of all regulations, but the debate was adjourned on the motion of W. H. Kitson, Chief Secretary and Minister in charge of the Aborigines Department (later Department of Native Affairs) since August 1936. His violent attack on Christian missions, delivered the following afternoon,[15] was clearly an attempt to split the ranks of the "anti-department" coalition; by concentrating all criticism on one partner, he hoped to drive a wedge between the missions and other critics of aboriginal administration, notably the pastoral lobby. The Chief Secretary started by defending his action as having been forced on him by the anti-government propaganda of certain missions and churches; for some years past, he said, "we have remained silent in spite of the unwarranted criticism of a large number of people both in the State and out of the State, when, to have replied to that criticism, would have disclosed matters that the department did not desire to make public in the interests of the persons concerned". Warming to his theme, Kitson went on to say that most missions had been established on unsuitable sites and did little to uplift their inmates; he also criticized some missionaries for their "lack of fitness for their work and knowledge of the natives" and for "lacking in training in almost every walk of life". The government had in the past painstakingly refrained from interfering with the spiritual nature of missionary undertakings, and had no desire to do so in the future, but it had a duty to ensure that the job was done efficiently and by those best qualified to do it. Presumably to emphasize the last point, the Chief Secretary proceeded to bring to light a number of relatively recent incidents concerning mission staff. At one mission, a boy was allegedly thrashed for a minor breach of discipline until he fell to the ground and was then kicked by the missionary in charge, who had boots on. At the same mission, a man was flogged for a breach of marital relations and chained by the neck to a post; his wife ran away but was brought back and publicly thrashed in front of her husband and the assembled inmates. At the same mission, men had been chained by the neck to a post, and women had been chained for minor offences. Parties had

brought liquor to the mission and consumed it, the missionary
joining in. At another mission, according to a police report based on
statements of the inmates, the superintendent had misconducted
himself on several occasions with a female inmate. Serious irregularities had been reported from yet another mission, such as homosexual
practices between a male missionary and missionary boys, immorality between a male member of the staff and aboriginal women and
girls, liquor being supplied to female inmates by a missionary, and
drinking and fighting between members of the staff. The Chief
Secretary further referred to a case where a mission superintendent
had stripped the clothing from a young half-caste girl, cut off her
hair, and sent her in that condition to live with bush aborigines, as
a punishment for having run away with an aborigine. Next, he
mentioned the shooting of an inmate by a missionary. The incident
occurred when the mission staff attempted to chain another inmate
for a minor breach of discipline. When he escaped, others took
advantage of the situation and ran away, and one of them was shot.
The missionary was subsequently prosecuted for manslaughter but
was acquitted, the principal witness (also a missionary) having committed suicide before the trial. The accused continued in the employ
of the mission, though undoubtedly he shot the aborigine. The
department, concluded the Chief Secretary, had never publicly
criticized the missions; on the contrary it had sought to hide their
imperfections. The policy in the past had been to allow the churches
to work out such matters for themselves, but this had obviously
failed. "If the missions are to work in co-operation with the department and if they are to receive increased financial support from the
Government, it is imperative, in my view, to exercise more control
over their activities."

Kitson's speech, as suggested earlier, was an attempt to split the
opposition by attacking one partner of the coalition, the missionaries.
His main target was the United Aborigines' Mission, since, as he
put it, "the whole opposition to the regulations arises from the one
source".[16] Kitson's attack on the U.A.M. was thus understandable,
but the ammunition which he used had been supplied by other
missions — some of the most serious incidents referred to in his
speech had in fact occurred at Forrest River. Kitson's speech,
naturally enough, precipitated a great furore. On 24 November a
group of leading churchmen, in a rebuttal published by the *Daily
News,* protested in the strongest terms against the "mud-slinging"

tactics of the administration. On 29 November the Legislative Council passed a motion calling for the appointment of a Royal Commission to report on the relationship between the Department of Native Affairs and Christian missions, and to inquire into the allegations made by the Chief Secretary and the member for the northeast province; just before Christmas, when it became clear that the administration was not prepared to consider the appointment of a Royal Commission, parliament disallowed most of the regulations. To break the impasse, the department suggested the convening of yet another conference, which would include representatives of women's organizations and other bodies interested in aboriginal welfare, to discuss the objectionable features of the regulations. The conference, held in February 1939, broke up in an uproar following the refusal of the administration to withdraw the charges or, alternatively, to agree to the appointment of a Royal Commission.

After years of apathy about natives in Australia [commented the *West Australian* on the premature ending of the conference] it is good to see a number of people getting excited about the matter. The doubt is whether they got excited about the conditions of the natives or about their own personal feelings.[17]

The conference, however, was not altogether wasted. Early in March the organizations which had taken part in the proceedings formed the Native Welfare Council of Western Australia which subsequently circularized the candidates at the March 1939 general election, asking them to support an amendment of the Native Administration Act to implement all recommendations of the Moseley Royal Commission. Since the aborigines were not an election issue, the circular had little effect, and the government was safely returned. Following a reorganization of the cabinet, the department became the responsibility of the new Minister for the North-West, A. A. M. Coverley, who had held the Kimberley seat since 1924. Coverley was a man of strong opinions, and was not afraid to speak his mind. In 1927, as we have seen, he criticized in parliament the "stupid system of protecting the aborigines to the detriment of the settlers as a whole";[18] two years later he led the opposition to the bill to amend the 1905 Aborigines Act and was largely instrumental in its defeat; in 1932 he was responsible for the deletion from the Land Act of a clause giving the aborigines the right to enter the unenclosed and otherwise unimproved parts of all pastoral leases to seek their sustenance in their accustomed manner;[19] in 1937 he led the attack

on the Natives' Medical Fund, and in the following year he took
a prominent part in the manoeuvres which led to the disallowance
of the 1938 regulations. The appointment of Coverley was, in fact,
little short of a sell-out by the administration to the pastoralists.
In September 1939, after the regulations had been regazetted with
a few minor alterations, four members moved that they be disallowed,
but events took a different turn on this occasion. One motion was
defeated in the Legislative Council on 28 September, while another
was withdrawn on 16 November after Coverley had assured the
Pastoralists' Association that the powers conferred by the regulations
would not be exercised in the pastoral regions except in special circumstances. The remaining motions were defeated in the Legislative
Assembly on 23 November, following a statement by Coverley that
regulations which proved unworkable would be withdrawn. The
passing of the regulations, after a delay of almost twenty months,
was a victory for the administration, but the price it had to pay
may have been too high. It was forced to make several concessions
to the pastoral lobby and, by insisting on the retention of the provisions relating to the licensing of missionaries, it incurred the wrath
of the churches and the missions. With the passing of the infamous
regulations by parliament, announced the Australian Aborigines'
Amelioration Association, in a pamphlet published shortly after,

the question ceases to be a merely native question; it becomes a religious
question which affects the whole of the churches. The Minister, Mr.
Coverley, may think that he is acting according to his conscience, but he
must remember that "conscientious" devotion to the cause of secular
control in religious matters cannot be justified and that other people have
consciences . . . Not for 300 years has any Parliament in the British Empire
dared to bring in laws so drastic and far-reaching, attacking those cherished
principles of free and unfettered preaching of the gospel, which we consider
to be our inalienable right—bestowed upon us by God.[20]

The department

If the powers with which the department finally emerged from the
tussle with parliament and the humanitarian and pastoral lobby were
not quite what it had hoped for, it had little ground for complaint
in the matter of finance. In 1933–1934 Western Australia spent only
$56,680 on its 19,021 estimated aborigines (excluding those "beyond
the confines of civilization") — slightly more than one-half of what
New South Wales spent on half that number, and only a little more
than South Australia expended on its 3,407 aborigines. Four years

later the government gave the department $102,038, and in 1939–1940, $135,550. Much of this increase was swallowed by expenditure on relief ($38,738 in 1939–1940) and by the mounting cost of running aboriginal settlements. Some of the funds were channelled into capital works, and the remainder was used to pay the salaries and wages of the permanent and temporary employees of the department (55 in 1938, not counting the 102 honorary protectors). The missions received very little ($3,776 in 1939–1940).

The expansion of departmental establishment which this financial bonanza made possible, however, did not occur along the lines envisaged by the Moseley Royal Commission. Moseley suggested the initial appointment of three divisional protectors, so as to decentralize aboriginal administration and to lessen the dependence of the department on honorary protectors and the police. Neville's public reaction to the proposal was to label it impracticable: it would "impose altogether too great a strain upon the Minister in charge. It would involve three separate clerical staffs, offices and accounting systems... There might even be three contending policies, thus rendering it impossible for the Minister to co-ordinate the whole matter..."[21] — the real reason for his opposition was that the reforms would have reduced the position of the Commissioner to that of a departmental secretary. Instead, Neville revived the system of inspectorship, by appointing the manager of Moola Bulla, A. T. Woodland, as travelling inspector for the northern districts; he also spoke of making another appointment for the southern half of the state, but this had to wait until July 1943. More importantly, nothing was done to reduce the number of honorary protectors and to abolish the police protectors ("if the present system is to be continued", said Moseley, "then this report may I think be regarded as valueless...").[22] Indeed, the department was gradually moving in the opposite direction. In May 1940 existing police districts were proclaimed "native districts" for the purpose of the Native Administration Act, and thirty-six additional police officers were appointed as protectors. As a result, the department became for all practical purposes an appendage of the Police Department. This emerges clearly from the account of an incident which occurred in West Kimberley. Early in 1940 a young constable knocked down an aborigine before the eyes of some twenty employees of the Freeney Oil Company and then kicked him until he lost consciousness. A departmental investigation disclosed that the aborigine had not provoked the constable in any way and had offered no resistance whatsoever during the assault. Bray, who had just replaced Neville as Commissioner, instructed the travelling inspector, C. L. McBeath, to lay charges against the constable. The inspector (a former policeman himself) procrastinated; first he suggested that the police ought to prefer the charges since they were "generally thought and recognized to be the proper authorities who should prosecute offences against the various acts", and later counselled Bray to drop the case because of its likely effect on the "administration of the act". After consulting the Solicitor-General, who reassured him that there was a *prima facie* case against the constable, Bray formally instructed the inspector to prefer the charges. Soon after a somewhat distraught field superintendent of the Freeney Oil Company called on Bray to complain that the inspector of police in Broome had questioned the veracity of his evidence. He had been told that four years in the north were not "sufficient experience" and that he must have been mistaken when he testified that there was no provocation on the part of the aborigine. The police, he was told, would be quite happy to accept evidence to that effect from any employee of the company prepared to testify. The charges were eventually heard in Derby before the resident magistrate and a local justice of the peace. The magistrate described the constable as a "decent type" who had committed the offence largely through "lack of experience in the north", and bound him over to be of good behaviour for six months.[23]

The pastoral north

The rapprochement between the department and the pastoralists, sealed by the appointment of A. A. M. Coverley as Minister for the North-West, was precipitated by several factors. One was Neville's impending retirement. For about eighteen months before relinquishing office, in March 1940, Neville had not been in the best of health, and delegated much of his work to F. I. Bray, his deputy. Bray joined the public service in 1896, as John Forrest's personal messenger, became clerk-in-charge of records in the Chief Secretary's Department in 1923, was promoted to ministerial clerk soon after, and became Deputy Commissioner of Native Affairs in 1937. Bray was a public servant personified, thorough if somewhat pedestrian, and anything but forceful. In Neville's time the permanent head tended to dominate the Minister; under his successor the reverse was to be the case.

A second reason for the rapprochment between the department and the pastoralists was the concern they shared on the preservation of the full-blood as an economic asset. In 1930 there were 5,855 aborigines in pastoral employment; by 1939 the number had decreased to 3,190, and not because there were not enough jobs to go around (in 1937 the Pastoralists' Association came out publicly against the policy of white Australia and for the introduction of limited quotas of coloured labour from the Empire). In the past most pastoralists thought that the problem was one for the government alone to tackle, but now many had become aware of their obligations towards their aboriginal workers and of the role they could play in a more progressive aboriginal administration in the pastoral regions. For this reason the majority welcomed the new act and regulations, if only because they spelled out in detail their obligations towards their aboriginal employees. By the time the Royal Commission on the Pastoral Industry presented its report, in 1940, all major areas of conflict between the pastoralists and the department had been resolved, including the question of rationing indigents on pastoral properties. The pastoralists agreed to look after all destitute aborigines on their stations; as a *quid pro quo* the administration pegged wages in the pastoral industry and instructed protectors to "discourage" aboriginal station hands from leaving pastoral employment for other occupations.

The long-range results of this alliance, as will be shown in chapter nine, were an unmitigated disaster, but the short-term results were not unimpressive. With more than two-thirds of employers of native labour contributing to the Natives' Medical Fund, most aboriginal workers were assured of minimum medical and hospital attention and maintenance if injured on the job (employees not covered by the fund were still entitled to free treatment under the Native Administration Act, and, at least on paper, to workers' compensation). Hospital facilities were improved: in 1937 the department opened two new hospitals for aborigines, at Broome and Wyndham, and clinics at Moola Bulla and Munja. In 1938 an aboriginal ward was added to the Port Hedland general hospital, with financial assistance from the Lotteries Commission. In 1939 the federal government seconded Dr L. A. Musso to assist with the medical inspection of aborigines, though after the resignation of Dr A. P. Davis, in February 1941, the former had to carry on the work alone. Earlier, the Commonwealth had contributed $10,000 toward the capital cost of the Derby leprosarium, opened in 1937 and staffed by the sisters of the order of Saint John of God, under the control of the Medical Department. The eradication of leprosy, unfortunately, turned out to be more than a question of money. "Some natives", complained Neville in 1938, "having been brought in, have decamped only to be recovered more than once until complete cure has resulted."[24] Many others, upon discovering themselves to be afflicted, did not wait to be brought in. Even more disquieting was the reappearance of the disease in the northwest. In 1936 several cases were reported from Mount Vernon, and in 1940 one case was reported from as far south as Mullewa. In 1941 the Native Administration Act was amended to prohibit the movement of aborigines south of the 20th parallel which became known as the "leper line". The Minister was given the right to issue temporary permits allowing movement across the line for the purpose of droving stock, and for specialist medical attention and legal action.

The concern with the preservation of the full-blood as an economic asset had some unexpected results in the legal field. The appointment of Courts of Native Affairs and the recognition of aboriginal custom as a source of law (but not as a part of the law of the land) is a good case in point. The idea behind the experiment went back to the 1840s when Governor Hutt instructed his officials to ignore acts of violence committed by aborigines *inter se*. Governor Broome, in 1887, proposed the creation of a new criminal offence, "killing of an aboriginal native in pursuance of a native custom or superstition",[25] but nothing came of it. In 1899 a commission inquiring into the penal system of the colony questioned the wisdom of prosecuting for tribal murders: "It seems unjust that not only should an offender suffer punishment at the hands of his tribe, but that he should be punished a second time for the same offence by the white law."[26] This was also the opinion of white juries who, more often than not, acquitted the accused by bringing in a verdict of "murder in accordance with tribal custom".[27] The administration, on its part, wavered between its stated policy of prosecuting for tribal murders whenever they had been brought to light, and the expedient of allowing the aborigines to settle their disputes in their own way. Neville, at least during the twenties, supported the hard line, whereas most senior police officers tended to intervene only if an aborigine appealed for the protection of the law. The legal profession was also against strict application of criminal law to tribal murders. Mr. Justice Burnside, in a 1921 judgment, said: "I do not propose to pass a sentence of death on a native for doing what he has been doing almost since the time he has been on earth and what he will continue to do during the time he is on earth".[28] Two years later Mr. Justice Draper, in another judgment involving tribal murder, called for legislation which would recognize tribal custom as defence in criminal proceedings. The suggestion, as we have seen, was taken up by the Moseley Royal Commission and implemented by the 1936 Native Administration Act. The legislation empowered the Governor to appoint Courts of Native Affairs to hear all cases involving criminal offences committed by aborigines against aborigines. The courts were to consist of a magistrate and a nominee of the Commissioner of Native Affairs and were empowered to impose sentences of up to ten year's hard labour. Subsequent regulations laid down the following: a separate court must be appointed in every magisterial district, the trial must be held in the presence of the accused, the procedure should be as nearly as practicable the same as in proceedings before justices, and the court may seek the assistance of the head-man (*sic*) to ascertain tribal aspects, if any, of the case. This was a considerable improvement on past practice. The recognition of tribal custom as a source of law implied greater respect for aboriginal values. The stipulation that the court must be held in the district in which the offence had been committed reduced the cost of transporting the accused to Perth or, alternatively, of sending a Commissioner of the Supreme Court and a defence lawyer to remote parts of the state; it also ensured that the accused remained in his own country, with its benevolent and familiar spirits, instead of being removed to strange lands with spirits he did not know how to approach. Finally, the introduction of simple procedure did away with the formalism and legalism of the Supreme Court rules and enabled the accused and the witnesses to understand, at least to some extent, the real nature of the proceedings.[29]

Although the Courts of Native Affairs were intended to deal only with criminal offences involving tribal aspects, their scope was broadened as a result of the Dinah case. In 1941 a detribalized aborigine, A. R. Dinah, was committed for trial at the Perth criminal sessions for the murder of an aboriginal soldier, Maitland Warmaden. The prosecution refused to proceed with the case, however, on the grounds that it should have been dealt with by a Court of Native Affairs. Bray would not recommend the appointment of such a court, since there were no tribal aspects involved, and the Crown subsequently entered a *nolle prosequi* with respect to the Perth criminal sessions. This altered the whole concept of the Courts of Native Affairs and set a precedent for the appointment of such courts for the trial of offences by aborigines against aborigines irrespective of tribal considerations.

The appointment of Courts of Native Affairs was one aspect of the deliberate policy of preserving aboriginal groups *qua* aboriginal groups to which the 1936 Native Administration Act subscribed; the recognition of the importance of aboriginal marriage laws was another. The act gave the Commissioner of Native Affairs the right to prohibit aboriginal marriages which contravened tribal custom, thereby preventing certain missionaries from marrying aboriginal partners on the basis of "romantic" considerations alone. As applied by Neville, the provision meant two things: insistence on proper tribal relationships as far as the choice of partners was concerned, and obtaining the elders' consent before a marriage was celebrated. Although the act did not go so far as to recognize tribal marriages as legally valid, the 1938 regulations very nearly did: regulation 106 (drawn up after consultation with A. P. Elkin) stipulated that if a deceased aborigine was not married in accordance with the law of the land, his or her "estate" should be distributed to surviving relatives "in accordance with the social structure" of his or her tribe. The 1936 Native Administration Act also provided that an aboriginal wife should not be a compellable witness in proceedings before Courts of Native Affairs. This was later extended to normal Supreme Court proceedings. In 1937 the Crown used the evidence of tribal wives to secure the conviction of two aborigines for the murder of a European prospector. Three aborigines were implicated in the murder but the ringleader, Chunga, escaped. The other two were tried and sentenced to death but the sentences were commuted to ten years' hard labour, following protests from women's organizations. Chunga was eventually arrested in 1941. Since the case against him rested on the evidence of his tribal wife, the Minister for Justice, following new representations from women's organizations, instructed the prosecution to file a *nolle prosequi*. Since that time it has been the practice of the Supreme Court not to admit evidence of tribal wives unless they have agreed to testify voluntarily.[30]

Christian missions

Stripped of emotional verbiage, the conflict between the department and the missions which came to a head over the question of licensing of missionaries, boiled down to one fundamental issue.

These missionaries [said the Chief Secretary in 1938] virtually claim that they own the natives body and soul . . . We claim, however, that the natives are first and last a charge upon the State, whoever may subsequently be delegated more directly to handle them, and our duty is to ensure that the job is efficiently undertaken by those best qualified to do it.[31]

From the government's point of view the licensing of missionaries was not only justified but absolutely essential, to control locations of proposed missions and to ensure that they were not staffed by men and women who were either temperamentally unsuited or not properly trained for the task. The requirements that missions had to comply with departmental policy if they wanted to be subsidized was necessary because of the emphasis most missions placed on evangelizing, to the neglect of practical training of the aborigine. "They stress his inherent ability, and cite many individual cases to prove it. Let them do their best to develop such ability and remember that a Christian outlook . . . will not of itself fit the native for the life to which the missionaries say he is entitled".[32] The missions, of course, had grievances of their own: lack of financial support, obstacles being placed in their way when starting new stations, discrimination, real or imaginary, between the denominations, and the absence of clear and positive directives of what the government really expected of them.

The chief actors in this encounter were Neville and Schenk: his mission was the largest and the most active of all missionary societies. Both were headstrong and self-righteous men, and came to regard each other over the years with almost paranoid suspicion. In 1937, as we have seen, Schenk applied for a lease to start a mission at Wodjina, south of Port Hedland, but was flatly turned down — even though the government had been trying for decades to attract a mission to the northwest. In 1938 Schenk wanted to start a mission station somewhere between Mount Margaret and the Warburton Range, but was beaten to it by Neville: with a speed which would have been most commendable had it been applied in other directions, the department opened an institution of its own at Cosmo Newbery, about sixty miles northeast of Laverton, just to thwart Schenk's "imperialist" designs. In Kellerberrin, on the other hand, it was Schenk who got the better of Neville. Early in 1938 the Kellerberrin Ministers' Fraternal asked the Department of Education to build

a simple schoolroom on the local reserve, the Ministers' Fraternal
being prepared to find and pay a suitable teacher. When the school
was completed, the local member of parliament persuaded the Department of Education to staff the school. Soon after a missionary couple
from Mount Margaret arrived to look after the spiritual welfare
of the Kellerberrin aborigines, and another U.A.M. mission — the
sixth — was in existence. Neville raised immediate objections to
this "back-door attempt" to start a new mission without official
sanction,[33] but since the missionaries kept away from the aboriginal
reserve (unauthorized entry would have been an offence against the
Native Administration Act), he had to remain content with verbal
protests. The incident did little to improve relations between the
U.A.M. and the department. Late in 1939 an official party visiting
Mount Margaret was snubbed by the missionaries and the inmates,
in what Neville later described as an act of serious disloyalty to the
department. In January 1940 the department cancelled Schenk's
protectorship because of his "subversive propaganda" against the
government[34] and transferred to the police the distribution of government rations to the local indigents.

The Roelans Native Farm, opened in July 1938, was initially also
linked with the U.A.M. (the superintendent and his assistant came
from Mount Margaret). It was the brain-child of a Perth businessman, Albany Bell, the first president of the Native Welfare Council
of Western Australia. Early in 1938 Bell bought a 1,500 acre farm
near Collie, previously occupied by the Chander Boys' Scheme, and
converted it into a co-operative farm for aborigines of "superior
type". According to an elaborately drawn constitution, the farm
was to be administered by a council, responsible for the apportioning
of land. Each member was to be entitled to a reasonable share of
produce at cost price (to be determined by the council) and to a
share of profits, depending on the size of his allotment. Admirable
on paper, these arrangements apparently did not work in practice.
Bray, when he inspected the farm in October 1938, found the aborigines disgruntled and dispirited; they were paid $2 a week and had
to buy their groceries in the farm store. "You work for a dead horse
all the time", said one; another called the superintendent a "no
good nigger-driver".[35] The farm struggled on until 1941 when it
was turned into a home for quadroon children and given a subsidy
by the department.

After Neville's retirement, in March 1940, there occurred a temporary rapprochement between the government and the missions. "The Department believes in missions", said Neville's successor, F. I. Bray, "as it is vitally necessary to have spiritual and moral guidance in the native question, particularly for the half-castes."[36] Even while Neville was in office, there were signs that improved relations were round the corner. In 1939 Neville promised "greater support" for the Gnowangerup mission, and early in 1940, following a favourable report from the district inspector of schools, he made a similar promise to New Norcia. Bray was prepared to go further. In May 1940 the Native Welfare Council appealed to the government to do more for the education of aboriginal children; it should either provide schools of its own, or, if it was unable or unwilling to do so, it should subsidize missions and other welfare groups, at a rate half the cost of educating a white child in a country district (then about $24 per annum). The petition gave Bray an opportunity to air his views on aboriginal education in general. The provisions of the Native Administration Act notwithstanding, he advised Coverley, aboriginal education should become the responsibility of the Department of Education, since it was better equipped for the task; furthermore, it should not only have the right to exclude aboriginal pupils, as at present, but also the responsibility for their subsequent education (similar recommendation was made in 1938 by the select committee on education which will be mentioned later on). If the government decided against the recommended transfer, then it should increase subsidies to missions so that they could appoint qualified teachers.[37] Bray's proposals were agreed to, in principle, by the Director of Education in July 1940, with one qualification: whenever the number of aboriginal pupils warranted a separate aboriginal school, such school would be established as a matter of policy. More than a decade was to pass before the decision was finally put into effect, under radically different circumstances. As for mission subsidies, they too remained at 1940 levels for almost ten years.

The part-aborigines

The framers of the 1936 Native Administration Act had two precepts for the solution of the part-aboriginal problem: "tutored assimilation" and the "breeding out of colour". The first precept permeated the whole act: all its provisions, insofar as they applied to part-aborigines, were meant to uplift them, by force if necessary, to the level of our civilization. It was an old idea, going back at least to

1905. The second precept, also known as "assimilation by organized breeding", was more recent, and enjoyed a certain popularity throughout Australia under such less offensive names as physical or ethnic assimilation, absorption or amalgamation. Among its supporters could be found Sir Raphael Cilento, the Director of Health in Queensland, Professor J. B. Cleland of the University of Adelaide, and N. B. Tindale of the South Australian Museum, who produced a scientifically based "scale of absorbability" of the various types of cross-breeds, ranging from "high" for the 1/8, 1/4, 3/8 and Fl (first generation half-caste) types to "low" for the 3/4 and 7/8 types.[38] The policy was based on the assumption that there were "no strictly biological reasons for the non-acceptance in the white community of a people with a dilute strain of Australian aboriginal blood";[39] the popular catch-phrase was "black blood breeds out in three generations". In Western Australia, one of the foremost advocates of this solution was Dr. C. P. Bryan.

We must choose [he said before the Moseley Royal Commission] between the setting up of a black population in our so called "White Australia", or the policy of miscegenation—a mixing of Blacks and Whites . . . With the gradual disappearance of the black colour and the other physical characteristics that go with it, it is more likely to eventuate and more certain to be tolerated than the deliberate raising up of a separate black population that might threaten to last for all time and raise problems that confront the United States today.[40]

Although Moseley was lukewarm towards the idea — he appears to have misunderstood the real meaning of the doctor's remarks — the Department of Native Affairs was not. Indeed, Neville was the leading protagonist of the idea. "It was the increasing numbers of near-white children", he said in *Australia's Coloured Minority,* "which finally turned the scale in giving the deciding answer to the question as to whether the coloured should be encouraged to go back to the black, or be advanced to white status to be eventually assimilated into our own race".[41] To Neville assimilation meant "racial mixture", to be achieved preferably by intermarriage, otherwise by miscegenation, as "that happens whatever we may think about that". The process would be completed when "there are no more virile full-bloods remaining alive".[42] The well-known "destiny of the race" resolution of the 1937 Canberra conference of aboriginal authorities had been proposed by Neville; it expressed the belief that the destiny of "natives of aboriginal origin" (but not of the full-bloods) lay in their "ultimate absorption by the people of the Commonwealth".

The idea of "organized breeding" was given official sanction by s.45 of the 1936 Native Administration Act. It gave the Commissioner of Native Affairs the right to object to the celebration of marriages involving a "native", and widened the grounds on which consent could be withheld; he could now object to a marriage if it contravened tribal custom, if one of the parties was afflicted with a communicable or hereditary disease, or if there were "any other circumstances" which rendered it inadvisable that the marriage should take place. Increased penalties for cohabitation and sexual intercourse (up to two years' imprisonment or a penalty not exceeding $400 for a third or subsequent offence), and the broadening of the term to cover relations between white women and aboriginal men, would appear to run counter to the idea of absorption, and in a sense they did. But the provision was largely a sop to the humanitarians to whom miscegenation spelt untold horrors and was rarely applied outside the pastoral areas except in cases of public scandal.

"Uplift by force" and "absorption" remained the motto of the administration until the early fifties when they were replaced by the policy of "assimilation into the general community on the basis of reasonable equality in all facets of community life".[43] In the pre-war period, the policy was an unequivocal failure. Writing in 1940, N. B. Tindale had this to say about the situation in Western Australia:

There seems to be increasingly an insistence on a policy of segregation. . . Even in the closely settled districts, no general attempts are being made at education. . . No endeavour seems to be made to provide housing for half-castes or aborigines . . . Illiteracy is extremely high . . . even persons who might in other circumstances pass as whites may be ill-clothed, uneducated nomads.[44]

The policy failed for several reasons. Some were inherent in the 1936 Native Administration Act, since many of its provisions were inconsistent with the act's professed aim. In particular, criticism could be levelled at the new, wider, definition of a "native", although it must be remembered that the framing of such a definition is always fraught with hazards: it must be flexible enough not to harden the caste barrier, and it has to be sufficiently wide to cover those in need of guidance and protection. The new definition was certainly wide enough, and the provisions relating to exemptions could have easily assured the necessary flexibility, but the department maintained that most aborigines were unfit for the privilege. Neville, for one, was convinced that exemptions, if used unwisely, would retard rather than speed up assimilation. "The persons thus exempted will be the first to suffer and suffer badly. It will debar them from the benefits which the Native Administration Acts provide without compensating advantages from the other side".[45] Between 1937 and 1944, the date of introduction of "citizenship" rights for aborigines, 276 certificates of exemption were issued, covering perhaps 600 individuals; 75 certificates were revoked in the same period. Some of the exempted aborigines failed to show the gratitude that was expected of them. They objected to the production upon demand of what they called "dog licences", claiming that if a person was fit to be exempted he should not have to carry a piece of paper to prove it — an unfortunate notion, said Neville, since the white man must treat him as an aborigine "until he can prove that he is not".[46]

The policy also failed for economic reasons. Although the economic situation improved considerably during the late thirties, southern aborigines continued to form an economically under-privileged group, eking out a precarious existence on casual work and government rations. In June 1938 roughly two-thirds of the adult male population along the Great Southern were unemployed, and in some parts of the region the proportion was even higher; around Pingelly, for instance, only two of the twenty-two men were in permanent employment. Here again, some of the difficulties were the direct result of the 1936 Native Administration Act which tightened the provisions regarding employment permits; Tindale, who had visited the southwest in the late thirties, found that some aborigines blamed their inability to get work on the new laws governing employment. The situation improved somewhat in 1940 when the department agreed first to waive the fees for casual permits and later extended the scope of such permits to cover temporary employment not exceeding the period of one month (the old maximum was two weeks) within each three consecutive months. Significantly, the reform came only after the wartime shortage of labour and the resulting practice of employing aborigines without a permit made the relevant part of the Native Administration Act a dead letter.

The most important reason for the failure of the policy of uplift and absorption during the pre-war years, however, was the growth of racial prejudice. "With the increase of mixed bloods in Australia", to quote N. B. Tindale once more, "the attitude of whites towards mixed blood aborigines seems to be trending increasingly to align

itself with the general American attitude towards the negro."[47]
Prejudice was most pronounced along the Great Southern where
even the horses allegedly refused to drink from troughs used by
aborigines. In February 1939 a conference of representatives of
Great Southern road boards and municipalities asked the government to permanently segregate all aborigines in government settlements or, alternatively, to establish Native Boards of Control in
all country towns with substantial aboriginal population and to
endow these bodies with practically absolute powers over such
matters as distribution of rations and employment. The conference
also resolved that the Native Administration Act should be applied
to all coloured people, irrespective of the degree of admixture of
aboriginal blood. Finally, the conference asked the government to
prohibit aborigines from occupying houses in white residential areas,
including those exempted from the act, "for such fact does not alter
the colour of these people".[48]

Prejudice manifested itself particularly in the field of education.
Late in 1936, as a result of concerted pressure from parents' and
citizens' associations along the Great Southern, the Minister of
Education reversed the earlier ruling of the Director of Education
which prohibited teachers from expelling aboriginal pupils on their
own initiative; they were now allowed to suspend aboriginal children
who did not conform to the standards required of white pupils and
who, "because of their home surroundings or low morals are not
fit for association with white children".[49] Early in 1937 several
quadroons were expelled from the Quairading school when the local
parents' and citizens' association complained that they "lacked the
elements of knowledge of physical and moral cleanliness and for
most part came from abodes which, to say the least, did not approach
the standard of our meanest dwellings".[50] In Carnarvon, all aboriginal children were sent home following similar complaints from
white parents. Among the unfortunate children were three part-
aboriginal boys who were expelled on somewhat unusual grounds:
the family lived in a one-room house. When the father complained
he was told that he would have to have a four-room house before
he could send his children to school.

The select committee inquiring into the educational system of the
state, which presented its report late in 1938, made two important recommendations regarding the education of aboriginal children. Firstly,
it proposed to transfer the statutory responsibility for aboriginal

education from the Department of Native Affairs to the Education Department. Secondly, it recommended that every district with more than twenty aboriginal children of school age should have a separate aboriginal school, and that such schools should follow a special curriculum, adjusted as far as possible to local needs.[51] These recommendations were not put into effect: the Education Department was lukewarm about the proposed arrangements, while the Department of Native Affairs was dead against them, on the ground that the poor living conditions of most aboriginal families would only result in opposition from white parents, even if the aboriginal children were given separate instruction. This state of affairs could not continue much longer, however. In 1939 the Education Department started regular inspections of mission and settlement schools, the latter having adopted the state school curriculum some time earlier. In the following year the Education Department undertook an inquiry into the "educability" of aboriginal children. The result showed that most aboriginal pupils were considerably retarded; where attendance had been regular, however, and home background satisfactory, their performance was found to be only a fraction below that of the average white child.[52] Unfortunately, there was no change of policy regarding attendance. In July 1940, following a "school strike" threat by the local parents' and citizens' association the district inspector of education suspended all coloured children from the Brookton school, on the ground that they had "contagious sores";[53] records show that the local doctor had diagnosed the sores as impetigo (a harmless complaint common among white and aboriginal children alike) and that the Director of Education was aware of this fact. On another occasion, at Culbin, the parents' and citizens' association forced the Education Department to segregate the aboriginal pupils, all "in perfect health",[54] in an old abandoned classroom; it was divided from the white school by a wire fence and provided with separate wash-basins and toilets.

Given these circumstances, it would be pointless to dwell on the reasons why the policy of "organized breeding" was quietly dropped. Interbreeding of races is normally one of the incidents of culture contact, and "amalgamation" one of the indices, perhaps the ultimate index, of the extent of cultural fusion. But it is almost invariably an outcome rather than the cause of assimilation. Western Australian advocates of interbreeding were putting the sexual cart before the cultural horse, in a manner of speaking. In spite of repeated assertions that there was no danger of reversion in white-coloured unions, the idea had but little appeal to the average white man; certainly he did not want to be prosecuted and sent to prison for "supplying" his part-aboriginal wife with a glass of beer. This is what happened to an unfortunate husband in Perth. "Perhaps the prosecution in that case was justified because of the habitual drunkeness of the woman", said Neville, "but the case certainly raised some fine points."[55] The idea found little support among the humanitarians because of its immoral undertones. And it had no appeal whatsoever for the part-aboriginal males whom it would have relegated to lifelong celibacy. Part-aboriginal women may have found the prospect of marrying white men attractive, but their way of life as a rule precluded contacts which could have led to such marriages. So the coloured people turned back to their own; marriages between part-aborigines and full-bloods increased; instead of being bred out, colour was being bred in.

Towards a national policy for aborigines

The 1927 Royal Commission on the Constitution did not slam the door completely on all forms of Commonwealth-state co-operation in aboriginal affairs: while recommending that the states should retain control of aboriginal affairs, it stated that "every endeavour should be made to ensure the adaption of the best method of administration by periodical conferences".[56] This was in 1929, when the "best method of administration" was segregation and protection — and they were obviously failing. The 1931 meeting of the Association for the Protection of Native Races showed the way towards better methods, by calling for a less negative policy for the aborigines as the only effective means of ensuring their protection and securing their advance and welfare. This new programme was gradually adopted by most of those who had special association with the care, administration, or study of the aborigines — outside this very limited circle of the "initiated", as W. E. H. Stanner has stressed recently, the new ideas had very little impact.[57] But it was a beginning. Late in 1933 the National Missionary Council of Australia, in a manifesto subsequently endorsed by the Aborigines' Friends' Association and the Association for the Protection of Native Races, appealed to the federal government to assume "oversight and control" of the aborigines of Australia and to establish an advisory board, with representatives from all states, to assist it in matters of policy. Published in

1934 under the title *A National Policy — For the Protection, Education, Health, Control and Better Government of the Aborigines,* the manifesto also called for special laws to deal with the half-caste problem, more inviolable reserves for the full-bloods, increased mission subsidies, and an aboriginal policy directed towards "ultimate incorporation into full citizenship". This was followed by other representations too numerous to mention save one: a 1935 deputation from the Australian Aborigines' League (formed in Victoria in 1932 and composed entirely of aborigines) which appealed to the Minister for the Interior to establish a federal Department of Native Affairs, so that Australia might have a national aboriginal policy; it also asked for parliamentary representation for aborigines in both federal and state parliaments. The growing agitation for a national policy for aborigines was noted by the 1936 Premiers' Conference. Owing to the "different stages of evolution" of the aborigines in the different states, the conference rejected centralized control as impracticable; instead, it recommended periodical conferences of state and federal aboriginal authorities to discuss methods of control and the general questions of the welfare of aborigines and to submit recommendations to the various governments.[58]

Envisaged as the first of regular annual meetings, the now historical first conference of state and federal aboriginal authorities met in Canberra in April 1937. The question of federal control was not put to a vote at the meeting. It was quite clear to those who attended the conference, said Neville with a certain disappointment, "that the question of National control was a subject to be avoided, in other words that the Commonwealth was not then prepared to assume such control. . ."[59] Instead, the meeting passed a resolution asking the Commonwealth to give financial assistance to states "most requiring it to assist them in the care, protection and education of natives which, unless extended, will bring discredit upon the whole of Australia".[60] Other resolutions called for uniformity of legislation, abolition of corporal punishment and chaining of aboriginal prisoners, stricter supervision of missions, appointment of female protectors, and establishment of Courts of Native Affairs. These were straightforward enough. Others were not so clear. For instance, the conference recommended that children of detribalized full-bloods living near centres of white population should be educated to "white standard" and subsequently placed in employment which "will not bring them into economic or social conflict with the white community".[61] The famous "destiny of the race" resolution was equally devoid of clarity: it expressed the belief that the future of the part-aborigines (but not of the full-bloods) lay in their "ultimate absorption by the people of the Commonwealth". Finally, the conference agreed that similar meetings should be held annually, and the Commonwealth government offered to establish a secretariat to provide liaison between the states and the administration of the Northern Territory.

For those who expected quick and tangible results, the meeting was a disappointment. "One might reasonably infer", said an observer in 1939, "that the Conference felt that no particular urgencies were involved . . . It is significant, too, that the Conference concerned itself almost entirely with highly general questions of policy, and postponed for a year such matters as control and prevention of disease, diet, working conditions, the fixation of a minimum aboriginal working wage, and several other matters of primary importance".[62] The postponed consultations never took place, so that "any action that may have followed that conference was so slight as to bear little relation to its decisions".[63] Yet the momentum was not lost. In November 1937 the Aborigines' Protection League forwarded a petition to the Commonwealth government (with 1,814 signatures, of which 500-odd were from Western Australia) for presentation to the King, imploring the Sovereign "to prevent the extinction of the Aboriginal race and better conditions for all and grant us power to propose a Member of Parliament in the person of our own Blood, or White man known to have studied our needs . . ."[64] In 1938, while the National Health and Pensions Insurance Bill was before federal parliament, the government introduced an amendment proposing to bring detribalized aborigines within the scope of the legislation, but the bill was subsequently abandoned. In February 1939 the federal government published the so-called McEwen Memorandum, the "New Deal for the Aborigines in the Northern Territory", which replaced the objective of "merely dealing with the physical needs of the natives" by the long-range policy of raising their status so as to entitle them, "by right and by qualification", to citizenship. But there was still no sense of urgency: "One must not", cautioned the document, "think in terms of years but of generations."[65] The 1940 federal Electoral (War-Time) Act gave a voluntary vote to aboriginal soldiers, and in the following year children of detribalized aborigines were included within the scope of the Child Endowment Act. The legislation marked the beginning of the end of an era during which the aborigine had been regarded as a human being essentially different from the European: by tacitly recognizing that his backwardness was due mainly to historical and environmental factors, it opened promising vistas for the future. A new concept of assimilation came into being, but it took another decade before its effect became noticeable.

9. The War and Aftermath
1941-1947

"A healthy awakening of the consciousness of the white man's duty to the aborigines"

The outbreak of hostilities in Europe, in September 1939, had little immediate effect on the lives and security of most Western Australians: for Australia, the war began in earnest only in December 1941 when it ceased to be a question of helping Britain and became one of survival. During the panic which followed the fall of Singapore and the occupation of the Netherlands East Indies, aboriginal administration in the parts of the state threatened by Japanese invasion came to a virtual standstill. The aboriginal hospitals at Broome, Wyndham, and Derby were closed and medical inspection was suspended. The Sunday Island and Kalumburu missions were evacuated, and Forrest River struggled on with only one staff member. The entire aboriginal population of Broome was moved to Beagle Bay, taken over late in 1940 by the Intelligence Branch of the Army, after the internment of all priests and missionaries of German nationality. The travelling inspector for northern districts enlisted in the Army "for duty in the north on native matters", and the position remained vacant until July 1943. The staffs at aboriginal cattle stations were reduced to a bare minimum and the school at Moola Bulla was closed, not to reopen until 1950. Outside the threatened areas the work of the department suffered from an acute shortage of personnel, due partly to enlistments and partly to low salaries. In 1943 the entire teaching staff at the Moore River and Carrolup aboriginal settlements resigned, and the schools remained closed until March 1945.

As the war progressed two influences were making themselves increasingly felt: a "healthy awakening of the consciousness of the white man's duty to the aborigines",[1] and an improvement in the economic position of most part-aborigines and some full-bloods. The change in white attitudes was largely the outcome of developments outside Australia. Stirred by the plight of oppressed peoples in Europe, many Australians came to see the inconsistency between their solicitude for the suffering of these people and their lack of interest in the plight of Australia's aboriginal population. One symptom of this change was the extension of Commonwealth social services to certain categories of aborigines. In 1941 children of de-tribalized aborigines became eligible for child endowment; in 1942 exempted aborigines were made eligible for old-age and invalid pensions and for maternity benefits (in states where exemptions did not exist an aborigine qualified for these benefits if he had attained standards which would have entitled him to an exemption); in the same year the Child Endowment Act was amended to extend its application to aboriginal children in missions and government settle-ments; in 1944 the Unemployment and Sickness Benefit Act was applied to all aborigines who, in the opinion of the Director-General of Social Services, had qualified for benefits under the act "by reason of character and the standard of intelligence and social develop-ment".

Another symptom of a change in attitude was the revival of the demand for federal control of aborigines — itself a reflection of the war conditions which forced the federal government to assume control over almost the whole of the national life, and, at the same time, increased its legal and political opportunities for doing so. Pay-as-you-go income tax was introduced in 1940. Manpower con-trol and regulation of non-essential industries were established in 1941. In the following year the federal parliament passed a series of acts which excluded the states from the field of income tax and made in return a grant to the states on condition that they did not themselves levy taxation on incomes. All this, of course, was in keeping with the general philosophy of the Labour Party as a centralizing party, but the war encouraged it to move faster than it would otherwise have done in its economic and social experiments. In November 1942 the federal government convened a meeting of representatives of Commonwealth and state parliaments to discuss the referral by the states to the Commonwealth of adequate powers to make laws in relation to postwar reconstruction for a period of five years after the end of hostilities. The meeting agreed that this was desirable, and approved a draft bill listing such powers. The fate of the proposal, including the 1944 abortive referendum made necessary by the refusal of the majority of the states to pass the bill in the prescribed form, is too familiar to require repetition here except for two minor facts. The first concerns the original draft of the 1942 Commonwealth Powers Bill which did not mention federal control of aborigines: it was added to the list only after representations from A. P. Elkin and others.[2] The second is related to the passage of the bill through Western Australian parliament. It was referred to a select committee which recommended against federal control of aborigines and, at the same time, called for Commonwealth financial assistance "to enable such plans as are agreed upon between the Commonwealth and the State to be carried out by the State for the protection and betterment of the people of the aboriginal race".[3] In its final form, the 1943 Commonwealth Powers Act ceded to the Commonwealth the power to legislate with respect to the people of the aboriginal race "in co-operation with the State", and with a rider calling on the federal government to avail itself, as far as practicable, of the assistance of state officers and instrumentalities in the execution of laws made by the federal parliament.

On the state level, too, the idealism generated by the war brought a change in white attitudes. One example was the upsurge in mission activities which became noticeable very early in the war. In 1938, as we have seen, the Perth businessman Albany Bell opened the Roelands Native Farm which was later taken over by the U.A.M. and converted into a home for quadroons. The year 1939 saw the opening of a U.A.M. mission at Kellerberrin and of a Pallotine mission at Balgo Hills in the Kimberleys. The closing of opportunities for missionary work in China and the Pacific diverted staff and funds from these areas, while the generous assistance of the federal government, in the form of child endowment payments to aboriginal institutions, including missions, gave an additional incentive to missionary work in Australia. In 1942 the Federal Aboriginal Missions Board of the Church of Christ started a children's mission at Norseman, with the definite aim of preparing the inmates for rural and pastoral employment, and a second mission in Carnarvon in 1946, after a delay of several years due to opposition of local residents. During 1943 and most of 1944 the board gave token financial assistance to the Perth Native Mission, a small volunteer organization which operated from a vacant shop in East Perth (situated in the same street as Bray's residence, a fact which the Commissioner found slightly annoying). Early in 1944 the board acquired a block of land in Bassendean, a Perth suburb, with a view to opening a hostel for aboriginal transients (an aboriginal visitor foolish enough to look for accommodation in those days was lucky if he was allowed to spend the night at the police stables near Herdsman Lake). The proposal fell through when the local road board, unhappy about the influx of aborigines from the country, refused to issue the required building permit. In the same year the Federal Aboriginal Missions Board of the Church of Christ started negotiations with the department regarding a new mission station at Roebourne, but the department lost interest when the Pastoralists' Association protested: "A mission does little to add to the natives' real welfare and usefulness but rather results in the loss of their natural bushcraft and encourages laziness."[4] Other churches did not have to face the same opposition. In 1944 the Apostolic Church, a non-conformist body which had originated in Wales in 1904, was given land for a mission near Jigalong, on the edge of the Gibson Desert; it opened in 1946. In 1944 the Roman Catholic Church started a children's mission at Wandering in the southwest, and in the following year the Pallotines applied for a permit to establish a boys' institution at Saint Joseph's Farm near Tardun. It was opened, after some delay, in 1948.

The department, not to be outdone, set in motion grandiose planning to improve its service as soon as the emergency was over. In the past, said Bray before the select committee on social security in February 1942, "we have viewed the local native question as a black question, forgetting the necessity for more humane consideration to the social outcast, the half-caste". To accord him better treatment the state needed more training institutions and settlements, a "more far-reaching organization for the native question in all its aspects, including segregation of types and classes", as well as a "scheme of warm-blooded welfare work in districts outside our settlements".[5] In 1943, before the select committee on the Commonwealth Powers Bill, Bray listed the following as the minimum new staff requirements for his department: one assistant commissioner, two medical officers, two travelling inspectors (one for the southwest and one for the eastern goldfields and the Murchison), an inspectress to deal with matters affecting women and children, and an itinerant magistrate for the north to preside over Courts of Native Affairs and over cases involving assaults by whites against aborigines. He also spoke of two new settlements in the southwest land division, a settlement in the Port Hedland-Marble Bar area, a new training institution in West Kimberley, new premises for the Native Girls'

Home in East Perth (opened in 1931 as a transit home for girls from Moore River on their way to domestic service), and substantial improvements at Carrolup and Cosmo Newbery. Since the plan was largely conditional on Commonwealth financial assistance (advocated by Bray before the 1942 select committee on social security and again, in 1943, before the select committee on the Commonwealth Powers Bill), little of it was implemented during the war. In July 1943 a travelling inspector for the southern districts was appointed, and in 1944 the department acquired Udialla station in West Kimberley, to be used as a training institution for part-aboriginal children. But the impetus did not last long. With the departmental grant stationary about the $150,000 mark during the war years, it was easy to blame inactivity on lack of finance: "The greatest handicap we suffer in the administration of native affairs is that of £ s.d.", said Coverley in 1943.[6] What Bray and his Minister failed to grasp was that not only money but new ideas would be required to cope with the unsettling effect of the war. Opposing a complete transfer of aboriginal administration to the Commonwealth, Bray said: "I can well imagine that if my department lost the power to issue warrants [to remove aborigines to settlements] the whole effort of local administration in Western Australia would be nullified and broken down ... at present our organization is largely worked through the police department."[7]

Improvement in the aborigines' economic status

The second wartime development to be noted was the improvement in the economic position of most part-aborigines and some aborigines. According to official returns, based on employment permits, aboriginal employment increased from 3,198 in June 1939 to 5,625 in June 1944, but these figures do not reflect the situation accurately since many employers did not bother to apply for permits. In the south, many aborigines found unskilled or semi-skilled work at award rates in the construction and manufacturing industries, as surface workers in the mines, and as drivers and general labourers with local authorities; in 1944, in the southwest, it was "difficult to get a native who is able to do anything at all for a wage of under £3 [$6] a week", with meat supplied.[8] On the Murchison there was ample work on the roads and railways. In northern townships, above-award rates were common during the last two years of the war. However, there was no corresponding improvement in the rural and pastoral industries. Wages in the pastoral industry were pegged late in 1940, and protectors were instructed to "discourage" workers from leaving rural and pastoral employment for other jobs. As a result many aborigines simply moved to country towns and the metropolitan area in search of better paid employment, while others refused to work at all, preferring to subsist on child endowment or to live "socialist fashion" with other aborigines. Early in 1943 some of the loafers were removed to settlements and the department, under pressure from farming interests, asked for a bill to be drafted which would have authorized protectors to order adult male aborigines residing south of the 26th parallel to obtain "approved" employment. The bill was not proceeded with, but in June 1943 the department instructed all protectors to ensure that aborigines in rural and pastoral employment, while allowed to change jobs, should not be permitted to leave the industry. Those who had taken up other occupations should be ordered to return.[9]

The "healthy awakening of the consciousness of the white man's duty to the aborigines", mentioned earlier, was unfortunately limited largely to those who had little to do with the flesh-and-blood aborigines. In most country areas the drift of aborigines to towns led to an escalation rather than the opposite of the "cold war" between the races. Some aboriginal parents apparently believed that the payment of child endowment was conditional on school attendance, and the administration did nothing to discourage this assumption. Initially there was no overt reaction among the white town-dwellers to the influx of aboriginal schoolchildren — indeed, much of the opposition to aboriginal parents seeking education for their children came from their own people. On one Great Southern reserve a family who moved their tent to a more isolated position had it burnt for being "above themselves" in having their children attending school.[10] European opposition was most pronounced at Pingelly. In September 1942 the Pingelly Parents' and Citizens' Association asked the Education Department to provide separate facilities for the aboriginal children attending the local state school, because of their "verminous condition";[11] when the department refused, the parents withdrew their children from school. Early in December the senior medical inspector of schools examined the pupils at the Pingelly school and found two cases of impetigo, one being a white child. Immediately afterwards the Director of Education, who had accompanied the senior medical inspector to Pingelly, told a special meeting of the parents' and citizens' association that the aboriginal children would not be segregated; his department was "blind to colour" and only required that children attending school be clean and free from infection.[12] The parents tried another tack: their real complaint, they told the Director of Education, was the conditions in the aboriginal camp. The senior medical inspector offered to inspect the camp but, as he recalled in his report, "various obstacles were put in my way, as for example, I was told that it was impossible for me to go there without an authorization from the Department of Native Affairs".[13] On 31 December 1942 the Director of Education, with the full support of the Conference of Inspectors, issued a ruling on the subject of school attendance of aboriginal children. The provision enabling parents to object to the presence of coloured children, he told all headmasters, must be read in conjunction with the rest of the relevant regulations; consequently, future objections would have to be substantiated by proof that the child being objected to was "habitually unclean or infected with disease".[14] The firm stand taken by the Education Department transformed the question of aboriginal education into a political issue. Late in January 1943 the opposition member for Pingelly, H. S. Seward, moved in the Legislative Assembly that the government should establish separate schools on aboriginal reserves, thereby implementing the recommendations of the Moseley Royal Commission. The motion was lost on party lines, with three future Ministers of Native Affairs (later Welfare) voting against the government.[15]

Some of the newcomers bought or built homes inside town boundaries and were often followed by friends or relatives, much to the annoyance of white townfolk. "The native problem is difficult in practically every town I have the honour to represent", said the member for the southeast province in 1944.[16] The white folks' complaints, now that many aborigines were better-off, took a different line: they did not have "any moral code at all",[17] they were unreliable, and they spent their time "twirling the pennies in the air".[18] The government was too lenient; the Commonwealth had made a "ghastly error" when it made child endowment available for payment direct to the aborigines.[19] Yet, significantly, the demands for the removal of aborigines to settlements had ceased; because of the considerable spending power of the aboriginal population (an estimated $3 million in 1947), most local authorities welcomed their presence in towns during business hours, preferring them safely back on reserves after dark. This was the arrangement in York, for instance; in Katanning one day a week was set aside for aboriginal shopping; and, since there was no train until midnight, they had to obtain a permit to remain in town after dark.

It was a different story on the Murchison where the influx of aborigines to towns was a more recent phenomenon. In May 1945 the annual conference of the Murchison Road Boards Association appealed to the government to declare all townships within its area out of bounds to aborigines and to provide housing on reserves of a standard comparable to that prescribed for shearers by the Shearers and Agricultural Labourers Accommodation Act; a few months later the association added a request for separate aboriginal schools. In this, the association had the support of the Teachers' Union which, at its 1944 annual meeting, endorsed the policy of special aboriginal schools in districts with a sizeable aboriginal population, staffed by properly trained teachers. At Carnarvon, the presence of coloured children led to a somewhat unusual incident. The headmaster, in his zeal to promote goodwill between the races, adopted an arrangement which involved seating a boy next to a girl, irrespective of colour. A hurried meeting of the municipal council followed, and the headmaster adjusted the seating arrangements in accordance with the council's wishes — except in the case of the mayor's daughter. In the end most white parents withdrew their offspring from the state school and enrolled them in the local convent which "practised segregation on a minor scale".[20]

The reaction of the trade unions to the increased demand for aboriginal labour should also be noted here. In September 1943 the W.A. branch of the Australian Workers' Union applied for an award to cover workers in rural and pastoral industries not already covered by other federal and state awards. On the insistence of the Department of Native Affairs, the union included in its application a clause which would have permitted the employment in the rural industry of "less efficient" aboriginal workers at under-award rates, subject to the approval of the local protector and the overriding right of the Commissioner of Native Affairs to disallow any contract entered into. The state Arbitration Court which heard the application ruled that it did not have jurisdiction over rural workers, and the union took the case to the federal Arbitration Court. The first submission to the court said nothing about the employment of aborigines at under-award rates, for the union was convinced that the farmers were unlikely to employ white labour if they could hire aboriginal workers for lower wages. After repeated representations from the department the union agreed to incorporate the proposal in its application, albeit in a modified form: the employment of aborigines at under-award wages was to be conditional on the consent of the union rather than the department. This proved unacceptable to the department, and in the end the union agreed to the provision in the form in which it had been first introduced in 1943. The case was finally heard in November 1945, and the award was handed down early in 1946. It provided for the employment of aborigines in the southwest land division at less than award rates and conditions, subject to the approval of the Commissioner of Native Affairs.[21] The 1944 application by the A.W.U. for a new federal pastoral award also betrays the white workers' concern with competition from "cheap" aboriginal labour. Arguing that the number of aborigines in pastoral employment had greatly increased since the last award (1938) and that aborigines were increasingly called upon to perform work involving greater responsibility and even supervisory duties, the union asked the federal Arbitration Court to expunge the "unjust" exclusion of aborigines from the definition of a station hand. "I perceive an inconsistency in the Union's attitude", said Judge Kelly, rejecting the claim. "In one breath it avers that the native is capable of performing the various duties of a station hand as efficiently as a 'white' employee; yet, in the next it suggests that equality of opportunity for employment will be lost, to the detriment of the 'whites', unless the cost of employing natives is brought up to the level of the cost of award rates and conditions."[22]

The war and official policy

The ambivalence displayed during the war by many white Australians was reflected in official policy: the department acknowledged the need for reform but maintained that all change should be gradual, and that it would have to come from above, not below. A good case in point is the question of aboriginal housing. In June 1943 the State Advisory Committee on Post-War Housing recommended that group housing of a special type should be provided for detribalized aborigines in a number of country towns. Aborigines "capable of taking their place in the community" should be given houses of a standard comparable to the "reasonable standard" laid down by the committee for European housing, the government making a contribution towards the rent. Bray's reaction speaks for itself. Most aborigines, said the Commissioner, had "a definite tendency to live under camping conditions" and had retained most of their old superstitions, so that it was likely that they would abandon a house where a death had occurred. "In any case the Department is not prepared to recommend expenditure of moneys for the provision of housing for natives within one hundred miles of a Native Settlement."[23]

An even better example is the question of exemptions. In October 1941 the secretary of the Barmen and Barmaids' Union wrote to Bray about the dilemma facing the members of his union when asked to serve drinks to aboriginal soldiers. If they complied they broke the law; if they refused the white soldiers in the aborigines' company would invariably start a brawl. The only solution, suggested the secretary, was to grant exemptions to all aborigines in uniform. This was rejected by Bray because "as a body they were unsuitable for that privilege".[24] But the question was bound to come up again sooner or later. In October 1942 two aboriginal soldiers, Miller and Hill (the latter had served overseas with the 2nd 11th Battalion), were charged with a minor offence before the Perth Police Court. After the proceedings the magistrate suggested that it was a grave mistake for a protector to appear in court on behalf of aboriginal soldiers. Once they had been admitted to the forces, said the magistrate, aboriginal soldiers were treated by the Army as whites. All their mates were white, and any action which made it publicly known that a soldier was legally an aborigine could only result in ridicule from the members of his unit who previously may not have given the matter a thought. Bray agreed that in future aboriginal soldiers charged with minor offences would be asked if they wished a protector to appear on their behalf, but failed to take up the fundamental issued raised by the magistrate, obsessed as he was, or appeared to be, with the "sad story of their moral ineptitude", their "native habits and inclinations, and . . . the disabilities of their native ancestry".[25] By 1943 Bray's ideas had undergone a radical change, however. In May he told his Minister that the time had come to extend the franchise to all persons of the half-blood since, as he put it, "in recent years there has been an improvement in the intelligence of the half-castes".[26] This was too radical a departure for A. A. M. Coverley, but by 1944 he, too, became convinced of the need for reform. In September 1944, in moving the second reading of the Natives (Citizenship Rights) Bill, he told the Legislative Assembly that the time had come to give those aborigines "prepared to adopt a higher standard of living"[27] an opportunity to uplift themselves, by satisfying a magistrate that they were entitled to full citizenship. Most of his colleagues agreed; the bill will be a "charter for the natives in Western Australia",[28] said one member, while another called it a "milestone in the social progress of this country and this Commonwealth. We will be the cynosure of all eyes."[29] Passed with hardly a dissident voice (one member thought that there should be a qualifying period of two years before the granting of "full" citizenship rights), the 1944 Natives (Citizenship Rights) Act gave an adult aborigine the right to apply, under certain conditions, to a magistrate or government resident for a certificate of citizenship. He had to satisfy the magistrate that, for two years immediately preceding the date of his application, he had "dissolved all tribal and native associations except with respect to lineal descendants or native relations of the first degree", and had either served in the armed forces or was otherwise a "fit and proper" person to obtain the certificate. In addition, the magistrate had to assure himself that the applicant was able to speak and understand the English language and was not suffering from active leprosy, syphilis, granuloma, or yaws. Applicants had to supply two recent references from "reputable" citizens to show that they were of industrious habits and good behaviour and reputation, and reasonably capable of managing their own affairs.

Hailed by the *West Australian* as "something new in Australia",[30] and described in the 1945 annual report of the Department of Native Affairs as a "most modern piece of legislation",[31] the act was one of the strangest enactments ever passed by the Western Australian parliament. Some of its provisions were lifted almost verbatim from U.S. legislation promulgated in 1886 relating to American Indians (supplied obligingly by the U.S. consul in Perth) and repealed by Congress a decade earlier. One would have thought that the act had made exemptions superfluous, but they were nevertheless retained, even though, as Coverley put it during the debate, a "certificate of exemption is really of no use to a native".[32] There was a curious clause stating that a holder of a certificate of citizenship "shall be deemed to be no longer a native or aborigine and shall have all rights, privileges and immunities and shall be subject to the duties and liabilities of a natural born or naturalized subject of His Majesty", while at the same time making provisions for the revocation or suspension of such certificates. The act was equally confusing from a legal point of view. Since 1608 (*Calvin's Case*) every person born within the territorial limits of the dominions of the King or Queen of Great Britain and whose parents did not come within a few special categories, such as foreign diplomats or prisoners of war, was by common law deemed to be a British subject by birth. The principle was reaffirmed in 1914 by the British parliament and in Australia by the 1920 Nationality Act which followed the lines of British legislation by restating the common law position that birth within the dominions of the Crown created British nationality, unless there were special circumstances removing the child from British allegiance. On these principles, every aborigine born in Australia after the whole continent had become part of the dominions of the Crown was a British subject by birth. From a purely legal point of view, however, being a British subject is by itself of little value; it is merely the foundation on which further conditions of qualification or disqualification can be built, such as being a member of a particular race or meeting certain residential requirements. In spite of its imposing language, the Natives (Citizenship Rights) Act intended simply to free all holders of certificates of citizenship not only from the restrictions of the Native Administration Act but from all other legal disabilities, thereby granting full civil rights.[33]

Aboriginal reaction to the war

Aboriginal response to the war was complex. Although the Army had initially shown little enthusiasm for aboriginal volunteers, even for non-combatant duties, a number of "better class" aborigines and part-aborigines enlisted during the first year of the war.[34] The first to join was one Cecil Fitzgerald on 10 October 1939; by June 1940 sixteen part-aborigines had enlisted in Broome, five in Katanning, and over fifty in the metropolitan area. After Pearl Harbour the Army became less selective and accepted aborigines in larger numbers (altogether some four hundred aborigines had joined the ranks during the war, about fifty had served overseas, and two had died in Japanese prison camps). At no stage, however, even when the Japanese invasion seemed imminent, did the Army consider arming the northern aborigines. In April 1942, when the entire military force in the Kimberleys consisted of approximately one hundred men, the Army created a number of commando units to organize defences on some of the larger pastoral properties. On the suggestion of a journalist, C. Langmore, the commander of a unit visiting Liveringa station agreed to an experiment in the training of the station aborigines. The experiment was so successful (70 per cent of the "aboriginal platoon" averaged three hits out of five shots at a head and body target 400 yards away) that Langmore subsequently wrote to the Prime Minister, suggesting the formation of an aboriginal auxiliary force in the Kimberleys. But the Army would have nothing to do with the idea, even though Curtin himself had apparently asked for it to be considered "on the highest plane".[35] The other two services, on the other hand, used aboriginal manpower freely. The Air Force organized a number of unofficial aboriginal units at its northern airfields, while in the Northern Territory the Navy had an aboriginal patrol trained in drill, care of arms, seamanship, and land patrol work, whose members did extremely valuable work and had even absorbed the naval tradition of being inclined to patronize the men in the junior services.

After the danger of invasion had passed, the Army discharged most of the "camping type" aborigines for rural and pastoral employment, because of their "unsuitablility for sustained service, with its attendant Army discipline".[36] By then aboriginal attitudes had undergone a noticeable change. As usually happens when an oppressed group gains some of the rights withheld from it in the past, the moderate improvement in the aborigines' status during the early war years led to expectations of further reforms. When these were not forthcoming the aborigines reacted resentfully, in the only way open to a numerically insignificant minority. In June 1942 the Port Hedland police were asked to investigate rumours that the "Japs were going to come and that all black-fellows would be all right"; the Japanese were going to teach the aborigines to read and write, give them women, both Japanese and white, and "see we were alright for tucker".[37] In October 1942 Jack Egan, one of the Northam aborigines who had been removed to Moore River in 1933, said publicly in Geraldton that "we will be better off when the Japs come — the Japs will do me"[38] — a statement which earned him another trip to Moore River, under military escort. Late in 1942 an elderly Bassendean aborigine, when a white man told him not to walk across his paddock, retorted: "I remember last time big war on you skite how we win the war, this time maybe we don't win the war, then I walk across your paddock when I like you be our servant then."[39] At nearby Guildford a white and an aboriginal woman collided when leaving the ladies' toilet at the railway station. The white woman apologized and the aboriginal woman replied: "Oh certainly, when the Japs win the war you will be our servants."[40] Another case investigated by the police concerned two elderly aboriginal women who announced in the main street of Guildford that Japan was going to win the war; when asked for the source of this information, they said they "knew by studying the stars".[41]

How representative these opinions were of the aboriginal population as a whole we shall probably never know. The Army, for its part, decided to take no risks. In June 1942 a Special Mobile Force stationed at Moora rounded up all unemployed aborigines from the Midlands and interned them in Moore River as "possible potential enemies";[42] those in employment were forbidden to leave their place of residence without special permission. A few weeks later the Deputy Director of Security for Western Australia asked Bray to compile a register of all aborigines so that they could be kept under observation, as the "possibility of natives becoming subversive in the event of invasion by means of bribery or propaganda cannot be overlooked".[43] In August the Army, without consulting the department, issued an order regarding the control of aboriginal population between the mouth of the Murchison River and the northern boundary of the metropolitan area. Employed aborigines were to reside on the properties of their employers who were made responsible for their conduct and movements. Unemployed aborigines were to be confined to the Moore River settlement or, if residing north of the Dongara-Mingenew line, to camp permanently on aboriginal reserves under the direction and supervision of the police. The scheme was put into operation in spite of Bray's objections which were later substantiated by the unnecessarily harsh methods ("nigger hunting")[44] used by Army personnel in the execution of their duties. In January 1943 the Army sought to extend the scheme to the northwest and the West Kimberley. Aborigines on pastoral stations were to become the responsibility of the pastoralists, while unemployed aborigines were to be interned in detention camps at Milly Milly, Bangemal, Ashburton Downs, Mulga Downs, Warrawagine, and Fossil Downs stations. This time there was opposition not only from the department but also from the Commissioner of Police, and the proposal was abandoned once the danger of invasion had passed.

The improvement in the military situation brought to the fore-

front another problem — that of communist influence among the
aborigines. The Communist Party was declared an illegal organization[45] in June 1940 but continued to operate underground, and emerged in a powerful position after Germany's declaration of war on
Russia. Later in 1943 the party included in its platform a plank of
complete economic and legal equality for aborigines, except for
voluntary rather than compulsory franchise. In Western Australia,
the party found two fertile areas for its activities: the metropolitan
area and the Port Hedland-Marble Bar region. In the metropolitan
area the party took up the plight of the part-aborigines in Bassendean,
Bayswater, and Guildford. Most of these were new arrivals attracted
by better employment opportunities and the bright lights of Perth,
and lived mainly on the South Guildford reserve. In May 1943 the
land was taken over by the Army and the camp was moved to the
vicinity of Wydgie Road. Early in 1944 the Bayswater and Midland
Junction branches of the party made several representations to the
Guildford municipal council and the Department of Native Affairs,
pointing out the deplorable living conditions at the Wydgie Road
camp (the aborigines lived in bush-type wurlies) and the complete
lack of sanitary facilities. The only outcome was the eviction of
several aboriginal families from condemned houses. Subsequently
the party organized a "protest movement" among the aborigines,
"led" by a part-aboriginal woman called Mrs. Morden, but the
ringleaders were promptly deported to Moore River.[46]

The "Morden affair" was rather insignificant when compared with
events in the Port Hedland-Marble Bar area where the war had
created extremely favourable conditions for the party's activities.
There was much latent discontent among the local aborigines because
of the ban on their transfer from pastoral to other employment.
Aboriginal station hands were "getting ideas" — they wanted to
earn more money, to "knock about" the country, doing contract
work or almost anything rather than the humdrum work on the
stations. Dissatisfaction was widespread throughout the pastoral
north, but it was most pronounced on the Pilbara where a somewhat
unusual combination of circumstances, past and present, created an
ominous situation. The Pilbara aborigines, as we have seen, had a
long tradition of active opposition to white man's rule: the generation of the 1860s put up a gallant fight when the pastoralists invaded
their lands; their sons, in 1904, organized an abortive rebellion to
"shoot the bloody government";[47] the generation of the 1920s and

1930s was equally recalcitrant.[48] Since the turn of the century, too,
the Pilbara aborigines had enjoyed a modicum of economic inde-
pendence, for they could always walk out on the pastoralists and
yandy for alluvial tin around Marble Bar. The war created additional
tensions, particularly in Port Hedland where the local part-aborigines
had joined forces to establish the Euralian Association in 1934. By
the time of Pearl Harbour the town's aboriginal labour force had
approximately doubled, with predictable results; for instance, there
were the usual demands for "separation of scholars" and "separate
lavatory accommodation". When the Army took over it wanted to
evacuate all aborigines (as in Broome), but the aboriginal workforce had by then become practically indispensable. A compromise
solution was arrived at late in October 1942 when it was decided to
declare Port Hedland a "prohibited area" and to issue passes to
"good conduct natives" allowing them to remain in town.[49] Immediate and well-organized protest followed. Early in November a
meeting of the town's part-aborigines, chaired by the president of the
Euralian Association, declared its opposition to the pass system,
but the local Roman Catholic Priest, Father Bryan, eventually persuaded the rebels to acquiesce in the regulations. This might have
been the end of the story had it not been for an unassuming, quiet
white man, Donald McLeod. McLeod was born in 1908 at Meeka-
tharra and had spent most of his adult life prospecting, well-sinking,
and doing contract work. His somewhat belated interest in aborigines and their welfare is difficult to explain. He was something of a
rough anthropologist and, on his own admission, an active member
of the Communist Party from 1945 until 1948;[50] in 1946 he described
the aboriginal strike then in progress as a "struggle for the fundamental rights of all workers".[51] He may have had political ambitions
(in 1944 he stood for the Pilbara seat as a "Progressive Labour"
candidate) and may have seen the enfranchisement of aborigines,
which the Communist Party stood for, as a means of fulfilling his
aspirations. He also appears to have craved notoriety, or so it would
seem from a statement he made shortly before his arrest in May
1946: "While I am inside, as I am likely to be, I will become a
martyr to a very vocal section of citizens particularly the female
species and will be a continual pain in the neck to the government."[52]

McLeod came to the notice of the authorities shortly after the
May 1943 abortive strike of Port Hedland part-aborigines which he
had almost certainly helped to organize. The upheaval was sparked

off by a half-caste, Jack Coffin (or Coppin), one of "three brothers, big strong men, forceful and vigorous".[53] On discovering that he was employed under a permit, Coffin walked off his well-paid job with the local road board and found casual employment with a private firm. He was later interviewed by the police and told them that he objected to being treated as an aborigine, since he paid rates and taxes like any white man. Reporting the matter to Perth, the local constable warned about the widespread unrest among the part-aborigines: they "bridle at the very thought that they should come under the Department".[54] In Port Hedland, the news of Coffin's "victimization" by the police was followed by another meeting of the town's part-aborigines who decided to stage a strike in Coffin's support. Although the "strikers" had some support from the local business community (abolition of permits would have been in the employers' interests as well), the police were instructed to deal sternly with any disturbances, and the aborigines were warned that they would be evacuated en masse if they did not adopt a more "reasonable" attitude.

If Bray hoped that his firm stand would end the dispute once and for all, he was mistaken. In June 1943 McLeod came down to Perth to discuss the aborigines' grievances with the Commissioner. He told Bray that it was common knowledge that a "general agreement existed with the pastoralists to keep wages low",[55] and asked him to lift the prohibition which prevented aborigines from taking on better-paid jobs in Port Hedland. While in Perth, McLeod applied to the Lands Department for a lease of 28,500 acres near Port Hedland, but the application was turned down on the ground that the area was too small for an economical holding (McLeod subsequently claimed that he intended to establish aborigines on the land, in a scheme combining intense cultivation and grazing, but his application does not mention this fact). Later in the month, after returning to Port Hedland, McLeod established a branch of the Anti-Fascist League (the Euralian Association became affiliated with it soon after) and invited Bray to Port Hedland to discuss with him a number of demands agreed upon by the aborigines, and in particular the abolition of employment permits, better housing, and the grant of full citizenship rights to all holders of certificates of exemption. By then McLeod had come to the notice of the Security Service who asked the local police to keep an eye on his activities. In October, acting on Bray's instructions, the police refused to grant McLeod a permit to employ aboriginal labour to fulfil a contract for the supply of timber to a Nullagine mining company. In January 1944 McLeod applied for a general permit to employ ten aborigines to assist him with contract work, but was turned down because, in the opinion of the department, he was not a fit and proper person to employ aborigines. McLeod appealed, and the decision was reversed by the Nullagine police court in November 1944. After that McLeod disappeared from the public eye, but not for long. In July 1945, following the Port Hedland "Race Time", McLeod wrote another letter to Bray. He told the Commissioner that the assembled aborigines had asked him to become a protector, to look after their conditions of employment, and that he had explained to them that the appointment would have to come from Perth. He also raised the question of establishing an aboriginal settlement under his superintendency, preferably on Abydos station, one of the eight properties foreclosed by Dalgety and Co. some time earlier.[56] About the same time vague rumours of a strike by aboriginal stockmen, to take place at an unspecified date, began to circulate in the district. In October the local constable reported that on every station he had inspected the aborigines had heard of the proposed strike and knew that "they all must sit down on May 1st and refuse to work until McLeod visited them and told them what to do",[57] adding that McLeod himself was staying out, while his trusted "lieutenants" — Clancy McKenna, Captain, Dougal, Dooley, and Kitchener — made the rounds of the stations. In November Bray sent the travelling inspector for northern districts, the former policeman L. O'Neill, to investigate the reports further. O'Neill concluded that the rumours had been grossly exaggerated and that McLeod's influence in the district was on the wane. McLeod had no interest in the welfare of the aborigines but endeavoured to set himself up as their champion, and "in this regard he is somewhat dangerous in that he is by no means a fool, can speak well and has a fair amount of influence particularly among the semi-educated half-castes".[58] O'Neill recommended that no special precautions were necessary as the aborigines simply lacked an organization to act in unison; all that was required was to keep a close watch on McLeod and "throw the book" at him for the slightest infringement of the Native Administration Act or any other law.

Aborigines, missionaries, and politicians

Recurring official statements about the importance of Christian missions notwithstanding, departmental policy towards missions remained basically unchanged during the war. Early in the war there was a brief period of fairly cordial relations between the administration and the missions, but by 1942 the old animosities reasserted themselves. One of the causes of renewed friction was the alleged refusal of certain missions to "release" their inmates for work in the pastoral industry, thereby hampering the war effort. Mount Margaret came in again for a lion's share of criticism. Late in 1942, after the local police had reported "unfavourably on the influences of the mission in respect to employment matters",[59] Bray decided to expand the facilities at nearby Cosmo Newbery so as to reduce the mission, in time, to a children's home and a preaching station. Other missions incurred departmental displeasure by continually disregarding the provisions of the Native Administration Act requiring prior approval from the Commissioner for the celebration of marriages between aborigines. In June 1943, following a number of tribal murders at the Forrest River mission, said to be the result of marriages arranged by the missionaries in disregard of tribal custom, the department called to the attention of the missions its powers under the act, promising drastic action if they continued to celebrate marriages which did not conform to tribal custom. Although there was a shortage of appropriate marriage partners everywhere in the Kimberleys, most aboriginal groups, including the Nyul-Nyul at Beagle Bay and the Worora at Kunmunya, managed to modify their traditional marriage rules without much attending violence. These rules had been framed primarily in terms of kinship and varied from tribe to tribe; each had its ideal preferences but each tribe, traditionally, permitted alternative marriages. Depopulation forced the aborigines to modify these rules by resorting to irregular unions (such as marriages with classificatory mother, father's sister, and sister) which gradually became recognized as being of almost equal legality with the traditionally correct marriages; among the six East Kimberley tribes studied by Phyllis Kaberry in the mid-thirties, irregular marriages constituted 4 per cent – 24 per cent of all tribal marriages and were generally accepted or at least tolerated.[60] At Forrest River, where the missionaries did their utmost to suppress the authority of the old men and to foster contempt for the old ways among the young people, irregular marriages caused much dissension and dissatisfaction, for the old men were not reconciled to them.

Although the stern tone of the departmental directive appears to

have been well justified, the missions were quick to retaliate in their
own way. The opening shot was fired by the Moore River Church
of England resident missionary, deaconess Heath. In a letter to the
Anglican Synod, later made public, the deaconess described the
settlement as an "all-night and all-day brothel". Education was at
a standstill (all teachers had resigned in 1943 and were not replaced),
and there was a constant stream of girls absconding and being brought
back under police escort. "I think", concluded the deaconess, "it
is time we realized our responsibility in a more practical way than
sympathetic remarks and masterly inactivity."[61] A description of the
conditions at Carrolup, from the pen of the daughter of a Presbyterian clergyman who spent two months at the settlement as a voluntary worker, was just as damaging: "There are no sheets on the
beds . . . They are locked up like fowls after an early tea every night,
winter and summer — no light, no fire, no recreation at all — just
an animal existence . . . I have never seen kiddies with such dull,
unhappy eyes, hang-dog expression and surly looks. It is a veritable
prison to them."[62] These allegations (and some others) were taken
up by the Anglican Synod, in the form of a resolution calling for the
improvement of conditions in aboriginal settlements, and in October
1944 the Native Welfare Council published them in pamphlet form,
under the title *The Tragedy of Native Affairs*. The pamphlet accused
the government of allowing the pastoralists to dictate aboriginal
policy; more specifically, it criticized the department for its continued
refusal to undertake the education of half-caste children, called for
the removal of all children from the Moore River and Carrolup
settlements to children's institutions under church control and
assisted financially by the government, and appealed to the Commonwealth government to assume responsibility for aborigines on a
national basis. Finally, the pamphlet listed the council's "18 Points"
as the foundation for an enlightened aboriginal policy, to be based
on the assumption that the aborigine was "fully human" and had
the right to a "place in Australia's National Economy in accordance
with his capacity to fit in it". All efforts to uplift him should be
"constructive" and directed towards the creation of a self-reliant
race through employment in the primary and "associated" industries.
Selected aborigines should be given the opportunity to settle on the
land. Reserves should be declared inviolable and developed by
modern industrial methods "for the advantage of, and, where
possible, by the aborigines".

Admirable as most of these suggestions were, there was "much more than meets the eye"[63] in the council's manoeuvre. It was not a coincidence that the pamphlet was published shortly after the 1944 referendum on increased federal powers, including the right to legislate with respect to the people of the aboriginal race. The missions and churches everywhere in Australia had hoped for a "yes" vote, having in the past found the federal government more amenable than the various state governments to their lobbying. The allegations in the pamphlet were no doubt true, but the record of some missions was not any better. "Immorality", in the form of boys' visits to girls' dormitories, was probably just as common as in government settlements, and discipline equally difficult to enforce. In 1943, for instance, the superintendent of the Forrest River mission put a "lazy" stockboy in chains, having first "struck him across the face with an open hand", and thrashed a girl for "consistent laziness and deliberate disobedience".[64] Other missions enforced discipline by sending the trouble-makers away, sometimes after a beating administered by "senior men", or called the police to deal with them. Since these incidents, unlike similar happenings in government settlements, were not public knowledge, it was not difficult for the missions and the churches to exploit, for their own ends, the poor record of the administration. On 14 September 1944 the *Daily News* published extracts from the letter by deaconess Heath, including the statement that Moore River was no better than a day and night brothel. On 21 September the member for Williams-Narrogin, Victor Doney, asked the Minister for the North-West to comment on the recent charges by the Anglican Synod and the Native Welfare Council, alleging the breakdown of control in aboriginal settlements where "conditions are spoken of as appalling and resembling a brothel".[65] Coverley replied a week later — by introducing the Natives (Citizenship Rights) Bill; in a more flippant vein, he told the house that if there was any truth underlying the scandal, then the deaconess's efforts of a spiritual nature failed because she had been the resident missionary at Moore River for ten years. On 10 October Mrs. Cardwell-Oliver, the member for Subiaco, returned to the brothel theme by quoting at great length from the letter which started it all. But there were other, more serious voices asking to be heard. In the *West Australian,* the authoress Mary Durack spoke of past "policy of neglect and apathy", adding that we have "at least reached the stage wherein everyone agrees that there is 'something wrong somewhere' with our native administration and is indignantly passing the blame on to someone else".[66] But the best of this game of guilt-projection was yet to come. On 1 November the member for central province, E. H. H. Hall, during the debate on the Supply Bill, called upon the government to clear the name of Western Australia from the "shocking reflections" cast upon it by the allegations of the Native Welfare Council. Two days later the *West Australian* urged parliament to make its own inquiries, irrespective of any action the government might take. The climax came on 22 November when the leader of the Nationalist Party, R. R. McDonald, moved in the Legislative assembly that the house should request the federal government to appoint a Royal Commission to report on the policy pursued in regard to the people of the aboriginal race, and in particular to determine what financial support should be made available to the states by the Commonwealth. The member for West Perth came well prepared. He based his motion on two considerations. The first was the "recognition on the part of many responsible people in this State of the obligation they have to our aboriginal population". The second was the recent offer of the Commonwealth to assume responsibility for aboriginal affairs — "something new in the history of our native problem".[67] The motion, said McDonald, was simply an invitation to Commonwealth parliament to make good that offer by accepting a share of the responsibility for the aboriginal population, under s.96 of the constitution which enabled the federal government to grant financial assistance to any state on such terms and conditions as the Commonwealth thinks fit. Coverley, in reply, opposed the motion as having no other purpose than to appease certain organizations which desired federal control, not in the interests of the aborigines themselves, but because it would give them "a greater chance of getting control through the Commonwealth Government than they would through the State Government". Hysteria and extremism, he said, would not solve the aboriginal problem — this should be left to the department, which had a commonsense policy "founded on years of experience. It is not a policy formulated by theorists or itinerant missionaries or dreamers. It is not a policy put forward by anthropologists."[68] The motion was eventually defeated after a debate during which Coverley, in a style reminiscent of Kitson's 1938 attack, brought to light certain recent "scandals" which had allegedly taken place on several missions, to remind the critics of the department that those "who live in glass houses should not throw stones".[69] On 6 November the house passed a compromise motion asking the federal government to make available to the state a sum of not less than $100,000 per annum for three years to supplement state expenditure and enable necessary reforms to be put into effect. The reply of the federal government was not unexpected: the existing financial commitments of the Commonwealth, said the Prime Minister, made it impossible for his government to provide the requested sum.

The 1946 Pilbara "strike"

The work of the department during the immediate postwar years was characterized by the same attitude of "sympathetic remarks and masterly inactivity" which marked aboriginal administration during the war. The Labour government, in office since 1924 (except for the period from 1930 to 1933), was running out of steam — certainly, as far as aboriginal affairs were concerned, neither Coverley nor Bray had contributed anything positive during the last two years of Labour rule. When they did act, the results were usually nothing short of disastrous. In the second half of 1946, following an increase in the departmental grant, Bray appointed two additional travelling inspectors, bringing the total number to four (their respective districts were north, northwest, Murchison, and southwest). It was an ideal opportunity for injecting new blood into the department, but the positions were filled by men whose training and experience did not exactly fit them for welfare work — they were former policemen (when the State Executive of the Australian Labour Party appealed to him to appoint an anthropologist, Bray replied: ". . . the welfare of the natives is not bound up with the advice and guidance of trained anthropologists, and it is not apparent just what advantages would result to the natives").[70] The department was obviously thinking of returning to the pre-war system, with only minor modifications. The 1946 strike of aboriginal stockmen shattered this illusion. Starting on the Pilbara, in May 1946, the upheaval had repercussions throughout the state: it was without doubt the most important single event in the history of aboriginal affairs in Western Australia to that date.

Described by John Wilson as a "number of tentative stop-work meetings" rather than a strike in the usual sense,[71] the events on the Pilbara had taken the department by complete surprise. In November 1945, as we have seen, Bray sent a senior official to investigate the rumours of a planned aboriginal strike; his report dismissed them as grossly exaggerated, concluding that the aborigines lacked the necessary organization to act in unison. This turned out to be a serious miscalculation: the strike took place almost exactly as planned. On 27 April over-anxious musterers on the De Grey station struck for higher pay but returned to work when the manager agreed to increase wages from $2 to $3 a week and found. Two days later Warrawagine station aborigines refused to work but returned the following day, without having achieved anything, after the manager called in the police. On 30 April the Pippingara station aborigines won a 50 cents wage increase. On 2 May natives from Tabba Tabba, Strelley, and several other stations were granted a similar increase. On 30 April McLeod, in a letter timed to reach Perth at the same time as the news of the strike, asked the Premier to give immediate effect to the strikers' demands and to appoint him as their "spokesman and representative".[72] Meanwhile, unrest had spread to other stations on the Pilbara and to Roy Hill on the Nullagine, and by 5 May some twenty stations were affected, in spite of the efforts of the police to "persuade" the strikers to go back to work. When persuasion failed, the police resorted to legal action. On 7 May Clancy McKenna, one of McLeod's aboriginal "lieutenants", was sentenced to three months' imprisonment for breach of s.47 of the Native Administration Act (prohibiting enticing of aborigines from their employment); on 16 May Dooley, another of McLeod's assistants, was given the same sentence for a similar offence; and on 17 May McLeod himself was arrested, charged with three offences under s.47, and refused bail. The reprisal turned out to be a serious miscalculation. In Perth, McLeod's arrest led to the formation of the Committee for the Defence of Native Rights, with Rev. H. P. V. Hodge as secretary and an imposing membership which included the Very Rev. Dean Moore, Professor A. C. Fox, the authoress K. S. Prichard, the President of the Women's Christian Temperence Union, and other public figures, including several members of the Communist Party. On 28 May a public meeting, held in the Perth Town Hall and attended by about four hundred people, endorsed the aborigines' claim for a minimum weekly wage of $3 and found, and passed a resolution protesting against the imprisonment of the strike leaders. Soon after, the committee engaged a Perth lawyer, Fred Curran, to lodge appeals on behalf of the imprisoned aborigines and to defend McLeod, still in prison awaiting trial. Early in June the committee organized an appeal for funds and moral support for the strikers, in the form of a circular letter to trade unions, women's organizations, churches, and local authorities, and, after an unsatisfactory reply from the Premier (to the effect that McLeod's actions were not in the best interests of the aborigines), it took the strikers' cause to the World Federation of Trade Unions and to the United Nations.[73]

The government, obviously taken aback by the support the strikers had been able to mobilize, beat a partial retreat. On 21 June McLeod was sentenced to a nominal fine, and soon after McKenna and Dooley were released before the expiration of their sentences, on the instruction of the Minister for Justice. The resulting sense of victory among the strikers was reinforced, late in June, by the introduction of an improved scale of rations for aboriginal indigents, approved before the strike but seen by the aborigines as the outcome of the strike. Early in July more pastoralists agreed to increase wages, but some of the strikers refused to return to pastoral employment. Gradually, the striking aborigines sorted themselves out into two groups. One was based on the Twelve Mile camp near Port Hedland, and lived by hunting kangaroos, fishing, and dry-shelling; the other had its headquarters at Moolyella, near Marble Bar, and supported itself mainly by mining alluvial tin. Why did the aborigines refuse to return to their stations, in spite of the higher wages offered? What did they hope to achieve? According to a story current at the time of the strike, which may be apocryphal but which is nevertheless highly revealing, an aborigine who was already getting $3 a week told his boss: "Me go on strike, me wantum thirty bob [$3] a week."[74] John Wilson, in his study of the later stages of the strike movement, described it as "reformist, highly organized, non-millenarian, coordinated and, if consideration to the predominant value emphasis is added, egalitarian."[75] While expressing their demand mainly in economic terms, the aborigines fought for human dignity, for an aboriginal version of assimilation — an aim summed up by Donald Stuart in the novel *Yaralie,* when he spoke of the *"real* people" of the northwest, people "with their roots in the country, people who have all the forward-thrusting attributes of the European, and the wise love of the country that the old blackfeller always had".[76] But the department and most pastoralists saw the strike as a Communist-inspired plot which had to be dealt with accordingly. Early in August the police refused to issue ration coupons for tea and sugar to the Port Hedland group of strikers (these were "wartime" rations, not rations issued to aboriginal indigents); the coupons, they were told, were with their bosses on the stations, and if they wanted them they would have to go back to work. On 14 August the strikers held a protest meeting, attended by McLeod and Hodge, at which McLeod agreed to discuss the aborigines' grievances with the police. Both men were immediately arrested for a breach of s.39 of the Native Administration Act (prohibiting a European from frequenting an aboriginal camp without permission or lawful purpose), and were subsequently tried before the police court at Port Hedland. Hodge was fined $20, and McLeod was sentenced to three months' imprisonment but was allowed to remain free pending appeal. Meanwhile, many more aborigines had abandoned their stations, and in November 1946 there were about two hundred strikers at Moolyella alone, and almost as many at the Twelve Mile camp. By the end of the year, however, signs of disunity appeared among the striking aborigines: some, believing that McLeod "could do no good for them", wanted to "follow the government"[77] and return to work, providing the pastoralists made certain concessions, while the majority were against returning under any circumstances. The dispute came to a head in January 1947 when a group from the Twelve Mile camp, led by McKenna, forcibly removed some of the "moderates" from Moolyella to the camp. The ringleaders were immediately arrested for a breach of s.9 of the Native Administration Act (forbidding unlawful removal of aborigines from one district to another) and sentenced to two months' imprisonment. Other aborigines from the Port Hedland group became involved in an incident of a different kind. In January 1947 McLeod, with the help of the Port Hedland station master, a certain Bonham, arranged for some of the strikers to help unload the State Shipping Line steamer *Dorrigo*. The police ordered the aborigines from the wharf, but McLeod persuaded the lumpers to refuse to work without the aborigines, providing they were given union tickets. Next the police organized a group of returned servicemen, but when they tried to unload the cargo, the seamen refused to work with non-unionists. The strike ended after a few days when the local branch of the A.W.U., acting on instructions from Perth, reversed its earlier decision to admit aborigines.[78] McLeod lost a battle, but the campaign was far from over. His little army was intact, and another shearing season just around the corner.

Postwar difficulties in the south

Outside the pastoral regions, the immediate postwar years were marked by continued demand for aboriginal labour. In the southwest, aborigines dominated the casual labour market, doing most of the clearing, burning off, fencing, and crutching, and providing the bulk of hands in the shearing sheds. In the metropolitan area many continued to work in factories as unskilled labourers; in the Midlands and around Wongan Hills "reliable" aborigines found permanent employment on farms; in the Murchison ample work was offering on the roads and railways. All this did nothing to improve the already strained race relations in most country areas. In May 1945, as we have seen, the Murchison Road Boards' Association appealed to the government to declare all townships within its area out of bounds to aborigines. In June the Country Municipal Councils Association asked the government to permanently confine all unemployed aborigines to reserves. In August the York police removed twelve "insolent" aborigines to the Carrolup settlement.[79] In 1946 the Northam municipal council, only a few weeks after the mayor had spoken publicly in favour of citizenship rights for aborigines, took objection to a departmental suggestion to cancel the declaration of Northam as a prohibited area — a good example of the "we're all for aboriginal rights but not in our neighbourhood" attitude, so popular in Western Australia after the war. In these circumstances, the life of an aborigine trying to carve out a new life for himself and his family was full of misery and disappointment. F. B. Vickers, in the novel *The Mirage,* set in Arkoola (almost certainly Mullewa), described with insight and compassion the struggle of a part-aboriginal couple attracted to Arkoola by high wages and the vision of a better life. Freddie was the son of a white station overseer from the northwest, brought up by his father as "proper white feller"; Nona was a Moore River "graduate" who had run away from her "missis". She had known Freddie only for a day or so before she asked him to take her with him. "I ain't going back there. . ." [to Moore River], she told him. "I wouldn't go! I'd kill myself. All they does is tell ya how bad ya are an' how good they is. They makes ya say prayers to Jesus, but he don't never listen to 'em. I don't reckon he's everybody's God like they say he is."[80] The couple worked hard, saved most of their wages, and eventually bought a small house on the outskirts of Arkoola. Then everything went wrong. Freddie lost several jobs

in succession through no apparent fault of his own. Their house
was damaged by a mob of drunken aborigines and the couple
had to move to the local reserve, only to find themselves snubbed
by the "permanents". The reserve was

hard as rock now, and a quagmire in winter, for the marks of bare feet
were baked into it. There was a well with a windlass over it; the windlass
was broken, the iron handle gone. Not far from the well was the wooden
frame of a building that had once been a washhouse and lavatory. The
iron had gone from its walls now. All around the skeleton framework was
a litter of rubbish — old boots, old clothes, a broken bed-frame, tins and
scraps of dirtied paper. And, rising out of this rubbish tip, from which
they seem to have been built, was a shambles of humpies, shacks made of
anything that might keep out weather. Some of the humpies were like
wig-wams with boughs and old bags thrown on them. Others were made
of bush timbers nailed and wired together to make the frame of a house.
Their walls and roofs were of anything — slabs of paper-bark stripped
from the swamp trees, rusted iron, boughs and old bags. One humpy was
built of hammered-out tar-drums collected from some roadmakers' camp.
Some had doors, but most had a bag curtain over their entrances. None
had windows, and the smoke of their fires curled through a thousand
chinks in the walls and roofs.[81]

Nona became pregnant. When her confinement was due she had
the opportunity to go to the local hospital, but refused because "it
ain't proper for us". It is hard to believe that any aboriginal woman
could have ever entertained such thoughts. The Mullewa aboriginal
ward, known locally as the "meat box", was an uninviting structure
of square design, enclosed in fly-wire from halfway up. Patients were
given no sheets and only one blanket. They did their own laundry,
got their own meals, and were expected to fetch wood for the "fire
tins" used to heat the building during winter. An aboriginal woman,
taken to the hospital for a post-partum operation, described her
experience in these words:

I was put in the Native Ward and instead of putting me on a mackintosh
the Matron put me on some old newspaper. After the operation, the new
sister asked Matron if she could give me a wash and Matron shook her head
and said, "We don't do that." The new sister seemed startled. So I had
to lie in my own mess, until I ran away . . . I don't know how I managed to
get home. There was another native woman in the hospital at the time,
also a native boy of about ten years age, who had to empty my pans,
and Rosie, the other woman, had to attend to my baby and sponge her
over for me.[82]

What did the department do for the countless unfortunate Freds and Nonas? For the "most pathetic and degenerate"[83] there were always the government settlements, overcrowded and understaffed. "Often enough a new superintendent, cook, or storekeeper would arrive [in Carrolup] on Tuesday's train and after a brief, despairing look round would take the return train on Thursday. For the most part the skeleton staff consisted of people who were unable to find better accommodation for a short period."[84] Discipline was a constant problem, the food monotonous (the "evening" meal, served at half-past four in the afternoon, consisted regularly of "tea, bread and jam, porridge if they want it"),[85] and the wages paid to inmates purely nominal, ranging from 20 cents to 75 cents a week, depending on the "length of service".[86] Every evening at five, the inmates were "drafted into dingy, stone dormitories, where they cursed and fought and battered at the doors. They crowed like fowls and sang the *Prisoners' Song*. They slept in filth, inadequately covered in winter, stifling hot in summer." It was not all unhappiness, of course: sometimes there were "good times in the camp . . . laughter and play almost in the old corroboree spirit of former days"[87] — behind the back of the staff. The government itself could claim credit for only one alleviating feature: the reopening of settlement schools, early in 1945, under the auspices of the Education Department (even here inter-departmental wrangling and the opposition from the Under-Treasurer, A. Reid, who was of the opinion that the "education of native children is something quite apart from the education of ordinary white children",[88] postponed the reopening of the schools for one year). In a sense, the new arrangement only added to the difficulties, since the new teachers, eager and enthusiastic, did not get on with the settlement staff. But the results were remarkable, especially at Carrolup where the headmaster, Noel White, so managed to arouse the interest of his pupils that they frequently returned to school after hours. Sensing their aptitude for drawing and painting, White encouraged the children to express themselves freely: "The song, the dance, the dramatization of simple stories, animal impersonation — these things were close to them still and had formed part of their broken, wandering, sometimes hunted lives."[89] In less than three years the fame of the "child artists of the Australian bush" spread all over Australia. In October 1947 the Native Arts Committee held a well-patronized exhibition of their work in Perth at which over $200 was realized in sales. Other paintings were later shown in Sydney where they created a minor sensation in artistic circles; subsequently they were exhibited in Melbourne, Hobart, and Launceston. In 1949 selected paintings were shown overseas by UNESCO, and in July 1950 an exhibition was arranged at Overseas House in London, receiving enthusiastic reviews.

Outside the settlements the work of the department was limited almost entirely to the policing of the Native Administration Act. Hospital facilities outside the metropolitan area remained inadequate. The department forgot about its plans for aboriginal housing, discussed enthusiastically and at some length in 1943 by the State Advisory Committee on Post-War Housing and later by the Commonwealth Commission on Post-War Housing. As regards education, in the words of the Minister for the North-West himself, "all that was necessary was primary education, to be followed by manual training for the boys and domestic training for the girls".[90] But even this modest aim was out of reach for some: because of the insistence of the Education Department on a policy of "non-segregation", many an aboriginal child outside the metropolitan area found itself debarred from school by parental opposition (in June 1947, 650 aboriginal children were enrolled in state schools, including about 250 in settlement schools, and over 100 in the metropolitan area). Here the Education Department found itself opposed by the powerful Teachers' Union which, perhaps more realistically, believed that some sort of segregation was desirable if the aboriginal child was to be given any education at all. In September 1945 the union, at its annual meeting, endorsed the establishment of properly staffed aboriginal schools in all country towns with a large aboriginal population, to be followed by the introduction of a special curriculum suited to the abilities and adapted to the needs of aboriginal pupils. The first suggestion was rejected out of hand by the Minister for Education when he told parliament that the policy of "non-segregation", would be continued;[91] the second was acted upon early in 1946 when a special curriculum for schools in aboriginal settlements and for state schools with large numbers of aboriginal pupils was adopted by the Education Department. The curriculum had the following aims: to provide "rudiments of our civilization", to attain literacy, to inculcate "desirable habits of hygiene and living", to secure a training in rural pursuits, and to provide "desirable moral and spiritual attitudes".[92] The aboriginal child was still to be conditioned rather than educated.

The 1947 general election

By the beginning of 1947 it was obvious that the department was moving into a blind alley; something more than "masterly inactivity" was needed to cope with the vastly different conditions of the postwar years. What was to be done? The defeat of the Labour government, after four successive electoral victories and fourteen years of continuous rule, provided the answer, though no one knew it at the time. While in opposition the Nationalist (after 1945 Liberal) Party and the Country and Democratic League were increasingly critical of the government's handling of the aboriginal question; on assuming office, on 1 April 1947, the coalition found it difficult to translate their criticism into concrete proposals. The Premier, Ross McLarty, did the best possible thing under the circumstances: he created a separate Portfolio of Native Affairs and appointed R. R. McDonald, the leader of the Nationalist Party, as Minister. Some of the early actions of the new government were discouraging. For instance, following the resignation of the travelling medical inspector and the subsequent blacklisting of the position by the British Medical Association (the salary offered was too low), serious consideration was given to a merger of the Department of Public Health and the Department of Native Affairs. Late in April 1947 the Minister for Education announced in parliament that while co-education of white and aboriginal children would continue in principle the situation would always be dealt with "in the light of local conditions".[93] In May cabinet decided that separate aboriginal schools would be established whenever requested by white parents, with the proviso that under no circumstances would the children of exempted aborigines or of holders of citizenship rights be forced to attend such schools. On the Pilbara, the new government adopted a conciliatory attitude. Late in April, following a formal offer by the Pastoralists' Association to increase musterers' wages to $3 a week (conditional on the reintroduction of compulsory contracts of service), McDonald sent the Acting Commissioner, C. L. McBeath, to Port Hedland, in an attempt to persuade the strikers to return before the start of the shearing season. He found the strikers well entrenched, especially at the Twelve Mile camp where they had erected a number of permanent buildings and started a school for the camp children, without any outside help (the teacher, a part-aboriginal named Tom Sampie, was educated at the Beagle Bay mission). "They would take a lot of moving",[94] said the travelling inspector Jensen in March 1948, and in the following month McBeath advised McDonald: "So far we have been acting on the assumption that the strikers will return, but now it appears that they will remain."[95] Finally, the new government took a more flexible line as regards Commonwealth-state co-operation in aboriginal affairs. At the 1946 Premiers' Conference Western Australia was the leading opponent of federal control (New South Wales and Queensland were also opposed to it); at the 1947 conference McDonald came out openly for greater Commonwealth participation in aboriginal affairs, and was instrumental in the calling of a meeting of federal and state aboriginal welfare authorities to consider common matters of policy and administration, including the feasibility of transferring the responsibility for aboriginal affairs to the Commonwealth. The conference, held in February 1948, decided against federal control and recommended instead that the federal government should subsidize the states on a pound for pound basis; it also decided against uniformity in administration but suggested that the state authorities should keep each other informed of legislation in force. The 1948 Premiers' Conference, once again on McDonald's initiative, passed a motion asking the Commonwealth to implement the resolution of the 1948 aboriginal welfare conference which called for financial assistance by the Commonwealth to the states. The Prime Minister, in what the *West Australian* later described as a "contemptuous rejection of moral responsibility",[96] declared the motion carried but not accepted: his government already shouldered more than a fair share of the burden, in the form of $840,000 it spent annually on social welfare services for the aborigines.

But all these problems were in a sense marginal: the overriding question was that of a successor to Bray who retired on 13 April 1947. In July McDonald, in what can be only described as a stalling operation, appointed the Perth magistrate F. E. A. Bateman to undertake a survey of the aboriginal problem and to make appropriate recommendations to the government. In the following month, while attending the Premiers' Conference in Sydney, McDonald called on A. P. Elkin at the University of Sydney. According to the latter, the Minister told him that "his government had to do something about native affairs; but what? Its members had no more ideas about what to do than did the other party. Having, in opposition, used my name in debates, he now came to ask me."[97] Elkin advised

McDonald to appoint a good Commissioner, from outside the state, and back him to the full — and drew the attention of several old Papuan "Hubert Murray trained" hands to the advertisement. In July 1948 the Bateman report cleared whatever obstacles there may have been to an appointment from outside the public service, by recommending that the vacant position of Commissioner of Native Affairs should go to a man with sound anthropological training and a thorough administrative experience. This was done in August when S. G. Middleton, Assistant Director of the Papua-New Guinea Department of Native Affairs and District Services, was appointed to the position. Middleton was born in New South Wales and spent his childhood in southwestern Queensland. Before joining the Papuan public service, in 1926, he was a clerk with the Queensland railways and a journalist with the *Northern Miner,* and his first job in Papua was a brief engagement as clerk with New Guinea Mines Ltd. at Bootless Inlet. He was forty-six at the time of his appointment as Commissioner for Native Affairs.

10. Middleton's New Broom
1948 - 1954

The Bateman Report

Whatever ideas Middleton may have had when he arrived in Western
Australia in September 1948, he found that his future course of
action had been pretty well mapped out by magistrate Bateman. The
Bateman Report,[1] presented in July 1948, followed what had by then
become something of a tradition on such occasions: it was cautious
and non-controversial. "It seems that in dealing with the aboriginal
question as a whole", said the magistrate, "there is a danger of
becoming too idealistic. While admitting that the aborigines have
been badly treated in the past and that our treatment of them today
leaves much to be desired, I believe that it is important to realize their
limitations and to approach the problem in a practical way." Not
that Bateman was reluctant to criticize whatever shortcomings he had
unearthed during his inquiry. Even a cursory inspection of Moore
River, said the magistrate, would convince anyone that the outlook
from an institutional viewpoint was absolutely useless: "sanitation
and hygiene are merely words without meaning at Moore River."
He found similar conditions at the aboriginal cattle stations: "To
refer to Moola Bulla as a native institution in its present run-down
state would be palpably absurd." The magistrate also criticized,
in words almost identical with those used by the Moseley Royal
Commission thirteen years earlier, the dual position of police protectors which required them to prosecute an aborigine and at the same
time to defend him. "This objection is so obvious and so well founded
as to require no further comment." Perhaps more damaging, in the
long run, was the tendency to staff the head office with former policemen, the practice being to appoint them as inspectors in the field
and to promote them shortly after to Perth, on the basis of seniority
in the public service, thereby depriving promising young officers
of the department of their natural line of promotion. The pastoralists,
too, came in for their share of criticism. Noting that the Kimberleys

were the only part of Australia where aboriginal workers were not paid in cash, the magistrate volunteered the opinion that sustenance in return for service was "not in accord with modern civilization"; the customary objection that the aborigines had no idea of the value of money and of its function was "really an indictment against ourselves". But he absolved the Pilbara pastoralists from any direct responsibility for the strike, blaming the departmental system of supervision, or lack of supervision, for the upheaval. Finally, the magistrate took the missions to task for their tendency to encourage idleness. "The day of evangelizing the natives unaccompanied by other activities to uplift them has gone": something more than religious training, accompanied by rudimentary education, was necessary if the aborigines and the community at large were to benefit from missionary endeavour.

Bateman's recommendations are too detailed to be discussed here in full. Among the more important ones were the following: the establishment of a departmental field organization independent of the police; the introduction of a cadet system for field officers; the replacement of employment permits by an annual registration of employers; the introduction of a small cash wage in the Kimberleys and some regulation of wages in the rest of the state; transfer of aboriginal hospitals to the Department of Public Health; the abolition of the Natives' Medical Fund; and higher subsidies to missions, on condition that they comply with the official policy of uplift. But the most important recommendations were those pertaining to town aborigines. North of Geraldton, the expedient of "discouraging" aborigines from towns should be replaced by a definite policy of compelling employers to provide adequate accommodation for their aboriginal workers. South of Geraldton, the magistrate suggested a government housing scheme for selected aboriginal families, and the removal to settlements of all aborigines residing on reserves, for they were, as a body, beyond redemption, "idle, unreliable, fond of drinking and gambling and generally useless". Education in the pastoral north should not aim at too high a standard and should be limited to instruction in reading, writing, money values, and weights and measures, and training in cleanliness, thrift, and social behaviour. In the south, education should be geared toward assimilation, "to fit these people into our economic and social structure". More specifically, education should aim to eradicate laziness and indolence and replace them with industry and effort; higher education, in the magistrate's opinion, was unnecessary "except in rare cases". Noting that in the closely settled areas there existed "all the seeds of racial hatred", Bateman thought that the policy of "non-segregation" in state schools should be abandoned, as it was in everyone's interest that these seeds did not germinate. Instead, aboriginal children should be educated in special institutions, known as colleges, to be established in good farming and grazing country, where they would be changed "from a nomadic, idle and discontented race to a settled, industrious, contented section of the community".

Middleton's early reforms

Middleton had brought from Papua-New Guinea the concept of a purely welfare department, with an independent and well-staffed field organization of its own. Accordingly, in October 1948, he asked McDonald to approve a plan envisaging the transfer to other departments of the police, health, and educational functions of the Department of Native Affairs, followed by the establishment of a decentralized field organization approximating fairly closely the existing district administration in Papua-New Guinea. The state was to be divided into two regions (with the 26th parallel as the separating line), each under the control of a regional protector who was to be the co-ordinating authority responsible for the supervision of departmental activities throughout the region. The regions were to be divided into districts, each in the charge of a district officer whose staff would include one or several cadets and travelling inspectors and appropriate clerical and welfare personnel. The first step towards the implementation of the new scheme was taken in February 1949 when the aboriginal hospitals at Broome, Wyndham, Derby, and Port Hedland were handed over to the Department of Public Health (already responsible, since February 1948, for the "general" health of aborigines). The establishment of regions and districts was approved by the cabinet in March 1949 and put into effect in June, with minor modifications. The regional protectors envisaged in the original plan were not appointed: the northern region, consisting of the East Kimberley, West Kimberley, and Pilbara districts (the latter included the Gascoyne sub-district) was placed under the control of the Senior Administrative Officer stationed at Broome, and the southern region, embracing the Great Southern and central districts (the latter included the Murchison and the eastern goldfields subdistricts) under the control of the Deputy Commissioner, in his capacity as "Control-

ling Officer, Southern Region". In mid-1951, following the resignation
of the Senior Administrative Officer in charge of the northern region,
the regions were quietly dismantled. In October 1951 the north-
central district was created from parts of the Pilbara district and the
Murchison sub-district, bringing the number of districts to six.

All this, of course, required money, but for the first time since 1897
finance was no real problem: the government, having committed
itself to reform, was bound to be generous. Staffing was not much
of a problem, either: Middleton brought with him his own "branch"
of the Papua-New Guinea Department of Native Affairs, appointing
two of his former colleagues as district officers, one as the Senior
Administrative Officer in Broome, and one as superintendent of the
Moore River settlement (another newly appointed district officer
was formerly a magistrate in India). As could be expected, the
appointments created dissatisfaction among the Western Australian
officers of the department, and were subsequently attacked in parliament by the former Minister for the North-West, A. A. M. Coverley,
as having a detrimental effect on the morale of local officers.[2] But
there still remained the task of replacing the police with departmental
officials or other suitable persons. Early in 1949 Middleton mooted
the appointment of local solicitors as protectors in country areas,
but this was turned down by McDonald, a lawyer himself, on the
grounds that they would have to be paid fees which the department
could not afford. With the appointment of additional field staff, the
problem in the end solved itself: by June 1956 there were in the whole
of Western Australia only twenty-nine police protectors (mainly in
the southwest), as compared with seventy-seven five years earlier.
Some police, finding it difficult to adjust to the new order of things,
gave up their protectorship voluntarily; the constable at Beverley,
for instance, resigned when Middleton accepted the recommendation
of the district officer, rather than his own, on some minor matter.
Other policemen, however, continued to treat the field staff of the
department as their subordinates. The situation in Western Australia,
said Middleton after one particularly galling incident, early in 1949,

is such that I do not consider any useful purpose can be served by pursuing
the point of a Sergeant of Police being disrespectful to a Departmental
Head. It is a new one on me, but I am afraid that we must be prepared
to suffer indignities at the hands of subordinate officers of other Departments, local authorities officials and others whose views towards natives
are reflected in their attitudes towards officers of this Department.[3]

Concurrently with the administrative reorganization just described, Middleton tried to do something about the aboriginal settlements and cattle stations, so severely criticized by magistrate Bateman. His first impulse was to rehabilitate Carrolup and Moore River by removing some of the more troublesome inmates to Cosmo Newbery, converted into an institution for "criminally minded" aborigines late in 1948 (it was also to be used as a detention centre for aborigines sentenced to gaol terms and released into the custody of the Commissioner of Native Affairs). The use of ministerial warrants was discontinued, except in most unusual circumstances; they were replaced by court orders committing the aborigine in question to the care of the department. Facilities and accommodation at the settlements were improved, and an aboriginal foreman was appointed at Carrolup early in 1949.[4] Wages paid to inmates were increased, and even the detainees at Cosmo Newbery were given a small monthly allowance. But the settlements were seemingly beyond rehabilitation. In Carrolup the new superintendent — a graduate of the Muresk Agricultural College appointed by Middleton, with training in agricultural pursuits in mind — found the aborigines "beyond him" and was dismissed by the cabinet after suffering a nervous breakdown. At Moore River there was friction between the headmaster and the superintendent (also a Middleton appointee) over school-leaving age, the former insisting that the children should remain in school until sixteen. In October 1950, after a well-publicized mass escape from Cosmo Newbery, the local road board asked the department to withdraw all inmates until proper detention facilities had been constructed. By this time Middleton had become convinced that aboriginal settlements were a burden politically, as well as wrong in principle, since they postulated a policy of isolation and segregation.[5] Towards the end of 1950 girls of school age were transferred to missions, and during the first part of 1951 adult males from Carrolup and Moore River were found employment outside the settlements, while those requiring medical attention were directed to report to the nearest hospital in the district in which they normally resided. In August 1951 the Moore River settlement was closed and handed over on a walk-out-walk-in basis to the Methodist Overseas Mission. Carrolup, on the other hand, was retained as a farm training institution for boys, known as the Marri-bank farm school. In spite of intensive canvassing by the field staff, aboriginal parents showed no enthusiasm for sending their children to the new school — in fact, not a single volunteer came forward. The presence of state wards kept it going for little over a year, until it was closed, in June 1952, and handed over to the Baptists Aborigines' Mission five months later.

If the closing of the Carrolup and Moore River settlements was largely the result of political considerations, the even earlier abandonment of Udialla and Munja was almost entirely a matter of expediency. Udialla had always been regarded as something of a joke by all the settlers of West Kimberley, except the pastoralists on adjoining properties; the soil was badly eroded, "little better than a dust bowl",[6] and the officer-in-charge made no secret of the fact that Udialla sheep would not survive if he were to keep the boundary gates shut. The station was closed in December 1949 and the inmates were transferred to the La Grange feeding depot south of Broome. In April 1949 Munja was handed over to the Presbyterian Church which later transferred the Kunmunya mission to Wotjulum on the Munja reserve. Moola Bulla, on the other hand, was retained. In August 1949, almost a year before the Kimberley pastoralists started to pay cash wages, Moola Bulla station hands were given $2.50 a month, and tradesmen $8.00 a month; the school, closed early in 1942, was reopened in the following year. In 1952, after Moore River and Carrolup had been handed over to missions, Middleton thought of similarly disposing of Moola Bulla but decided to keep it, since it gave him little trouble. It was probably the right decision. "The concept of the place was excellent", said Dr. Ida Mann when she visited the station soon after with a medical team; ". . . it was the best attempt to solve the native problem we had seen so far."[7]

Middleton, McLeod, and the pastoralists

The Pilbara strike, well in its third year when Middleton took office, was a crucial test for the new administration: the strikers had defied the government and would have to be treated firmly, but they were also displaying the very spirit of self-reliance which the new administration hoped to kindle and foster among all aborigines. More importantly, the strike had by then affected the frame of mind of many aborigines outside the Pilbara. In December 1946 a group of Perth aborigines, led by Helen Clarke (and encouraged by McLeod), formed the Coolbaroo League;[8] it was primarily a social club, but its offshoot, the Coolbaroo York Club for adolescents, organized evening classes in industrial art, elocution, and deportment, and the

league itself hoped to establish a community settlement near Arma-
dale, an outer Perth suburb. On the Murchison, seventeen aborigines
were arrested in April 1947 after a "protest march" through Mount
Magnet in support of two mates arrested earlier on a drunk and
disorderly charge. On the Ashburton, aboriginal station hands were
abandoning pastoral properties in droves to work in the lead mines,
and the pastoralists complaining that mining was an "unsuitable"
occupation for aborigines. Even the "unspoilt" aborigines of the
Kimberleys were showing signs of unrest; early in 1948 there were
rumours of a planned strike at Derby, and even further inland
aboriginal station hands wanted to know exactly what wages they
were getting.

Luckily for the new administration, McLeod kept away from the
strikers during the second half of 1948, while maintaining contact
with them through Dooley whom he met from time to time in Port
Hedland (in August 1948 McLeod was reported in the De Grey
River area, but when the police tried to trace him he could not be
found). This gave Middleton a breathing space. In November 1948
he instructed the Pilbara district officer not to place obstacles in the
way of aboriginal workers who wanted to leave pastoral employment.
Soon afterwards he enlisted the support of Father Bryan, the Roman
Catholic priest at Port Hedland, in an attempt to undermine McLeod's
influence in the district. The government would lease to the church
an abandoned pastoral station, White Springs, for the purpose of
establishing a mission, and would give it a lump sum for capital
expenditure, whereupon the church would assume the responsibility
for running costs. In December, while the White Springs mission
was still in the planning stage, Middleton made his first mistake:
following a complaint from the manager of Pippingara station that
the striking aborigines were constantly trespassing on the property,
he declared the Twelve Mile camp a "prohibited settlement"[9] (under
regulation 107 which enabled him to declare any settlement on
Crown land — the camp was technically a forestry reserve — a
prohibited settlement, for any reason whatsoever). If Middleton
expected the Twelve Mile aborigines to return to their stations, he
badly miscalculated. The strikers refused to move, and, joined by
McLeod who suddenly appeared in the camp, threatened "industrial
action" if the department closed the camp.[10] Then Middleton made
his second mistake: he decided not to enforce the proclamation for
the time being, and to proceed speedily with the establishment of the

White Springs mission. In March 1949 the property was vested in the Roman Catholic Church, and the department gave it $6,000 towards initial capital expenditure, with a promise of more to come. In 1950 the Bishop of Geraldton asked the Premier for $20,000 to enable the church to complete the building operations; the government gave him $8,000, on the understanding that he should not expect further assistance. But finance was only one difficulty the mission had to face. For one thing, it was slightly outside the area normally frequented by the Pilbara aborigines. More importantly, it was a direct threat to McLeod's standing with the Pilbara aborigines, and he did his utmost to turn them against the mission. It was abandoned towards the end of 1951.

The failure of the White Springs mission was not the only setback for the administration. In March 1949 there occurred a new outbreak of violence on the Pilbara, caused by the insistence of the strike leaders that the aborigines should not return to pastoral employment without first obtaining their consent. Later in March 1949 a group of strikers removed an aboriginal stockman from Corunna Downs to the Twelve Mile camp, apparently against his will, and in April some thirty strikers abducted two aboriginal employees from Meentheena station. The arrest of the culprits and their trial at Marble Bar, on 21 April, was followed by a walk-out of the remaining station aborigines, bringing the Pilbara pastoral industry to a virtual standstill. On 26 April the Seamen's Union called for the immediate release of the imprisoned strikers, threatening to impose a ban on wool from the stations where "slave conditions still apply that brought about the present strike".[11] Expecting the worst, Middleton flew to Port Hedland, only to find that the situation had been exaggerated by the press and the radio. He returned to Perth convinced that some of the difficulties could have been averted had the department been represented in the district by someone with a more realistic appreciation of the situation than the former policeman O'Neill, whose "view towards the requirements of his position is diametrically opposed to ours".[12] He also concluded that nothing short of removing the root causes of aboriginal discontent would bring lasting peace to the Pilbara; since the aborigines were now conscious of their value to the pastoral industry, the belief that "no . . . nigger is worth more than a quid [$2] a week",[13] so widespread among the pastoralists, was an obvious source of aboriginal dissatisfaction. The arrest, on 22 June, of another group of strikers, on charges of enticement, gave Middle-

ton an opportunity for putting his new ideas into practice. As soon
as the news of the arrest reached Perth, he asked McDonald for
permission to suggest to the Marble Bar police that the charges
should be withdrawn; if they refused, he intended to appear in court
in the aborigines' defence and to argue that they had acted in
accordance with tribal custom involving "mob rule", as well as to
point out to the court that s.48 of the act (relating to enticement) did
not apply to aborigines, its sole purpose being to prevent the pirating
of aboriginal labour by other employers. In the meantime, on 28
June, the Seamen's Union placed a ban on wool from the "black"
stations on the Pilbara, and on 1 July the Independent Labour
member for Bourke, Mrs. D. A. Blackburn, brought the issue to
the attention of federal parliament.[14] The trial itself, held early in
July, was something of an anti-climax. The aborigines were defended
by the Senior Administrative Officer, S. Elliot-Smith; they were
acquitted, on the ground that the abductions did not involve violence
or even intimidation, but only moral suasion.[15] Three weeks later
McLeod and Elliot-Smith concluded an unofficial agreement, the
former undertaking not to stir up more trouble among the aborigines
in return for a pledge that the administration would do its utmost
to persuade the pastoralists to accept the "Limestone and Mount
Edgar rates" ($6 per week for station hands and $2 per week for
domestics, in addition to keep valued at $4 per week), negotiated
some time earlier by McLeod with the managers of the two stations.
But the truce came too late to prevent adverse publicity overseas.
In August the Czech newspaper *Svobodné Slovo* reported that the
Roman Catholic church was "buying Australian aborigines and
selling them at a profit as slaves".[16] In October the Soviet Foreign
Minister, Andrei Vishinsky, accused Australia in the United Nations
of openly violating "fundamental freedom and human rights";
instead of "slinging mud" at the peoples' democracies, the Australian
government would be well advised to pay more attention to its own
backyard.[17]

Late in 1949 McLeod joined a group of about twenty-five aborigines
mining for tin on the Cooglegon field near Marble Bar. Helped by
the war in Korea and the resulting worldwide shortage of metals, the
group expanded its mining activities, switching from tin to tantalite,
columbite, and wolfram, the latter readily marketable at $3,000 a
ton. By August 1951 the group had about six hundred members,
and its gross earnings for the year were $96,000. The profits were

reinvested into real estate and mining machinery. Working through two interlocking companies established for that purpose, the Northern Development and Mining Co. Pty. Ltd. and the Glen Ern Pastoral Co. Pty. Ltd., McLeod acquired five pastoral properties for about $40,000. Yandyerra station was chosen as a base for the group's social service projects including a school, a hospital, and accommodation for old people. Yandyerra fired the imagination of many sympathizers all over Australia. Among those who had spent some time on the station were the novelists Max Brown and Donald Stuart, and at one stage McLeod had sixteen Europeans on his staff, all of whom "envisaged the scheme in either Socialist or Communist terms".[18] Late in 1951 McLeod entered into an agreement with Western Wolfram, a company formed by an Adelaide syndicate headed by the financier George McDonald, regarding the joint exploitation of the group's mineral deposits. In February 1952 McLeod lodged further mineral claims covering tungsten, tin, gold, and molybdenum, and applied for a general permit to employ aboriginal labour on a large scale. It was a move of such importance that the cabinet referred the application to a special committee consisting of F. E. A. Bateman and Sir Ross McDonald (he had resigned his portfolio in October 1949 and was knighted shortly after). Before the committee could conclude its inquiry, however, new circumstances had arisen which changed its frame of reference: by April 1952 the group was on the verge of bankruptcy, owing $13,000 on the purchase price of Yandyerra station alone, and proceedings had been initiated against it by Western Wolfram for the recovery of a substantial sum, said to be $60,000. The report of the committee, presented in August 1952, dealt with several issues. Starting with McLeod's claim that he spoke on behalf of the Pilbara aborigines, the committee thought that his motives must be accepted "with some reserve", adding that it saw no reason to doubt the sincerity of his belief that he had a mission in aboriginal welfare; indeed, it was his very sincerity which probably accounted for his impact on the aborigines. While the pastoralists had every reason to resent his activities, they themselves were not without blame, for as a body they "have almost for a century taken native labour for granted". The committee recommended that McLeod should be allowed to stand or fall on the outcome of the situation which he himself had created, and that the aborigines should not be held responsible for the fact that he had become their leader.

The group should be allowed to work out its own salvation, and if the group failed it would be preferable that the reasons for lack of success should be inherent in the group itself and its present leadership rather than there should be any pretext arising or suggested in the minds of natives for attributing such lack of success to intervention or interference of the Government.[19]

The committee also recommended that the State Mining Engineer should become a shareholder in the Northern Development and Mining Co. Pty. Ltd., and that the Treasury should be asked to lend the group $6,356 on the condition that it accepted an accountant nominated by the government. These salvage operations, however, did little to improve the group's financial position, for the litigation initiated against it by Western Wolfram was eventually won by the latter on appeal, bringing the group close to complete financial collapse.

Compared with the complex situation which the new administration had to cope with on the Pilbara, the problem of the Kimberleys was but child's play. The department held most of the trumps: the Bateman Report had ventured the opinion that the practice of paying station workers in kind "cannot continue forever";[20] organized public opinion was squarely on the aborigines' side; and their living conditions were palpably sub-standard. There were, of course, the pastoralists to reckon with, but their stock arguments that the aborigines should not be interfered with, that they were happy and contented, and that money would only unsettle them, lacked the conviction of days past. Middleton played his cards with considerable skill. In October 1948 he told the Pastoralists' Association: "From a Departmental point of view I am not in favour of paying high wages at this stage . . . not until the natives learn the value of money . . ."[21] In February 1949, however, at a conference with the association's representatives, he thought that the time had come for a close look at the question of cash wages, but agreed not to take any action pending a departmental survey of working conditions in the Kimberley pastoral industry. Completed in October 1949, the survey established the fact that some West Kimberley pastoralists were already paying their aborigines in cash and that all were convinced that cash wages were inevitable; the aborigines themselves were anxious to be paid in cash and "jingle a few coins in their pockets to be able, when they feel inclined, to buy something for the wife and kids and to feel that they are an important unit on the station".[22] The survey recommended the immediate introduction of a nominal cash wage (supplemented by a fixed issue of food and clothing) and the compulsory provision of housing of a prescribed standard by the pastoralists for their employees. This was rejected by the Pastoralists' Association as unsuited to the "present development of the natives in the Kimberleys".[23] Two months later the fight was over: a special meeting of pastoralists, held in January 1950, having noted the pressure brought on the department "by various interests and public opinion, even though for the most part entirely misinformed",[24] agreed to the introduction of a "standard" wage of $2 a month for stockmen and $1 a month for domestics. The agreement was put into effect in July 1950, without much enthusiasm on the part of the pastoralists. "The Company pays in so much a week for everyone", complained a character in Mary Durack's novel *Keep Him My Country*. "It goes into a sort of trust fund like a bank account and instead of having things given you out of the store like the old days, you pay for them — comes to much the same thing in the end — only more book-keeping for the manager."[25]

Aboriginal welfare

The stated goal of Middleton's policy outside the pastoral areas was "assimilation into the general community on the basis of reasonable equality in all facets of community life".[26] It was a long-range goal, to be achieved in several stages, and culminating in equality before the law. The road was strenuous and often discouraging. Within his own department Middleton found considerable opposition to his ideas from officers who resented the appointment of outsiders to most of the key positions. Other government departments, with the exception of the Department of Public Health and the Department of Education, were equally unenthusiastic, while some police, as we have seen, were openly hostile. The general public was indifferent. All these were facts which could not be wished away. Accordingly, Middleton decided to work initially through missions — to be more precise, missions catering for aboriginal children.

I regard Missions as being valuable and important administrative adjuncts of the Department [he said in 1951, echoing his mentor, Sir Hubert Murray] and missionaries as being vitally essential to the welfare of the native race . . . We all must have religion in some form or another; take that away and you leave a spiritual vacuum which would be soul and body destroying . . .[27]

In January 1949 the department increased the subsidy for approved mission inmates from 30 cents to 40 cents a week (there was an increase in July 1947, from 26 cents a week to 30 cents — the first since 1917), in addition to free drugs, clothing, and blankets, and promised an annual review of subsidies based on the variation in the cost of living. In March 1950 the cabinet approved a new scale of financial assistance to missions catering for children, ranging from 90 cents to $1.25 per week, depending on location; significantly, subsidies for adult inmates remained unchanged. Late in 1949 Middleton introduced mission grants-in-aid for approved capital expenditure, and in the following year he sought to institute special educational grants to missions ($500 per teacher annually) similar to those in operation in Papua-New Guinea. Since such grants would have conflicted with the provisions of the 1895 Assisted Schools Abolition Act, the Education Department agreed, early in 1951, to second staff to mission schools instead, the cost to be debited to the Department of Native Affairs. The first mission to avail itself of this opportunity was Mount Margaret, and by early 1953 all except the Roman Catholic missions had been brought under the scheme. In February 1953 the Education Department established a special section responsible for all aspects of aboriginal education, including attendance and the supply of teaching aids, and compiled a *Provisional Curriculum for Coloured Pupils in Caste Schools*. Based on the assumption that there was a considerable gap between the white and the aboriginal child, not only in skills, habits, and attitudes but also in "potential", the curriculum aimed to equip aboriginal children with skills which would enable them to "support themselves and their families within the economic structure of the State", to inculcate desirable habits of hygiene and desirable moral and spiritual attitudes, and generally "help ultimate assimilation".

Middleton's calculated encouragement of Christian missions attracted several new missionary societies to the state. Early in 1949 the Australian Aborigines' Evangelical Mission, a breakaway group from the United Aborigines' Mission, opened a mission for tribal aborigines on Madura station, an abandoned pastoral property near the Transcontinental Railway; it was later moved to the Cundeelee reserve north of Zanthus. In 1950 the influential Methodist Overseas Mission applied for a permit to establish a mission near Kellerberrin in the eastern wheatbelt, but the insistence of the mission council on what the department regarded as an unreasonably high initial capital grant wrecked the scheme. Early in 1951, after the government had decided to close the Moore River settlement, Middleton offered the Methodists the first option on the property; it was handed over to the mission in August 1951. Renamed Mogumber Methodist mission, the institution catered almost exclusively for children of both sexes and became known for its emphasis on vocational training, hitherto largely neglected by other missions. In 1952, following the failure of the Marribank farm school at Carrolup, the department offered the institution to the Baptist Aborigines' Mission, in preference to the U.A.M. and the Australian Board of Missions, both of whom had shown interest in the property. It was reopened in November 1952 as the Marribank Baptist mission.

In addition to increased financial support for children's missions the administration tried, wherever possible, to ensure the attendance of aboriginal children at state schools. By 1951 practically all children in the southwest were receiving regular schooling; there was still sporadic opposition to their presence in state schools but it often took such subtle form as the manipulation of the school bus service to the disadvantage of aboriginal pupils. Outside the southwest old attitudes persisted. In Carnarvon, for instance, most aboriginal children went to church schools which were segregated. In the northwest, outside Port Hedland, it was practically impossible for a full-blood child to receive even a rudimentary education. In the Kimberley, a few part-aboriginal children were allowed to attend schools in Broome, Derby and, until 1950, also at Wyndham, although aboriginal parents were given every encouragement to send their children to the nearest mission school.

Strangely enough, it was in the field of higher education that the department met with the most outspoken opposition to its efforts to secure for the aboriginal child a "reasonable equality" of opportunity. During the thirties and forties the administration had shown no interest in secondary schooling of aborigines,[28] and as late as 1948 the Bateman Report expressed the opinion that the aboriginal child lacked the ability to benefit from secondary studies. For Middleton, on the other hand, the scholastic difficulties of the aboriginal students were largely a matter of motivation and environment.[29] In April 1949, on the recommendation of the Minister for Native Affairs, the cabinet authorized the department to purchase a house in East Perth and to convert it into a hostel for aboriginal girls attending secondary schools. The violence of public reaction was quite un-

expected. "McLarty Dumps Natives into East Perth", complained
the *Westralian Worker,* suddenly espousing the cause of East Perth
ratepayers.[30] Following a public protest meeting, held in July, the
cabinet rescinded its decision, but in August 1950 the department was
given permission to buy a house in Alvan Street, Mount Lawley,
for the same purpose. Once again, local residents were displeased.
Early in September sixty Mount Lawley ratepayers petitioned the
Perth road board not to allow the establishment of an aboriginal
hostel in a white residential suburb, and some angry letters appeared
in the correspondence columns of the metropolitan press. One correspondent went to considerable length to explain that, while
opposed to the hostel, he was not motivated by "racial prejudice
or self-interest"; the house was too small for a hostel and the girls
would have little privacy, since it was too close to the street.[31] Another correspondent, signing himself "Indignant, Mt. Lawley",
while admitting that he was "not without consideration for natives",
pleaded for a lowering of rates if no other site could be found for
the hostel.[32] But the "hostel party" was equally determined and
organized a public meeting at the Perth Town Hall, at which a
number of distinguished figures, including Sir Ross McDonald and
Paul Hasluck, spoke in support of the scheme. The cabinet upheld
its decision and the hostel, known as Alvan House, was officially
opened in January 1951; a similar hostel for boys, named after Sir
Ross McDonald, opened in West Perth in February 1952.

"Reasonable equality" in other spheres proved even more difficult
to attain, partly for reasons inherent in the aborigines themselves,
such as apathy and reputation for unreliability, and partly because
of continued opposition from the white community. In the economic
sphere, one of the first steps taken by the new administration was
to discontinue indiscriminate rationing, since it only perpetuated
pauperism, and to limit the distribution of relief to genuinely needy
aborigines. Every effort was made by the field staff to find permanent
work for able-bodied men, with varying success. Late in 1948
Middleton secured the repeal of s.9 of the Land Act which limited
to 200 acres the area of Crown land the government could grant
or lease to an aborigine or a person of aboriginal descent (a white
Australian was entitled to 1,000 acres), expecting that some of the
more ambitious aborigines would welcome this opportunity to
become landowners, but the fear that the amendment would be
followed by a flood of applications, voiced in parliament by an

opponent of the measure, turned out to be without foundation. So most aborigines continued to work as "hewers of wood and drawers of water" for the white farmers.[33] Since they lacked skills, the department could do little to improve their position; in 1951 the field staff were instructed to secure "equivalent conditions" for aboriginal farm workers,[34] without any apparent results. The large-scale immigration of "New Australians" made the position of aboriginal workers even more tenuous, and by 1952, for the first time since the outbreak of the war, they ceased to dominate the labour market in the southwest.

Provision of adequate housing and hygiene facilities for aborigines was another facet of the policy of assimilation. This was central to Middleton's thinking. Poor housing, apart from its obvious effect on health, produced in the aborigines an apathy towards their own betterment, and bred juvenile delinquency and a general lack of social standards; allied to the insecurity of employment, it helped to produce instability, encouraged migratory habits, and had a devastating effect on the education of their children. In December 1948 the cabinet approved the construction of ten houses (two each on the Narrogin, Katanning, Gnowangerup, Beverley, and Moora reserves), to be rented for 50 cents a week to aboriginal families selected by ballot, but the scheme was abandoned because of an alleged shortage of building materials. Next, the department set up three mobile workshops to assist aborigines who wanted to build cottages on their own land, only to find that there was very little interest in the scheme. Early in 1951 the department came up with another proposal: a housing scheme for aborigines similar to that administered by the State Housing Commission, with some minor modification, such as the selection of applicants by the department rather than the commission. This was rejected by the cabinet in May 1951, allegedly on the grounds of shortage of building materials.[35] The real reason for the decision is not difficult to find. "No plan designed to raise the living standards of natives", said Middleton, "and to improve their status in the white community could succeed without the whole-hearted co-operation, sympathy and support of the white community and particularly the local authorities."[36] And these bodies were unsympathetic, to say the least. In July 1950 several aboriginal families were refused building permits by the Bassendean road board; "apparently it is quite all right for them to live in bag and kerosene tin humpies as long as they are out of sight, but they must not have houses which do not conform to road board stand-ards."[37] In the country, several municipalities asked to be declared prohibited areas; Geraldton made such a request in 1949, Kalgoorlie in 1950, Mandurah in 1951, and in the following year Mullewa asked the Local Government Department to draft a by-law to prevent aborigines from remaining in town after dark. In 1950 the Bruce Rock road board prevented the department from building several cottages for aboriginal families because the specifications were "sub-standard". In 1951 the Ongerup road board objected to the erection of Nissen huts for seven aboriginal families, on the same grounds. Even aborigines with citizenship rights were not to be spared; in 1950 the Brookton road board passed a resolution calling for the establishment of aboriginal compounds on the outskirts of major country towns where all aborigines, including those with citizenship rights, should be compelled to reside. The opposition of local authorities forced Middleton to abandon all plans to provide housing for aborigines within town boundaries and to adopt instead the policy of "qualified segregation",[38] by which he meant the con-struction of simple dwellings on reserves, with adequate ablution and sanitary facilities. This was probably the most realistic course of action under the circumstances, for there existed in most country areas a "deep-rooted and at times almost militant prejudice" against the aborigines as a race.[39] A Korean veteran, in uniform, found it impossible to get a meal in a Williams cafe: "Sorry, not allowed to serve natives . . .", the waitress told him, "not even a native who is a Korea soldier, and even holders of citizenship rights."[40] Through-out the southwest the white folk were complaining that the aborigines were "getting a bit above themselves".[41] Nothing apparently can be done, announced the *Narrogin Observer,*

to improve them to become respectable members of the community. They appear to lack all sense of responsibility and decency. Even in the case of individual members who display an attitude of respect for the rules and regulations which govern society, it is almost invariably found to be based on pretence, sooner or later to give way to the pressure of sordid inclina-tions which are fundamentally natural to them.[42]

In the field of public health, "reasonable equality" was easier to attain: success was largely a matter of finance and organization. Early in 1949 the Department of Public Health took over the four aboriginal hospitals formerly administered by the department; at the same time it became responsible for the supervision of mission hospitals and medical aid posts, liaison with the flying doctor service and infant welfare centres. The Commissioner of Public Health, Dr. C. E. A. Cook, conceived the responsibility of his department in broad terms: it should provide not only medical and hospital facilities, but also impart to the aborigine "a sense of hygienic responsibility which means education in citizenship with a view to his eventual integration into the white community".[43] Of the many achievements of the public health authorities only two will be mentioned here: the virtual eradication of leprosy and trachoma. Having little faith in the value of the "leper line", the Department of Public Health embarked on active treatment of all known cases of leprosy, discharging the patients as soon as possible. This increased the confidence of other sufferers and made it easier to discover new cases, while the follow-up of discharged patients and of all known contacts of new patients, acted as a check on the spread of the disease. The anti-trachoma campaign began in earnest after a pilot survey of the Wotjulum mission, undertaken in 1951 by Dr. Ida Mann. The survey showed such a high incidence of trachoma that the Department of Public Health ordered a similar survey of the entire Kimberley population, during which 2,866 persons were examined; it confirmed the suspicion that the aborigines formed a dangerous reservoir from which a spread-back to the white population could occur (56.49 per cent of all full-bloods examined showed traces of trachoma). A survey of the eastern goldfields and the Murchison was undertaken soon after, and a survey of the southwest was completed in 1955.[44]

Where the work of the public health authorities depended on the co-operation of the public, the results were not so satisfactory. Aboriginal women seeking admission to maternity wards in government hospitals found various obstacles placed in their way. "Many of these women are in filthy condition", said the matron of the King Edward Memorial Hospital in 1949. "It is all very well to talk about the rights of the natives, but I do not think that people who talk in this way would like to be in the next bed to some of these women."[45] In 1950 a deputation led by the member for Avon Valley and supported by the National Council of Women, asked the government to provide a separate ward for aboriginal women at the York government hospital. It was not uncommon for medical practitioners in country towns to have two waiting rooms, one for white and another for aboriginal patients. A few doctors, notably Dr. Jacobs at Narrogin,

Dr. Constable at Guildford, and Dr. Jolley in Midland Junction, had flourishing aboriginal practices, but the majority regarded aboriginal patients as something of a nuisance, since the fees they were allowed to charge under the Natives' Medical Fund were low (they had remained unchanged since 1937) and their collection entailed too much paperwork, not to mention frequent and irritating delays. In March 1950, following representations from the State Health Council, the department increased the fees to the level charged under the Workers' Compensation Act. This strained the resources of the fund to the utmost, and in July 1952 the department raised the employers' contribution from $2 to $6 with respect to every aborigine permanently employed, with a maximum annual contribution of $300 from any one employer, irrespective of the number of aborigines employed. Even this did not rescue the fund from insolvency; in 1952–1953 it had to be subsidized to the extent of $2,660, and in the following year the deficit reached a staggering $18,298. The practice of some employers of engaging aboriginal workers without an employment permit added another complication. When an aboriginal not covered by the fund and who was not a recognized indigent consulted a private doctor, the latter, in the first instance, tried to collect his fee from the patient; if he did not succeed he claimed the fee from the department which in turn attempted to recover it from the aborigine. In practice, the cost was almost always borne by the department, since most aborigines, accustomed to regard free medical service as their birthright, made no attempt to meet their financial responsibilities. Consequently, when this arrangement was discontinued, in January 1953, many doctors refused to treat aborigines who were not covered by the Natives' Medical Fund except for cash, and the burden of "free" medical service fell somewhat unfairly on the shoulders of the more idealistic section of the medical profession.

Middleton and citizenship rights

The new administration placed considerable emphasis on the improvement of the aborigines' legal status: if assimilation was not to remain just another empty slogan, equality before the law was imperative. The position, at the time of Middleton's arrival in September 1948, was as confusing as it was unsatisfactory. By virtue of the 1948 Nationality and Citizenship Act a Western Australian aborigine was a subject of His Majesty and a citizen of the Commonwealth of

Australia; unless he possessed a certificate of exemption he was also subject to the restrictive provisions of the 1936 Native Administration Act which at the same time conferred upon him certain privileges to which a white citizen was not entitled. An exemption, furthermore, freed the aborigine only from the restrictions of that act, for he still remained subject to the special provisions of the Criminal Code, the Evidence Act, the Firearms and Guns Act, the Mining Act, the Dog Act, the Fauna Protection Act, the Fisheries Act, and the Land Act, as well as the federal Social Services Act (some were protective in intention, others restrictive, and all were discriminatory). It was only by securing a certificate of citizenship under the provisions of the 1944 Natives (Citizenship Rights) Act that an aborigine could secure full civil rights, although until 1951 all "persons of the half-blood", irrespective of whether or not they possessed such a certificate, were denied the right to vote at state elections.

Middleton approached the problem in a piecemeal fashion. In October 1949 the Minister for Native Affairs asked the Minister for the Interior to extend old-age pensions and maternity benefits under the Commonwealth Social Services Act to all detribalized aborigines; the latter replied that this could be achieved by a more judicious grant of exemptions by the department. Since an exempted aborigine found himself not only outside the jurisdiction but also outside the protection of the department, Middleton did not accept the advice; in his opinion, an aborigine should not have to renounce the protection of the department merely to qualify for social service benefits. In February 1953, after another unsuccessful representation to the federal government, the department started to issue exemptions to all elderly, invalid, and widowed aborigines, irrespective of caste. In June 1954 the Solicitor-General reversed his earlier ruling that an exempted "native" was to be no longer deemed a native for the purpose of the Native Administration Act: he was exempted only from its restrictive provisions and was still entitled to the welfare benefits it conferred. The ruling opened the way for a wholesale grant of exemptions to enable all aborigines to qualify for social service benefits.

But exemptions did not bestow full civil rights, for it was only by obtaining a certificate of citizenship in accordance with the provisions of the 1944 Natives (Citizenship Rights) Act that an aborigine could shed the status of a second-class citizen. Introduced in an atmosphere of wartime idealism, citizenship rights for aborigines turned out to be something of a sham, however. Although only 206 certificates had been issued before mid-1948, local authorities were increasingly concerned with the liberality of certain magistrates in granting citizenship rights. In December 1949, for instance, a deputation from the Beverley, Brookton, and Pingelly road boards told the Minister for Native Affairs that aborigines should not be granted citizenship rights without the approval of the local authority concerned. In May 1950 a conference of representatives of Great Southern road boards resolved that applicants for citizenship rights should undergo a five-year probationary period to prove that they were worthy of the privilege. Citizenship rights for aborigines had by then become a political issue. In September 1950 the former Minister for the North-West, A. A. M. Coverley, introduced a private members' bill which provided for an automatic extension of citizenship rights to children of aborigines who had been granted such rights. The bill was passed with the support of two independent members, in the face of determined opposition from the government. In 1951, however, the government pushed through another amendment which provided for the appointment of citizenship boards to deal with applications for citizenship rights. The boards consisted of a resident or stipendiary magistrate and a representative of the road board or municipality in which the applicant resided, and there was no appeal from their decision.

Middleton's ideas had by this time undergone a radical change. He had never had any illusions as to the value of the 1944 Natives (Citizenship Rights) Act: he thought that the application procedure was humiliating in the extreme, and the certificate itself a mixed blessing, for an aboriginal citizen was required to sever his aboriginal associations without in any tangible way improving his status in the white community. After the 1951 amendment of the act, Middleton concluded that the existing concept of aboriginal administration throughout Australia was "basically, fundamentally and entirely wrong", for it tended to inculcate in the aborigines a sense of inferiority and a shame of their own race and colour; they were citizens by birth, and the only bar to full civil rights lay in the discriminatory clauses of specific acts.[46] The meeting of the state and Commonwealth Ministers in charge of aboriginal affairs, convened in Canberra in September 1951 by the Minister for Territories, Paul Hasluck, provided Middleton with an ideal platform for an elaboration of his views; in a well-argued statement, he told the conference that the time had come for the repeal of all discriminatory legislation throughout Australia and its replacement by special welfare acts, to be applied to all aborigines in need of the benefits they conferred.[47] The failure of the conference — its only tangible result was the formation of the Native Welfare Council consisting of state and Commonwealth ministers concerned with aboriginal affairs — and, closer to home, the reluctance of the government to commit itself to reform, convinced Middleton that the only course of action open to him was to appeal directly to public opinion. In January 1952 he was instrumental in the formation of the Native Welfare Council of Western Australia, an umbrella organization embracing all groups interested in aborigines and their welfare, with E. H. B. Lefroy as president, which was subsequently recognized by the Minister for Native Affairs as the body authorized to speak on behalf of the affiliated welfare organizations.[48] Later in the year the Narrogin District Welfare Council and the Wagin District Welfare Council were formed, with some encouragement from the department; this was followed in 1953 by the formation of the Native Welfare Association at Kojunup, the Native Welfare Committee at Mount Barker and the Native Welfare Group in Collie.

Middleton's direct appeal to the public, which was to earn him the wrath of the politicians, was well organized. Believing that the aboriginal question was as much a "white problem" as it was an "aboriginal problem", he had from the beginning tried to re-educate the public, using every conceivable medium and technique. He and his officers wrote articles for the press, lectured at meetings, and spoke on the radio, appealing to Christian values or to the creed of equal rights, emphasizing the contributions of aborigines in sport and art, telling his audiences that cultural differences were learned and not biologically inherent; it was on Middleton's representation that the Education Department deleted from its text books all passages describing the aborigines as the lowest and most degraded of human beings.[49] Some time in 1952 Middleton joined the Labour Party which had been slowly moving in the direction of full citizenship rights for aborigines. A few weeks before the meeting of the platform revision committee of the party, scheduled for October 1952, Middleton wrote two articles entitled "Not Slaves, Not Citizens" and gave them to Des Stuart, the Indian-Fijian wife of the novelist Donald Stuart. Des, whose ancestry was not publicly known (she was thought to be part-aboriginal) sent them to Ernest de

Burgh, the editor of the *West Australian,* pretending she was the author. The first article appeared on 10 October, and the second was published the following morning:

Not Pagans, not Christians; not white, not black; not half-castes, but outcastes. Such are we, who are the descendants of the original "half-castes", the progeny of white man — and not always the "degenerate" types, my masters — mating with aboriginal women. . . We are natives whether we like it or not. Well then — Hath not (a native) eyes? Hath not (a native) hands, organs, dimensions, senses, affections, passions? Fed with the same food, hurt with the same weapons, subject to the same diseases, healed by the same means? If you prick us, do we not bleed, if you tickle us, do we not laugh? If you poison us, do we not die? . . . Have we not been turned away from your places of worship, and other public places? Is it not a fact that in this very city "natives" have been asked to stay away from churches because certain white Christian ladies objected to "natives" sitting next to them in Church?[50]

The articles had the desired impact. On 18 October the *West Australian* accused the government and the opposition of utter disregard for the welfare of the aboriginal population, and criticized the churches and the University for their complacency. Two days later the platform revision committee of the Labour Party drew up an eight-point aboriginal welfare plank which included full citizenship rights for all aborigines, adequate housing and education, encouragement of aboriginal land settlement, and a "fair" wage for aboriginal workers.[51] On 22 October a Labour member gave notice in the Legislative Council that he intended to introduce a private members' bill to extend citizenship rights to all part-aborigines.[52] On 5 November a public meeting, chaired by the Lord Mayor of Perth, declared its support for the bill, and the *West Australian* spoke of the need for a "new charter" for the aborigines. The bill was defeated on 26 November but the impetus was not lost. Early in December the State Congress of the Labour Party ratified the changes in the party platform. A public meeting, held on 12 December under the auspices of the Women's Service Guild, elected a committee which was given the job of drafting a new bill to replace the existing Native Administration Act, and appointed a deputation which later asked Middleton to assist the committee with the drafting of the bill. On 15 January 1953, a month before the general election, another deputation waited on the Minister for Native Affairs. It was led by the Anglican Archbishop of Perth, Dr. Moline, the president of the Native Welfare Council, E. H. B. Lefroy, and the state president of the Women's

Service Guild, Mrs. Kastner. The deputation asked for an assurance that the proposed amendment of the Native Administration Act would incorporate the principle that Australian-born children, regardless of race, had the full privileges and obligations of citizenship. It received none whatever.

Labour and aboriginal welfare

It is against this background that the 1953 electoral victory of the Labour Party should be viewed. Of the three major parties contesting the election only Labour had a forward aboriginal policy;[53] the Liberal Party stood almost entirely on its record,[54] while the policy of the Country Party, if indeed it can be termed such, amounted to little more than verbose platitudes.[55] The Hawke government wasted little time in translating into concrete proposals the party's electoral promise to give aboriginal welfare the utmost consideration. It increased the departmental vote (reduced by the previous government in 1951–1952 and again in 1952–1953) to $472,642; in the following financial year, 1954–1955, the vote was $792,000, almost 1 per cent of all expenditure from the Consolidated Revenue Fund (total expenditure on native welfare was probably in excess of 1 per cent of all expenditure — other departments, such as the Department of Public Health, spent a part of their budget on services for aborigines, the Lotteries Commission contributed $39,654 for specific welfare projects in 1954–1955 alone, and missions received a subsidy from the federal government in the form of child endowment for children in their care).[56] In July 1953 the department increased mission subsidies for children to $2.25 a week, including a clothing and blanket allowance, and a new rate of $1 a week for adults was approved. Parity with white children's institutions was achieved in June 1954 when the subsidy was raised to $3.08 a week — an increase of over 1,000 per cent in six years. In April 1955 the Lotteries Commission agreed to pay an additional 50 cents a week to any mission whose principles did not debar it from accepting this form of subsidy; missions unable to accept the payment on religious grounds were given an equivalent grant by the government. Earlier still, in June 1954, the administration gave missions greater security of tenure, by offering them an option on a ninety-nine year lease of up to 1,000 acres of land held by any mission at that time, with the qualification that the land so leased would automatically revert to the Crown if it ceased to be used for mission purposes.

During the first two years of Labour rule four new missions were founded and two departmental institutions were handed over to existing missions. In September 1953 the Assembly of Gospel Brethren, with missions in New South Wales and South Australia, opened the Kurrawang mission on a reserve near Kalgoorlie. In 1954 the Seventh Day Adventists' Conference of Western Australia established a mission at Karalundi, about thirty-five miles north of Meekathara, designed to cater for children from nearby pastoral properties; its Wiluna mission opened early in the following year. The Wonguntha mission training farm was started in 1954 by R. W. Schenk, the son of the founder of Mount Margaret, as an inter-denominational institution for boys of post-primary standard. The two departmental institutions handed over to missions were the Cosmo Newbery corrective institution and the La Grange feeding depot. The former was closed in December 1953 and handed over to the U.A.M.; La Grange was transferred to the Beagle Bay missionaries in January 1955.[57] By this time most missions had changed their philosophy. There was less evangelizing and more practical training, as well as an increasing emphasis on work with children, even at such "adult" missions as Mount Margaret (in November 1953 the twenty-five missions then in existence had 1,125 children and 1,074 adult inmates). By the end of 1954 all missions in the southern half of the state had become children's institutions, having gradually replaced the old dormitory system, with its dreary atmosphere, by modern and humane methods of institutional care. A few missions made a modest start in the direction of replacing European staff with aborigines. The Roelands mission farm appointed a part-aboriginal kindergarten teacher as early as 1945; the Warburton Range mission employed a "fully accredited" aboriginal missionary in 1950, and Mount Margaret brought out a part-aboriginal teacher from South Australia. In 1954 the U.A.M. employed a linguist, W. H. Douglas, for translation work at the Warburton Range mission, as a first step in the direction of establishing an indigenous church. The only mission not affected by the winds of change was the "unproductive, futureless"[58] Forrest River. Randolph Stow, in the novel *To the Islands,* captured some of the feeling of futility hanging over the mission. After a lifetime of work among the aborigines the superintendent, Heriot, realized that he no longer believed in the values which had till then supported him and that he had lived into a new age in which the legend of his former ruthlessness had become an anathema. "I've given half my life . . .", he told a group of inmates who came to remonstrate with him for sending away a "trouble maker". "My wife gave all hers. I've lived in poverty, half-starved at times, been lonely, been overworked, been forgotten by everyone in the world except you."[59]

In the field of education, the early years of Labour rule were marked by a steady if unspectacular progress, as the policies initiated by the previous government were gradually bearing fruit. By mid-1955 2,200 aboriginal children were enrolled in primary and secondary schools. In the southwest the last vestiges of discrimination had disappeared, and the main problem was now irregularity of attendance and the resulting retardation of aboriginal pupils, due largely to the migratory habits of most native families. On the goldfields 54.4 per cent of aboriginal children of school age were attending school in June 1954. In the northwest and the Kimberleys the old white attitudes were still in evidence; early in 1954, for instance, a handful of aboriginal children were admitted to the state school at Roebourne, only to be segregated soon after. About the same time the Education Department decided to establish schools on selected pastoral properties, but it was not until 1957 that the first such school was opened on Gogo station near Fitzroy Crossing. There was also some progress in the field of secondary education. In 1952 one girl passed the Junior Examination of the University of Western Australia, and in the following year a second girl passed the same examination in six subjects. In 1954 three girls were successful in the Junior Examination and one gained the Leaving Certificate. By mid-1955 seventy-two aboriginal students were enrolled in state and private high schools in Perth, Bunbury, Kalgoorlie, and Geraldton, where a subsidized hostel for aboriginal girls attending the local state high school was opened by the Church of England early in 1954. The church was also indirectly responsible for the first aboriginal University student. In 1953 it awarded a bursary to Irwin Lewis, who became the first aboriginal matriculant in Western Australia and later joined the department as a patrol officer.

In the field of housing Labour did only a little better than the previous government. In June 1953 six State Housing Commission homes earmarked for aborigines were under construction, four at Port Hedland, one at Bassendean, and one at Kwolyin, and the cabinet had approved the building of another twenty-five. They were to be constructed in European residential areas and cost between $3,700 and $4,000, with a fortnightly rental ranging from $10 to $12. In 1954 the commission designed a new "intermediate" type of aboriginal housing, costing about $3,200, and by mid-1955 thirty-two commission homes had been rented to aborigines, and another twenty-nine were under construction. There was also some improvement in the standard of amentities on reserves; in 1954–1955 over $12,000 was spent on water supply, lavatories, and laundry and shower facilities, mainly in the southwest. Finally, in 1954, the last of the prohibited areas were cancelled, including the city of Perth from which the aborigines had been barred since 1927.[60]

On the Pilbara, Labour was called upon to preside over the liquidation of McLeod's empire. The financial position of the group, already precarious as a result of the litigation with Western Wolfram, took another turn for the worse after the loss in transit of four drums of tantalite, worth about $3,000 each. Expecting the group to go bankrupt, the department began to make preparations for the reopening of White Springs as a government settlement, but a lucky find of rich columbite deposits staved off the collapse. The group was also plagued by increasing internal dissension as more and more aborigines began to demand "cash money in hand".[61] In June 1954, after conditions had reached near-starvation level, there occurred a mass exodus from the group's camps,[62] and in August the shareholders of the Northern Development and Mining Co. Pty. Ltd. voted to put the company into voluntary liquidation. The group then split into three factions: the Yandyerra "mob", with a membership of about three hundred, which remained under McLeod's control, and two breakaway groups in the Moolyella-Marble Bar area with a membership of about a hundred each. The collapse of the group solved one problem and created another. As a senior departmental official remarked shortly before the voluntary liquidation of the Northern Development and Mining Co. Pty. Ltd.,

in the past three years the company had earned big money, but the only apparent material results are a record of expensive litigation, a number of non-producing pastoral properties, and a quantity of largely idle machinery and plant. . . On the credit side there is the confidence and self-reliance which has been engendered in these people. It is tangible, and something the value of which I do not attempt to assess. It is probably unique in the history of this State and, if the company fails, it may rest with this Department whether this spirit is nurtured or crushed.[63]

Middleton opted for the first alternative. In the face of vociferous opposition from McLeod, the department opened a rationing depot at the Twelve Mile camp and provided transport for all former members of the group who wanted to move to the camp. In December 1954, at McLeod's request, Middleton agreed to take over the management of the group's affairs, having first obtained an explicit promise from McLeod that there would be no interference on his part. In April 1955 the department helped the aborigines to form the Pilbara Natives' Society which was later incorporated as a business concern, and established marketing and purchasing agencies in its name, under a written agreement with the aborigines. In May the department, on behalf of the aborigines, purchased Riverdale station near the township of Nullagine, formerly owned by the group, for use by the members of the society, and made arrangements for the opening of a hostel and a school on the property. But McLeod would not admit defeat. In April 1955 he went to Hall's Creek, apparently to organize a protest march across the "leper line". Late in May he returned to the Pilbara and held a series of meetings with the former members of the group. The aborigines of the Pilgangoora-Yandyerra area then repudiated their agreement with the department and signed a contract with McLeod which gave him the exclusive control of their mining and other business activities, whereupon the department withdrew from the group marketing scheme.[64]

The 1954 Native Welfare Act

In November 1953, in keeping with its electoral promise to grant citizenship rights to aborigines, the Labour government brought down the long-awaited bill to amend the 1936 Native Administration Act. The essence of the bill can be gauged from its terminology: the department was to be known as the Department of Native Welfare, and its permanent head was to have the title of Commissioner of Native Welfare. As a welfare measure, the bill sought to repeal most of the restrictive clauses of the old act, as well as a number of other clauses which were discriminatory in that they applied only to aborigines. Specifically, the bill proposed to abolish employment permits and agreements (by then Western Australia was the only state to retain penal sanctions for breaches of employment contracts), prohibited areas, Courts of Native Affairs, and the Natives' Medical Fund; it also sought to end the prohibition on the supply of liquor to aborigines and to abolish the right of administration to remove aborigines to reserves, while retaining the provisions of the 1936 legislation pertaining to cohabitation, aboriginal marriages, leprosy control, aboriginal evidence, and the right of the department to supervise the economic affairs of aborigines. The bill did not propose to confer citizenship rights on all aborigines but only on part-aborigines, with the qualification that any part-aborigine unfit for such a responsibility could be classed as a "native" by magisterial order, or could apply to the Minister to be classified as such.

The debate centred on the twin issues of citizenship rights and liquor. The opposition came out openly against both proposals, using a variety of arguments: the aboriginal problem could not be solved by legislation; the reforms were "not in the best interest of the native population"; the part-aborigines would be denied the guidance of the department; the extension of citizenship rights would decrease mission subsidies, for only full-blood inmates would be subsidized.[65] The Legislative Assembly passed the bill with a comfortable majority, but in the Legislative Council, where the government was in a minority, the bill was given an unfriendly reception. "People in the Great Southern towns", said L. Craig, "complain that, if the Bill is passed, there will be riots and drunken orgies, and that it will not be safe for women to walk out after dark."[66] The member for the southwest province was no doubt exaggerating, but his concern was not without foundation. There was a danger in granting liquor consumption rights to aborigines: in the absence of the moderating influence of group disapproval, they were likely to adopt the worst drinking habits of the uninhibited white "swillers", the group with which they were in most intimate contact.[67] The member for the southwest province, H. L. Roche, quoted figures from the latest annual report of the Police Department to document his concern about the growing disregard for the law among the part-aborigines, largely "the result of the policy followed by the Native Affairs Department and its officers".[68] Much of the debate, however, was quite unrelated to the bill before the house. Several members were highly critical of the work of the department in general, and of Middleton's public criticism of certain aspects of aboriginal administration in particular. "I feel that the present Commissioner of Native Affairs has been foolishly intemperate in his statements", said L. Craig. "One might almost say he has been impertinent in his public statements. No one doubts his earnestness, but his folly in publicly making statements about the Act which it is his duty to administer is obvious."[69] The former Minister for Trans-

port, Railways, and Mines, C. H. Simpson, attacked Middleton for
the frankly propagandist nature of his latest annual report which,
by implication, accused both parliament and the government of
lack of sympathy for the aborigines. He also disclosed that Des
Stuart, the author of the articles "Not Slaves, Not Citizens", was
not an aborigine; he did not go as far as to state the articles had been
written by Middleton himself, but the import of his remarks that
the Commissioner's part in the episode had been the subject of an
inquiry by the Public Service Commissioner was well understood.[70]

My own feelings of Mr. Middleton are that he is a very earnest officer,
somewhat of an idealist and a little inclined, at times, to haste when
a more cautious approach to his objective would be better. The last-
mentioned trait still needs to be curbed, as it can easily lead to intolerance
and general misunderstanding.[71]

The defeat of the bill, late in session, was the politicians' revenge
for Middleton's manipulation of public opinion: for the first time
since 1948, the department was clearly on the defensive. In September
1954 a watered-down version of the bill was sent back to parliament
and passed by both houses, after a perfunctory debate. The price
which the department had to pay for the parliamentarians' complaisance was high, for citizenship rights were not mentioned in the bill,
the prohibition on the consumption of liquor was left intact and
cohabitation and sexual intercourse with aborigines remained a
punishable offence. And yet, for all its shortcomings, the 1954
Native Welfare Act, promulgated on 20 May 1955, was a landmark
in the history of Western Australia's aborigines: by freeing them
from the shackles and humiliations of a legal status likened by
Paul Hasluck to that of a born idiot,[72] it gave them reasonable
equality before the law without which all other attempts to advance
them would have been but a sham.

11. Conclusion

Much water has flowed under the bridge of white-aboriginal relations in Western Australia, or for that matter, in Australia as a whole, since 1954. In one sense, the changes in the aboriginal situation have been so radical that they can be only described as a revolution. But, as W. E. H. Stanner put it, "the great reforms of the recent past — the full suffrage, the end of discriminatory laws, and other such things — all real, all valuable, all in their way courageous, did not damage real interests or pockets to an alarming extent . . ."[1] Their main effect was psychological: they raised hopes and expectations which remain to be fulfilled — or repudiated. In the United States of America similar reforms of the not too distant past are now bearing fruit in the negro "revolution of rising expectations". Already, in Australia, there are signs among the aborigines of "anger born of frustration".[2] Aboriginal leaders are losing patience. They have given up asking for what they think is due to their people; they now urge their followers to stand up and fight.

But this book is not concerned with the present. It is an attempt to describe past endeavours to solve the aboriginal problem, and wherever possible, to account for their success or failure. Its practical value, if any, lies in the hardly original suggestion that some of the present-day difficulties may have their roots in the past: both ourselves and the aborigines are in some sense prisoners of collective experience. In Western Australia, the aborigines' collective experience since the arrival of the white man has been marked by several persistently recurring themes. One such theme centres on the rigidity of the underlying assumptions which had moulded our attitudes towards the aborigines. "Once the idea was to kill them off", said Peter Coleman, speaking with reference to Australia as a whole, "then the more humane programme was to let them die peacefully and meanwhile to smooth the dying pillow, now the policy is to assimilate them."[3] This summing up of our record may be something of an over-simplification, but it contains an important element of truth: we have never envisaged the aborigines as having any right of choice, and our attitudes towards them have always involved a physical, spiritual, or cultural imperialism of one kind or another. In our abhorrence of pluralism, we have not only convinced ourselves that the aborigines would be better off through adopting all our ways; we have also come to believe in the existence of "The Wistful Aboriginal",[4] whose main ambition in life was to become a brown Australian. At the same time, "it was always typical of our approach to require the aborigines to give up something as the price of good relations with us":[5] their land, their religion, their kin, and their friends, the prospect of adequate schooling for their children and of minimum medical care and decent living conditions for themselves, their cultural and their racial identity. Even those whom we have attempted to segregate on reserves were to pay a price for our benevolence: they were to be debarred from the material blessings of our civilization. In Western Australia, during the 1830s, we had deprived the southwest coast aborigines of their tribal lands, thereby damning them to the role of shiftless vagrants and economic pests. Under Governor Hutt we had offered them protection "in their persons and in the free enjoyment of their possessions" but also the dubious benefits, from their point of view, of a planned "advancement in civilization".[6] It was during Hutt's tenure of office, too, that we had started debating with one another about the best means of promoting this goal. Hutt himself, foreshadowing today's critics of the policy of assimilation, believed that, left to themselves, the aborigines would, by constant contact, become "infected" with civilization,[7] whereas Lieutenant (later Sir George) Grey and his followers were convinced that civilization was something which could be taught, by force if necessary; it was the latter precept which prevailed in the end. But the attempt was doomed to failure, for most of Her Majesty's aboriginal subjects had shown little inclination to abandon the ways of their fathers, while for many others "civilization was a cloak they donned easily enough, but they could not wear it and live".[8] Reinforced by pseudo-Darwinian notions of the survival of the fittest, rapid depopulation among the coastal tribes confirmed the settlers' suspicion that the aborigines were destined to vanish from the face of the earth; this led in turn to the abandonment of the policy of planned advancement in civilization and its replacement, by the middle sixties, by the expedient of "humanitarian care of the unfortunate".[9] This change of outlook coincided with the beginnings of territorial expansion into the vast pastoral regions north of the Tropic of Capricorn, marked by unprecedented violence on both sides. It was on the pastoral frontiers that the settlers found the final proof of their moral and intellectual superiority, and that the "white man's attitudes were confirmed to a pattern which has damned the descendants of Aborigines ever since . . ."[10] Only a few years ago a Pilbara pastoralist, writing under a pseudonym, complained in all seriousness about the people down south who were

blind as bats where coons is concerned. Half of 'em never seen a nigger in their lives, yet all they talk about these days is how to "uplift" the pore blackfeller. . . I've known a few that needed it, and I've uplifted 'em — on the toe of my boot.[11]

And there is little reason to believe that the past cruelties do not live in the memories of many people of aboriginal descent, and that much of their cynicism and fatalism today does not derive from the harsh treatment they had received at the hands of the white man in the past. "In a period of anxious good-will, with a widespread desire to do what is 'good for' the Aborigines it is perhaps too easy to assume that these things are forgotten."[12]

During the last quarter of the nineteenth century the protective element of official policy had undergone an important change. Under Governor Hutt protection was conceived in humanitarian terms; the pearl-shell fishery acts of the early seventies and the subsequent special aboriginal legislation of 1886, 1897 and 1905 sought to protect the aborigine as an economic asset, by discouraging abuses on the part of employers of aboriginal labour. Not infrequently, the policy involved protection of white interests as well; the appointment of police as "protectors" of aborigines and the introduction of contracts of service with penal sanctions are two cases in point. The latter example, however, should not be pressed too far, for in Western Australia, in contrast with most other parts of the world affected by European contact, "free" rather than contract labour was the norm, and the provision of labour for European enterprise only a minor aspect of aboriginal administration. Indeed, pastoral employment was not without appeal for the aborigines, since many had abandoned their tribal lands voluntarily in order to secure a share in the novel and desirable goods which only the pastoralist (or the missionary) could provide. It is therefore misleading, as the humanitarians and other well-intentioned critics had done so frequently in the past, to raise the question of slavery and exploitation in this context. The aborigines were "free" to leave, and in any case they worked no harder than the minimum the "boss" would stand for. Admittedly their "wages", in the form of rations, were barely sufficient to keep body and soul together, but the pastoralist had always many more mouths to feed in addition to those employed on his station. As far as the aborigines were concerned, the pastoralist was there to be "exploited" as part and parcel of the new environment, and so were other persons or institutions; this is implied in the term "intelligent parasitism"[13], coined by A. P. Elkin to describe aboriginal attitudes during this stage of European conquest.

Sometime before the First World War three new elements were added to our already complex attitudes towards the aborigines. The first was the postulate of partial segregation or social isolation, manifesting itself in the existence of a colour bar in schools and hospitals in the southwest, particularly along the Great Southern, and in the establishment of the Carrolup and Moore River aboriginal settlements, in 1915 and 1918 respectively. It is important to remember the origins of this phenomenon, for it was a spontaneous reaction on the part of the white country folk to the rapid growth of the part-aboriginal population and their subsequent demand for education for their children and a "fair go" for themselves. Although the numbers of part-aborigines involved in this process of integration were fairly small, it was brought to a halt, almost as soon as it had started, by a lack of intelligent appreciation of its real nature on the part of the white Western Australians. The resulting disillusionment was a causal factor behind many aboriginal attitudes which can be observed even today in any southern township or aboriginal reserve: resentment, aggressiveness, lack of dependability, irresponsibility in situations concerning payment of rent, food, and hospital bills, various forms of ambivalence such as demanding assistance as a birthright and resenting all help proffered — all these attempts to reinforce personal and group integrity are in some way related to our failure to accept the southern aborigine on equal terms.

The second element to be added to official policy during this period was the principle of "tutored" assimilation. Formulated along somewhat different lines by Lieutenant Grey soon after the establishment of the colony and abandoned during the 1860s, the policy was resuscitated by the 1886 Aborigines Protection Act and given official blessing by the 1905 Aborigines Act which made provision for individuals who had dissolved their tribal associations to become exempted from the application of legislation pertaining to the control of aboriginal population; another clause of the same act gave the Chief Protector the power to remove an aboriginal child from the custody of the parents. Of little importance initially, this provision was later applied with increasing ruthlessness, in an attempt to suppress all individual and social characteristics different from those of the average Australian, thereby ensuring the eventual disappearance of aborigines by a process of thin spreading of colour among the white population. The heyday of this policy was the twenties and the thirties, but as late as 1944 the Natives (Citizenship Rights) Act required that a candidate for citizenship rights should have dissolved all "tribal and native" associations, except with respect to lineal descendants or relations of the first degree, and even four years later the Bateman Report saw the splitting of generations as the only solution to the aboriginal problem.

The third new component of official policy to emerge before the First World War was the postulate of complete segregation of tribal aborigines on gazetted reserves. Humanitarian in intention, the policy entailed a partial protection of white interests as well, at least in the case of aboriginal cattle stations established primarily as buffers between the nomadic tribes and the marginal pastoral regions. Since segregation was not its main purpose, the experiment proved to be fairly successful, in marked contrast with the aboriginal reserves proper which became increasingly denuded of aboriginal population as time went on, since the aborigines would not forsake certain material items, such as stimulants, which they could obtain only by contact with the white man. Put into cold storage in the late thirties and abandoned officially during the fifties when most of the large reserves were cancelled, the policy suffered from other inherent drawbacks. Almost invariably, the reserves were of extremely low potential, and in any case the aborigines were not given legal title to the land; nor could they claim, by right, to share the new assets discovered on them. It is true that in the early thirties Neville, probably inspired by developments in Indian administration in the United States, had on several occasions attempted to have the larger aboriginal reserves declared "A Class" reserves under the Permanent Reserves Act, and had even tried to secure for the aborigines a share in the royalties derived from minerals found on reserves, but the spirit of the times was against such bold innovations.

The inter-war years were largely unproductive in terms of ideas.

Some of the old formulas, such as the policy of complete segregation, were quietly dropped, while others were refined to a point of perfection. At the back of these developments was the realization that something had gone wrong; in spite of concerted efforts to preserve them, the tribal aborigines were still dying out, while the southern coloured people continued to adhere to their own ways with a tenacity bordering on the rebellious. The prescribed remedy was more and better protection, and a more vigorous "tutoring" towards assimilation: such was the tenor of the 1936 Native Administration Act which conferred upon the Commissioner of Native Affairs greatly increased powers over the daily lives of his aboriginal charges, and established a regime of benevolent tyranny and an efficient administrative machinery to enforce it. But changing conditions, particularly during and after the Second World War, made this concept of aboriginal administration outmoded: the 1946 strike of aboriginal stockmen and the subsequent developments on the Pilbara are examples which speak for themselves. Not until 1948, with the appointment of S. G. Middleton as Commissioner of Native Affairs, was there a break with the past, but it was not as complete as might appear at first sight; the emphasis on welfare should not obscure the fact that the Middleton system was basically paternalistic, even though the tyranny of former days had gone forever. It is worth noting, for instance, that the 1954 Native Welfare Act, in defining the duties of the Department of Native Welfare, empowered it

to exercise such general supervision and care over all matters affecting the interests and welfare of the natives as the Minister in his discretion considers most fit to assist in their economic and social assimilation *by* [italics supplied] the community of the State, and to protect them against injustice, imposition and fraud.

The obvious benevolence of the formula cannot hide the fact that it was still dictatorial, and worlds apart from Léopold Senghor's admirable precept: "assimiler, non être assimilé."[14]

The second *leit-motif* in the history of white-aboriginal relations in Western Australia focuses on the absence of any noticeable influence of aboriginal culture on the shaping of the emerging colonial society. Future historians may well conclude that, except for the incorporation of aboriginal place names and of a few words of aboriginal origin into the language which the white man had brought with him as part of his cultural baggage, the aborigines had added nothing to the variety of Australian life. Admittedly, the way of life of a few isolated individuals, such as small pastoralists and missionaries, had undergone some change as a result of their daily contact with the aborigines (Sydney Hadley is a good example), and there was considerable interaction between the two groups as groups, but only in the sense that official policy and individual attitudes were to some extent shaped by the aborigines' reaction to earlier policies or attitudes. And yet, there is the nagging suspicion that the aborigines must have had some causality in Australian life. If, as W. E. H. Stanner has said, the aborigines were as irrelevant to Australian development as we believe, an explanation is necessary.

Perhaps another kind of "history" is called for — one that is less ethnocentric and more sensitive to the contributions which ideas, morals and values make to events. The characteristics of aboriginal mentality, life and society were at least among the enabling conditions of Australian development.[15]

Extending this argument into the realm of the specific, could we not ask, for instance, if there existed a causal connection between the policy of white Australia, "the indispensable condition of every other Australian policy", and the self-knowledge on the part of Australians, stemming from the recollection of their past cruel treatment of the aborigines, that they could not "trust themselves to be merciful and just in their dealings with a weaker people on their own soil"?[16] And was it not a fact that in legislating against the entry into Australia of the "servile nations of the world",[17] the Australians knew themselves obedient to the laws of God and the laws of science — and had not much of post-Darwinian thought been grounded in fieldwork undertaken in Australia, and had not most of the scientists engaged in it approached their task with preconceptions which damned the aborigines as a miserable, disgusting, filthy, and degraded remnant of primitive humanity?

Allied to the above comments is the third broad theme in the history of white-aboriginal relations in Western Australia. "Native" administration, that is to say the institutions set up by the governments for the control of the indigenous population, had always signified administration for rather than by the aborigines, even on the lowest rungs of organization. It could be argued, of course, that the acephalous structure of aboriginal societies foredoomed to failure any attempt to associate the aborigines with the process of enforcing the new laws and obligations which the government found necessary to impose, and the fate of the aboriginal "governors" or "kings" appointed in the 1850s certainly supports this view. But the difficulties were not insurmountable; for instance, it would not have required any special gifts of insight to arrange for the participation of traditional leaders in the administration of aboriginal reserves, cattle stations, and settlements. As Don McLeod said in an interview with John Wilson:

When you want to get something through with the mob, you have to hint, or make minor suggestions, talk over points. You can't introduce innovations directly yourself. If you try to force it on them they will baulk up on you and they won't change. If you make these suggestions . . . they have to come from a key figure, someone who is important to the people, and he has to think of it himself.18

There was also room for advice from non-traditional leaders as regards new ideas or the implementation of existing policy. The part-aboriginal "elite" which emerged around the First World War could have made a contribution here, as can be seen from the intelligent suggestions put forward by a deputation of part-aboriginal leaders which waited on the Premier in 1928. But our aim has been to prevent, at almost any cost, the emergence of an aboriginal elite: we ourselves have provided all the "leadership" thought necessary, debating with one another about how the aborigines should be protected, exploited, or developed. The startling success of McLeod or such missionaries as Schenk at Margaret River and Hadley on Sunday Island is conclusive evidence of the vacuum so created.

The last thread which can be traced through the history of white-aboriginal relations in Western Australia concerns race, the "hidden premise" behind our attitudes towards the aborigines. While constantly preoccupied with colour, we had often protested that skin coloration was irrelevant, or tried to convince ourselves (and others) that racialism was in a sense un-Australian, for it could be "traced to the playing fields of Eton".19 Even at our enlightened best, we tended to regard race as something a person could give up or forget when he shared the advantages, real or imaginary, of living with a community of another race; the 1944 Natives (Citizenship Rights) Act which provided that a successful applicant for citizenship rights "shall be deemed no longer a native or aborigine", is the clearest expression of this pious belief. Only occasionally were we prepared to admit that *they* smell "sweetish and dusty, more like stale vegetables in the sun", whereas *we* are like "something cooking, roast meat and onions and grease".[20] Even today, policy planners appear determined to cancel out this fact by social measures; assimilation, said C. D. Rowley, "appeals to the same sentiment as that which upholds the white Australia policy. For it involves a vague promise that in some way these coloured people will disappear, and that this process can be expedited."[21]

White racialism, not surprisingly, evoked a corresponding aboriginal racialism. Some aborigines, conditioned by our attitudes, found "self-respect" in looking down on their darker brethren, while the few on the top of the colour hierarchy became assimilated by "passing", that is through denial and concealment. Trilby, one of the characters in Nene Gare's novel *The Fringe Dwellers*,[22] identifies with her two white grandfathers and has only one ambition, to cease to be a nigger, even if this means becoming a white man's prostitute; K. S. Prichard's half-caste heroine N'Goola also dreams of what it would be like to be a white woman.[23] But this was exceptional, for most aborigines tried to find self-respect in reverting to a broader, non-tribal, aboriginal identification, consciously reusing those elements in their past which could serve to build up cohesion and to express difference or defiance. And colour provided the most powerful symbol of this difference, as well as an outward expression of the unity of all castes and classes. In response to our colour bar, the aborigines had even laid down a corresponding bar of their own; between 1952 and 1956, for instance, whites were excluded from all social functions organized by the New Coolbaroo League.[24]

It could be argued, of course, that the humanitarian strain, always conspicuous in our relations with the aborigines, has provided something of a counterbalance to the more repressive features of official policy. In a sense it has. Yet it could be said that "our present concern with the aborigines makes us stand rather better with ourselves than we once stood, but it comforts us rather more than we have any reason to suppose it will comfort the aborigines".[25] If we think of a man as naked, we cannot imagine him failing to accept the first garment with utmost joy and gratitude. And so it was in the past. Most missionaries, in their failure to admit that the old way had an element of truth, were not really different from other agents of change; the net result of almost a century of their endeavour was summed up by a northwest aborigine in one sentence: "This one God, he new chum, he no more bin leave him corroboree"[26] — our God is a stranger in aboriginal Australia since the missionaries had

failed to provide a connecting link between Him and anything known
to the aboriginal mind. As for other humanitarians, they were often
men and women without any personal knowledge of the aborigines;
the greater their distance from the flesh and blood aborigines, the
more liberal were their prescribed remedies likely to be. So it is
hardly surprising that their altruistic suggestions should have appeared unrealistic to those in daily contact with the aborigines. It
was the people "on the spot" who really counted, for it was their
preconceptions and actions which fashioned the aborigines' attitudes
in the past, and still continue to do so. Kathleen Harrison, in her
study of the culture contact situation at Collie, has shown that social
contacts between the white folk and the local part-aborigines are
limited almost entirely to prostitution.[27] Nene Gare's *The Fringe
Dwellers* depicted a separate aboriginal society in the heart of Geraldton, "only touching the white community when the law and social
services are concerned".[28] Winston Charles, one of the characters of
Gavin Casey's novel *Snowball,* a northwest part-aboriginal who
had settled in the fictional but nonetheless tangibly real town of
Gibberton, found that he could not become a white man, though
he had ceased being wholly a black one: it was always ". . . the same
old stuff — keep away from the settlement, keep out of the town,
git off the face of the earth".[29]

Is it surprising, then, if the aborigines are still in a struggle with us,
"for a different set of things, differently arranged, from those which
most European interests want them to receive"?[30] No one can predict
the outcome of this struggle, or say with certainty whether or not
the aboriginal groups will eventually lose their separate identity.
But one thing is clear; there is ample evidence of the aborigines'
determination to maintain their separateness, even in the case of
groups which had almost completely lost their aboriginal culture.
What is the mainspring of this will to resist?

Is there a perceptual block [asks W. E. H. Stanner] of such a kind that
capital-building and other type-conceptions of our culture just do not
make sense, since the form-ideas either do not exist or, if they do, are
hooked up with contrary conceptions? Or shall we accept the easier hypo-
thesis: that it is because they resent our denial to them of decent opportunities of education and participation in our life?[31]

These are complex questions, and we do not know enough about
some of the problems they raise. It may be that the respective "styles"
of western and aboriginal societies are so different as to be virtually

incompatible, as the gulf between the aboriginal conception of "the dreaming" and our conception of the ultimate social reality suggests. It may be that the aborigines' way of life is eminently "unadaptable" and that the aborigine cannot "unlearn" to be himself; some groups, said R. Taft in his study of social assimilation problems, "may be shed or donned like one's coat, others like one's skin".[32] But, as with all learning or change, the presence or absence of an inner impulse or motivation is of importance here. It is the contention of this book that if a central thread can be traced throughout the history of white-aboriginal relations in Western Australia, it is the failure on our part to provide this motivation. C. D. Rowley said as much when he remarked that much of what looks like stubborn adherence to the non-materialistic interest of aboriginal culture may be due to the lack of opportunity for a choice.[33] Could we not explain the aborigines' "perceptual block" to capital-building by the absence of opportunity to accumulate wealth, or relate their "lack of innate drive or personal incentives"[34] to our discouragement of initiative? Could the aboriginal child's "passive resistance to formal schooling"[35] not be traced to the "brooding suspicion that while pretending to encourage his education we have in reality withheld the secret of some essential tribal increase rite by which separate acquisitions, instead of ending on the scrap heap, multiply to include all the good things of life"?[36] Do not aboriginal groups, even after more than a century of contact, cling to the belief that life is a "one-possibility thing with a once-for-all character"[37] because the choices we had offered them were not real? And if the aborigines cannot, in fact, "cease to be themselves"[38], are we not responsible to some extent for what they are today? It would be comforting to be able to conclude, with Marjorie Barnard, that

we are what our ancestors and the continuing circumstances of Western civilization have made us. The aboriginal is what aeons of isolation in the last and most difficult of continents have made him . . . We destroyed his adjustment and, confused and beggared, he lost the will to live. In all conscience we owe him a great deal, but it is difficult to pay the debt because our coin is not his.[39]

Or shall we admit that we have tried to repay our debt with a coin which turned out to be a counterfeit?

Appendices

Appendix I

POPULATION OF WESTERN AUSTRALIA,
1830–1960

Year	Aborigines, including part-aborigines (approximate numbers[1])	Part-aborigines (approximate numbers)	Whites (including part-aborigines)
1830	55,000		1,172
1890		600	48,502
1900	24,000	1,000	179,967
1910	23,000	1,500	276,832
1920	21,500	2,100	331,323
1930	19,000	3,500	431,610
1940	17,500	4,800	474,076
1950	16,500	6,500	572,649
1960	17,000	8,100	730,581

1 Including aborigines "beyond the confines of civilization". During the first decade of this century official estimates put their numbers at 20,000; from 1917 until 1947 at 10,000, and from 1948 up to 1958, at 6,000. In 1959 the official estimate was reduced to 2,000 but the actual numbers were about one-third of that figure (*Oceania,* December 1959, p. 85; *Report from the Select Committee on the Voting Rights of Aborigines,* p. 2).

Appendix II

WESTERN AUSTRALIAN MINISTRIES, 1890–1954

December 1890	John Forrest
February 1901	George Throssell
May 1901	George Leake
November 1901	Alfred E. Morgan
December 1901	George Leake
July 1902	Walter H. James
August 1904	Henry Daglish
August 1905	Cornthwaite H. Rason
May 1906	Newton J. Moore
September 1910	Frank Wilson
October 1911	John Scaddan
July 1916	Frank Wilson
June 1917	Henry B. Lefroy
April 1919	Hal P. Colebatch
April 1924	Phillip Collier
April 1930	James Mitchell
April 1933	Phillip Collier
August 1936	John C. Willcock
July 1945	Frank J.S. Wise
April 1947	Duncan R. McLarty
February 1953	Albert R.G. Hawke

Appendix III

THE EXPENDITURE OF THE ABORIGINES DEPARTMENT AND ITS SUCCESSORS, 1898–1954

Financial year	Departmental expenditure	Total expenditure from the Consolidated Revenue Fund
	$	$
1898[1]	10,000	6,513,832
1899	21,648	5,078,714
1900	20,050	5,231,352
1901	20,612	6,328,294
1902	21,426	6,982,032
1903	23,038	7,773,604
1904	25,990	8,255,946
1905	28,128	8,291,250
1906	30,250	8,094,922
1907	28,028	7,863,430
1908	35,898	7,796,006
1909	45,118	7,813,346
1910	49,718	8,121,220
1911	91,876	7,468,896
1912	71,426	8,202,164
1913	64,130	9,574,126
1914	66,172	10,681,508
1915	53,956	11,413,084
1916	49,502	11,410,402
1917	51,398	10,553,528
1918	54,274	10,656,558
1919	64,936	11,193,730
1920	61,720	13,063,450
1921	69,388	14,952,582
1922	68,618	15,278,484
1923	55,440	15,225,712
1924	52,612	16,189,506

1 April–June only.

Financial year	Departmental expenditure	Total expenditure from the Consolidated Revenue Fund
	$	$
1925	49,288	16,879,688
1926	55,436	17,814,618
1927	55,790	19,445,176
1928	58,502	19,668,830
1929	60,724	20,447,838
1930	69,464	20,537,036
1931	56,430	20,214,590
1932	55,038	19,186,424
1933	54,476	18,392,468
1934	56,680	18,541,218
1935	61,384	18,997,050
1936	70,400	19,890,686
1937	80,438	21,113,276
1938	102,038	21,659,470
1939	109,000	22,340,204
1940	135,550	22,533,536
1941	167,772	22,841,914
1942	157,304	23,876,762
1943	151,586	26,254,484
1944	150,890	27,110,308
1945	159,368	27,898,680
1946	183,468	28,815,114
1947	214,020	30,056,854
1948	224,666	36,124,784
1949	259,210	42,755,814
1950	344,866	51,574,406
1951	423,206	55,993,668
1952	408,024	69,093,536
1953	361,232	78,784,238
1954	512,642	86,497,038

Appendix IV

ABORIGINES EMPLOYED UNDER PERMITS,
1914–1954

Financial year	Numbers of aborigines employed	Financial year	Numbers of aborigines employed
1914[1]	3,606	1935	3,996
1915	2,907	1936	3,992
1916	2,558	1937	4,135
1917	5,450	1938	3,665
1918	4,988	1939	3,949
1919	4,650	1940	4,075
1920	3,910	1941	4,138
1921	4,528	1942	4,366
1922	4,805	1943	4,628
1923	5,134	1944	5,625
1924	4,862	1945	5,351
1925	4,509	1946	5,463
1926	5,069	1947	5,636
1927	4,259	1948	5,648
1928	4,303	1949	6,095
1929	4,279	1950	6,294
1930	4,272	1951	5,677
1931	4,212	1952	5,430
1932	3,856	1953	4,677
1933	4,054	1954	4,785
1934	3,942		

1 Statistics for 1906–1913 have not been preserved.

Appendix V

ABORIGINES PERMANENTLY RELIEVED, 1898–1954

Financial year	Numbers of aborigines permanently relieved	Cost[1] $
1898	750	
1899	747	14,394
1900	605	11,786
1901	778	12,590
1902	516	13,242
1903	833	14,476
1904	975	16,578
1905	956	16,266
1906	837	17,066
1907	996	15,890
1908	1,200	19,608
1909	1,504	19,720
1910	1,497	17,624
1911	1,939	13,830[2]
1912	2,456	15,766
1913	3,121	14,308
1914	3,320	15,556
1915	3,319	19,988
1916	1,205	17,454
1917	1,012	16,204
1918	1,035	14,626
1919	820	12,334
1920	948	16,968
1921	901	17,560
1922	907	16,940
1923	895	13,444
1924	959	15,016
1925	1,088	16,704
1926	1,104	17,468

1 Excluding blankets, clothing, and medicine.
2 Between 1911 and 1914 the cost of rations on aboriginal cattle stations was recorded separately.

Financial year	Numbers of aborigines permanently relieved	Cost $
1927	1,197	18,730
1928	1,551	19,824
1929	1,403	20,138
1930	1,415	22,614
1931	1,950	23,444
1932	2,271	25,902
1933	2,210	24,396
1934	1,866	24,356
1935	2,657	24,720
1936	2,776	27,200
1937	1,847	30,886
1938	2,012	34,232
1939	2,224	38,038
1940	2,254	38,730
1941	1,794	34,618
1942	1,239	28,712
1943	1,064	27,650
1944	1,145	29,072
1945	1,021	28,854
1946	1,222	33,942
1947	1,369	34,468
1948	1,445	47,794
1949	1,179	43,624
1950[3]		

3 Exact figures for 1950–1954 are not available.

APPENDIX VI

ABORIGINAL RESERVES OVER 2,500 ACRES
(in 1929)

Name	Locality	Area (in acres)
Admiralty Gulf	North Kimberley	600,000
Beagle Bay Mission	West Kimberley	700,000
Central Australian Reserve	Central Australia	14,933,334
Collier Bay	West Kimberley	414,000
Drysdale River Mission	North Kimberley	300,000
Forrest River Mission	East Kimberley	100,000
Lyndon River	Ashburton	2,625
Marndoc	East Kimberley	3,000,000
Mount Hann	Central Kimberley	1,000,520
Moola Bulla	East Kimberley	1,119,000
Moore River Native Settlement	Midlands	11,756
Munja	West Kimberley	706,000
Pia	Murchison	50,000
Port George IV Mission	West Kimberley	58,000
Violet Valley	East Kimberley	251,460
Wilgi Mia Cave	Murchison	10,500

Appendix VII

CHRISTIAN MISSIONS, 1898–1954[1]

Name and location	Date established	Controlling authority (in 1954)
Aborigines Rescue Mission, Jigalong	1946	A.R.M. Board
Beagle Bay Mission	1891	Roman Catholic Church
Church of Christ Mission, Carnarvon	1946	C. of C. Federal Aborigine Mission Board
Cundeelee Mission	1950	Australian Aborigines Evangelical Mission Board
Forrest River Mission	1913	Church of England
Holy Child Orphanage, Broome	1912	Sisters of St. John of God
Kalumburu (formerly Drysdale River)	1907	Benedictine Community, New Norcia
Karalundi Mission	1954	Seventh Day Adventists' Conference of W.A.
Kunmunya (formerly Port George IV; transferred to Wotjulum in 1950)	1910	Australian Presbyterian Board of Missions
Kurrawang Native Mission	1952	Kurrawang Mission Trust
La Grange Mission	1955	Pious Society of Missions, Inc.
Lombadina	1911	Pious Society of Missions, Inc.
Marribank Mission, Katanning	1952	Baptist Aborigines Mission of W.A.
Mogumber Mission	1951	Methodist Overseas Mission

---

1 Ellensbrook (1878–1917), Swan Native and Half-Caste Home (1870–1921), and Dulhi Gunyah (1909–1917) were industrial schools within the meaning of the 1874 Industrial Schools Act.

Name and location	Date established	Controlling authority (in 1954)
New Norcia Mission	1846	Roman Catholic Church
Norseman Mission	1942	C. of C. Federal Aborigines Mission Board
Pallotine Mission, Balgo	1939	Pallotine Fathers
Pallotine Mission School, Tardun	1948	Pallotine Fathers
Roelands Native Mission Farm	1938	Council of Native Mission Farm
St. Francis Xavier Native Mission, Wandering	1944	Roman Catholic Archbishop of Perth
United Aborigines Mission, Badjaling	1930[2]	U.A.M. Federal Council
——, Cosmo Newbery	1953	U.A.M. Federal Council
——, Fitzroy Crossing	1952	U.A.M. Federal Council
——, Gnowangerup	1928	U.A.M. Federal Council
——, Kellerberrin	1939[2]	U.A.M. Federal Council
——, Mount Margaret	1921	U.A.M. Federal Council
——, Sunday Island	1898	U.A.M. Federal Council
——, Warburton Range	1933	U.A.M. Federal Council
Wonguntha Mission Training Farm, Esperance	1954	Council of Wonguntha Mission Training Farm, Inc.

---

2 Abandoned during the early fifties.

Appendix VIII

FINANCIAL ASSISTANCE TO MISSIONS,
1898–1954

Financial year	Subsidy $	Grants-in-aid $
1898[1]	842	
1899	2,440	
1900	2,670	
1901	2,886	
1902	2,748	
1903	3,120	
1904	3,328	
1905	3,454	
1906	5,950	
1907	3,948	
1908	3,758	
1909	4,190	
1910	4,972	
1911	4,648	
1912	5,498	
1913	4,468	
1914	5,454	
1915	3,964	
1916	3,872	
1917	3,766	
1918	3,606	
1919	2,742	
1920	2,632	
1921	2,204	
1922	2,044	
1923	2,000	
1924	2,192	
1925	2,172	
1926	2,102	
1927	2,220	

1 April-June only.

Financial Year	Subsidy	Grants-in-aid
	$	$
1928	2,328	
1929	1,888	
1930	2,038	
1931	1,718	
1932	1,350	
1933	1,862	
1934	2,000	
1935	1,776	
1936	1,976	
1937	2,470	
1938	2,844	
1939	3,082	
1940	3,776	
1941	3,614	
1942	3,564	
1943	3,486	
1944	4,272	
1945	4,120	
1946	5,200	
1947	5,696	
1948	6,830	
1949	13,670	
1950	23,156	15,058
1951	40,220	24,756
1952	71,270	21,174
1953	84,428	39,512
1954	150,480	34,222

Notes to Text

Note to Preface

1 T. Hodgkin, *Nationalism in Colonial Africa* (London, 1956), p. 19.

Notes to Chapter One

1 *Commonwealth Yearbook,* 1930, p. 689.
2 *Proceedings of the American Philosophical Society,* 1938, p. 452.
3 The figure is Davidson's. R. M. Berndt, in *Oceania,* December 1959, p. 86, estimated the pre-contact population of the area "extending from the Rawlinsons north-west past Lakes Gregory, Naberru and Carnegie to Wiluna, and to Jigalong near the Great Northern Highway, and bounded on the north . . . by the southern and eastern Kimberley" at roughly 10,000 persons.
4 R. M. and C. H. Berndt, *From Black to White in South Australia* (Melbourne, 1951), p. 34.
5 W. E. H. Stanner, "Continuity and Change Among the Aborigines", *Australian Journal of Science,* December 1958, p. P.107.
6 R. L. Sharp, quoted in R. M. and C. H. Berndt, *The World of the First Australians* (Sydney, 1964), p. 303.
7 *Ibid.,* p. 302.
8 Quoted in P. Hasluck, *Black Australians* (Melbourne, 1942), p. 49.
9 Burton, J., in *R. v. Jack Congo Murrell* (1836) 1 Legge (New South Wales) 72, quoted in M. C. Kriewaldt, "The Application of the Criminal Law to the Aborigines of the Northern Territory of Australia", *University of Western Australia Law Review,* December 1960, p. 18.
10 J. A. Barnes, "Indigenous Politics and Colonial Administration with Special Reference to Australia", *Comparative Studies in Society and History,* January 1960, p. 139.
11 *Ibid.*
12 *Ibid.*
13 C. M. H. Clark, *A History of Australia,* vol. 1 (Melbourne, 1962), p. 5.
14 *Ibid.*
15 A. P. Elkin, "Reaction and Interaction: a Food Gathering People and European Settlement in Australia", *American Anthropologist,* April 1951, p. 165. See also Berndt and Berndt, *The World of the First Australians,* pp. 420–46; Barnes, "Indigenous Politics and Colonial Administration with Special Reference to Australia"; Stanner, "Continuity and Change Among the Aborigines"; and M. Reay, "The Background of Alien Impact", in *Aboriginal Man in Australia* (Sydney, 1965), pp. 377–95.
16 O. Mannoni, *Prospero and Caliban* (New York, 1964), p. 23.
17 Elkin, "Reaction and Interaction", p. 174.

18 *Ibid.,* p. 179.
19 W. E. H. Stanner, *After the Dreaming* (Sydney, 1968), p. 7.
20 Stanner, "Continuity and Change Among the Aborigines", p.P. 104.
21 Berndt and Berndt, *The World of the First Australians,* p. 443.
22 *Ibid.,* p. 442.
23 Elkin, "Reaction and Interaction", p. 171.
24 Berndt and Berndt, *The World of the First Australians,* p. 422. For an account of early contacts in Western Australia see the article by M. E. Wood, "First Contacts Made with Western Australian Natives", *Journal and Proceedings of W.A. Historical Society,* December 1943, and the manuscript by D. M. Bates, "First Meetings with W.A. Aborigines" (Papers, X111/2).
25 Elkin, "Reaction and Interaction", p. 167.
26 F. K. Crowley, *Australia's Western Third* (London, 1960), p. 8.
27 J. S. Battye, *Western Australia* (Oxford, 1924), pp. 132–33, and a series of articles in the *Journal of the Historical Society of Western Australia,* 1927.
28 C.S.O. vol. 159, 18 January 1847.
29 Elkin, "Reaction and Interaction", p. 168.
30 Hasluck, *Black Australians,* p. 47.
31 *Ibid.,* p. 74.
32 *Ibid.,* p. 75.
33 S. Mitchell, *Looking Backwards* (Geraldton, 1911), p. 25.
34 D. M. Bates, *The Passing of the Aborigines* (Melbourne, 1966), p. 89.
35 B. Smith, in the book *European Vision and the South Pacific, 1768–1850* (Oxford, 1960), has shown how this humanitarianism was combined with a reaction against primitivism which all but obliterated the earlier fiction of the noble savage. Missions and welfare groups now stressed the abomination of savage society, and any suggestion that a fallen race awaiting its redemption possessed nobility of character was considered un-Christian.
36 Great Britain. Parliament. *Report from the Select Committee on Aborigines (British Settlements), with Minutes of Evidence* (C. 425, 1837), p. 45.
37 Hasluck, *Black Australians,* p. 57.
38 *Ibid.,* p. 86.
39 Kriewaldt, "The Application of the Criminal Law to the Aborigines of the Northern Territory of Australia", p. 17.
40 Reprinted in G. Grey, *Journals of Two Expeditions of Discovery in North-West and Western Australia,* 2 vols. (London, 1841), 2: 373–88.
41 Hasluck, *Black Australians,* p. 58.
42 L. R. Marchant, "Native Administration in Western Australia 1886–1905" (B.A. [Hons.] thesis, University of Western Australia, 1954), p. 1.
43 Hasluck, *Black Australians,* p. 103.
44 Berndt and Berndt, *The World of the First Australians,* p. 128.
45 R. Maunier, *The Sociology of Colonies,* 2 vols. (London, 1949), 1: 80.
46 Bates, *The Passing of the Aborigines,* p. 80.
47 Berndt and Berndt, *The World of the First Australians,* p. 422.
48 A. P. Elkin, *Citizenship for the Aborigines* (Sydney, 1944), pp. 39–40.
49 Marquis de Condorcet, in the book *Esquisse d'un tableau historique des progrès de l'esprit humain* (Paris, 1795) outlined how humanity had risen from primitiveness, through the stages of animal husbandry and agriculture, to literacy and ultimately to "enlightenment". G. Klemm, whose main work was the *Allegemeine Kultur-Geschichte der Menschheit* (10 vols.; Leipzig, 1843–52), discerned three stages in the history of human development: savagery, tameness, and freedom. The ideological basis for the superiority of the white race was furnished by Compte de Gobineau, whose best known

work is the *Essai sur l'inégalité des races humaines* (4 vols.; Paris, 1853–1855). Since he had formulated his theory before Darwin, Gobineau assumed that the differentiation of man into races was brought about by the violence of climatic forms.

50 D. J. Mulvaney, "The Australian Aborigines 1606–1929: Opinion and Field-work", in *Historical Studies: Selected Articles* (Melbourne, 1964), pp. 29–30.

51 *Ibid.*, p. 31.

52 Hasluck, *Black Australians*, p. 91.

53 *Ibid.*, p. 193.

54 *Ibid.*, p. 197.

55 Maunier, *The Sociology of Colonies*, 2: 567.

56 G. C. Bolton, *Alexander Forrest* (Melbourne, 1958), p. 23.

57 Hasluck, *Black Australians*, pp. 188–89.

58 *Ibid.*, p. 172; *Western Mail*, 6 March 1886, p. 13.

59 Hasluck, *Black Australians*, p. 64.

60 *Ibid.*

61 *Ibid.*, p. 66.

62 Crowley, *Australia's Western Third*, p. 48.

63 *G.G.*, 24 August 1864.

64 R. D. Sturkey, "Growth of the Pastoral Industry in the North-West 1862–1901" (B.A. [Hons.] thesis, University of Western Australia, 1957), p. 14.

65 C. H. Berndt, *Women's Changing Ceremonies in Northern Australia* (Paris, 1950), pp. 11, 15.

66 J. R. B. Love, *Stone-Age Bushmen of To-day* (London, 1936), pp. 31–32.

67 Hasluck, *Black Australians*, p. 163.

68 Elkin, "Reaction and Interaction", pp. 180–81.

69 R. Allen, "Reminiscences of the Kimberley District, 1900–1920, and Impressions of Certain Goldfields before 1900" (typescript in the Battye Library of West Australian History), p. 15.

70 Pacific Books edition, p. 127.

71 I. L. Idriess, *Outlaws of the Leopolds* (Sydney, 1952).

72 G. C. Bolton, "A Survey of the Kimberley Pastoral Industry from 1885 to the Present" (M.A. thesis, University of Western Australia, 1954), p. 64.

73 *W.A. Church News*, 1 October 1925.

74 Police 3548/1897.

75 *Ibid.*

76 Bolton, "A Survey of the Kimberley Pastoral Industry from 1885 to the Present", p. 64. See also A. L. Haydon, *The Trooper Police of Australia* (London, 1911), pp. 318–24; G. Buchanan, *Packhorse and Waterhole* (Sydney, 1934), pp. 172–73; M. Durack, "The Outlaws of Windginna Gorge", *Walkabout*, June 1941; and the memoirs of R. H. Pilmer in *Countryman*, 6 and 13 September 1956.

77 *Report of a Commission Appointed to Inquire into the Treatment of Aboriginal Native Prisoners of the Crown and into Certain Matters Relating to Aboriginal Natives, V. & P.,* 32 (1884): 4.

78 *V. & P.,* 33 (1882): 11.

79 E.M. Curr, *The Australian Race*, 4 vols. (Melbourne, 1886), 1: 290, 296.

80 *V. & P.,* 32 (1884): 5–6.

81 Hasluck, *Black Australians*, p. 165.

82 Marchant, "Native Administration in Western Australia 1886–1905", p. 36.

83 Hasluck, *Black Australians*, p. 203.

Notes to Chapter Two

1 *A.R.*, 1899, p. 9. This is the most reliable estimate of "civilized" aborigines for the period. Other estimates can be found in Aborigines Protection Board, *Annual Report*, 1897, and in the *Seventh Census of Western Australia, Taken for the Night of 31st March, 1901* (Perth, 1904).

2 A.F. 331/1912. *A.R.*, 1908, p. 3, put the number of aborigines "outside civilization" at about 20,000. A. O. Neville, in *Australia's Coloured Minority* (Sydney, 1947), p. 203, claimed that the aboriginal population of Western Australia about the turn of the century was about 40,000. See also his assertion in H. Colebatch, ed., *A Story of a Hundred Years* (Perth, 1929), p. 119, that the pre-1829 population of the state was about 100,000.

3 The figures which follow are based on sources listed under fn. 1.

4 *Reports on Stations Visited by the Travelling Inspector of Aborigines* (Perth, 1903), p. 78.

5 *A.R.*, 1908, p. 15.

6 Bates, *The Passing of the Aborigines*, pp. 78, 120.

7 In 1899 there were in the northwest 2,603 natives "in employment", and 258 were listed as "relieved by the government".

8 Bates, *The Passing of the Aborigines*, p. 53.

9 Curr, *The Australian Race*, 1: 288.

10 Bates, *The Passing of the Aborigines*, p. 22.

11 Neville, *Australia's Coloured Minority*, p. 68.

12 C. D. Rowley, *The New Guinea Villager* (Melbourne, 1965), p. 8.

13 In 1899 there were in West Kimberley 959 aborigines "in employment" (as shearers, shepherds, and domestic servants in and around Broome and Derby), and 102 were rationed by the government. Figures for East Kimberley are not available but they were negligible.

14 A. 137/1901.

15 On the unreliability of aboriginal evidence in general, see A. P. Elkin, "Aboriginal Evidence and Justice in North Australia", *Oceania*, March 1947, and T. G. H. Strehlow, "Notes on Native Evidence and its Value", *Oceania*, March 1936.

16 *S.T.*, 16 October 1904.

17 M. Durack, *Kings in Grass Castles* (Corgi Books, 1967), p. 369. In 1908 the Kimberley police force consisted of 27 constables and 29 native trackers.

18 *V. & P.*, 5 (1905): 109, 116.

19 *Ibid.*, pp. 13, 88. In this context note the opinion stated in *Tuckiar* v. *King* (*Commonwealth Law Reports*, 52: 352), that "rules of English law cannot be cited in support of this action".

20 *V. & P.*, 5 (1905): 47.

21 *Countryman*, 9 November 1961, p. 11.

22 *W.A.*, 30 June 1909.

23 Elkin, "Reaction and Interaction", pp. 170–71.

24 J. Wilson, "Authority and Leadership in a 'New Style' Australian Aboriginal Community: Pindan, Western Australia" (M.A. thesis, University of Western Australia, 1961), p. 36.

25 F.W. Gunning, *Lure of the North* (Perth, 1952), p. 141.

26 Wilson, "Authority and Leadership in a 'New Style' Australian Aboriginal Community", p. 36.

27 *Ibid.*

28 *Australasian*, 5 March 1927. The quotation is from *Walkabout*, 1935, p. 23.

29 *A.R.*, 1901, p. 5.

30 *S.T.*, 3 September 1899.
31 *V. & P.*, 5 (1905): 6.
32 C.S.D. 1096/1905. This appears to be the first reference to what has become known as the Kurangura cult. According to Hallet, the aborigines on Pyramid, Mount Florence, Millstream, and other stations had evolved a new ceremony called the "poison" or "sulky fellow" corroboree. In April 1905 a meeting was held at Millstream station and later another at Yarraloola station where natives from properties farther west were made "doctors". Subsequent references to the cult can be found in R. Piddington, "Karadjeri Initiation", *Oceania*, June 1932, p. 81; A. Lommel, "Modern Culture Influences on the Aborigines", *Oceania*, September 1950; H. E. Petri, *Kurangura* (Braunschweig, 1950); *A.R.*, 1955, p. 34; and W. H. Edwards, "Aboriginal Education: Aims and Principles", *Journal of Christian Education*, June 1961, p. 27.
33 Marchant, "Native Administration in Western Australia 1886–1905", p. 91.
34 H. G. B. Mason, *Darkest West Australia* (Kalgoorlie, 1909), p. 59. For contemporary criticism of the conditions in pastoral employment, see J. B. Gribble, *Dark Deeds in a Sunny Land* (Perth, 1886), pp. 32–37, and Sturkey, "The Growth of the Pastoral Industry in the North-West 1862–1901," pp. 28–29.
35 See also *P.D.*, 40: 3248: "It takes a very smart blackfellow to shear 100 sheep a day, while a white man will shear 200."
36 Elkin, "Reaction and Interaction", p. 167.
37 In W. Kloosterboer, *Involuntary Labour Since the Abolition of Slavery* (Leiden, 1960), p. 1.
38 Stanner, "Continuity and Change Among the Aborigines", p. P.101.
39 *All-About* (Sydney, 1935), *Chumuna* (Sydney, 1936), *Son of Djaro* (Perth, 1940), and *Keep Him My Country* (London, 1955). The first three were written in association with E. Durack.
40 *Walkabout*, June 1945, pp. 13–14.
41 Hasluck, *Black Australians*, p. 103.
42 *A.R.*, 1903, p. 8.
43 *Reports on Stations Visited by the Travelling Inspector of Aborigines* (Perth, 1903), p. 25.
44 Quoted in Hasluck, *Black Australians*, p. 22.
45 *Ibid.*, p. 95.
46 Maunier, *The Sociology of Colonies*, 1: 71.
47 *Oceania*, December 1958, p. 92.
48 A. 640/1906.

Notes to Chapter Three

1 In 1890 he had delivered the presidential address to the Anthropology section of the Melbourne meeting of the Australasian Association for the Advancement of Science, and was the author of several learned articles, including "On the Natives of Central and Western Australia", *Journal of the Anthropological Institute*, 1876, and "The Marriage Laws of the Aboriginals of North-Western Australia", *Report of the 2nd Meeting of the Australasian Association for the Advancement of Science* (Melbourne, 1890). The Battye Library of West Australian History has an undated manuscript by Forrest entitled "Notes on the Aborigines, and Their Customs and Legends".
2 Hasluck, *Black Australians*, p. 119, states that in 1900, "when under Section 70 of the 1889 Constitution Act the amount for aborigines would have been nearly £30,000 [$60,000], the actual vote by the Parliament was £5,000

[$10,000]". This is correct only in the sense that the "statutory" vote was $10,000; since there was also a supplementary vote of $10,000, the "actual" vote amounted to $20,000 (*A.R.*, 1900, p. 10).

3 *G.G.*, 10 June 1898.

4 *A.R.*, 1899, p. 6.

5 *M.H.*, 6 July 1901.

6 Bates, *The Passing of the Aborigines*, pp. 6–7.

7 *Ibid.*, p. 6.

8 From just over $6,000 to $2,440.

9 Amounting to about 50 per cent during the last years of the Aborigines Protection Board; subsequently their share of subsidies fluctuated between 42 per cent and 48 per cent.

10 A. 156/1898.

11 Marchant, "Native Administration in Western Australia 1886–1905", pp. 17–18, 78.

12 *Ibid.*, p. 83.

13 A. 830/1900.

14 *P.D.*, 83: 2101.

15 *The Australian Commonwealth* (Melbourne, 1956), p. 2. "It has been very nearly literally true", said the author, "that aboriginal natives are not counted as human beings, in Australia ."

16 *Report from the Select Committee on Voting Rights of Aborigines* (Canberra, 1961), p. 39. Section 127, incidentally, did not apply to half-castes, whose numbers were included in census returns. "Civilized" aborigines were counted at every census but their numbers were not included in "white" totals and were published separately. The relevant part of s.51 and the whole of s.127 were repealed by the 1967 Constitution Alteration (Aboriginals) Act.

17 *A.R.*, 1902, p. 3. Similar comments in *A.R.*, 1901, p. 3.

18 *A.R.*, 1903, p. 4.

19 *Ibid.*

20 P. 68.

21 "Reports of the Chief Protector Concerning the Mission Stations on the Dampier Peninsula" (undated typescript in the W.A. State Archives). See also E. A. Gibson, "Culture Contact on Sunday Island" (M.A. thesis, University of Sydney, 1951), pp. 61–65.

22 A. 10/1901.

23 A. 8/1902.

24 Hasluck, *Black Australians*, p. 62; Mason, *Darkest West Australia*, p. 59.

25 A. R. Richardson, *Early Memories of the Great Nor-West* (Perth, 1914), p. 20.

26 Mason, *Darkest West Australia*, pp. 58–59.

27 1906, p. 6.

28 Richardson, *Early Memories of the Great Nor-West*, p. 63.

29 Quoted in J. T. Reilly, *Reminiscences of Fifty Years' Residence in Western Australia* (Perth, 1903), p. 312.

30 5 October 1893.

31 *P.D.*, 28: 562.

32 *P.D.* (Commonwealth), 4: 3150.

33 *Ibid.*

34 17 August 1901.

35 *P.D.*, 19: 62.

36 4 December 1901.

37 Bates, *The Passing of the Aborigines*, p. 2.

38 *P.D.*, 21: 1901.

39 6 October 1902.
40 22 January 1904 (weekly edition).
41 *V. & P.*, A8 (1904).
42 *W.A.*, 1 February 1905.
43 *W.A.*, 4 February 1905.
44 16 February 1905.
45 *W.A.*, 2 February 1905.
46 *Report of the Royal Commission on the Conditions of Natives, V. & P.*, 5 (1905).
47 *W.A.*, 23 February 1905. Captain Hare's suspension was largely the result of an article in the *Morning Herald,* published on 10 February. It must have given considerable satisfaction to many former goldminers who remembered his role, as warden of the Coolgardie goldfield, in the "Ivanhoe trouble" of 1899.
48 Police 3036/1905.
49 *M.H.*, 1 April 1905.
50 *V. & P.* A8 (1904): 4. It should be noted that the administration already possessed the right to declare aboriginal reserves of unlimited size under the provisions of the 1898 Land Act.
51 *P.D.*, 28: 275.

Notes to Chapter Four

1 J. I. Patterson, "Native Administration and Welfare in Western Australia, 1905–1936" (B.A. [Hons.] thesis, University of Western Australia, 1957), p. 5.
2 31 January.
3 A. C. Staples, "Henry Charles Prinsep", *Journal and Proceedings of the W.A. Historical Society,* 1955, p. 43.
4 A.F. 2026/1914.
5 *Ibid.*
6 *Ibid.*
7 *P.D.*, 35: 1845–46.
8 *V. & P.*, A2 (1915).
9 Neville, *Australia's Coloured Minority*, pp. 98–99.
10 *Ibid.*, pp. 80–81.
11 A.F. 406/1911.
12 *A.R.*, 1918, p. 4.
13 Neville, *Australia's Coloured Minority*, p. 22.
14 Over $40,000 of this amount was non-recurring capital expenditure. The sum spent on "all services in connection with aborigines" was $51,100.
15 E. Morrow, *The Law Provides* (London, 1937), p. 36.
16 Quoted in Patterson, "Native Administration and Welfare in Western Australia, 1905–1936", p. 23.
17 Neville, *Australia's Coloured Minority*, p. 215.
18 Buchanan, *Packhorse and Waterhole*, pp. 173–74.
19 *Oceania,* June 1938, p. 461.
20 Marchant, "Native Administration in Western Australia 1886–1905", p. 17.
21 A.F. 870/1910.
22 The relevant files here are A. 412/1927, N.A. 451/1933 and Treasury 1954/1929.
23 Earlier pastoralists' pressure groups were the Kimberley Pastoral Association, in the 1880s, and the Northerners' Association, formed in 1893.
24 Marchant, "Native Administration in Western Australia 1886–1905", p. 89.
25 *Ibid.*, p. 90.
26 A. 45/1933.

27 *W.A.,* 12 September 1912.
28 *P.D.,* 66: 891, 1903.
29 7 July 1911.
30 *A.R.,* 1907, p. 6.
31 *Ibid.*
32 A.F. 70/1907.
33 Bates, *The Passing of the Aborigines,* p. 22.
34 *Times,* 9 July 1907.
35 *W.A.,* 21 December 1907.
36 5 December 1907.
37 6 December 1907.
38 The report was not tabled in parliament. A typescript copy can be found in the Battye Library of West Australian History (PR 452).
39 *W.A.,* 22 February 1908.
40 *Daily Telegraph,* 12 December 1911.
41 A.F. 517/1912.
42 A.F. 473/1915.
43 M. R. Cullen, "The Life of Daisy Bates", typescript, 1962 (Battye Library of West Australian History, HS/PR/1485).
44 C. L. M. Hawtrey, *The Availing Struggle* (Perth, 1949), p. 179.
45 Bolton, "A Survey of the Kimberley Pastoral Industry from 1885 to the Present", p. 224.
46 *Report of Royal Commission of Inquiry into Alleged Killing and Burning of Bodies of Aborigines in East Kimberley, and into Police methods when Effecting Arrests, V. & P.,* 3 (1927): XV.
47 R. Stow, *To the Islands* (Penguin Books, 1962), p. 57.
48 27 January 1927.
49 *S.T.,* 26 November 1926.
50 *W.A.,* 10 March 1928.
51 *W.A.,* 12 March 1928.
52 Bolton, "A Survey of the Kimberley Pastoral Industry from 1885 to the Present", p. 218.
53 G. Drake-Brockman, *The Turning Wheel* (Perth, 1960), pp. 222–23.
54 21 August 1925.
55 *P.D.,* 76: 454.
56 *P.D.,* 83: 2163.
57 R.M. Crawford, *Australia* (London, 1955), pp. 169–170.
58 N.W. 170/1943.
59 *A.B.M. Review,* 15 February 1911.
60 *Report of the 14th Meeting of the Australasian Association for the Advancement of Science* (Melbourne, 1914), p. 451.
61 N.A. 238/1927. Western Australia agreed to the proposal, providing no expenditure on its part was involved. In 1910 both Gale and Connolly opposed federal control as impracticable (A.F. 938/1910). The 1913 proposal, on the other hand, was received favourably: in July 1913 cabinet agreed, "in principle", to transfer aboriginal affairs to the Commonwealth, providing the request came through proper channels, and in June 1914 the Premier formally notified the Prime Minister that his government was prepared to relinquish aboriginal affairs at any time (A.F. 1538/1914).
62 *P.D.* (Commonwealth), 116: 507–13. Leopold, King of Belgium, said one member, when the British government brought to his notice the atrocities in the Congo Free State, allegedly replied: "Have you ever read Dr. Roth's report of the treatment of Western Australian aboriginals?" (p. 509.)

63 *V. & P.* (Commonwealth), 19 (1929).
64 *V. & P.* (Commonwealth, 16 (1929): 270 (majority report), 303 (minority report). Neville, who appeared as a witness before the commission, supported the minority view (N.A. 412/1927).
65 Aborigines' Friends' Association, *Annual Report,* 1927, p. 6.
66 *Ibid.,* 1926, pp. 3–4.
67 *Report of the 18th Meeting of the Australasian Association for the Advancement of Science* (Perth, 1928), p. 508.
68 *V. & P.* (Commonwealth), H. of R. I.F 1276/1927.
69 There is a wealth of literature dealing with the growth of anthropology in Australia as an academic discipline. Some of the more important contributions are A. P. Elkin, "Anthropology in Australia, Past and Present", *Report of the 22nd Meeting of ANZAAS* (Melbourne, 1935); "Anthropological Research in Australia and the Western Pacific, 1927–1937", *Oceania,* June 1956; "Anthropology in Australia: One Chapter", *Mankind,* October 1958; "A Darwin Centenary and Highlights of Field-Work in Australia", *Mankind,* November 1959; Mulvaney, "The Australian Aborigines 1606–1929: Opinion and Fieldwork"; and R. M. and C. H. Berndt, "A.P. Elkin — The Man and the Anthropologist", in *Aboriginal Man in Australia* (Sydney, 1965).
70 *Australian Encyclopaedia,* 5: 22.
71 A. L. Pitt-Rivers, quoted in Mulvaney, "The Australian Aborigines 1606–1929: Opinion and Field-work", p. 37.
72 *Ibid.,* p. 54.
73 *Ibid.,* p. 55.
74 H. R. Lowie, *The History of Ethnological Theory* (London, 1937), p. 226. A more recent and detailed assessment of his work can be found in Elkin, "A.R. Radcliffe-Brown, 1880–1955", *Oceania,* June 1956.
75 *Ibid.,* p. 238.
76 *Ibid.,* p. 251.
77 April 1930, editorial.
78 *A.R.,* 1927, pp. 4–5.
79 N.A. 1011/1945.
80 Stanner, *After the Dreaming,* p. 14.
81 G. M. Morant, "Study of Australian and Tasmanian Skulls Based on Previously Published Measurements", *Biometrika,* 1927; H. Woolard, "The Aboriginal Brain", *Journal of Anatomy,* 1929.
82 S. D. Porteus, *Psychology of a Primitive People* (London, 1931), p. 420. Porteus constructed the well-known "maze test", in 1913, and was probably the first to administer intelligence tests to aborigines. See his article, "Mental Tests with Delinquents and Australian Aboriginal Children", *Psychological Review,* 1917, where he attributed retardation of aboriginal children to a shorter period of brain growth; and the book, *Porteus Maze Test* (Palo Alto, 1965).
83 *Oceania,* September 1932, p. 112. The Kimberley group scored an average of 7.22 years on the Goddard form test, and the Moore River group 9.18.
84 *Oceania,* March 1932, p. 358.
85 Stanner, *After the Dreaming,* p. 15.
86 Pacific Books edition, p. 204.
87 R. Sadleir, "The Novels of Katharine Susannah Prichard", *Westerly,* 1961, no. 3, p. 34.
88 H. M. Green, *A History of Australian Literature,* 2 vols. (Sydney, 1962), 2: 1000.
89 See also the comment by another humanitarian controversialist, C. E. C.

Lefroy: The Roth report was so damaging "that it was never given to the public". (*Contemporary Review,* February 1929, p. 221.)
90 *World* (Sydney), 14 January 1932; *Argus,* 16 January 1932; *Anti-Slavery Reporter and Aborigines' Friend,* July 1932.
91 *W.A.,* 17 May 1932. In this context see Kaberry, *Aboriginal Woman,* which shows that the lot of aboriginal women was on the whole not an unhappy one.
92 *V. & P.,* 2 (1935): 22.
93 N.WT. 100/1925.
94 17 June 1933. Full text of the paper is in A. 166/1932.
95 *V. & P.,* 2 (1935): 11.

Notes to Chapter Five

1 Stanner, *After the Dreaming,* p. 12.
2 Kaberry, *Aboriginal Woman,* p. x, estimated the Kimberley population (in 1935) at about 6,000 — a far more realistic estimate than the official figure of 7,639. The official estimate for the northwest was 3,452.
3 See, for instance, Colebatch, *A Story of a Hundred Years,* p. 119.
4 *A.R.,* 1928, p. 9.
5 Kaberry, *Aboriginal Woman,* p. 40.
6 Drake-Brockman, *The Turning Wheel,* pp. 194–95.
7 *A.R.,* 1920, p. 14.
8 Wilson, "Authority and Leadership in a 'New Style' Australian Aboriginal Community", p. 37.
9 Mason, *Darkest West Australia,* p. 58.
10 *W.A.,* 30 June 1909.
11 Police 2896/1909.
12 A. 337/1913.
13 *A.R.,* 1910, p. 4.
14 Elkin, *Citizenship for the Aborigines,* p. 98.
15 Crowley, *Australia's Western Third,* p. 177.
16 Up to 1923, with a record profit of $8,632 in 1917–1918. After 1923 the station operated at a loss.
17 A.F. 406/1911.
18 *Ibid.*
19 Australian Aborigines' Amelioration Association, *Putting Back the Hands of the Clock 300 Years* (Perth, n.d.).
20 For the negotiations which led to this step, see N.A. 49/1929.
21 *Man,* 1920, p. 191.
22 Wilson, "Authority and Leadership in a 'New Style' Australian Aboriginal Community", p. 21.
23 N.WT. 199/1921.
24 *G.G.,* 23 January 1920.
25 N.WT. 353/1921.
26 For details, see chapter four.
27 *A.R.,* 1927, p. 3.
28 N.W. 437/1935.
29 P. 147.
30 *W.A.,* 9 December 1935.
31 N.A. 258/1930.
32 *A.R.,* 1909, p. 15.
33 *A.R.,* 1910, p. 4.
34 A. 135/1901.

35 A.F. 870/1910. This was in reply to an offer to pay aboriginal labour 6d. per hour, made by a Franco-German syndicate in its application to employ aborigines in large-scale cotton cultivation it hoped to start near Derby.
36 *A.R.,* 1911, p. 5.
37 N.A. 451/1933.
38 *G.G.,* 12 May 1916.
39 N.A. 451/1933.
40 From a 1927 departmental survey of conditions in the pastoral industry, in A. 412/1927.
41 N.W. 437/1935.
42 Crowley, *Australia's Western Third,* p. 176.
43 *Ibid.,* p. 255.
44 Hasluck, *Black Australians,* p. 105.
45 *Ibid.*
46 Crowley, *Australia's Western Third,* p. 50.
47 J. E. Hammond, *Winjan's People* (Perth, 1933), pp. 71–72.
48 *A.R.,* 1907, p. 5.
49 *A.R.,* 1908, p. 4.
50 Bates, *The Passing of the Aborigines,* p. 102.
51 *Ibid.*
52 A.F. 58/1911.
53 *A.R.,* 1908, p. 4.
54 In 1908 the travelling inspector of aborigines reported several cases from Cygnet Bay, but these were not bacteriologically proven.
55 A. H. Baldwin and L. F. Cooling, *An Investigation Into Hookworm Disease, Malaria and Filaria in Western Australia* (Melbourne, 1922).
56 N.WT. 695/1922.
57 *W.A.,* 25 June 1934.
58 *V. & P.,* 2 (1935): 11.
59 *W.A.,* 25 June 1934.
60 *A.R.,* 1920, p. 12.

Notes to Chapter Six

1 *A.R.,* 1910, p. 16.
2 C. Price Conigrave, *Walk-About* (London, 1938), pp. 120–21.
3 A. M. Catalan, *Lecture on the Origin and Development of the Drysdale River Mission* (New Norcia, 1935), p. 12.
4 E. Perez, *Kalumburu* (New Norcia, 1959), p. 27.
5 N.WT. 242/1927.
6 Before going to Cygnet Bay Father Emo ran a small unofficial mission in Broome, from 1901 until 1907, catering for part-aborigines and the local "Manilamen". Father Jany remained for several years at Disaster Bay.
7 A.F. 548/1912.
8 *W.A. Church News,* 1 October 1925.
9 E. J. Telfer, *Amongst Australian Aborigines* (Sydney, 1939), p. 104.
10 *Ibid.,* p. 113.
11 *Ibid.,* pp. 115, 116, 122.
12 N.WT. 6/1920.
13 Premier's 13/1928.
14 H. P. Smith, ed., *The First Ten Years of Mount Margaret Mission, Western Australia* (Melbourne, 1933), p. 65.
15 Police 1972/1921.

16 A. 484/1926.
17 *P.D.,* 102: 2331.
18 Porteus, *The Psychology of a Primitive People,* p. 5.
19 A.F. 813/1911.
20 *A.R.,* 1908, p. 22.
21 Perez, *Kalumburu,* p. 31.
22 *Ibid.,* 53.
23 *A.R.,* 1908, pp. 19–20.
24 *Ibid.,* p. 19.
25 *Ibid.,* p. 20.
26 "Reports of the Chief Protector Concerning Mission Stations on the Dampier
    Peninsula".
27 *M.H.,* 3 April 1908.
28 Porteus, *The Psychology of a Primitive People,* p. 6.
29 *Ibid.,* pp. 7–8.
30 N.WT. 242/1927.
31 *W.A.,* 23 April 1938.
32 Love, *Stone-Age Bushmen of To-day,* p. 32.
33 S. R. Marks, "Mission Policy in Western Australia, 1846–1959", *University
    Studies in Western Australian History,* 1960, p. 82.
34 P. 193–94.
35 P. 82.
36 E. R. B. Gribble, *Forty Years With the Aborigines* (Sydney, 1930), p. 88.
37 E. R. B. Gribble, *The Problem of the Australian Aboriginal* (Sydney, 1932),
    p. 117.
38 A. 308/1928.
39 It was thought at the time that he was transferred as a result of his role in the
    1927 Royal Commission on alleged police atrocities. See M. M. Bennett,
    Australian Aboriginal as a Human Being (London, 1930), p. 69; and Bolton,
    "A Survey of the Kimberley Pastoral Industry from 1885 to the Present",
    p. 226. Hawtrey, *The Availing Struggle,* p. 155, says "he felt too tired to carry
    on longer".
40 A. 99/1930.
41 *A.R.,* 1935, p. 15.
42 A. 140/1904.
43 *A.R.,* 1908, p. 18.
44 Gibson, "Culture Contact on Sunday Island", p. 103.
45 *A.R.,* 1908, p. 18.
46 E. J. Stuart, *A Land of Opportunities* (London, 1923), p. 17.
47 A. 151/1934.
48 R. S. Schenk, *The Educability of the Native* (Perth, 1936), p. 37.
49 Marks, "Mission Policy in Western Australia, 1846–1959", p. 86.
50 *Ibid.,* p. 83.
51 Smith, *The First Ten Years of Mount Margaret Mission,* p. 67.
52 N.A. 219/1932.
53 *Ibid.*
54 A.F. 1471/1911.
55 Neville, *Australia's Coloured Minority,* p. 99.
56 C.S.D. 2384/1904.
57 A. 606/1906.
58 *A.R.,* 1907, p. 4.
59 *A.R.,* 1911, p. 7.
60 A. 690/1906.

61 Neville, *Australia's Coloured Minority,* p. 98.
62 N.A. 431/1928.
63 Quoted in Smith, *The First Ten Years of the Mount Margaret Mission,* p. 14.
64 A. 315/1928.
65 N.A. 219/1932.
66 *P.D.,* 102: 2249.

Notes to Chapter Seven

1 Crowley, *Australia's Western Third,* p. 49.
2 G. Greenwood, ed., *Australia* (Sydney, 1955), pp. 253–54.
3 Marchant, "Native Administration in Western Australia 1886–1905", p. 89.
4 N. B. Nairn, in the article "A Survey of the History of White Australia Policy
   in the 19th Century", *Australian Quarterly,* September 1956, stresses the
   economic factors behind the introduction of the policy, while C. Kellaway's
   " 'White Australia' — How Political Reality Became a National Myth",
   ibid., June 1953, regards the policy as a "matter of principle for political
   action". Racial factors behind the policy are stressed by B. C. Mansfield in
   the article "The Origins of 'White Australia' ", *ibid.,* December 1954 and,
   more recently, by A. T. Yarwood in the book *Asian Migration to Australia:
   the Background to Exclusion 1896–1923* (Melbourne, 1967).
5 *P.D.* (Commonwealth), 4: 4807.
6 A. 830/1900.
7 *A.R.,* 1901, p. 3.
8 *Ibid.,* 1903, p. 4.
9 *Ibid.,* 1904, p. 4.
10 *V. & P.,* 5 (1905): 25.
11 *P.D.,* 25: 558.
12 A.F. 95/1912.
13 *P.D.,* 28: 553.
14 A.F. 762/1912.
15 *S.T.,* 24 June 1900; *W.A. Record,* 23 June 1900.
16 Durack, *Kings in Grass Castles,* p. 371.
17 A. 1076/1906.
18 A. 827/1906.
19 *M.H.,* 14 October 1902.
20 *Report on Stations Visited by the Travelling Inspector of Aborigines* (Perth,
   1901), pp. 129–30; *A.R.,* 1900, p. 8.
21 P. 95.
22 Lands 15124/1908.
23 A.F. 1435/1911.
24 *Seventh Census of Western Australia* (Perth, 1904), pp. 206–7.
25 A. 170/1905.
26 C. Gye, *The Cockney and the Crocodile* (London, 1962), p. 138.
27 A. 170/1905.
28 A.F. 753/1914.
29 *W.A.,* 28 May 1912.
30 A.F. 753/1914.
31 Education 4259/1915.
32 *Ibid.*
33 Elkin, "Reaction and Interaction", p. 174.
34 *Ibid.*
35 Police 4378/1918.

36 A.F. 419/1915.
37 Education 4259/1915.
38 *Ibid.*
39 *Ibid.*
40 *Ibid.*
41 *Ibid.*
42 Stow, *To the Islands,* p. 61.
43 A.F. 817/1918.
44 *A.R.,* 1919, p. 10.
45 Neville, *Australia's Coloured Minority,* p. 113.
46 *A.R.,* 1919, p. 25.
47 A. 261/1927.
48 *Ibid.*
49 Neville, *Australia's Coloured Minority,* pp. 177–81.
50 *V. & P.,* 2 (1935): 8.
51 N.WT. 681/1923.
52 N.WT. 811/1923.
53 *S.T.,* 26 November 1926.
54 *W.A.,* 9 February 1906.
55 *Ibid.,* 13 March 1913.
56 *S.T.,* 6 April 1913.
57 *Ibid.*
58 *Ibid.,* 26 November 1926.
59 Premier's 155/1928.
60 *Ibid.*
61 *W.A.,* 10 March 1928.
62 But it gave the local scandal rag, the *Mirror,* an excellent opportunity to poke fun at the Premier. According to a *Mirror* reporter, Harris concluded his speech with the following sentence: "The Helots of Sparta were better established in their native soil than are the aborigines of Western Australia", to which Collier allegedly replied: "Yes, that's so, but I have not yet had time to visit that place as sparse settlement does not yet warrant the building of a state hotel there. In any case that point is one for my colleague the Hon. Minister for Agriculture, who tells me that he is about to initiate some experiments in shallot growing in the South-West." (10 March 1928.)
63 *W.A.,* 12 March 1928.
64 N.WT. 2260/1919.
65 *P.D.,* 83: 1523.
66 *Ibid.,* p. 2101.
67 For example, 327 in 1918, 732 in 1919, 379 in 1926, 310 in 1930, and 823 in 1935.
68 *V. & P.,* 2 (1935): 8.
69 *Worker,* 1 March 1934.
70 Neville, *Australia's Coloured Minority,* pp. 136–37.
71 P. Hasluck, *Our Southern Half-Caste Natives and Their Conditions* (Perth, 1939), p. 16.
72 *W.A.,* 13 March 1934.
73 N.A. 827/1938.
74 Hasluck, *Our Southern Half-Caste Natives and Their Conditions,* p. 11.
75 N.A. 231/1933.

Notes to Chapter Eight

1 *V. & P.,* 2 (1935).

2 *P.D.*, 97: 710.
3 Hasluck, *Black Australians,* pp. 160–61.
4 N. B. Tindale, "Survey of the Half-Caste Problem in South Australia", *Proceedings of the Royal Geographical Society of Australia, South Australian Branch,* 1940–1941, p. 126.
5 Neville, *Australia's Coloured Minority,* p. 246.
6 *W.A.,* 23 August 1937.
7 *P.D.,* 99: 724.
8 *W.A.,* 14 May 1938.
9 *Ibid.,* 17 June 1938.
10 30 June 1938.
11 1 August 1938.
12 *W.A.,* 28 August 1938.
13 N.A., 815/1937.
14 *P.D.,* 102: 2241.
15 Kitson's speech in *P.D.,* 102: 2326–57.
16 *Ibid.,* p. 2327.
17 *W.A.,* 17 February 1939.
18 *P.D.,* 74: 454.
19 *Ibid.,* 89: 2559. The clause was restored in 1934 though in a somewhat different form, limiting the aborigines' right of entry to unenclosed parts of pastoral leases.
20 Australian Aborigines' Amelioration Association, *Putting Back the Hands of the Clock 300 Years.*
21 *A.R.,* 1938, p. 4.
22 *V. & P.,* 2 (1935): 20.
23 The whole incident in N.A. 320/1940.
24 *A.R.,* 1938, p. 7.
25 *G.G.,* 1887, p. 537.
26 *V. & P.,* 16 (1899): 23–24.
27 For instance, *W.A.,* 17 November 1908.
28 A. 417/1927.
29 In this context see *R.* v. *Dyson,* referred to in *R.* v. *Pritchard* (1836) and quoted in Kriewaldt, "The Application of Criminal Law to the Aborigines of the Northern Territory of Australia", p. 21: "If the accused cannot understand the nature of the proceedings of the trial he cannot be tried, and if he cannot be tried, he cannot be punished."
30 Crown Law 1749/1941.
31 *P.D.,* 102: 2331, 2336.
32 *V. & P.,* 2 (1935): 18.
33 N.A. 216/1938.
34 N.A. 151/1934.
35 N.A. 778/1938.
36 *A.R.,* 1940, p. 11.
37 N.A. 231/1933.
38 Tindale, "Survey of Half-Caste Problem in South Australia", p. 85.
39 *Ibid.,* pp. 71–72.
40 *W.A.,* 23 March 1934.
41 Neville, *Australia's Coloured Minority,* p. 54.
42 *Ibid.,* p. 56.
43 S. G. Middleton, "The Problem of our Native People" (roneoed, 1951).
44 Tindale, "Survey of the Half-Caste Problem in South Australia", p. 126.
45 Neville, *Australia's Coloured Minority,* p. 243.

46 *Ibid.,* p. 244.
47 Tindale, "Survey of the Half-Caste Problem in South Australia", p. 122.
48 *Minutes of Proceedings of a Conference of Delegates of Great Southern Road Boards* (Perth, n.d.).
49 N.A. 330/1936.
50 N.A. 486/1935.
51 *V. & P.,* A2 (1938): 10.
52 N.A. 246/1940. The survey was not the first of its kind undertaken in Western Australia. In 1929 the State Psychologist, Dr. E. T. Stoneman, tested the pupils of the Moore River settlement. She found that 20 per cent did as well as the average white child; approximately 40 per cent equalled the performance of "dull" white children; the remainder did very poorly. She recommended three separate courses of instruction: an ordinary course up to standard four level for the first group; a practical course in hygiene, cooking, and animal husbandry for the second group; and instruction in the children's own dialect, wherever possible, for the third group (*W.A.,* 24 March 1934).
53 N.A. 346/1936.
54 N.A. 1170/1940.
55 Neville, *Australia's Coloured Minority,* p. 242.
56 *V. &. P.* (Commonwealth), 16 (1929): 270.
57 Stanner, *After the Dreaming,* p. 21.
58 *A.F.A. Annual Review,* 1936, p. 17.
59 Neville, *Australia's Coloured Minority,* p. 207.
60 *A.F.A. Annual Review,* 1937, p. 39.
61 *Ibid.*
62 J. C. G. Kevin, ed., *Some Australians Take Stock* (London, 1939), p. 24.
63 P. M. C. Hasluck, *Native Welfare in Australia* (Perth, 1953), p. 10.
64 Quoted in M. T. Clark, *Pastor Doug* (Melbourne, 1965), p. 97.
65 *Commonwealth Government's Policy with Respect to Aborigines* (Canberra, 1939).

Notes to Chapter Nine

1 *S.T.,* 13 February 1944. Note also the introduction in January 1940 of a regular "Aboriginal Sunday" — the Sunday preceding the Australia Day holiday.
2 Elkin, *Citizenship for the Aborigines,* p. 7.
3 *V. & P.,* A/2 (1943): 15.
4 N.A. 1045/1945.
5 Quoted in *P.D.,* 114: 1907.
6 Quoted *ibid.,* p. 1910.
7 N.W. 170/1943.
8 *P.D.,* 114: 1279.
9 N.A. 563/1943.
10 *Education,* November 1961, p. 42.
11 N.A. 246/1936.
12 *W.A.,* 11 December 1942.
13 N.A. 246/1936.
14 Education 451/1941.
15 *P.D.,* 111: 2835.
16 *Ibid.,* 114: 1408.
17 *Ibid.,* p. 1280.
18 *Ibid.,* 113: 825.
19 *Ibid.,* 114: 1409.

20 N.A. 330/1936.
21 Award 6/1946. Negotiations with the union in N.A. 956/1943.
22 *Commonwealth Arbitration Reports,* 53: 216.
23 N.A. 1137/1942.
24 N.A. 939/1941.
25 Quoted in *P.D.,* 113: 856–57.
26 N.A. 463/1944.
27 *P.D.,* 113: 825.
28 *Ibid.,* p. 969.
29 *Ibid.,* p. 972.
30 *W.A.,* 29 September 1944.
31 *A.R.,* 1945, p. 9.
32 *P.D.,* 113: 826.
33 *Report from the Select Committee on Voting Rights of Aborigines,* p. 47.
34 The 1939 National Registration Act which provided for a census of male population between the ages of eighteen and sixty-five, did not specifically mention aborigines. This oversight (if it was one) was subsequently clarified by an official ruling that all aborigines except full-bloods were under an obligation to register. See also the 1909 Defence Act which exempted from military service persons who were not "substantially" of European origin or descent, and the 1951–1965 National Service Act which exempted from registration persons of the half-blood and persons of aboriginal extraction living as aborigines. Any exempted aborigine living as white could register voluntarily, however, and was liable to serve if called up.
35 *W.A.,* 14 August 1945.
36 *P.D.,* 113: 856.
37 Police 1391/1942.
38 N.A. 43/1931.
39 N.A. 592/1943.
40 *Ibid.*
41 *Ibid.*
42 *Ibid.*
43 *Ibid.*
44 *Ibid.*
45 Another "subversive" organization which acquired some influence among the aborigines was the sect of Jehovah's Witnesses. It was banned early in the war but the ban was lifted in July 1943. The sect was active around Brookton, Pingelly, and Narrogin, particularly between 1945 and 1950 (*Narrogin Observer,* 25 August 1950).
46 *D.N.,* 10 October 1944.
47 C.S.D. 1096/1905.
48 In 1934 the secretary of the Marble Bar road board told the Moseley Royal Commission: "The native question should be handled entirely by the Police Department." (*W.A.,* 14 August 1934.)
49 *G.G.,* 30 October 1942.
50 *Record,* 14 July 1955.
51 Mines 3785/1935.
52 *Ibid.*
53 D. Stuart, *Yandy* (Melbourne, 1959), p. ii.
54 N.A. 460/1943.
55 *Ibid.*
56 N.A. 800/1945.
57 *Ibid.*

58 *Ibid.*
59 N.A. 431/1938.
60 Kaberry, *Aboriginal Woman*, p. xxiv. In the language of an old woman portrayed in Mary Durack's *Keep Him My Country,* there were "straight marriages and crooked marriages and little-bit crooked marriages and little-bit straight marriages." (Pacific Books edition, p. 9.)
61 *P.D.*, 113: 1012.
62 *Ibid.*, 114: 1461–62.
63 *Ibid.*, p. 1912.
64 N.A. 409/1943.
65 *P.D.*, 113: 733.
66 21 October 1944.
67 *P.D.*, 114: 1905, 1908.
68 *Ibid.*, p. 1912.
69 *Ibid.*, p. 1916.
70 N.A. 1011/1945.
71 Wilson, "Authority and Leadership in a 'New Style' Australian Aboriginal Community", p. 53. His thesis focuses on the later stages of the strike movement but has an extremely valuable historical section. The strike is also the subject of D. Stuart's novel *Yandy.*
72 N.A. 800/1945.
73 Committee for the Defence of Native Rights, *Story the Press Did Not Tell* (Perth, 1946).
74 *S.T.,* 8 November 1951.
75 Wilson, "Authority and Leadership in a 'New Style' Australian Aboriginal Community", p. 388.
76 D. Stuart, *Yaralie* (Melbourne, 1962), p. 68.
77 N.A. 621/1943.
78 N.A. 1194/1940.
79 N.A. 4/1942.
80 F. B. Vickers, *The Mirage* (Melbourne, 1955), pp. 183–84. The novel was written soon after the war.
81 *Ibid.*, pp. 230–31.
82 N.A. 68/1935.
83 M. Durack, *Child Artists of the Australian Bush* (Sydney, 1952), p. 29.
84 *Ibid.*, p. 31.
85 N.A. 1294/1945.
86 *Ibid.*
87 Durack, *Child Artists of the Australian Bush,* pp. 31, 33.
88 N.A. 745/1942.
89 Durack, *Child Artists of the Australian Bush,* p. 37.
90 *P.D.*, 114: 1913.
91 *Ibid.*, 116: 1739.
92 Education 631/1944.
93 *P.D.*, 119: 502.
94 N.A. 305/1947.
95 *Ibid.*
96 26 August 1948.
97 A. P. Elkin, "Australian Aboriginal and White Relations: A Personal Record", *R.A.H.S. Journal and Proceedings,* July 1962, p. 226. Earlier, in 1946, Elkin had been asked by several welfare organizations to "survey" the state's aboriginal administration but declined the invitation because the state government would not co-operate.

Notes to Chapter Ten

1 *V. & P.*, 19 (1948).
2 *P.D.*, 123: 356.
3 N.A. 376/1945.
4 This modest step towards the "aboriginalization" of the department was followed, in September 1949, by the appointment of two clerical assistants at the head office. By June 1954 eleven aboriginal clerks were employed by the department; the first aboriginal patrol officer, Irwin Lewis, was appointed in the late fifties.
5 *A.R.*, 1951, p. 5.
6 N.A. 712/1943.
7 Gye, *The Cockney and the Crocodile*, p. 100.
8 The league disintegrated in 1947 and was revived in 1950 as the New Coolbaroo League, with the Mudalla Youth Club taking the place of the Coolbaroo York Club. In 1952 the league established branches at Narrogin and Geraldton and in the following year started publishing the monthly *Westralian Aborigine*, edited by the journalist Lyndall Hadow. The last issue appeared in 1956.
9 *G.G.*, 10 December 1948.
10 N.A. 732/1948.
11 N.A. 621/1943.
12 *Ibid.*
13 *Ibid.* Dorothy Hewett expressed similar feelings in the poem "Clancy and Dooley and Don McLeod":

> The squatters are riding round in the night
> Crying "Load up your guns and, wrong or right,
> Let's teach these niggers that they can't rob
> The big white bosses of thirty bob".

14 *P.D.* (Commonwealth), 203: 1908.
15 *W.A.*, 7 July 1949.
16 Quoted in *D.N.*, 8 August 1949.
17 N.A. 252/1949.
18 Wilson, "Authority and Leadership in a 'New Style' Australian Aboriginal Community", p. 82.
19 N.A. 686/1951.
20 *V. & P.*, 19 (1948): 15.
21 N.A. 34/1949.
22 *Ibid.*
23 *Ibid.*
24 *Ibid.*
25 P. 12.
26 Middleton, "The Problem of Our Native People".
27 *A.R.*, 1951, p. 21. In 1960, addressing a conference at the University of New England, Middleton quoted Sir Hubert Murray: "Even if I were an atheist I would have to admit that Christianity was of tremendous value and importance as a civilizing influence and aid in the assimilation of natives into our way of life." (Address to a Conference on Australian Aborigines, University of New England, 27th to 29th May, 1960, p. 11.)
28 The first aborigine (a girl) passed the Junior Examination of the University of Western Australia in 1943 — the only successful candidate until 1952.
29 This was later substantiated by two students of the University of Western

Australia, A. H. West and F. Goddard, whose B.Ed. theses, "The Education of the Native Child in Western Australia" (1953) and "The Retardation of Native Children in South-West of Western Australia" (1954), demonstrated that aboriginal education was primarily a sociological problem.

30 10 June 1949.

31 *W.A.,* 15 September 1950.

32 *D.N.,* 2 September 1950.

33 *A.R.,* 1951, p. 11.

34 N.A. 834/1951.

35 N.A. 991/1947.

36 *W.A.,* 5 April 1950.

37 *W.A.,* 22 July 1950.

38 N.A. 115/1938.

39 Middleton, "Address to a Conference on Australian Aborigines" (roneoed, 1960), p. 4.

40 *W.A.,* 2 December 1952.

41 N.A. 596/1949.

42 13 January 1950.

43 *W.A.,* 17 May 1949.

44 The results of the surveys are tabulated in I. Mann, *Opthalmic Survey of South-Western Portion of Western Australia* (Perth, 1956), p. 27. In the Kimberleys 44.38 per cent of the part-aborigines and 56.49 per cent of the full-bloods examined showed various traces of trachoma. Corresponding figures for the goldfields survey were 56.52 per cent and 58.9 per cent while in the southwest 64.36 per cent of the part-aborigines and 59.81 per cent of the full-bloods examined were affected by the disease. Dr. Mann recorded her personal impressions in Gye, *The Cockney and the Crocodile.*

45 *D.N.,* 29 July 1949.

46 *A.R.,* 1952, p. 5.

47 *Ibid.,* p. 3.

48 This body should not be confused with the first Native Welfare Council of Western Australia, formed in 1939, which disintegrated after the war. The following organizations were affiliated with the second council: the Federated Progress Association of Western Australia, the Native Rights and Welfare League, the Society of Friends, the State Women's Council of the Liberal and Country League, the National Council of Women, Toc H, Women's Service Guild, the University Society of Native Welfare, the Western Australian Association of University Women, Labor Women's Central Executive, and the New Coolbaroo League.

49 N.A. 92/1949.

50 *W.A.,* 10 October 1952.

51 *Ibid.,* 21 October 1952.

52 *P.D.,* 132: 1483. The bill was drafted in August by the parliamentary draftsman for private members and submitted for the approval of the parliamentary Labour Party on 9 October, one day before the publication of the first "Not Slaves, Not Citizens" article in the *West Australian.* It was not approved, but the decision was reversed on 21 October.

53 *W.A.,* 23 January 1953.

54 *Ibid.,* 24 January 1953.

55 *Ibid.,* 28 January 1953.

56 McLeod, in *Westerly,* 1957, No. 2, p. 7, predicted that the aborigines will one day claim what he called the "accumulated deficit" due to them (amounting to some $20 million), that is the difference between the sum spent on native

aboriginals since 1897, and the amount which Western Australia would have so spent if the provision requiring that 1 per cent of government revenue should be set aside for the aborigines had not been abolished in 1897.

57 Moola Bulla was closed in 1954, largely because of staffing problems, and sold for $200,000 to a Queensland pastoralist, Allan Goldman, who later resold the property at a substantial profit (*D.N.*, 17 August 1961).

58 N.W., 1266/1944.

59 P. 72.

60 *G.G.*, 18 March 1927. The prohibition originally covered the whole of the city of Perth but the area was reduced in 1948 to the inner city bounded by the Swan River and Milligan, Newcastle, and Bennett streets, with a view to strict enforcement of the prohibition.

61 *A.R.*, 1955, p. 8.

62 "I bin wait too long", said an old aborigine to a departmental officer. "McLeod a liar . . . all the time chook food, beans, beans, beans, no meat." (N.A. 127/1951.)

63 *Ibid.*

64 In 1958 McLeod's group located a big manganese field on Nimmingara station, east of Port Hedland, and Pindan Pty. Ltd. and a Sydney metal merchant, A.G. Sims, formed a company called Simdan to exploit the deposits. For an account of McLeod's activities after 1955 see Wilson, "Authority and Leadership in a 'New Style' Australian Aboriginal Community".

65 *P.D.*, 135: 1796–97; 136: 2112–13, 2311.

66 *Ibid.*, 136: 2776.

67 T. G. H. Strehlow, *Nomads in No-Man's-Land* (Adelaide, 1961), p. 26.

68 *P.D.*, 136: 2480.

69 *Ibid.*, pp. 2775–76.

70 The inquiry, instigated by Simpson himself, was concluded, significantly, two days after the election in which the Liberal-Country Party government was defeated. The Public Service Commissioner cleared Middleton of all complicity in the affair: "He has denied having been instrumental in any way in writing or assisting in the preparation of these articles." (*P.D.*, 136: 2762–63.)

71 *Ibid.*, p. 2763.

72 Hasluck, *Black Australians*, pp. 160–61.

Notes to Chapter Eleven

1 Stanner, *After the Dreaming*, p. 38.

2 *Australian*, 8 April 1969.

3 *Observer* (Sydney), 13 June 1959.

4 Stanner, "Continuity and Change Among the Aborigines", p. P.104.

5 M. Reay, ed., *Aborigines Now* (Sydney, 1964), p. ix.

6 Hasluck, *Black Australians*, p. 57.

7 *Ibid.*, p. 58.

8 Bates, *The Passing of the Aborigines*, p. 67.

9 Hasluck, *Black Australians*, p. 101.

10 C. D. Rowley, "Aborigines and Other Australians", *Oceania*, June 1962, p. 249.

11 J. Doughty, *The Green Stick* (London, 1960), pp. 17, 124.

12 Rowley, "Aborigines and Other Australians", p. 249. Note, however, Wilson's comment that while mass reprisals (in the north-west) were thought deplorable, especially when children were shot by the settlers, they were partially

excused on the grounds that members of both cultures were "wild old fellows". The atrocities were not resented as much as being "knocked back", that is the refusal by the station owners of clothing, tobacco and other amenities "Authority and Leadership in a 'New Style' Australian Aboriginal Community", p. 36.

13 Elkin, "Reaction and Interaction", p. 158.
14 Quoted, in translation, in R. Emerson, *From Empire to Nation* (Cambridge, Mass., 1960), p. 428.
15 Reay, *Aborigines Now,* p. viii.
16 W. K. Hancock, *Australia* (Brisbane, 1964), pp. 59, 61.
17 *Ibid.,* p. 60.
18 Wilson, "Authority and Leadership in a 'New Style' Australian Aboriginal Community", p. 73.
19 M. Harris, "Are We All Murderers?", *Nation,* 11 April 1959.
20 Gye, *The Cockney and the Crocodile,* p. 36.
21 Rowley, "Aborigines and Other Australians", p. 259.
22 N. Gare, *The Fringe Dwellers* (London, 1961).
23 K. S. Prichard, *N'Goola and Other Stories* (Melbourne, 1959).
24 Despite the fact that *coolbaroo* was a Murchison word for magpie and was apparently chosen as a symbol of "black and white" integration.
25 Stanner, "Continuity and Change Among the Aborigines", p. P.104.
26 A. Capell, "Christian Missions and Australian Aboriginal Religious Practice", *International Review of Missions,* April 1950, p. 177.
27 C. Harrison, *A Study of the Culture Contact Situation in Collie* (B.A. [Hons.] thesis, University of Western Australia, 1960).
28 Review by R. Stow in *Australian Book Review,* November 1961, p. 3.
29 G. Casey, *Snowball* (Sydney, 1958), p. 7.
30 Stanner, "Continuity and Change Among the Aborigines", p. P.99.
31 *Ibid.,* p. P.107.
32 R. Taft, "A Psychological Model For the Study of Social Assimilation", *Human Relations,* 1957, p. 154.
33 Rowley "Aborigines and Other Australians", p. 253.
34 R. Rose, *Living Magic* (London, 1957), p. 193.
35 *Ibid.*
36 M. Durack, "From Yallangonga to Namatjira: a Noted Author Surveys Native Education", *W.A. Teachers Journal,* April 1961, p. 53.
37 Stanner, "Continuity and Change Among the Aborigines", p. P.105.
38 *Ibid.,* p. P.104.
39 M. Barnard, *A History of Australia* (Sydney, 1962), p. 666.

Selected Bibliography

Official Sources

1. Printed

a) Western Australia

Annual Reports of the Aborigines Department and its successors, most of which were printed as Parliamentary Papers. Those which were not printed can be consulted in the J. S. Battye Library of West Australian History.
Acts of Parliament.
Blue Books.
Census of the colony of Western Australia for the years 1848, 1854, 1861, 1870, 1881, 1891, and 1901, respectively.
Notes on Primary Curriculum for Teachers in Native Schools. Perth, 1960.
Parliamentary Debates.
Parliamentary Papers.
Provisional Curriculum for Coloured Pupils in Caste Schools. Perth, 1953.
Reports on Stations Visited by the Travelling Inspector of Aborigines. Perth, 1901.
Reports on Stations Visited by the Travelling Inspector of Aborigines. Perth, 1903.
Rottnest Gaol: General Rules and Regulations. Perth, 1879.

b) Commonwealth of Australia

Commonwealth Government's Policy with Respect to Aborigines: Issued by the Honourable J. McEwen, Minister for the Interior, February 1939. Canberra, 1939.
Commonwealth Yearbooks.
Native Welfare: Meeting of Commonwealth and State Ministers held in Canberra, 3rd and 4th September, 1951. Canberra, 1951.
Notes on Conference of Commonwealth and State Aboriginal Welfare Authorities held at Parliament House, Canberra, on Tuesday, 3rd February, 1948. Canberra, 1948.
Parliamentary Debates.
Parliamentary Papers.

Report from the Select Committee on Voting Rights for Aborigines. Canberra, 1961.

Royal Commission on Espionage. Canberra, 1954.

c) International organizations

International Labour Conference. *Conventions and Recommendations 1919–1949.* Geneva, 1949.

International Labour Office. *Living and Working Conditions of Indigenous Populations in Independent Countries.* Geneva, 1955–1956.

————. *Penal Sanctions for Breaches of Contract of Employment.* Geneva, 1953–1954.

————. *Protection and Integration of Indigenous and Other Tribal and Semi-tribal Populations in Independent Countries.* Geneva, 1953–1954.

2. Departmental records

Files of the Aborigines Department and its successors, located in the State Archives or in the registry of the Department of Native Welfare.

Selected files of the Chief Secretary's Department, Colonial Secretary's Department, Crown Law Department, Education Department, Mines Department, Police Department, and Premier's Department.

Unofficial Sources

1. Books, Pamphlets and Articles

"Aboriginal Labour in Western Australia", *International Labour Review,* May 1936.

Aborigines' Friends' Association. *The Aborigines: a Commonwealth Problem and Responsibility.* Adelaide, 1934.

"Administrative Classification of Australian Aborigines", *Nature,* 24 October 1936.

Alexander, F., ed. *Four Bishops and Their See: Perth, Western Australia, 1857–1957.* Perth, 1957.

Anderson, A. F. "Police Patrol in the 'Never, Never'", *Walkabout,* September 1948.

Ashley-Montague, M. F. "The Future of the Australian Aborigines", *Oceania,* March 1938.

Australian Association of Social Workers (W.A. Branch). *A Review of the Welfare, Progress and Assimilation of Aborigines with Particular Reference to the Position in Western Australia.* Perth, 1953.

"Australia's Burden", *Nature,* 18 December 1937.

Baldwin, A. H., and Cooling, L. F. *An Investigation into Hookworm Disease, Malaria and Filaria in Western Australia.* Melbourne, 1922.

Balfour, H. R. *Kunmunya Mission, Port George IV, Western Australia.* Melbourne, 1935.

Barnes, J. A. "Indigenous Politics and Colonial Administration with Special Reference to Australia", *Comparative Studies in Society and History,* January 1960.

Basedow, H. *The Australian Aboriginal*. Adelaide, 1925.

Bates, D. M. *Efforts Made by Western Australia Toward the Betterment of Her Aborigines*. Perth, 1907.

———. "The Marriage Laws and Some Customs of the West Australian Aborigines", *Victorian Geographical Journal*, 1905.

———. *The Passing of the Aborigines: a Lifetime Spent Among the Natives of Australia*. London, 1938.

———. "The Possibilities of Tropical Agriculture in the Nor'-West: the Beagle Bay Mission Experiments", *W.A. Yearbook*, 1900–1903.

———. "Social Organization of Some Western Australian Tribes", *Report of the 14th Meeting of the Australasian Association for the Advancement of Science*. Melbourne, 1914.

———. "Trappist Mission at Beagle Bay (W.A.)", *The Australasian*, 27 July 1929, 3 August 1929, 10 August 1929, 17 August 1929.

Bateson, F. W. "The Story of the Canning Stock Route", *Journal of the Historical Society of Western Australia*, 1942.

Battye, J. S. *Development of the Pastoral Industry in Western Australia*. Perth, 1923.

———, ed. *The History of the North West of Australia*. Perth, 1915.

———. *Western Australia: a History from its Discovery to the Inauguration of the Commonwealth*. Oxford, 1924.

Beckenham, P. W. *The Education of the Australian Aborigine*. Melbourne, 1948.

Beckett, J. "Marginal Men: a Study of Two Half-Caste Aborigines", *Oceania*, December 1958.

Bennett, M. M. *The Australian Aboriginal as a Human Being*. London, 1930.

———.*Human Rights for Australian Aborigines: How Can They Learn Without a Teacher*. Brisbane, 1957.

———. *Hunt or Die*. London, 1950.

———. *Teaching the Aborigines: Data from Mount Margaret Mission, W.A*. Perth, 1935.

Berndt, C. H. *Assimilation versus Apartheid: Paper Prepared for Pan Indian Ocean Science Association Congress, 1960*. Perth, 1960.

———. "Mateship or Success: an Assimilation Dilemma", *Oceania*, December 1962.

———. "The Quest For Identity: the Case of the Australian Aborigines", *Oceania*, September 1961.

Berndt, R.M. "The Concept of 'the Tribe' in the Western Desert of Australia", *Oceania*, December 1959.

———. "Influence of European Culture on Australian Aborigines", *Oceania*, March 1951.

———. "Native Welfare in Western Australia since the Warburton Controversy", *Australian Quarterly*, September 1959.

———. "The Status of Australian Aborigines", *Quadrant*, Summer 1960–1961.

———. "The 'Warburton Range' Controversy", *Australian Quarterly*, June 1957.

————, and Berndt, C. H. *The First Australians.* Sydney, 1952.

————, and ————. *From Black to White in South Australia.* Melbourne, 1951.

————, and ————. *Report on Survey of the Balgo Hills Area, South Kimberleys, Western Australia.* Perth, 1960.

————, and ————. *Social Anthropological Survey of the Warburton, Blackstone and Rawlinson Ranges.* Perth, 1959.

————, and ————. *The World of the First Australians: an Introduction to the Traditional Life of the Australian Aborigines.* Sydney, 1964.

————, and Fink, R. *Anthropological Survey of the Eastern Goldfields, Warburton Range and Jigalong Regions, January 26th-March 2nd, 1957.* Perth, 1957.

Bertram, H. *Flug in die Hoelle: Bericht von der "Betram-Atlantis-Expedition".* Berlin, 1933.

Birt, H. N. *Benedictine Pioneers of Australia.* 2 vols. London, 1911.

Bischofs, P. J. "Churinga and Totems in Nordwest-Australien", *Anthropos,* 1909.

————. "Die Niol-Niol, ein Eingebohrenenstamm in Nordwest-Australien", *Anthropos,* 1908.

Bleakley, J. W. *The Aborigines of Australia: Their History, Their Habits, Their Assimilation.* Brisbane, 1961.

Board of Missions of the Presbyterian Church of Australia, *Kunmunya.* Melbourne, 1937.

Bolton, G. C. *Alexander Forrest: His Life and Times.* Melbourne, 1958.

Briggs, T. J. *Life and Experience of a Successful West Australian.* Perth, 1917.

Brobham, A. *The First Australians and the New Australians.* Perth, 1959.

Buchanan, G. *Packhorse and Waterhole: With the First Overlanders to the Kimberleys.* Sydney, 1935.

Burges, L. C. *Pioneers of Nor'-West Australia, Pastoral and Pearling.* Perth, 1926.

Calvert, A. F. *The Aborigines of Western Australia.* London, 1894.

Campbell, T. D. "An Account of the Aboriginals of Sunday Island, King Sound, Kimberley, Western Australia", *Journal and Proceedings of the Royal Society of Western Australia,* 1914–1915.

————. "Need for Ethnological Survey of Western Australia", *Journal of the Western Australian Natural History Society,* January 1911.

Capell, A. "Christian Missions and Australian Aboriginal Religious Practice", *International Review of Missions,* April 1950.

————. "Interpreting Christianity to Australian Aborigines", *International Review of Missions,* April 1959.

Carnegie, D. W. *Spinifex and Sand: A Narrative of Five Years' Pioneering and Exploration in Western Australia.* London, 1898.

Catalan, A. M. *Lecture on the Origin and Development of the Drysdale River Mission, Western Australia, from 1908 to 1934.* New Norcia, 1935.

"Champion of the Aborigines: Stanley Guise", *People,* 7 October 1953.

Clark, M. T. *Pastor Doug: The Story of an Aboriginal Leader.* Melbourne, 1965.

Cleland, J. B. "The Australian Aboriginal: the Significance of His Past, the Present, His Future", *Report of the 27th Meeting of ANZAAS*. Hobart, 1949.

Coleman, P. "Making Black White", *Observer*, 13 June 1959.

Committee for the Defence of Native Rights, *Story the Press Did Not Tell*. Perth, 1946.

Cook, C. E. A. "The Native in Relation to the Public Health", *Medical Journal of Australia*, 30 April 1949.

————. "The Native Problem — Why is it Unsolved?", *Australian Quarterly*, December 1950.

Crowley, F. K. *Australia's Western Third: a History of Western Australia from the First Settlements to Modern Times*. London, 1960.

Curr, E. M. *The Australian Race*. 4 vols. Melbourne, 1886–1887.

Davidson, D. S. "Ethnic Map of Australia", *Proceedings of the American Philosophical Society*, 1938.

————. *A Preliminary Register of Australian Tribes and Hordes*. Philadelphia, 1938.

Davies, S. H. "The Problem of the Australian Aboriginal", *Australian Quarterly*, September 1935.

Despeissis, A. *The Nor'west and Tropical North*. Perth, 1921.

Doughty, J. *The Green Stick*. London, 1960.

Douglas, W. H. *Illustrated Topical Dictionary of the Western Desert Language, Warburton Ranges Dialect, Western Australia*. Perth, 1959.

————. *An Introduction to the Western Desert Language: a Pedagogical Description of the Western Desert Language Based on the Dialect Spoken at the Warburton Ranges, Western Australia*. Sydney, 1957.

————. *Wangka: a Set of Primers for Teaching Aborigines of the Warburton Ranges and the Western Desert to Read Their Own Language*. Perth, 1954.

Drake-Brockman, G. *The Turning Wheel*. Perth, 1960.

Drake-Brockman, H. "Broome and Its Tragic Yesterday", *Walkabout*, September 1946.

————. "Coloured Characters", *Walkabout*, June 1945.

Duguid, C. *The Future of the Aborigines of Australia*. Adelaide, 1941.

Dumas, R. J. *Report of a Committee Appointed by the Government to Investigate Measures Necessary to Promote the Development of the North-West*. Perth, 1945.

Durack, M. *Child Artists of the Australian Bush*. Sydney, 1952.

————. "From Yallagonga to Namatjira: Noted Author Surveys Native Education", *W.A. Teachers Journal*, April 1961.

————. *Keep Him My Country*. Pacific Books, 1966.

————. *Kings in Grass Castles*. Corgi Books, 1967.

————. "The Outlaws of Windginna Gorge", *Walkabout*, June 1941.

————. "The Priest Who Rode Away", *Westerly*, November 1962.

————. "The Vanishing Australian", *Walkabout*, August 1945.

————, and Durack, E. *All-About*. Sydney, 1935.

————, and ————. *Chumuna*. Sydney, 1936.

————, and ————. *Son of Djaro*. Perth, 1940.

Easton, R. *Report on the North Kimberley District of Western Australia.* Perth, 1922.

"Educating the Aborigine", *Times Educational Supplement,* 11 January 1941.

Edwards, W. H. "Aboriginal Education — Aims and Principles", *Journal of Christian Education,* June 1961.

Elkin, A. P. "A.R. Radcliffe-Brown, 1880–1955", *Oceania,* June 1956.

———. "Aboriginal Evidence and Justice in North Australia", *Oceania,* March 1947.

———. "Aboriginal Policy 1930–1950: Some Personal Associations", *Quadrant,* Spring 1957.

———. "Aborigines and the Ministers' Welfare Council", *Australian Quarterly,* December 1951.

———. "The Aborigines, Our National Responsibility", *Australian Quarterly,* September 1934.

———. "Anthropological Advance: Western Australia", *Oceania,* March 1956.

———. "Anthropological Research in Australia and the Western Pacific, 1927–37", *Oceania,* March 1938.

———. "Anthropology and the Future of the Australian Aborigines", *Oceania,* September 1934.

———. "Anthropology in Australia", *Oceania,* September 1939.

———. "Australian Aboriginal and White Relations: a Personal Record", *Journal and Proceedings of Royal Australian Historical Society,* July 1962.

———. *The Australian Aborigines: How to Understand Them.* Sydney, 1964.

———. *Citizenship for the Aborigines: a National Aboriginal Policy.* Sydney, 1944.

———. "Education in Aboriginal Australia", *Proceedings of the 7th Pacific Science Congress.* Christchurch, 1953.

———. "Native Education, with Special Reference to the Australian Aborigines", *Oceania,* June 1937.

———. "Native Reaction to an Invading Culture and its Bearers, with Special Reference to Australia", *Proceedings of the 7th Pacific Science Congress.* Christchurch, 1953.

———. "A New Anthropological Society", *Oceania,* March 1959.

———. *A Policy for the Aborigines.* Morpeth, 1933.

———. "Position and Problems of Aboriginal Mixed-Bloods in Australia", *Proceedings of the 7th Pacific Science Congress.* Christchurch, 1953.

———. "Reaction and Interaction: a Food Gathering People and European Settlement in Australia", *American Anthropologist,* April 1951.

———. "The Social Life and Intelligence of the Australian Aborigine: a Review of S.D. Porteus' 'Psychology of a Primitive People' ", *Oceania,* September 1932.

———. "Social Organization in the Kimberley Division, North-Western Australia", *Oceania,* March 1932.

———. "Totemism in North-Western Australia (the Kimberley Division)", *Oceania,* March and June 1933.

Elphinstone, J. J. *Report on Health and Nutrition of the Natives from Rawlinson Range to Lake McDonald, 1958.* Perth, 1958.

Ewers, J. K. *Bruce Rock: the Study of a District.* Perth, 1959.

———. "In and Around Marble Bar", *Walkabout,* February 1949.

———. "Yandying for Tin at Moolyella", *Walkabout,* May 1935.

Firth, R. "Anthropology and Native Administration", *Oceania,* September 1931.

Fitzpatrick, B. *The Australian Commonwealth.* Melbourne, 1956.

———. "Lesser Tribes Without a Law", *Meanjin,* Summer 1958.

Fletcher, R. W. "The Battle of Leveque", *Western Mail,* 30 May 1946.

Forrest, J. "The Marriage Laws of the Aborigines of North-Western Australia", *Report of the 2nd Meeting of the Australasian Association for the Advancement of Science.* Melbourne, 1890.

———. "On the Natives of Central and Western Australia", *Journal of the Anthropological Institute,* 1876.

Fowler, H. L. "Report on Psychological Tests on Natives in the North-West of Western Australia", *Australian Journal of Science,* April 1940.

Fox, J., and James, J. R. "The Educational Needs of the Integrated School", *Education,* November 1961.

Foxcroft, E. J. B. *Australian Native Policy: Its History, Especially in Victoria.* Melbourne, 1941.

Fry, H. K., and Pulleine, R. H. "The Mentality of the Australian Aborigine", *Australian Journal of Experimental Biology and Medical Science,* 1931.

Gare, C. E. "Educating the First Australians: Welfare Officer's Viewpoint", *W.A. Teachers Journal,* June 1961.

Gare, N. *The Fringe Dwellers.* London, 1961.

Geddes, W. R. "Maori and Aborigine: a Comparison of Attitudes and Policies", *Australian Journal of Science,* November 1961.

Gerard, A. E. *History of the United Aborigines' Mission.* Adelaide, 1950.

Gore, S. "Leper Colony", *Walkabout,* November 1951.

———. "Spanish Mission — the Story of New Norcia", *Walkabout,* December 1951.

Grey, G. *Journals of Two Expeditions of Discovery in North-West and Western Australia.* 2 vols. London, 1841.

Gribble, E. R. B. *A Despised Race: The Vanishing Aboriginals of Australia.* Sydney, 1933.

———. "The Forrest River Mission", *West Australian Church News,* 1 October 1925.

———. *Forty Years with the Aborigines.* Sydney, 1930.

———. *The Problem of the Australian Aboriginal.* Sydney, 1932.

Gribble, J.B. *Black but Comely: or, Glimpses of Aboriginal Life in Australia.* London, 1884.

———. *Dark Deeds in a Sunny Land: or, Blacks and Whites in North-West Australia.* Perth, 1886.

Groser, T. S. *The Lure of the Golden West.* London, 1927.

Gunning, F. W. *Lure of the North: Seventy Years' Memoirs of George Joseph Gooch and his Pioneer Friends of Western Australia.* Perth, 1952.

Gye, C. *The Cockney and the Crocodile.* London, 1962.

Hammond, J. E. *Winjan's People: the Story of the South-West Australian Aborigines.* Perth, 1933.

Harding, F. "Kimberley Teacher Writes on Native Education", *W.A. Teachers Journal,* July 1961.

Harris, M. "Are We All Murderers?", *Nation,* 11 April 1959.

Hasluck, A. "Yagan the Patriot and Some Notable Aborigines of the First Decade of Settlement", *Early Days,* 1961.

Hasluck, P. M. C. *Black Australians: a Survey of Native Policy in Western Australia, 1829–1897.* Melbourne, 1942.

————. "The Future of the Australian Aborigines", *Report of the 29th Meeting of ANZAAS.* Sydney, 1959.

————. "The Future of the Missions", *Australian Territories,* August 1961.

————. *Native Welfare in Australia.* Perth, 1953.

————. *Our Southern Half-Caste Natives and Their Conditions.* Perth, 1939.

Hawtrey, C. L. M. *The Availing Struggle: a Record of the Planting and Development of the Church of England in Western Australia, 1929–1947.* Perth, 1949.

Haydon, A. L. *The Trooper Police of Australia.* London, 1911.

Hendren, G. R. *Native Education in Queensland.* Brisbane, 1945.

Hernandez, T. "Children among the Drysdale River Tribes", *Oceania,* December 1941.

————. "Social Organization of the Drysdale River Tribes, North-West Australia", *Oceania,* March 1941.

Holmes, C. "Experiment in Survival: the Pindan Cooperative at Port Hedland", *Overland,* April 1960.

————. "Black Company Directors", *Nation,* 12 March 1960.

Idriess, I. L. *Outlaws of the Leopolds.* Sydney, 1952.

————. *Over the Range: Sunshine and Shadow in the Kimberleys.* Sydney, 1951.

"Intelligence among Australian Aborigines", *Nature,* 10 August 1940.

Jones, F. Lancaster. "The Demography of Australian Aborigines", *International Social Science Review,* 1965.

Kaberry, P. M. *Aboriginal Woman: Sacred and Profane.* London, 1939.

————. "The Forrest River and Lyne River Tribes of North-West Australia", *Oceania,* June 1935.

Kenyon, A. S. "Black and White Culture Contacts on the Australian Continent", *Report of the 23rd Meeting of ANZAAS.* Auckland, 1937.

Kevin, J. C. G., ed. *Some Australians Take Stock.* London, 1939.

King, A., et al. "A Survey of Australian Aborigines for Pulmonary Tuberculosis", *Medical Journal of Australia,* 30 June 1951.

Klaatch, H. *Ergebnisse meiner Australischen Reise.* Braunschweig, 1907.

————. "Schlussbericht ueber meine Reise nach Australien in den Jahren 1904–07", *Zeitschrift fuer Ethnologie,* 1907.

———. "Some Notes on Scientific Travel among the Black Population of Tropical Australia in 1904, 1905, 1906", *Report of the 11th Meeting of the Australasian Association for the Advancement of Science.* Adelaide, 1908.

Kriewaldt, M. C. "The Application of the Criminal Law to the Aborigines of the Northern Territory of Australia", *University of Western Australia Law Review,* December 1960.

Law, F. A. *The History of the Merredin District.* Merredin, 1961.

Lefroy, C. E. C. "Australian Aborigines, a Noble-Hearted Race", *Contemporary Review,* February 1929.

———. *Memoirs of Henry Maxwell Lefroy.* Guildford, 1934.

Lindsay, H. A. "Tragedy in Our North-West", *Bulletin,* 3 March 1954.

Lommell, A. "Modern Culture Influences on the Aborigines", *Oceania,* September 1950.

Love, J. R. B. *The Aborigines: Their Present Condition, as Seen in Northern South Australia, the Northern Territory, North-West Australia and Western Queensland.* Melbourne, 1915.

———. "Introduction to Worora Language", *Journal of the Royal Society of Western Australia,* 1930–1931 and 1931–1932.

———. "Mythology, Totemism and Religion of the Worora Tribe of North-West Australia", *Report of the 22nd Meeting of ANZAAS.* Melbourne, 1935.

———. "Notes on the Worora Tribe of North-Western Australia", *Transactions of the Royal Society of South Australia,* 1917.

———. *Our Australian Blacks.* Melbourne, 1922.

———. *Stone-Age Bushmen of To-day: Life and Adventure among a Tribe of Savages in North-Western Australia.* London, 1936.

———, Webb, T. T., and Gribble, E. R. B. "Aborigines of Australia: Symposium", *International Review of Missions,* July 1943.

McLeod, D. W. "Aboriginal Enterprise in the Pilbara", *Westerly,* 1957, No. 2.

McMahon, J. T. *Bishop Salvado: Founder of New Norcia.* Perth, 1943.

———. *One Hundred Years: Five Great Church Leaders.* Perth, 1946.

Mant, G., and Armitage, M. "Kabbarli: Short Biography of Daisy Bates", *South West Pacific Annual,* December 1945.

Marks, S. R. "Mission Policy in Western Australia 1846–1959", *University Studies in Western Australian History,* 1960.

Mason, H. G. B. *Darkest West Australia: A Treatise Bearing on the Habits and Customs of the Aborigines and the Solution of 'The Native Question'.* Kalgoorlie, 1909.

Middleton, S. G. "A Host on the Highroad of History", *W.A. Teachers Journal,* October 1961.

———. "Address to a Conference on Australian Aborigines, Held at the University of New England, 27th to 29th May 1960." Roneoed.

———. "The Problem of our Native People: Notes Used at Symposium Arranged by New Education Fellowship Conference in Winthrop Hall, University of Western Australia, on 12th October 1951." Roneoed, Perth, 1951.

Millet, E. *An Australian Parsonage: or, the Settler and the Savage in Western Australia.* London, 1872.

Mitchell, S. *Looking Backward: Reminiscences of 42 Years.* Geraldton, 1911.

Monachus. *New Norcia: Historical Guide to All its Institutions.* New Norcia, 1946.

Moore, D. "Native Outlaws Terrorised East Kimberley in 1907", *Countryman,* 9 November 1961.

Moore, G. F. *Diary of an Early Settler in Western Australia.* London, 1884.

Mulvaney, D. J. "The Australian Aborigines 1606–1929: Opinion and Fieldwork", *Historical Studies: Selected Articles.* Melbourne, 1964.

Murray, A. "The Old and the New", *Education,* November 1960.

"Native Tribes of Western Australia", *Nature,* 22 April 1920.

Native Welfare Council of W.A. *The Tragedy of Native Affairs.* Perth, 1944.

Neville, A. O. "The Aborigines". In H. Colebatch, ed. *A Story of A Hundred Years.* Perth, 1929.

———. *Australia's Coloured Minority: Its Place in the Community.* Sydney, 1947.

———. "Contributory Causes of Aboriginal Depopulation in Western Australia", *Mankind,* September 1948.

———. "The First Possessors of the Land: the Care of Natives", *Civil Service Journal,* 20 July 1929.

———. "The Half-Caste in Australia", *Mankind,* September 1951.

———. "Relations Between Settlers and Aborigines in Western Australia", *Journal and Proceedings of the W.A. Historical Society,* 1936.

Nicolay, G. G. *Notes on the Aborigines of Western Australia.* London, 1886.

Nomad. "White and Black: Australian Natives in the Kimberleys", *Golden West,* 1920–1921.

O'Brien, S. "Nuns Care for 240 Lepers at Derby: a Wonderful Work of Mercy in our Midst", *Record,* 8 August 1945.

Parry, H.H. *Suggestions with Reference to the Treatment and Employment of the Aboriginal Natives in the Northern Districts of Western Australia.* Perth, 1889.

Parsons, G. *Black Chattels: Story of the Australian Aborigines.* London, 1947.

Pastoralists' Association of Western Australia. *Annual Reports,* 1907–1955.

———. *The Pastoral Industry in North-West Australia: State Development Committee's Inquiry and Recommendations together with Case Presented by the Pastoralists' Association of Western Australia.* Perth, 1945.

Perez, E., ed. *Benedictine Items.* New Norcia, 1953.

———. *Kalumburu, "Formerly Drysdale River" Benedictine Mission, North-Western Australia.* New Norcia, 1959.

Petri, H. E. *Kurangura: Neue Magische Kulte in Nordwest-Australien.* Braunschweig, 1950.

——. *Sterbende Welt in Nordwest-Australien.* Braunschweig, 1954.

Piddington, R. "Karadjeri Initiation", *Oceania,* September 1932.

——. "Psychological Aspects of Culture Contact", *Oceania,* March 1933.

——. "Totemic System of the Karadjeri Tribe", *Oceania,* June 1932.

——, and Piddington, M. "Report on Field Work in North-West Australia", *Oceania,* March 1932.

Pilmer, R.H. "Northern Patrol (Compiled from the Diaries of R. H. Pilmer by C. F. Christie)", *Countryman,* 30 August, and 6, 13, 20, and 27 September 1956.

Pindan Pty. Ltd. *Have the Natives of W.A. Been the Victims of a Confidence Trick.* Perth, n.d.

Pink, O. "Open Letter to Defenders of the Tribes-people Anywhere in Australia", *Communist Review,* February 1950.

Pitts, H. *The Australian Aboriginal and the Christian Church.* London, 1914.

Pollard, J. "New Norcia Mission", *Walkabout,* May 1940.

Porteus, S. D. "Mentality of Australian Aborigines", *Oceania,* September 1933.

——. *Primitive Intelligence and Environment.* New York, 1937.

——. *The Psychology of a Primitive People: a Study of the Australian Aborigine.* London, 1931.

Powell, R. *The Intelligence of Our Aborigines: Tested under the Severest Conditions.* Perth, 1953.

Price Conigrave, C. *Walk-About.* London, 1938.

Prichard, K. S. *Coonardoo.* Pacific Books, 1961.

——. *N'Goola and Other Stories.* Melbourne, 1959.

"Protection of Aborigines in Western Australia", *Nature,* 11 May 1935.

Pulleine, R., and Woolard, H. "Physiology and Mental Observations on the Australian Aborigines", *Transactions of the Royal Society of South Australia,* 1930.

Reilly, J. T. *Reminiscences of Fifty Years' Residence in Western Australia.* Perth, 1903.

Reay, M., ed. *Aborigines Now.* Sydney, 1964.

Richardson, A. R. *Early Memories of the Great Nor-West.* Perth, 1914.

Rieman, H. E. *Nor'West o'West.* Sydney, 1924.

Rose, R. *Living Magic: the Realities Underlying the Psychical Practices and Beliefs of Australian Aborigines.* London, 1957.

Rourke, W. H. "The North-West Camp School, 1953", *Education,* March 1954.

Rowe, G. *Australian Aborigines Who Have Made Good.* Adelaide, 1954.

——. *How Can the Aborigines Be Assimilated?* Adelaide, 1956.

——. *Sketches of Outstanding Aborigines.* Adelaide, 1956.

Rowley, C. D. "Aborigines and Other Australians", *Oceania,* June 1962.

Rutter, F. *Little Black Fingers.* London, 1951.

Salvado, R. *Mémoires historiques sur l'Australie.* Paris, 1854.

Schenk, R. S. *The Educability of the Native.* Perth, 1936.

Sexton, J. H. *Aboriginal Intelligence: Has the Full-Blooded Aboriginal*

Sufficient Intelligence to Understand the Responsibilities of Citizenship. Adelaide, 1946.

——. *Aboriginal Problems.* Adelaide, 1940.

——. *Australian Aborigines.* Adelaide, 1944.

——. *Australia's Attitude Toward the Aborigines.* Adelaide, 1935.

Shackcloth, I. *The Call of the Kimberleys.* Melbourne, 1950.

Sharland, M. "Prison Trees of the North-West", *Walkabout,* January 1949.

Skinner, M. L. *Black Swans.* London, 1925.

——. *Men Are We.* Perth, 1927.

Smith, B. *European Vision and the South Pacific, 1768–1850: a Study in the History of Art and Ideas.* Oxford, 1960.

Smith, H. P., ed. *The First Ten Years of Mount Margaret Mission, Western Australia.* Melbourne, 1933.

Smith, W. R. "The Aborigines of Australia", *Commonwealth Yearbook,* 1910.

"Social and Economic Conditions of West Australian Aborigines", *Nature,* 11 May 1935.

Stanner, W. E. H. "Continuity and Change Among the Aborigines", *Australian Journal of Science,* December 1958.

——, and Sheils, H., eds. *Australian Aboriginal Studies: A Symposium of Papers Presented at the 1961 Research Conference.* Melbourne, 1963.

Staples, A. C. "A Fair Deal for Coloured Children", *W.A. Teachers Journal,* 14 February 1946.

——. "Henry Charles Prinsep", *Journal and Proceedings of the W.A. Historical Society,* 1955.

Stephens, R. "Nakina, Mokare, Waiter: Three Black Brothers of the King George's Sound Tribe of Aborigines", *Early Days,* 1961.

Stow, R. *To the Islands.* Penguin Books, 1962.

Street, J. M. G. *Report of Visit to Pindan Camps, June, 1957.* Perth, 1957.

——. *Report on Aborigines in Australia.* Sydney, 1957.

Strehlow, T. G. H. *Dark and White Australians.* Melbourne, 1957.

——. *Nomads in No-Man's-Land.* Adelaide, 1961.

——. "Notes on Native Evidence and Its Value", *Oceania,* March 1936.

——. *The Sustaining Ideals of Australian Aboriginal Societies.* Melbourne, 1956.

"Strike of 800 Native Workers in Western Australia", *Anti-Slavery Reporter and Aborigines' Friend,* October 1946.

Stuart, D. R. *The Driven.* London, 1961.

——. *Yandy.* Melbourne, 1959.

——. *Yaralie.* Melbourne, 1962.

Telfer, E. J. *Amongst Australian Aborigines: A Story of the United Aborigines Mission.* Sydney, 1939.

Thomson, D. F. *Justice for Aborigines.* Melbourne, 1946.

Thornbury, G. F. "Native Education in Western Australia", *Education,* July 1955.

Tindale, N. B. "Distribution of Australian Aboriginal Tribes: a Field Survey", *Transactions of the Royal Society of South Australia,* 1940.

————. "General Report on the Anthropological Expedition to the Warburton Range, Western Australia, July-September 1935", *Oceania*, June 1936.

————. "Survey of the Half-Caste Problem in South Australia", *Proceedings of the Royal Geographical Society of Australasia, South Australian Branch*, 1940–1941.

Tuckfield, T. "Forrest River Mission", *Walkabout*, August 1952.

————. "Kalumburu Mission", *Walkabout*, July 1952.

Turner, I. "Black-White Relations from Phillip to Hasluck", *Outlook*, August 1962.

Turner, V. E. *"Good Fella Missus": Missionary Work among the Aborigines of Central Australia*. Adelaide, 1937.

————. *Ooldea*. Melbourne, 1950.

United Aborigines' Mission. *Cut Out Without Hands, or the Miracle of the United Aborigines' Mission*. Melbourne, n.d.

————. *God Cares for the Aborigines*. Adelaide, 1946.

Vickers, F. B. "Can We Assimilate the Aborigines", *Westerly*, 1958, No. 1.

————. *The Mirage*. Melbourne, 1955.

"The West Australian Aborigines: Concerning their Haunts and Habits, and Other Characteristics", *Golden West*, 1906.

Wilson, J. "Kurungura: Aboriginal Culture Revival", *Walkabout*, May 1954.

Wilson, K. "The Blood Test", *Observer*, 24 January 1959.

Withnell, J. G. *The Customs and Traditions of the Aboriginal Natives of North Western Australia*. Roebourne, 1901.

Wood, M. E. "First Contacts Made with Western Australian Natives", *Journal and Proceedings of the W.A. Historical Society*, December 1943.

Wood-Jones, F. *Australia's Vanishing Race*. Sydney, 1934.

————. "The Claims of the Australian Aborigine", *Report of the 18th Meeting of the Australasian Association for the Advancement of Science*. Perth, 1928.

Worms, E. A. "Foreign Words in Some Kimberley Tribes in North-Western Australia", *Oceania*, June 1938.

————. "H. Nekes' and E. A. Worms' Australian Languages (Micro-Biblioteca Anthropos, vol. 10)", *Anthropos*, 1953.

Wright, T. "Fight for the Aborigines", *Communist Review*, April 1947.

Wright, T. *New Deal for the Aborigines*. Sydney, 1939.

Yabaroo. *Aborigines of North-West Australia*. Perth, 1899.

2. Typescripts and Manuscripts

[Unless otherwise stated, the items listed are in the J. S. Battye Library of West Australian History.]

Allen, R. "Reminiscences of the Kimberley District, 1900–1920, and Impressions of Certain Goldfields before 1900." Typescript, n.d. (448 A).

Anderson, A. F. "A Bush Patrol, 19 May–21 June 1947." Typescript, n.d. (PR 215).

Angelina, Sr. "Historical Outline of the New Norcia Mission." Typescript, 1957 (HS/PR/1242).

Bates, D. M. Papers.

Battye, J. S. "The Battle of Pinjarra." Typescript, 1927 (HS/673).

Bolton, G. C. "A Survey of the Kimberley Pastoral Industry from 1885 to the Present." M.A. thesis, University of Western Australia, 1953.

Calver, M. W. "The History of the Swan Homes." Typescript, 1957 (HS/PR/1317).

Cornish, H. "Pioneering in the Kimberleys: Reminiscences of Hamlet Cornish, 1880–1883." Typescript, n.d. (312 A).

Cullen, M. R. "The Life of Daisy Bates." Typescript (HS/PR/1485).

De Bilj, J. "History of the Beagle Bay Mission, 1890–1912." Typescript, 1957 (HS/PR/1304).

Dunne, J. P. "Investigation into Coloured Children's Backwardness in Primary School Subjects at Three Metropolitan Schools in Perth, Western Australia." B. Ed. thesis, University of Western Australia, 1958.

Fink, R. A. "The Changing Status and Cultural Identity of Western Australian Aborigines: a Field Study of Aborigines in the Murchison District, Western Australia", 1955–1957. Microfilm, Columbia University, 1960.

Forrest, J. "Notes on the Aborigines, and Their Customs and Legends." Manuscript, n.d. (390 A).

Gibson, E. A. "Culture Contact on Sunday Island." M.A. thesis, University of Sydney, 1951.

Gil, T. "A Concise Catechism of Christian Doctrine Written in the Pela Language (Drysdale River Mission), with English Translation." Manuscript, 1934 (PR 2867, microfilm).

Goddard, F. "The Retardation of Native Children in South-West of Western Australia, and Its Possible Amelioration by Better Housing." B. Ed. thesis, University of Western Australia, 1954.

Hammond, J. E. "Native Laws, Rites, Customs, Ceremonies and Religious Beliefs, When in Their Primitive State." Typescript, 1938 (PR 385).

Harrison, C. "A Study of the Culture Contact Situation in Collie." B.A. (Hons.) thesis, University of Western Australia, 1960.

Kelly, G. J. "A History of the Champion Bay District." M.A. thesis, University of Western Australia, 1958.

Marchant, L. R. "Native Administration in Western Australia 1886–1905." B.A. (Hons.) thesis, University of Western Australia, 1954.

Marks, S. R. "A Study of Mission Policy in Western Australia, 1846–1959: Being a Study of Ten Representative Missions." B.A. (Hons.) thesis, University of Western Australia, 1960.

Melrose, L. "Report on Mogumber Native Mission." Typescript, 1957 (HS/PR/1246).

Neville, A. O. "Relations Between Settlers and Aborigines in Western Australia." Typescript, 1936 (HS/377).

Patterson, J. I. "Native Administration and Welfare in Western Australia, 1905–1936." B.A. (Hons.) thesis, University of Western Australia, 1957.

Prosser, P. G. "A History of Norseman and Carnarvon Native Missions." Typescript, 1957 (HS/PR/1241).

Riches, D. J. "The History of the Warburton Range Native Mission." Typescript, 1956 (HS/PR/1318).

Staples, C. "History of Harvey District." M.A. thesis, University of Western Australia, 1947.

Sturkey, R. D. "Growth of the Pastoral Industry in the North West 1862-1901." B.A. (Hons.) thesis, University of Western Australia, 1957.

Tebbit, H. "An Historical Account of the Presbyterian Church in Western Australia." Typescript, 1957 (HS/PR/1300).

Timperley, W. H. "The Aborigines of Western Australia." Manuscript, n.d. (HS/698).

West, A. H. "The Education of the Native Child in Western Australia." B. Ed. thesis, University of Western Australia, 1953.

West, A. L. "Adjustment of Part Aborigines Trained on a Rural South-West Mission." Students' Investigation, University of Western Australia, 1958 (in the possession of the Department of Native Welfare).

Wilson, J. "Authority and Leadership in a 'New Style' Australian Aboriginal Community: Pindan, Western Australia." M.A. thesis, University of Western Australia, 1961.

——. "Cooraradale: a Study of Changes in Administration Structures in Relation to a Part-Aboriginal Housing Settlement Population: the Effects of Administrative Action on Aspects of Social Organisation of this Population; and the Social Interaction Pattern of the Settlement Residents with Members of the Wider Community." B.A. (Hons.) thesis, University of Western Australia, 1958.

Wilson, K. "The Allocation of Sex Roles in Social and Economic Affairs in a 'New Style' Australian Community: Pindan, Western Australia." M.Sc. thesis, University of Western Australia, 1961.

——. "Kinship at Cooraradale." B.Sc. (Hons.) thesis, University of Western Australia, 1958.

Wood, M. E. "First Contacts Made with Western Australian Natives." Typescript, n.d. (HS/376).

3. Newspapers and Periodicals

Daily News, 1921-1954.

Geraldton Guardian, 1949-1954.

Ladder: Official Organ of the Australian Aborigines' Amelioration Association, 1936-1939.

Morning Herald, 1902-1908.

Sunday Times, 1900-1920.

West Australian, 1897-1954.

Westralian Aborigine, 1953-1956.

Index